Lecture Notes in Computer

Commenced Publication in 1973
Founding and Former Series Editors:
Gerhard Goos, Juris Hartmanis, and Jan van.

Shengchao Qin (Ed.)

Unifying Theories of Programming

Third International Symposium, UTP 2010
Shanghai, China, November 15-16, 2010
Proceedings

 Springer

Volume Editor

Shengchao Qin
University of Teesside
School of Computing
Borough Road
Middlesbrough, TS1 3BA
UK
E-mail: s.qin@tees.ac.uk

Cover Illustration
The picture on the cover was taken by Wanhong Zhao and was supplied by
the publicity department (Xuan Chuan Bu) of East China Normal University.

Library of Congress Control Number: 2010937234

CR Subject Classification (1998): F.3, D.2, D.2.4, D.3, F.4.1, I.2.3

LNCS Sublibrary: SL 1 – Theoretical Computer Science and General Issues

ISSN	0302-9743
ISBN-10	3-642-16689-X Springer Berlin Heidelberg New York
ISBN-13	978-3-642-16689-1 Springer Berlin Heidelberg New York

springer.com

© Springer-Verlag Berlin Heidelberg 2010
Printed in Germany

Typesetting: Camera-ready by author, data conversion by Scientific Publishing Services, Chennai, India
Printed on acid-free paper   06/3180

Preface

This book constitutes the proceedings of the Third International Symposium on Unifying Theories of Programming (UTP 2010) held at East China Normal University, Shanghai, China, November 15–16, 2010 in conjunction with the 12th International Conference on Formal Engineering Methods (ICFEM 2010).

This symposium followed on the success of the first one, held at Walworth Castle (Durham, UK) in 2006, and the second, held at Trinity College (Dublin, Ireland) in 2008. Based on the pioneering work of C.A.R. Hoare, He Jifeng, and others on unifying theories of programming, the aims of this symposium series are, as stated in UTP 2008, to continue to reaffirm the significance of the ongoing UTP project, to encourage efforts to advance it by providing a focus for the sharing of results by those already actively contributing, and to raise awareness of the benefits of such a unifying theoretical framework among the wider computer science and software engineering communities.

The program for the UTP 2010 symposium includes one invited tutorial, three invited talks, and 12 regular paper presentations. I would like to warmly thank our invited speakers, Ana Cavalcanti, He Jifeng, Jeff Sanders and Jim Woodcock, as well as all the authors, for their enthusiastic and engaged participation in this event.

There were in total 25 submissions made to UTP 2010. Each submission was reviewed by at least three PC members. Based on the reviewers' comments, the Program Committee had careful online discussions and decided to select 12 papers to be included in the UTP 2010 proceedings. I would like to thank all Program Committee members, not only for the excellent work in the paper review and selection process, but also for their useful comments and suggestions on the organization of this symposium. It would not have been possible to form such a high-quality program without their hard work.

Thanks should also be given to Jim Woodcock and Huibiao Zhu for the help and discussions especially in the initial stage of the organization, to Jeff Sanders for valuable comments and suggestions on the UTP event, and to Geguang Pu and his colleagues for excellent local organization for both UTP and ICFEM.

This symposium was organized using, and these proceedings were assembled with the assistance of, EasyChair (www.easychair.org). I would like to thank them for being there all the time!

September 2010   Shengchao Qin

Conference Organization

Program Chair

Shengchao Qin   University of Teesside, UK

Program Committee

Bernhard K. Aichernig	Graz University of Technology, Austria
Hugh Anderson	National University of Singapore, Singapore
Andrew Butterfield	Trinity College Dublin, Ireland
Yifeng Chen	Peking University, China
Deepak D'Souza	IISC, India
Steve Dunne	University of Teesside, UK
Colin Fidge	Queensland University of Technology, Australia
Jeremy Gibbons	University of Oxford, UK
Lindsay Groves	Victoria University of Wellington, New Zealand
Will Harwood	University of York, UK
Ian Hayes	University of Queensland, Australia
Arthur Hughes	Trinity College Dublin, Ireland
Jeremy Jacob	University of York, UK
Xiaoshan Li	University of Macao, Macao SAR, China
Annabelle McIver	Macquarie University, Australia
David Naumann	Stevens Institute of Technology, USA
Geguang Pu	East China Normal University, China
Shengchao Qin	University of Teesside, UK (Chair)
Zongyan Qiu	Peking University, China
Bill Stoddart	University of Teesside, UK
Jun Sun	National University of Singapore, Singapore
Meng Sun	CWI, The Netherlands
Naijun Zhan	Institute of Software, CAS, China
Huibiao Zhu	East China Normal University, China

Local Organization

Jian Guo, Geguang Pu (Chair), Min Zhang, Huibiao Zhu,
East China Normal University, China

Webmaster

Mengying Wang, East China Normal University, China

Table of Contents

Specification Coverage for Testing in *Circus*

Ana Cavalcanti[1] and Marie-Claude Gaudel[2]

[1] University of York, Department of Computer Science
York YO10 5DD, UK
[2] LRI, Université de Paris-Sud
and
CNRS, Orsay 91405, France

Abstract. The Unifying Theories of Programming underpins the development of *Circus*, a state-rich process algebra for refinement. We have previously presented a theory of testing for *Circus*; it gives a symbolic characterisation of tests. Each symbolic test specifies constraints that capture the effect of the possibly nondeterministic state operations, and their interaction. This is a sound basis for testing techniques based on constraint solving for generation of concrete tests, but does not support well selection criteria based on the structure of the specification. We present here a labelled transition system that captures information about a *Circus* model and its structure. It is useful for testing techniques based on specification coverage. The soundness argument for the new transition system follows the UTP style, but relates the new transition relation to the *Circus* relational model and its operational semantics.

1 Introduction

We have recently proposed a theory of testing for *Circus* [24], a state-rich process algebra that combines Z [37], CSP [28], and a refinement calculus [22]. Its semantics is based on the Unifying Theories of Programming (UTP) [18]. Tutorial introductions to the UTP can be found in [35,9].

Formal specifications have been widely applied as a starting point for software testing; a few approaches can be found in [10,14,2,3,1,20]. Our testing theory for *Circus* [6] instantiates Gaudel's long-standing theory of formal testing [15]. Its foundation is the *Circus* operational semantics [36], which is described and justified in the context of the UTP theory for *Circus* [24].

The main distinguishing feature of the *Circus* testing theory is its symbolic nature: it provides a symbolic characterisation of traces, acceptances and initials, and, most importantly, tests and exhaustive test sets. This takes advantage of the symbolic nature of the *Circus* operational semantics, where unknown data values, such as an input or the result of a nondeterministic choice, are represented by loose constants, which we call symbolic variables. Tractability stems first from the use of alphabets (of symbolic variables) in a manner akin to the use of alphabets (of observational variables) in the UTP. Additionally, we exploit a characterisation of process states as predicates of the UTP theory of relations, using the light touch of the UTP approach for clarity and simplicity.

S. Qin (Ed.): UTP 2010, LNCS 6445, pp. 1–45, 2010.

The conformance relation considered in the *Circus* testing theory is process refinement, which is characterised using the UTP notion of refinement. As usual in testing, we consider divergence-free processes. We take the typical view that, in a specification (as opposed to the system under test) divergence is a mistake and should not be used. In other words, in the specification, divergence should not be indicated as an allowed behaviour. Furthermore, in a program (as opposed to a program model) divergence cannot be distinguished from deadlock.

In previous work, we have shown that, for divergence-free processes, refinement can be characterised by the conjunction of traces refinement and *conf*. This is justified in the UTP in [7], based on a relationship between the UTP and the failures-divergences models of CSP. The *conf* relation [3] has been widely explored in the testing community, and requires reduction of deadlock.

The (symbolic) exhaustive test sets for both traces refinement and *conf* are potentially infinite. Practical techniques rely on selection criteria both to generate and to select a finite set of tests. Together, exhaustiveness and the selection criteria justify the conclusions that can be reached from testing experiments.

The symbolic tests and test sets of *Circus* are ideal as a starting point to consider well-known selection criteria based on constraints decomposition and solving [1,11,17]. These allow us to explore the rich data models and ensure meaningful coverage of possible observations. They cater for the infinite data types of *Circus* models, with operations specified in the Z predicative style. The symbolic tests, along with the symbolic traces and acceptance sets used to define them, are a prerequisite for proposing and justifying test-data generation techniques in any language combining control and complex data types. They specify the constraint-solving problems that need to be addressed.

On the other hand, complementary selection criteria that have been widely explored are based on coverage of the syntactic structure of the specification: actions, transitions, paths that link variable assignments and uses, and so on. The labelled transition system defined by the *Circus* operational semantics, however, abstracts from this structure, including from the particular way in which variables are used. Moreover, it includes transitions that do not correspond to observable behaviour; their coverage is unlikely to be interesting for testing.

In this paper, we present a new labelled transition system for *Circus* that is appropriate for the definition of specification-based coverage criteria, and the associated algorithms for test-case generation. We define the new system in terms of two other new transition relations, which we also present here. We briefly discuss the soundness of the new transition rules, but leave a complete account as future work. For illustration purposes, we explain how we can use the new transition system to define a definition-use selection criterion [13].

Section 2 provides an introduction to *Circus*, its operational semantics, and testing theory. The specification-oriented transition system is described in Section 3. Its use in testing is the subject of Section 4. Soundness is discussed in Section 5. Finally, we present our conclusions in Section 6. Appendix A reproduces the rules of the operational semantics used in discussions and examples.

2   *Circus*, Its Operational Semantics, and Testing

The UTP has been the basis for a now ten-year-old research agenda on the development of the *Circus* family of languages based on a combination of Z and CSP. There have been extensions to cater for time [32], synchronicity [4], mobility [33], pointers [16], and object-orientation [8,29]. We give here a brief description of the original *Circus* language, and its operational semantics [36]. Our results, however, are a starting point to consider coverage of specifications for all *Circus* extensions. They are all justified using UTP theories.

2.1   *Circus* Notation

A *Circus* model is formed by a sequence of paragraphs, like in Z [37], but they can define channels and processes, like in CSP and its machine-readable version (CSP-M) [28]. Figure 1 presents a model of a resource manager. Its first paragraph introduces a given set *Resource* including the valid resources. The second paragraph declares two channels: *insert* is used to request the addition of a resource in the pool, and *get* to request a resource from the pool. The last paragraph is a basic (or explicit) definition for a process called *ResourceManager*.

A basic process definition is itself formed by a sequence of paragraphs. The first paragraph of *ResourceManager* is a Z schema *RM* marked as the **state** definition. *Circus* processes have a private state defined using Z, and interact with each other and their environment using channels, like CSP processes.

The state of *ResourceManager* includes two components: a *pool* of resources, and a *cache* that records a resource ready for delivery. The state invariant requires that the cached resource is not in the pool as well.

Operations over the state can be defined by schemas just like in Z. For instance, the schema *Cache* specifies an operation that caches a resource, if the pool is not empty. The schema *Cache* includes the schema ΔRM to bring into scope the names of the state components defined in *RM* and their dashed counterparts to represent the state after the execution of *Cache*.

State operations are called actions in *Circus*, and can also be defined using Morgan's specification statements [22] or guarded commands from Dijkstra's language [12]. The operation *Insert* in our example, for instance, is defined by an assignment. It adds a resource *r*? given as input to the pool.

CSP constructs can also be used to specify actions. For instance, the resource manager has two components: a *CacheManager* and a *PoolManager*, specified by separate actions. *CacheManager* accepts requests for a resource through the channel *get*. When such a request occurs, the cache becomes empty and the manager terminates. The *PoolManager*, on the other hand, accepts requests to insert a resource in the pool, which is carried by *Insert*. It also monitors requests for a resource (through *get*). When this happens, if the pool is not empty, the manager terminates, otherwise, it waits for an element to be inserted in the pool before terminating. The specification of *PoolManager* combines an assignment, the action **Skip**, which terminates immediately, without changing the state,

[*Resource*]

channel *insert, get* : *Resource*

process *ResourceManager* $\widehat{=}$ **begin**

$$\boxed{\begin{array}{l} \textbf{state } RM \\ \hline pool : \mathbb{P}\ Resource \\ cache : Resource \\ \hline cache \notin pool \end{array}}$$

$$\boxed{\begin{array}{l} Init \\ \hline RM' \\ \hline pool' = \varnothing \end{array}}$$

$$\boxed{\begin{array}{l} Cache \\ \hline \Delta RM \\ \hline pool \neq \varnothing \\ pool' = pool \setminus \{cache'\} \end{array}}$$

$Insert \widehat{=} r? : Resource \bullet pool := pool \cup \{r?\}$

$CacheManager \widehat{=} get!cache \rightarrow \textbf{Skip}$

$PoolManager \widehat{=}$
$$\left(\mu X \bullet \left(\begin{array}{l} insert?r \rightarrow Insert(r);\ X \\ \square \\ get?x \rightarrow (\textbf{if } pool \neq \varnothing \rightarrow \textbf{Skip} \ [\!]\ pool = \varnothing \rightarrow insert?r \rightarrow Insert(r)) \end{array} \right) \right)$$

$\bullet$ *Init*;
$(\mu X \bullet (CacheManager \ [\![\{cache\} \mid \{\!| get |\!\} \mid \{pool\}]\!]\ PoolManager);\ Cache;\ X)$
end

Fig. 1. Resource manager in *Circus*

a schema operation, a conditional (in Dijkstra's style), and an external choice ($\square$). Z and CSP constructs are intermixed freely in an action definition.

A main action at the end defines the behaviour of the *ResourceManager*. After a call to the initialisation operation *Init*, a parallel composition combines the *CacheManager* and the *PoolManager*. When the parallelism terminates, the *Cache* operation updates the cache to make a resource available.

Like in CSP, the parallel operator defines a synchronisation channel set: communications through channels in this set require agreement of both parallel actions. In our example, *get* is in the synchronisation set. To avoid race conditions, the parallel operator also associates with each action a partition of the variables in scope over which it has write control. Both parallel actions can access the value of the state before the parallelism starts. Both can write to all state components. An update, however, only becomes visible to other actions after the parallelism terminates, and then only if the action has write control over the changed variable. In our example, the *CacheManager* has control over *cache*, and *PoolManager* over *pool*. (In fact, *CacheManager* does not change *cache*, but we require the name sets to be a partition of the state.)

Processes can also be defined by composition using CSP constructs. For example, in a distributed setting, we can have two resource managers available.

process *Resources* $\hat{=}$ *ResourceManager* ||| *ResourceManager*

In this case, we have two copies of a *ResourceManager*, each with its own private state. A request to *insert* or *get* a resource is responded by either of them; the choice is nondeterministic. Nondeterminism in *Circus* may arise from data operations, like in Z, or from parallelism, like in CSP. We also have the explicit operator for nondeterministic choice of CSP. In our example, the data operation *Cache* is nondeterministic, as is the process *Resources* above.

A full account of *Circus* and its denotational semantics, including the UTP theory that underpins it, is given in [25]. The *Circus* operational semantics [36] is briefly discussed and illustrated in the next section.

2.2   *Circus* Operational Semantics

As usual, the operational semantics of *Circus* is based on a transition relation that associates configurations. For processes, the configurations are processes themselves. For actions, the configurations are triples. The first component is a constraint over symbolic variables used to define labels and the state. The second component is a total assignment in the UTP theory of relations of symbolic variables to variables. The last component is an action.

The constraints in the configurations are texts that denote predicates (over symbolic variables). Like in the UTP, we use typewriter font for pieces of text. The syntax used to define them is that of the UTP relational theory, and of *Circus* predicates, which are basically Z predicates [23].

State assignments are expressed using the UTP notation $x := e$ for relational assignments. They can also include declarations and undeclaration of variables using the UTP constructs **var** x and **end** x. The declaration of a variable is immediately followed by an assignment of a symbolic variable to it, so that state assignments are deterministic programs that define a specific value (represented by a symbolic variable) for all variables in scope. We use the notation **var** $x := e$ as an abbreviation for **var** x; $x := e$. It is the combination of the constraint over symbolic variables, and the state assignment of symbolic variables to all variables in scope that, together, specify the state of a configuration.

To give the operational semantics of a process, we use a novel construct for a basic process. It records the current local state of a process using a constraint and a state assignment. The first transition rule for processes shown below introduces the record of the local state. It is characterised using a (list of) fresh symbolic variable(s) w_0. The constraint defines that w_0 is (are) of the appropriate type(s), and in the state assignment w_0 is assigned to the state component(s) x. In all transition rules, the symbolic variables introduced are assumed to be fresh.

$$
\begin{pmatrix} \texttt{begin} \\ \quad \texttt{state}\,[\,x:T\,] \\ \quad \bullet\ A \\ \texttt{end} \end{pmatrix} \xrightarrow{\ \epsilon\ } \begin{pmatrix} \texttt{begin} \\ \quad \texttt{state}\,[\,x:T\,]\mid \texttt{loc}\ (w_0 \in T \mid x := w_0) \\ \quad \bullet\ A \\ \texttt{end} \end{pmatrix}
$$

The semantics of composed processes is defined by providing a corresponding basic process [23]. We, therefore, do not consider them here. The complete set of transition rules is in [36]; some are presented below and in Appendix A.

The second transition rule for processes, which we omit here for conciseness, applies to the extended form of a basic process. The rule allows a process to evolve in accordance with the evolution of its main action in the state defined by the loc clause. We therefore focus on the transition relation for actions.

The rule for designs (which are a simplified form of specification statement) is below. The hypothesis requires the constraint to hold, the precondition to hold in the current state s, and the design to be feasible. In this case, evolution to Skip is silent (not labelled, or labelled by ϵ). The constraint is strengthened by introducing fresh symbolic variables w_0 that satisfy the postcondition, and the state is updated by assigning w_0 to all variables in scope. The state s is not completely discarded, since it may contain variable declarations.

$$
\frac{c \wedge (s;\ p) \wedge (\exists\,v' \bullet s;\ Q)}{(c \mid s \models p \vdash Q) \xrightarrow{\ \epsilon\ } (c \wedge (s;\ Q\,[w_0/v']) \mid s;\ v := w_0 \models \texttt{Skip})} \quad v' = out\,\alpha s
$$

Another rule states that, if the precondition does not hold, the design evolves to **Chaos**, the action that diverges immediately.

The evolution of an output prefixing $d!e \rightarrow A$, an action that outputs the value of the expression e through channel d and then behaves like A, is labelled. The label $d.w_0$ involves the fresh constant w_0; the new constraint defines its value to be that of e in the current state s. The remaining action is A.

$$
\frac{c}{(c \mid s \models d!e \rightarrow A) \xrightarrow{d!w_0} (c \wedge (s;\ w_0 = e) \mid s \models A)}
$$

The transition rule for an input prefixing $d?x \rightarrow A$ is as follows.

$$
\frac{c \wedge T \neq \varnothing \qquad x \notin \alpha s}{(c \mid s \models d?x : T \rightarrow A) \xrightarrow{d?w_0} (c \wedge w_0 \in T \mid s;\ \texttt{var}\,x := w_0 \models \texttt{let}\,x \bullet A)}
$$

The label is $d?w_0$. In the new the state, x is declared and assigned w_0. The only restriction on w_0 is that it has the same type as d. The remaining action let x $\bullet$ A records the fact that x is in scope in A as a local variable. The construct let x $\bullet$ A has been introduced specifically for use in the operational semantics. When A terminates, a rule for let x $\bullet$ Skip closes the scope of x in the state and removes the let x declaration. This is Rule (8) in Appendix A.

The transition rules for sequences A_1; B are standard. Evolution of A_1 leads to evolution of the sequence. When it terminates, a rule for Skip; B allows a silent transition to B, thus removing the sequence.

$$\frac{(c_1 \mid s_1 \models A_1) \xrightarrow{1} (c_2 \mid s_2 \models A_2)}{(c_1 \mid s_1 \models A_1;\ B) \xrightarrow{1} (c_2 \mid s_2 \models A_2;\ B)} \qquad \frac{c}{(c \mid s \models \text{Skip};\ A) \xrightarrow{\epsilon} (c \mid s \models A)}$$

For an internal choice $A_1 \sqcap A_2$, silent transitions are available to either A_1 or A_2 (in a configuration with the same constraint and state assignment).

$$\frac{c}{(c \mid s \models A_1 \sqcap A_2) \xrightarrow{\epsilon} (c \mid s \models A_1)} \qquad \frac{c}{(c \mid s \models A_1 \sqcap A_2) \xrightarrow{\epsilon} (c \mid s \models A_2)}$$

The treatment of parallelism is more subtle. We introduce an extra form of action par $s \mid x \bullet A$ that records the local state s of the parallel action A, which has write control over the variables in x. The first transition rule for a parallelism defines a silent transition that rewrites it in terms of this new construct.

The rule below allows evolutions of the first parallel action A_1 that are either silent or do not involve a channel in the synchronisation set to be reflected in the parallelism. A similar omitted rule considers independent evolutions of A_2.

$$\frac{(c \mid s_1 \models A_1) \xrightarrow{1} (c_3 \mid s_3 \models A_3) \quad 1 = \epsilon \vee \text{chan}\, 1 \notin cs}{\left(\begin{array}{c} c \mid s \\ \models \\ \left(\begin{array}{c} (\text{par } s_1 \mid x_1 \bullet A_1) \\ [\![cs]\!] \\ (\text{par } s_2 \mid x_2 \bullet A_2) \end{array} \right) \end{array} \right) \xrightarrow{1} \left(\begin{array}{c} c_3 \mid s \\ \models \\ \left(\begin{array}{c} (\text{par } s_3 \mid x_1 \bullet A_3) \\ [\![cs]\!] \\ (\text{par } s_2 \mid x_2 \bullet A_2) \end{array} \right) \end{array} \right)}$$

The next rule is for when the parallel actions can evolve by synchronising. In particular, A_1 can carry out an input $d?w_1$, and A_2 an output $d!w_2$, where d is a channel in the synchronisation set, and the values communicated are equal. The transition rule establishes that, in this case, the parallelism as a whole actually performs an output. The new constraint records the restriction that $w_1 = w_2$.

$$\frac{(c \mid s_1 \models A_1) \xrightarrow{d?w_1} (c_3 \mid s_3 \models A_3) \quad (c \mid s_2 \models A_2) \xrightarrow{d!w_2} (c_4 \mid s_4 \models A_4)}{d \in cs \quad c_3 \wedge c_4 \wedge w_1 = w_2}$$

$$\left(\begin{array}{c} c \mid s \\ \models \\ \left(\begin{array}{c} (\text{par } s_1 \mid x_1 \bullet A_1) \\ [\![cs]\!] \\ (\text{par } s_2 \mid x_2 \bullet A_2) \end{array} \right) \end{array} \right) \xrightarrow{d!w_2} \left(\begin{array}{c} c_3 \wedge c_4 \wedge w_1 = w_2 \mid s \\ \models \\ \left(\begin{array}{c} (\text{par } s_3 \mid x_1 \bullet A_3) \\ [\![cs]\!] \\ (\text{par } s_4 \mid x_2 \bullet A_4) \end{array} \right) \end{array} \right)$$

Similar rules apply when A_1 can output and A_2 input, or when both A_1 and A_2 can output. When they can both input, the parallelism also performs an input. We refer to the Appendix A for an account of all transition rules for parallelism.

Perhaps the most interesting rule is the one that applies when both parallel actions have terminated. In this case, the parallelism terminates.

$$c$$

$$\left(\begin{array}{c} \text{c} \mid \text{s} \\ \models \\ \left(\begin{array}{c}(\text{par } s_1 \mid x_1 \bullet \textbf{Skip}) \\ [\![cs]\!] \\ (\text{par } s_2 \mid x_2 \bullet \textbf{Skip})\end{array}\right)\end{array}\right) \xrightarrow{\epsilon} (\text{c} \mid (\exists x_2' \bullet s_1) \wedge (\exists x_1' \bullet s_2) \models \textbf{Skip})$$

The state after the parallelism is defined by composing the local states of the parallel action. We keep from the local state s_1 of the first action only the changes to the variables in its name set x_1. This is achieved by hiding (quantifying) the final value of the variables in the complement set x_2. The same applies for the changes in s_2. The conjunction of the quantifications defines the new state. We observe that, alternatively, we can define the new state as s_1; $\textbf{end} \, x_2 \wedge s_2$; $\textbf{end} \, x_1$.

Rules for external choice require similar considerations. Actions in an external choice can evolve independently, with local access to all variables, until an event decides the choice, and consequently, makes the local changes global.

For a hiding $A_1 \setminus cs$, the rules allow evolution of A_1 to lead to evolution of the hiding itself. In the rule below, evolution does not involve a hidden channel, so the label for the hiding transition is that for the A_1 transition.

$$\frac{(c_1 \mid s_1 \models A_1) \xrightarrow{1} (c_2 \mid s_2 \models A_2) \quad \text{chan } 1 \notin cs}{(c_1 \mid s_1 \models A_1 \setminus cs) \xrightarrow{1} (c_2 \mid s_2 \models A_2 \setminus cs)}$$

If, on the other hand, A_1 can communicate on a hidden channel, the corresponding evolution of the hiding is silent. This is defined by Rule (20) in Appendix A. Finally, Rule (21) specifies that if A_1 terminates, so does the hiding.

Example 1. We consider the action defined below, in the context of a process that has a state with components x and y, of type $\mathbb{Z}$, for instance. Channels *inp* and *out* also of type $\mathbb{Z}$ are in scope and used in E.

$$E \mathrel{\widehat{=}} x := 2; \ (y > x \ \& \ out!(y - x) \rightarrow \textbf{Skip} \sqcap inp?z \rightarrow \textbf{Stop}); \ x := y$$

As suggested by the transition rule for processes, we consider the transitions from a state characterised by $(w_0 \in \mathbb{Z} \wedge w_1 \in \mathbb{Z} \mid x, y := w_0, w_1)$. We can justify the following transitions using the *Circus* operational semantics described above. The rule numbers mentioned refer to the list in Appendix A.

$$(w_0 \in \mathbb{Z} \wedge w_1 \in \mathbb{Z} \mid x, y := w_0, w_1 \models E)$$

$$\longrightarrow \hfill \text{[Rules (2) and (9)]}$$

$$\left(\begin{array}{c} w_0 \in \mathbb{Z} \wedge w_1 \in \mathbb{Z} \wedge w_2 = 2 \mid x, y := w_2, w_1 \\ \models \\ \textbf{Skip}; \ (y > x \ \& \ out!(y - x) \rightarrow \textbf{Skip} \sqcap inp?z \rightarrow \textbf{Stop}); \ x := y \end{array}\right)$$

$$\longrightarrow \hfill \text{[Rule (10)]}$$

$$\left(\begin{array}{l} w_0 \in \mathbb{Z} \wedge w_1 \in \mathbb{Z} \wedge w_2 = 2 \mid x, y := w_2, w_1 \\ \models \\ (y > x \; \& \; \text{out!}(y - x) \to \text{Skip} \sqcap \text{inp?}z \to \text{Stop}); \; x := y \end{array}\right)$$

At this point two rules for internal choice apply, corresponding to the two choices available. We pursue the first below, and the second afterwards.

$\longrightarrow$ [Rules (11) and (9)]

$$\left(\begin{array}{l} w_0 \in \mathbb{Z} \wedge w_1 \in \mathbb{Z} \wedge w_2 = 2 \mid x, y := w_2, w_1 \\ \models \\ (y > x \; \& \; \text{out!}(y - x) \to \text{Skip}); \; x := y \end{array}\right)$$

$\longrightarrow$ [Rules (12) and (9)]

$$\left(\begin{array}{l} w_0 \in \mathbb{Z} \wedge w_1 \in \mathbb{Z} \wedge w_2 = 2 \wedge w_1 > w_2 \mid x, y := w_2, w_1 \\ \models \\ (\text{out!}(y - x) \to \text{Skip}); \; x := y \end{array}\right)$$

$\overset{\text{out!}w_3}{\longrightarrow}$ [Rules (4) and (9)]

$$\left(\begin{array}{l} w_0 \in \mathbb{Z} \wedge w_1 \in \mathbb{Z} \wedge w_2 = 2 \wedge w_1 > w_2 \wedge w_3 = w_1 - w_2 \mid x, y := w_2, w_1 \\ \models \\ \text{Skip}; \; x := y \end{array}\right)$$

$\longrightarrow$ [Rule (10)]

$$\left(\begin{array}{l} w_0 \in \mathbb{Z} \wedge w_1 \in \mathbb{Z} \wedge w_2 = 2 \wedge w_1 > w_2 \wedge w_3 = w_1 - w_2 \mid x, y := w_2, w_1 \\ \models \\ x := y \end{array}\right)$$

$\longrightarrow$ [Rule (2)]

$$\left(\begin{array}{l} w_0 \in \mathbb{Z} \wedge w_1 \in \mathbb{Z} \wedge w_2 = 2 \wedge w_1 > w_2 \wedge w_3 = w_1 - w_2 \wedge w_4 = w_2 \mid x, y := w_4, w_1 \\ \models \\ \text{Skip} \end{array}\right)$$

Considering the second option of the internal choice, we can proceed as follows.

$\longrightarrow$ [Rules (11) and (9)]

$$\left(\begin{array}{l} w_0 \in \mathbb{Z} \wedge w_1 \in \mathbb{Z} \wedge w_2 = 2 \mid x, y := w_2, w_1 \\ \models \\ (\text{inp?}z \to \text{Stop}); \; x := y \end{array}\right)$$

$\overset{\text{inp?}w_3}{\longrightarrow}$ [Rules (5) and (9)]

$$\left(\begin{array}{l} w_0 \in \mathbb{Z} \wedge w_1 \in \mathbb{Z} \wedge w_2 = 2 \wedge w_3 \in \mathbb{Z} \mid x, y := w_2, w_1; \; \text{var} \, z := w_3 \\ \models \\ (\text{let} \, z \bullet \text{Stop}); \; x := y \end{array}\right)$$

From here, we cannot proceed, as there are no transition rules for Stop.

All transitions above are valid when the associated constraints are satisfied. $\square$

Example 2. We consider the action defined below, in the context of a process that has a state with a component x of type $\mathbb{Z}$. Channels $inpA$, $inpB$, int, and out, also of type $\mathbb{Z}$, are in scope and used in PA.

$$PA \mathrel{\widehat{=}} \left(x := 2; \left(\begin{array}{c} (inpA?y \to int!y \to out!(y-x) \to \mathbf{Skip}) \\ [\![\{\!|\, int\, |\!\}]\!] \\ (inpB?z_1 \to int?z_2 \to z_1 > z_2 \;\&\; out!(z_1 - x) \to \mathbf{Skip}) \end{array} \right) \right)$$

Strictly speaking, we would need to define the sets of names of variables that can be updated by each of the parallel actions. In this simple example, however, they update no variables, so we omit these sets.

We consider below the transitions from the state $(w_0 \in \mathbb{Z} \mid x := w_0)$. We can justify the following transitions using the *Circus* operational semantics.

$(w_0 \in \mathbb{Z} \mid x := w_0 \models PA)$

$\longrightarrow$ \hfill [Rules (2) and (9)]

$$\left(\begin{array}{l} w_0 \in \mathbb{Z} \wedge w_1 = 2 \mid x := w_1 \\ \models \\ \mathbf{Skip};\; \left(\begin{array}{c} (inpA?y \to int!y \to out!(y-x) \to \mathbf{Skip}) \\ [\![\{\!|\, int\, |\!\}]\!] \\ (inpB?z_1 \to int?z_2 \to z_1 > z_2 \;\&\; out!(z_1 - x) \to \mathbf{Skip}) \end{array} \right) \end{array} \right)$$

$\longrightarrow$ \hfill [Rule (10)]

$$\left(\begin{array}{l} w_0 \in \mathbb{Z} \wedge w_1 = 2 \mid x := w_1 \\ \models \\ \left(\begin{array}{c} (inpA?y \to int!y \to out!(y-x) \to \mathbf{Skip}) \\ [\![\{\!|\, int\, |\!\}]\!] \\ (inpB?z_1 \to int?z_2 \to z_1 > z_2 \;\&\; out!(z_1 - x) \to \mathbf{Skip}) \end{array} \right) \end{array} \right)$$

$\longrightarrow$ \hfill [Rule (13)]

$$\left(\begin{array}{l} w_0 \in \mathbb{Z} \wedge w_1 = 2 \mid x := w_1 \\ \models \\ \left(\begin{array}{c} \mathbf{par}\; x := w_1 \bullet inpA?y \to int!y \to out!(y-x) \to \mathbf{Skip} \\ [\![\{\!|\, int\, |\!\}]\!] \\ \mathbf{par}\; x := w_1 \bullet inpB?z_1 \to int?z_2 \to z_1 > z_2 \;\&\; out!(z_1 - x) \to \mathbf{Skip} \end{array} \right) \end{array} \right)$$

Now, there are two rules that are applicable (Rules (15) and (16)), reflecting the fact that either of the parallel actions can evolve independently. So, we can have the following sequence of transitions if the left-hand action evolves first.

$\xrightarrow{inpA?w_2}$ \hfill [Rules (5) and (15)]

$$\left(\begin{array}{l} w_0 \in \mathbb{Z} \wedge w_1 = 2 \wedge w_2 \in \mathbb{Z} \mid x := w_1 \\ \models \\ \left(\begin{array}{c} \mathbf{par}\; x := w_1; \mathbf{var}\, y := w_2 \bullet (\mathbf{let}\; y \bullet int!y \to out!(y-x) \to \mathbf{Skip}) \\ [\![\{\!|\, int\, |\!\}]\!] \\ \mathbf{par}\; x := w_1 \bullet inpB?z_1 \to int?z_2 \to z_1 > z_2 \;\&\; out!(z_1 - x) \to \mathbf{Skip} \end{array} \right) \end{array} \right)$$

$\xrightarrow{\text{inpB?}w_3}$ [Rules (5) and (16)]

$$
\left(
\begin{array}{l}
w_0 \in \mathbb{Z} \land w_1 = 2 \land w_2 \in \mathbb{Z} \land w_3 \in \mathbb{Z} \mid x := w_1 \\
\models \\
\left(
\begin{array}{l}
\text{par } x := w_1; \ \text{var } y := w_2 \bullet (\text{let } y \bullet \text{int}!y \to \text{out}!(y - x) \to \text{Skip}) \\
\llbracket \{ \text{int} \} \rrbracket \\
\left(
\begin{array}{l}
\text{par } x := w_1; \ \text{var } z_1 := w_3 \bullet \\
\quad \text{let } z_1 \bullet \text{int}?z_2 \to z_1 > z_2 \ \& \ \text{out}!(z_1 - x) \to \text{Skip}
\end{array}
\right)
\end{array}
\right)
\end{array}
\right)
$$

If the right-hand action evolves first, we have the following transitions. We choose the names of the symbolic variables carefully, so that the same communicated values are represented by variables of the same name. In our use of the operational semantics to define traces, initials, acceptances, and tests [6], this careful choice is guided and fixed by an alphabet of symbolic variables.

$\xrightarrow{\text{inpB?}w_3}$ [Rules (5) and (16)]

$$
\left(
\begin{array}{l}
w_0 \in \mathbb{Z} \land w_1 = 2 \land w_3 \in \mathbb{Z} \mid x := w_1 \\
\models \\
\left(
\begin{array}{l}
\text{par } x := w_1 \bullet \text{inpA}?y \to \text{int}!y \to \text{out}!(y - x) \to \text{Skip} \\
\llbracket \{ \text{int} \} \rrbracket \\
\left(
\begin{array}{l}
\text{par } x := w_1; \ \text{var } z_1 := w_3 \bullet \\
\quad \text{let } z_1 \bullet \text{int}?z_2 \to z_1 > z_2 \ \& \ \text{out}!(z_1 - x) \to \text{Skip}
\end{array}
\right)
\end{array}
\right)
\end{array}
\right)
$$

$\xrightarrow{\text{inpA?}w_2}$ [Rules (5) and (15)]

$$
\left(
\begin{array}{l}
w_0 \in \mathbb{Z} \land w_1 = 2 \land w_2 \in \mathbb{Z} \land w_3 \in \mathbb{Z} \mid x := w_1 \\
\models \\
\left(
\begin{array}{l}
\text{par } x := w_1; \ \text{var } y := w_2 \bullet (\text{let } y \bullet \text{int}!y \to \text{out}!(y - x) \to \text{Skip}) \\
\llbracket \{ \text{int} \} \rrbracket \\
\left(
\begin{array}{l}
\text{par } x := w_1; \ \text{var } z_1 := w_3 \bullet \\
\quad \text{let } z_1 \bullet \text{int}?z_2 \to z_1 > z_2 \ \& \ \text{out}!(z_1 - x) \to \text{Skip}
\end{array}
\right)
\end{array}
\right)
\end{array}
\right)
$$

The configurations reached in both options are the same. (If we did not choose the names of the symbolic variables appropriately, there would be syntactic differences in the text of the constraint and state assignment, arising (just) from the differentiated use of fresh names. For the sake of simplicity, we are choosing the names in an adequate way as explained before. With the support of simple pattern matching facilities, a tool can identify the commonality in any case.)

The next transition rule that applies is that for synchronisation of parallel actions, when we have a matching input and output.

$\xrightarrow{\text{int}!w_5}$ [Rules (4), (7), (5), and (17)]

$$
\left(
\begin{array}{l}
w_0 \in \mathbb{Z} \land w_1 = 2 \land w_2 \in \mathbb{Z} \land w_3 \in \mathbb{Z} \land w_4 = w_2 \land w_5 \in \mathbb{Z} \land w_4 = w_5 \mid x := w_1 \\
\models \\
\left(
\begin{array}{l}
\text{par } x := w_1; \ \text{var } y := w_2 \bullet (\text{let } y \bullet \text{out}!(y - x) \to \text{Skip}) \\
\llbracket \{ \text{int} \} \rrbracket \\
\left(
\begin{array}{l}
\text{par } x := w_1; \ \text{var } z_1, z_2 := w_3, w_5 \bullet \\
\quad \text{let } z_1, z_2 \bullet z_1 > z_2 \ \& \ \text{out}!(z_1 - x) \to \text{Skip}
\end{array}
\right)
\end{array}
\right)
\end{array}
\right)
$$

We now have two choices again corresponding to the independent evolutions of the parallel actions. If the left-hand action evolves first, we have the following.

$\xrightarrow{\text{out!}w_6}$ [Rules (4), (7), and (15)]

$$\left(\begin{array}{l} \left(\begin{array}{l} w_0 \in \mathbb{Z} \wedge w_1 = 2 \wedge w_2 \in \mathbb{Z} \wedge w_3 \in \mathbb{Z} \wedge \\ w_4 = w_2 \wedge w_5 \in \mathbb{Z} \wedge w_4 = w_5 \wedge \\ w_6 = w_2 - w_1 \end{array}\right) \mid x := w_1 \\ \models \\ \left(\begin{array}{l} \mathbf{par}\ x := w_1;\ \mathbf{var}\ y := w_2 \bullet (\mathbf{let}\ y \bullet \mathbf{Skip}) \\ \quad [\![\{\ \mathbf{int}\ \}]\!] \\ \left(\begin{array}{l} \mathbf{par}\ x := w_1;\ \mathbf{var}\ z_1, z_2 := w_3, w_5 \bullet \\ \quad \mathbf{let}\ z_1, z_2 \bullet z_1 > z_2\ \&\ \mathbf{out}!(z_1 - x) \rightarrow \mathbf{Skip} \end{array}\right) \end{array}\right) \end{array}\right)$$

And again we have a choice of the silent evolution of the left-hand action, or the evolution of the second action. Continuing with the evolution of the left-hand action, we proceed with the following sequence of transitions.

$\longrightarrow$ [Rules (8) and (15)]

$$\left(\begin{array}{l} \left(\begin{array}{l} w_0 \in \mathbb{Z} \wedge w_1 = 2 \wedge w_2 \in \mathbb{Z} \wedge w_3 \in \mathbb{Z} \wedge \\ w_4 = w_2 \wedge w_5 \in \mathbb{Z} \wedge w_4 = w_5 \wedge \\ w_6 = w_2 - w_1 \end{array}\right) \mid x := w_1 \\ \models \\ \left(\begin{array}{l} \mathbf{par}\ x := w_1;\ \mathbf{var}\ y := w_2;\ \mathbf{end}\ y \bullet \mathbf{Skip} \\ \quad [\![\{\ \mathbf{int}\ \}]\!] \\ \left(\begin{array}{l} \mathbf{par}\ x := w_1;\ \mathbf{var}\ z_1, z_2 := w_3, w_5 \bullet \\ \quad \mathbf{let}\ z_1, z_2 \bullet z_1 > z_2\ \&\ \mathbf{out}!(z_1 - x) \rightarrow \mathbf{Skip} \end{array}\right) \end{array}\right) \end{array}\right)$$

$\longrightarrow$ [Rules (12), (7) and (16)]

$$\left(\begin{array}{l} \left(\begin{array}{l} w_0 \in \mathbb{Z} \wedge w_1 = 2 \wedge w_2 \in \mathbb{Z} \wedge w_3 \in \mathbb{Z} \wedge \\ w_4 = w_2 \wedge w_5 \in \mathbb{Z} \wedge w_4 = w_5 \wedge \\ w_6 = w_2 - w_1 \wedge w_3 > w_5 \end{array}\right) \mid x := w_1 \\ \models \\ \left(\begin{array}{l} \mathbf{par}\ x := w_1;\ \mathbf{var}\ y := w_2;\ \mathbf{end}\ y \bullet \mathbf{Skip} \\ \quad [\![\{\ \mathbf{int}\ \}]\!] \\ \left(\begin{array}{l} \mathbf{par}\ x := w_1;\ \mathbf{var}\ z_1, z_2 := w_3, w_5 \bullet \\ \quad \mathbf{let}\ z_1, z_2 \bullet \mathbf{out}!(z_1 - x) \rightarrow \mathbf{Skip} \end{array}\right) \end{array}\right) \end{array}\right)$$

$\xrightarrow{\text{out.}w_7}$ [Rules (4), (7) and (16)]

$$\left(\begin{array}{l} \left(\begin{array}{l} w_0 \in \mathbb{Z} \wedge w_1 = 2 \wedge w_2 \in \mathbb{Z} \wedge w_3 \in \mathbb{Z} \wedge \\ w_4 = w_2 \wedge w_5 \in \mathbb{Z} \wedge w_4 = w_5 \wedge \\ w_6 = w_2 - w_1 \wedge w_3 > w_5 \wedge w_7 = w_3 - w_1 \end{array}\right) \mid x := w_1 \\ \models \\ \left(\begin{array}{l} \mathbf{par}\ x := w_1;\ \mathbf{var}\ y := w_2;\ \mathbf{end}\ y \bullet \mathbf{Skip} \\ \quad [\![\{\ \mathbf{int}\ \}]\!] \\ \mathbf{par}\ x := w_1;\ \mathbf{var}\ z_1, z_2 := w_3, w_5 \bullet (\mathbf{let}\ z_1, z_2 \bullet \mathbf{Skip}) \end{array}\right) \end{array}\right)$$

$\longrightarrow$ [Rules (8) and (16)]

$$
\left(
\begin{array}{c}
\left(
\begin{array}{l}
w_0 \in \mathbb{Z} \wedge w_1 = 2 \wedge w_2 \in \mathbb{Z} \wedge w_3 \in \mathbb{Z} \wedge \\
w_4 = w_2 \wedge w_5 \in \mathbb{Z} \wedge w_4 = w_5 \wedge \\
w_6 = w_2 - w_1 \wedge w_3 > w_5 \wedge w_7 = w_3 - w_1
\end{array}
\right) \mid x := w_1 \\
\models \\
\left(
\begin{array}{l}
\text{par } x := w_1; \; \text{var } y := w_2; \; \text{end } y \bullet \text{Skip} \\
\quad [\{ \text{int} \}] \\
\text{par } x := w_1; \; \text{var } z_1, z_2 := w_3, w_5; \; \text{end } z_1, z_2 \bullet \text{Skip}
\end{array}
\right)
\end{array}
\right)
$$

$\longrightarrow$ [Rule (14)]

$$
\left(
\begin{array}{c}
\left(
\begin{array}{l}
w_0 \in \mathbb{Z} \wedge w_1 = 2 \wedge w_2 \in \mathbb{Z} \wedge w_3 \in \mathbb{Z} \wedge \\
w_4 = w_2 \wedge w_5 \in \mathbb{Z} \wedge w_4 = w_5 \wedge \\
w_6 = w_2 - w_1 \wedge w_3 > w_5 \wedge w_7 = w_3 - w_1
\end{array}
\right) \mid x := w_1 \\
\models \\
\text{Skip}
\end{array}
\right)
$$

Various interleavings of the evolution of each of the parallel actions are possible. The above is just an example. A second option, for instance, carries out all the evolutions of the right-hand side action to Skip before evolving the left-hand action. In this case, the order of communication of $y - x$ and $z_1 - x$ on *out* changes. The end configuration, with a careful choice of the names of the symbolic variables as illustrated before, is the same in all cases.   □

In the next section, we explain how the operational semantics is used to define tests based on *Circus* models of a system.

2.3 Testing in *Circus*

In previous work, we have instantiated Gaudel's long-standing testing theory to *Circus* [15]. The conformance relation we have considered is process refinement. This is the UTP notion of refinement applied to processes, that is, to their main actions, where the state components are taken as local variables.

As already said, we take the view that, in specifications, divergences are mistakes. In programs, they are observed as deadlocks. We, therefore, consider a theory for divergence-free models and systems under test (SUT). In this case, the refinement relation of *Circus* can be characterised by the conjunction of a traces refinement relation, and a *conf* relation that requires reduction of deadlock. This is proved in [7], where both relations are defined in the UTP *Circus* theory.

Accordingly, we have defined separate exhaustive test sets for traces refinement and *conf*. We have taken advantage of the symbolic nature of the *Circus* operational semantics, and defined the tests symbolically. These definitions specify how concrete tests can be obtained by a process of instantiation.

A test for traces refinement is constructed by considering a trace of the *Circus* model and one of the events that cannot be used to extend that trace to obtain a new trace of the *Circus* model [5]. Such events are called the forbidden continuations of the trace. Traces and forbidden continuations are characterised symbolically. The exhaustive test set includes all the tests formed by considering all the traces and all their forbidden continuations.

For the process PA in Example 2, we have traces of communications over $inpA$, $inpB$, and int. Below, we present a symbolic trace that specifies some of them; it has an associated constraint over the symbolic variables used in the specification of the trace. We call these pairs constrained symbolic traces.

$$(\langle \, \mathtt{inpA.w_2, inpB.w_3, int.w_5} \, \rangle, \mathtt{w_2} \in \mathbb{Z} \wedge \mathtt{w_3} \in \mathbb{Z} \wedge \mathtt{w_5} = \mathtt{w_2})$$

Roughly speaking, the constrained symbolic trace can be obtained by evaluating the operational semantics, collecting the labels together, and keeping the constraint over the symbolic variables used in the labels. The ? and ! decorations that determine whether the communications are inputs or outputs are ignored.

There is a forbidden continuation of this trace for each of the channels in scope. The only possible continuations involve communications over out, but not all of them are allowed. For example, the following is the specification of the forbidden continuations involving $inpA$; it is a constrained symbolic event.

$$(\mathtt{inpA.w_6}, \mathtt{w_2} \in \mathbb{Z} \wedge \mathtt{w_3} \in \mathbb{Z} \wedge \mathtt{w_5} = \mathtt{w_2})$$

It records the constraint of the trace, and imposes no restriction on the value w_6 communicated via $inpA$, since no value is allowed. The specification for the forbidden continuations involving out, on the other hand, is as follows.

$$(\mathtt{out.w_6}, \mathtt{w_2} \in \mathbb{Z} \wedge \mathtt{w_3} \in \mathbb{Z} \wedge \mathtt{w_5} = \mathtt{w_2} \wedge \mathtt{w_6} \neq \mathtt{w_2} - 2 \wedge \mathtt{w_6} \neq \mathtt{w_3} - 2)$$

The symbolic tests corresponding to the above trace and the forbidden continuation above (involving out) is as follows.

$inc \rightarrow inpA?w_2 : w_2 \in \mathbb{Z} \rightarrow$
$inc \rightarrow inpB?w_3 : w_2 \in \mathbb{Z} \wedge w_3 \in \mathbb{Z} \rightarrow$
$inc \rightarrow int?w_5 : w_2 \in \mathbb{Z} \wedge w_3 \in \mathbb{Z} \wedge w_5 = w_2 \rightarrow pass \rightarrow$
$out?w_6 : w_2 \in \mathbb{Z} \wedge w_3 \in \mathbb{Z} \wedge w_5 = w_2 \wedge w_6 \neq w_2 - 2 \wedge w_6 \neq w3 - 2 \rightarrow$
$fail \rightarrow \mathbf{Stop}$

We use extra special events inc, $pass$ and $fail$ to indicate a verdict. In the execution of a testing experiment, the test is run in parallel with the SUT, with all the model events hidden, so that the interaction between the test and the SUT cannot be affected by the environment. In our example, the communications over $inpA$, $inpB$, and int are hidden. The last special event observed in a testing experiment provides the verdict. Due the possibility of nondeterminism, a trace of the model is not necessarily available in the SUT. The inc event indicates an inconclusive verdict: the SUT has not performed the proposed trace. If it does perform the trace, we have a $pass$ event, but if the SUT proceeds to engage in the forbidden communication, then we have a $fail$.

The last event is that observed before the testing experiment leads to a deadlock. As already hinted, we do assume that we can observe a deadlock. In practice, this requires the definition of a timeout.

A possible concrete test satisfying the test specification above is as follows.

$$inc \rightarrow inpA.0 \rightarrow inc \rightarrow inpB.1 \rightarrow inc \rightarrow int.0 \rightarrow pass \rightarrow out.2 \rightarrow fail \rightarrow \textbf{Stop}$$

There are, of course, infinitely many other choices, as there may be infinitely many test specifications, in the case, for example, of nonterminating processes.

In the tests for *conf*, we use the traces and acceptances of a process. In the exhaustive test set for *conf*, we have all tests formed by considering all traces of the model, and all the acceptance sets after each of them.

In a *conf* test we check that, after the trace, the *SUT* does not deadlock if it is offered all the events of an acceptance set. Acceptance sets, like refusals, are more interesting for nondeterministic processes. So, we consider the action E in Example 1. After the empty trace $(\langle \rangle, \texttt{True})$, the specification of the minimal sets of acceptances is the following set of constrained symbolic events. They record whether the communications are inputs or outputs. As explained below, this is important in the creation of the concrete acceptance sets and *conf* tests.

$$\{(\texttt{out!w}_3, \texttt{w}_3 > 0), (\texttt{inp?w}_3, \texttt{w}_3 \in \mathbb{Z})\}$$

Roughly speaking, this is obtained by picking one of the continuations from each of the stable states that can be reached via the empty trace. Stable states are those from which there is no silent transition available. In our example, the stable states are those from which just a transition with label $\texttt{out!w}_3$ or label $\texttt{inp?w}_3$ is available. These labels define the continuations.

The symbolic test for *conf* defined by the empty trace and the constrained symbolic acceptance set above is as follows.

$$fail \rightarrow (out!w_3 : w_3 > 0 \rightarrow pass \rightarrow \textbf{Stop} \,\square\, inp?w_3 : w_3 \in \mathbb{Z} \rightarrow pass \rightarrow \textbf{Stop})$$

Since the trace is empty, there is no need for *inc* events. Before offering the *SUT* all the events of the acceptance set, we have a *fail*. The *SUT* cannot deadlock when all events of an acceptance are available, so if it accepts any of them, then we have a *pass*. Otherwise, the *fail* verdict stands.

In instantiating the above test, we can obtain the concrete test below.

$$fail \rightarrow (out?w_3 : w_3 > 0 \rightarrow pass \rightarrow \textbf{Stop} \,\square\, inp.0 \rightarrow pass \rightarrow \textbf{Stop})$$

The output in the model becomes an input in the test, since any output produced by the *SUT* is acceptable as long as it satisfies the associated constraint. For the input, a concrete test chooses a particular value satisfying the constraint.

The constraints in the symbolic tests for both traces refinement and *conf* define the constraint-satisfaction problems that need to be solved to obtain concrete tests. They provide a concise account of the state operations and their properties. Selection of concrete tests can use criteria based on coverage of the symbolic transition system, for instance. In addition, we can use the constraints to apply standard techniques based on uniformity subdomains. A very simple approach, for instance, considers, to start with, just one concrete test for each symbolic test (so that the constraints are themselves taken as definitions of uniformity subdomains: sets of tests that provide the same verdict).

What the symbolic tests do not provide is support for criteria based on the structure of the models. For example, in the tests above, we have no record of the way in which the variables x, y, z and so on are used. For larger examples, uses of data operations can also be of interest. For instance, the symbolic tests for the *ResourceManager* presented in Section 2.1 do not keep a record of the use of the operations *Cache*, *Insert*, and so on. It is to address this issue that we define a new transition system for *Circus* in the next section.

3   Specification-Oriented Transition System

The main distinguishing feature of the new transition system is its labels. They record not only events, like in the operational semantics, but also guards and state changes. Additionally, they are expressed in terms of the expressions of the *Circus* model, rather than symbolic variables. For example, for the action E in Example 1, we have transitions with labels x := 2, y > z, and out!z.

Furthermore, the specification-oriented system has no silent transitions; they correspond to evolutions that are not guarded, and do not entail any communication or state change. These transitions do not capture observable behaviour, and so are not interesting from a testing point of view.

We first discuss the definition of the new transition system for processes (Section 3.1). It is specified in terms of a transition relation for actions (Section 3.4), which is itself defined in terms of two other relations (Sections 3.2 and 3.3).

3.1   Processes

Like in the operational semantics, we have a transition relation $\Longrightarrow$ between texts of process. It is defined in terms of the corresponding relation for actions by the transition rule below. The labels are triples including a guard, an event, and an action. As mentioned above, there are no silent transitions.

We have a single transition rule, which allows us to lift transitions of the main action of a process in its local state to the process itself.

$$\frac{(state(\text{P}_1) \models maction(\text{P}_1)) \overset{1}{\Longrightarrow} (state(\text{P}_2) \models maction(\text{P}_2))}{\text{P}_1 \overset{1}{\Longrightarrow} \text{P}_2} \quad (1)$$

The local state of a process is characterised by the syntactic function *state* (P). It is defined below for basic processes: those originally in the *Circus* notation, and the extended form of process with a loc clause used in the operational semantics.

$state(\text{begin state } [\text{x} : \text{T}] \bullet \text{A end}) = (\text{w}_0 \in \text{T} \mid \text{x} := \text{w}_0)$
$state(\text{begin state } [\text{x} : \text{T}] \text{ loc } (\text{c} \mid \text{s}) \bullet \text{A end}) = (\text{c} \mid \text{s})$

where w_0 is a fresh symbolic variable. As mentioned in Section 2.2, there is no need to consider the composed processes, which are defined in terms of basic processes. Another syntactic function *maction* extracts the main action of a basic process. Its simple definition is omitted.

Unlike in the operational semantics, we do not have a rule to introduce the extended form of basic process as a first step of the evaluation. That is a silent transition, which we do not keep in the specification-oriented system.

For actions, a transition $(c_1 \mid s_1 \models A_1) \xRightarrow{(g,e,A)} (c_2 \mid s_2 \models A_2)$ establishes that in the state characterised by $(c_1 \mid s_1)$, if the guard g holds, then in the execution of A_1 the event e takes place, and afterwards A is executed. The new state is then characterised by $(c_2 \mid s_2)$ and the remaining action to execute is A_2. In the label, if the guard is True, we can omit it, and write just (e,A). Similarly, we omit the event if its value is ϵ, and the action, if omitted, is Skip. We do not have silent transitions, here defined as transitions with label (True, ϵ, Skip). So, at least one of the components of a label has to be given explicitly. If it has only one component given explicitly, we do not use the tuple notation.

The language used to write guards, events, and actions is *Circus* [23]. For actions, however, we include the extensions necessary to express the operational semantics, add the UTP constructs for variable declaration (**var** $x : T$) and undeclaration (**end** x), and two new constructs for parallelism and external choice.

The definition of $(c_1 \mid s_1 \models A_1) \xRightarrow{(g,e,A)} (c_2 \mid s_2 \models A_2)$ uses a succession of other transition relations that we define in the next sections.

3.2   Specification Labels

The first relation $(c_1 \mid s_1 \models A_1) \xRightarrow{(g,e,A)}_L (c_2 \mid s_2 \models A_2)$ associates configurations that are already related by a transition of the operational semantics. It, however, records more information in the labels, as explained above, and formalised below by the transition rules that define this new relation.

Basic actions. There are three rules for basic actions presented below: one for designs, one for schemas, and one for assignment. They are basically the same as the corresponding rules of the operational semantics (see Appendix A). The difference is that we record the executed action (state change) in the label.

$$\frac{c \wedge (s;\ p) \wedge (\exists\, v' \bullet s;\ Q)}{(c \mid s \models p \vdash Q) \xRightarrow{p \vdash Q}_L (c \wedge (s;\ Q\,[w_0/v']) \mid s;\ v := w_0 \models \text{Skip})} \quad v' = out\alpha s \qquad (2)$$

$$\frac{c \wedge (s;\ \mathbf{pre}\ Op)}{(c \mid s \models Op) \xRightarrow{Op} (c \wedge (s;\ Op\,[w_0/v']) \mid s;\ v := w_0 \models \text{Skip})} \quad v' = out\alpha s \qquad (3)$$

$$\frac{c}{(c \mid s \models v := e) \xRightarrow{v := e}_L (c \wedge (s;\ w_0 = e) \mid s;\ v := w_0 \models \text{Skip})} \qquad (4)$$

What we do not have are rules corresponding to those in the operational semantics that cover the situation where the precondition of a design or schema is false, and the action diverges. These are not useful in our work on testing, where, as previously explained, we assume the absence of divergence.

Example 3. For components of our example action E introduced in Example 1, we have the two transitions below. The numbers refer to the transition rules of the new relation presented above, rather than those of the operational semantics.

$(w_0 \in \mathbb{Z} \wedge w_1 \in \mathbb{Z} \mid x, y := w_0, w_1 \models x := 2)$

$\overset{x:=2}{\Longrightarrow}_L$ [Rule (4)]

$(w_0 \in \mathbb{Z} \wedge w_1 \in \mathbb{Z} \wedge w_2 = 2 \mid x, y := w_2, w_1 \models \mathsf{Skip})$

$\left(\begin{matrix} w_0 \in \mathbb{Z} \wedge w_1 \in \mathbb{Z} \wedge w_2 = 2 \wedge w_1 > w_2 \wedge w_3 = w_1 - w_2 \mid x, y := w_2, w_1 \\ \models \\ x := y \end{matrix} \right)$

$\overset{x:=y}{\Longrightarrow}_L$ [Rule (4)]

$\left(\begin{matrix} w_0 \in \mathbb{Z} \wedge w_1 \in \mathbb{Z} \wedge w_2 = 2 \wedge w_1 > w_2 \wedge w_3 = w_1 - w_2 \wedge w_4 = w_2 \mid x, y := w_4, w_1 \\ \models \\ \mathsf{Skip} \end{matrix} \right)$

□

We do not use symbolic variables in labels. We still, however, keep the characterisation of the state in terms of symbolic variables. This allows the combined use of the operational semantics and the specification-oriented transition system. This is useful both in the definition of the new transition system, and in the testing techniques that we plan to explore, since as explained in Section 2.3, *Circus* tests are expressed in terms of the symbolic variables.

Guards and prefixings. As previously mentioned, guards are also recorded in labels. We present below a rule similar to Rule (12) of the operational semantics, but which records the guard in the label.

$$\frac{c \wedge (s;\ g)}{(c \mid s \models g \& A) \overset{g}{\Longrightarrow}_L (c \wedge (s;\ g) \mid s \models A)} \tag{5}$$

There is no rule here and in the operational semantics for when the guard does not hold. This is a deadlock, represented by the absence of available transitions.

Example 4

$\left(\begin{matrix} w_0 \in \mathbb{Z} \wedge w_1 \in \mathbb{Z} \wedge w_2 = 2 \mid x, y := w_2, w_1 \\ \models \\ y > x \& \mathsf{out}!(y - x) \rightarrow \mathsf{Skip} \end{matrix} \right)$

$\overset{y>x}{\Longrightarrow}_L$ [Rule (5)]

$$\begin{pmatrix} w_0 \in \mathbb{Z} \wedge w_1 \in \mathbb{Z} \wedge w_2 = 2 \wedge w_1 > w_2 \mid x, y := w_2, w_1 \\ \models \\ \text{out!}(y - x) \to \text{Skip} \end{pmatrix}$$

☐

As opposed to the transitions in the operational semantics, here the labels for the transitions that apply to output prefixings record the expressions e whose values are output (rather than symbolic variables representing those values).

$$\frac{c}{(c \mid s \models d!e \to A) \overset{d!e}{\Longrightarrow}_L (c \wedge (s; \, w_0 = e) \mid s \models A)} \tag{6}$$

As discussed before, in the labels of $\Longrightarrow_L$, there is no use of symbolic variables. These labels record the text of the specification, rather than events with evaluated values (represented by symbolic variables). In this way, they record, for instance, the specification variables used in the communication d!e.

Example 5

$$\begin{pmatrix} w_0 \in \mathbb{Z} \wedge w_1 \in \mathbb{Z} \wedge w_2 = 2 \wedge w_1 > w_2 \mid x, y := w_2, w_1 \\ \models \\ \text{out!}(y - x) \to \text{Skip} \end{pmatrix}$$

$$\overset{\text{out.}(y-x)}{\Longrightarrow}_L \qquad\qquad\qquad\qquad\qquad\qquad \text{[Rule (6)]}$$

$$\begin{pmatrix} w_0 \in \mathbb{Z} \wedge w_1 \in \mathbb{Z} \wedge w_2 = 2 \wedge w_1 > w_2 \wedge w_3 = w_1 - w_2 \mid x, y := w_2, w_1 \\ \models \\ \text{Skip} \end{pmatrix}$$

☐

In the case of an input, the label records the input variable.

$$\frac{c \wedge T \neq \varnothing \qquad x \notin \alpha s}{(c \mid s \models d?x : T \to A) \overset{d?x}{\Longrightarrow} (c \wedge w_0 \in T \mid s; \, \text{var}\, x := w_0 \models \text{let}\, x \bullet A)} \tag{7}$$

Just like in CSP, the input implicitly declares the input variable x.

Example 6

$$\begin{pmatrix} w_0 \in \mathbb{Z} \wedge w_1 \in \mathbb{Z} \wedge w_2 = 2 \mid x, y := w_2, w_1 \\ \models \\ \text{inp?}z \to \text{Stop} \end{pmatrix}$$

$$\overset{\text{inp?}z}{\Longrightarrow}_L \qquad\qquad\qquad\qquad\qquad\qquad \text{[Rules (5) and (9)]}$$

$$\begin{pmatrix} w_0 \in \mathbb{Z} \wedge w_1 \in \mathbb{Z} \wedge w_2 = 2 \wedge w_3 \in \mathbb{Z} \mid x, y := w_2, w_1; \, \text{var}\, z := w_3 \\ \models \\ \text{let}\, z \bullet \text{Stop} \end{pmatrix}$$

☐

Variables. To record a variable declaration in a label, we use the UTP variable declaration construct **var** x. It is not available in *Circus*, originally, but can be defined as $\exists\, x \bullet$ **Skip** in the UTP theory for *Circus*.

$$\frac{c \wedge T \neq \varnothing \qquad x \notin \alpha s}{(c \mid s \models \mathbf{var}\, x : T \bullet A) \overset{(\mathbf{var}\, x:T)}{\Longrightarrow}_L (c \wedge w_0 \in T \mid s;\ \mathbf{var}\, x := w_0 \models \mathbf{let}\, x \bullet A)} \tag{8}$$

Like in the operational semantics, we assume that variable names are not reused.

When the action in the scope of a variable declaration finishes, the end of the scope is also recorded. For that we use the UTP undeclaration construct **end** x.

$$\frac{c}{(c \mid s \models \mathbf{let}\, x \bullet \mathbf{Skip}) \overset{(\mathbf{end}\, x)}{\Longrightarrow}_L (c \mid s;\ \mathbf{end}\, x \models \mathbf{Skip})} \tag{9}$$

Action operators. There are standard rules that reflect the fact that evolution of a component action leads to the evolution of the composed action that uses it.

$$\frac{(c_1 \mid s_1 \models A_1) \overset{1}{\Longrightarrow}_L (c_2 \mid s_2 \models A_2)}{(c_1 \mid s_1 \models \mathbf{let}\, x \bullet A_1) \overset{1}{\Longrightarrow}_L (c_2 \mid s_2 \models \mathbf{let}\, x \bullet A_2)} \tag{10}$$

$$\frac{(c_1 \mid s_1 \models A_1) \overset{1}{\Longrightarrow}_L (c_2 \mid s_2 \models A_2)}{(c_1 \mid s_1 \models A_1;\ B) \overset{1}{\Longrightarrow}_L (c_2 \mid s_2 \models A_2;\ B)} \tag{11}$$

For the silent transitions of the operational semantics that are involved in the evolution of a composed action, we have no corresponding transition rule. For instance, we have no specific rule for an action $\mathtt{Skip};\ A$ or an action $A_1 \sqcap A_2$. In the following section, we give a transition relation that handles these actions.

Example 7. We consider again the action E of Example 1, and present below transitions that are justified by the rules for the specification-oriented relation. We observe that, in many cases, no such rule applies, and we indicate again the transitions of the operational semantics that are possible.

$$(w_0 \in \mathbb{Z} \wedge w_1 \in \mathbb{Z} \mid x, y := w_0, w_1 \models E)$$

$$\overset{x:=2}{\Longrightarrow}_L \qquad\qquad\qquad\qquad\qquad\qquad\qquad \text{[Rules (4) and (11)]}$$

$$\begin{pmatrix} w_0 \in \mathbb{Z} \wedge w_1 \in \mathbb{Z} \wedge w_2 = 2 \mid x, y := w_2, w_1 \\ \models \\ \mathbf{Skip};\ (y > x\ \&\ \mathrm{out}!(y - x) \to \mathbf{Skip} \sqcap \mathrm{inp}?z \to \mathbf{Stop});\ x := y \end{pmatrix}$$

$$\longrightarrow$$

$$\begin{pmatrix} w_0 \in \mathbb{Z} \wedge w_1 \in \mathbb{Z} \wedge w_2 = 2 \mid x, y := w_2, w_1 \\ \models \\ (y > x\ \&\ \mathrm{out}!(y - x) \to \mathbf{Skip} \sqcap \mathrm{inp}?z \to \mathbf{Stop});\ x := y \end{pmatrix}$$

As before, we consider each of the options of the internal choice in turn.

$\longrightarrow$

$$
\begin{pmatrix}
w_0 \in \mathbb{Z} \land w_1 \in \mathbb{Z} \land w_2 = 2 \mid x, y := w_2, w_1 \\
\models \\
(y > x \ \& \ out!(y - x) \rightarrow Skip); \ x := y
\end{pmatrix}
$$

$\stackrel{y \geq x}{\Longrightarrow}_L$ [Rules (5) and (11)]

$$
\begin{pmatrix}
w_0 \in \mathbb{Z} \land w_1 \in \mathbb{Z} \land w_2 = 2 \land w_1 > w_2 \mid x, y := w_2, w_1 \\
\models \\
(out!(y - x) \rightarrow Skip); \ x := y
\end{pmatrix}
$$

$\stackrel{out!(y-x)}{\Longrightarrow}_L$ [Rules (6) and (11)]

$$
\begin{pmatrix}
w_0 \in \mathbb{Z} \land w_1 \in \mathbb{Z} \land w_2 = 2 \land w_1 > w_2 \land w_3 = w_1 - w_2 \mid x, y := w_2, w_1 \\
\models \\
Skip; \ x := y
\end{pmatrix}
$$

$\longrightarrow$

$$
\begin{pmatrix}
w_0 \in \mathbb{Z} \land w_1 \in \mathbb{Z} \land w_2 = 2 \land w_1 > w_2 \land w_3 = w_1 - w_2 \mid x, y := w_2, w_1 \\
\models \\
x := y
\end{pmatrix}
$$

$\stackrel{x:=y}{\Longrightarrow}_L$ [Rule (2)]

$$
\begin{pmatrix}
w_0 \in \mathbb{Z} \land w_1 \in \mathbb{Z} \land w_2 = 2 \land w_1 > w_2 \land w_3 = w_1 - w_2 \land w_4 = w_2 \mid x, y := w_4, w_1 \\
\models \\
Skip
\end{pmatrix}
$$

For the second option of the internal choice, we proceed as follows.

$\longrightarrow$

$$
\begin{pmatrix}
w_0 \in \mathbb{Z} \land w_1 \in \mathbb{Z} \land w_2 = 2 \mid x, y := w_2, w_1 \\
\models \\
(inp?z \rightarrow Stop); \ x := y
\end{pmatrix}
$$

$\stackrel{inp?z}{\Longrightarrow}_L$ [Rules (7) and (11)]

$$
\begin{pmatrix}
w_0 \in \mathbb{Z} \land w_1 \in \mathbb{Z} \land w_2 = 2 \land w_3 \in \mathbb{Z} \mid x, y := w_2, w_1; \ var \ z := w_3 \\
\models \\
(let \ z \bullet Stop); \ x := y
\end{pmatrix}
$$

From here, we cannot proceed with either kind of transition.   □

Parallelism and external choice. For these, the use of global variables raises an important issue. As already explained, parallel actions have access to the values of the global variables before the start of the parallelism, and can change their values locally. The name partitions define the updates that become visible after the parallelism finishes. This raises an issue concerning the interpretation of labels of transitions that reflect the evolution of parallel actions.

Example 8. We consider the following action involving an interleaving. (In both the operational and denotational semantics, interleaving is treated as a parallelism with an empty set of synchronisation channels.)

$$PA \mathrel{\widehat{=}} x := 2; \; ((x := 3; \; out!x \rightarrow \mathbf{Skip}) \, \| [\, \{x\} \mid \{ \} \,] \| \, (x := 4; \; out!x \rightarrow \mathbf{Skip}))$$

A naive approach to recording the evolution of the parallelism could lead to a sequence of labels like $(x := 2), (x := 3), (x := 4), out!x$. A perhaps reasonable interpretation of this path of execution would then be that the value 4 is output via *out*. This is, however, not necessarily the case, since, if the output comes from the first parallel action, then the value output is 3, and after two outputs, the new value of x is 3, in spite of the intermediate $x := 4$. The sequence of labels is not an accurate description of a path of execution of *PA*.   □

Example 9. A similar situation arises with the external choice below.

$$ECA \mathrel{\widehat{=}} x := 2; \; ((x := 3; \; outA!x \rightarrow \mathbf{Skip}) \; \Box \; (outB!x \rightarrow \mathbf{Skip}))$$

A sequence of labels $(x := 2), (x := 3); outB!x$ would be misleading, because the assignment $x := 3$ is discarded once the choice for the other action is taken.   □

In both cases, the difficulty is related to the fact that labels expose expressions that occur in the local scope of alternative paths of execution. In the operational semantics, this has been addressed by recording in the symbolic variables the evaluated values of the expressions, and using the symbolic variables, rather than the expressions themselves, to write the labels. Here, to record information about the structure of the specification, we need to keep the expressions.

What we need is to record is the use of global variables as local variables in parallel actions and external choices. For *PA* in Example 8, for instance, we need local versions x_l and x_r of x for the left-hand and the right-hand parallel actions. They are declared at the start of the parallelism, and the parallel actions use the local instead of the global variables. When the parallelism terminates, the global variables are updated in accordance with the name sets, and the local variables undeclared. A possible path for the action *PA*, for instance, is as follows.

$$(\mathsf{x} := 2), (\mathsf{var}\, \mathsf{x}_1, \mathsf{x}_r := \mathsf{x}, \mathsf{x}),$$
$$(\mathsf{x}_1 = 3), (\mathsf{x}_r := 4), (\mathsf{out}!\mathsf{x}_1), (\mathsf{out}!\mathsf{x}_r),$$
$$(\mathsf{x} := \mathsf{x}_1; \; \mathsf{end}\, \mathsf{x}_1, \mathsf{x}_r)$$

A related problem arises from the use of local variables in parallel paths of execution. This is illustrated and explained in the example below.

Example 10. We consider the interleaving and external choice below.

$$PALV \mathrel{\widehat{=}} x := 2; \; (int?z \rightarrow out!z \rightarrow \mathbf{Skip}) \, \| \| \, (out!x \rightarrow \mathbf{Skip})$$
$$ECALV \mathrel{\widehat{=}} x := 2; \; ((\mathbf{var}\, z \bullet x := z; \; outA \rightarrow \mathbf{Skip}) \; \Box \; (outB \rightarrow \mathbf{Skip}))$$

In the case of *PALV*, the labels int?z and out!z refer to a variable z that is not in the scope of (the state of) *PALV*, but in the local state of its first parallel action. The same holds for the labels $\mathrm{var}\,z$ and $x := z$ in the case of $ECALV$, which correspond to state changes that are local to the first action in the choice, and that are discarded if an interaction on $outB$ occurs.   □

In the operational semantics, this is again addressed by recording the local state of parallel actions and of branches of an external choice. The local state is used to evaluate any predicates or expressions when defining the constraint on symbolic variables. Since only the symbolic variables are used in labels, their interpretation is clear. Once again, however, here we need to keep the expressions.

For that, we in fact consider a single global scope declaring all variables. The structure of the specification itself, and the fact that names are not reused, enforces the appropriate use of the variables. In the case, of $PALV$, for instance, we have the following possible sequence of labels $(x := 2)$, $(\mathrm{var}\,x_1, x_r := x, x)$, $\mathrm{int}?z$, $\mathrm{out}!x_r$, $\mathrm{out}!z$, $(\mathrm{end}\,z)$, $(x := x_r;\ \mathrm{end}\,x_1, x_r)$. In this case, the scope of z is declared inside that of the local versions x_1 and x_r of x.

In summary, we provide an alternative view of the parallelism. It no longer creates two local states as in the operational semantics. Instead, the parallelism gives rise to two local copies of the global variables, which coexist, and at the end of the parallelism are used to update the global variables. This is in contrast with the parallel by merge in the UTP, where the the parallel actions work on local copies of the global state, whose variables are undeclared, and the local states are reconciled when needed. This is the view adopted in the *Circus* denotational and operational semantics. Here, we keep an extended global state containing the original (global) variables and their local copies.

To provide a transition system with these characteristics, we use a new construct $\mathrm{spar}\ v \mid v_1 \mid v_2 \mid x := x_1 \bullet A$, which is used to represent a parallel action A in a state containing the original global variables v, copies v_1 of these variables that are only used by A, and copies v_2 of these variables that are not used by A. In addition, A has write control over the global variables x, which correspond to the variables x_1. In out example action $PALV$, for instance, for the first action v is x, v_1 is x_l, v_2 is x_r, and if we assume that this is the action that has write control over x, then x is itself the programming variable x, and x_1 is x_l.

The transition rule that introduces the use of this new construct is as follows. The label in this case records the declaration of the new variables.

$$
\cfrac{
c \atop
(\mathrm{c} \mid \mathrm{s} \models \mathrm{A}_1 \llbracket\, \mathrm{x1} \mid \mathrm{cs} \mid \mathrm{x2}\, \rrbracket \mathrm{A}_2)
}{
\begin{array}{c}
\overset{\mathrm{var}\ v_1, v_r := v, v}{\Longrightarrow}_L \\[4pt]
\left(
\begin{array}{c}
\mathrm{c} \mid \mathrm{s};\ \mathrm{var}\ v_1, v_r := v, v \\
\models \\
\left(
\begin{array}{c}
(\mathrm{spar}\ v \mid v_1 \mid v_r \mid \mathrm{x1} := \mathrm{x1}_1 \bullet \mathrm{A}_1[v_1/v]) \\
\llbracket \mathrm{cs} \rrbracket \\
(\mathrm{spar}\ v \mid v_r \mid v_1 \mid \mathrm{x2} := \mathrm{x2}_r \bullet \mathrm{A}_2[v_r/v])
\end{array}
\right)
\end{array}
\right)
\end{array}
}
\qquad
\begin{array}{l}
v' = out\alpha s \\
v = x1, x2 \\
\textit{fresh } v_l, v_r
\end{array}
\quad (12)
$$

As opposed to the transitions for parallelism in the operational semantics, the transitions here lead to change of state before the termination of the parallelism.

As defined above, the state is first changed by a declaration of fresh copies v_1 and v_r of the global variables v. The parallel action A_1 is transformed to record that the original global variables are v, that it uses v_1, but does not use v_r. There is also a record that the variables $x1$ in its name set take the value of the variables $x1_1$ upon termination of the parallelism. Finally, the variables v are renamed to v_1 in A_1. The other action A_2 is transformed in a similar way.

The renaming $A[y/x]$ substitutes y for x in the action A covering also decorated input, output, and dashed variables, to cater for the uses of x in schemas and specification statements. For instance, $(x : [x > 0, x' = x - 1])[y/x]$ is $y : [y > 0, y' = y - 1]$ and $[\Delta S; x! : \mathbb{Z} \bullet x! = 3][y/x]$ is $[\Delta S; y! : \mathbb{Z} \bullet y! = 3]$.

Example 11. We consider again the action *PA* of Example 2. We show the $\Longrightarrow_L$ transitions, and as before in Example 7 repeat the transitions of the operational semantics when no $\Longrightarrow_L$ transition is possible. We define that the first parallel action has control over x, even though neither action actually updates x.

$(w_0 \in \mathbb{Z} \mid x := w_0 \models PA)$

$\overset{x:=2}{\Longrightarrow}$ [Rules (4) and (11)]

$$\left(\begin{array}{l} w_0 \in \mathbb{Z} \wedge w_1 = 2 \mid x := w_1 \\ \models \\ \quad \text{Skip}; \quad \left(\begin{array}{c} (\text{inpA}?y \rightarrow \text{int}!y \rightarrow \text{out}!(y - x) \rightarrow \text{Skip}) \\ [\![\{x\} \mid \{\!|\, \text{int}\, |\!\} \mid \{\}]\!] \\ (\text{inpB}?z_1 \rightarrow \text{int}?z_2 \rightarrow z_1 > z_2 \,\&\, \text{out}!(z_1 - x) \rightarrow \text{Skip}) \end{array} \right) \end{array} \right)$$

$\longrightarrow$

$$\left(\begin{array}{l} w_0 \in \mathbb{Z} \wedge w_1 = 2 \mid x := w_1 \\ \models \\ \quad \left(\begin{array}{c} (\text{inpA}?y \rightarrow \text{int}!y \rightarrow \text{out}!(y - x) \rightarrow \text{Skip}) \\ [\![\{x\} \mid \{\!|\, \text{int}\, |\!\} \mid \{\}]\!] \\ (\text{inpB}?z_1 \rightarrow \text{int}?z_2 \rightarrow z_1 > z_2 \,\&\, \text{out}!(z_1 - x) \rightarrow \text{Skip}) \end{array} \right) \end{array} \right)$$

$\overset{\text{var } x_1, x_r := x, x}{\Longrightarrow}$ [Rule 12]

$$\left(\begin{array}{l} w_0 \in \mathbb{Z} \wedge w_1 = 2 \mid x := w_1; \ \text{var } x_1, x_r := x, x \\ \models \\ \quad \left(\begin{array}{c} (\text{spar } x \mid x_1 \mid x_r \mid x := x_1 \bullet \text{inpA}?y \rightarrow \text{int}!y \rightarrow \text{out}!(y - x_1) \rightarrow \text{Skip}) \\ [\![\{\!|\, \text{int}\, |\!\}]\!] \\ \left(\begin{array}{c} \text{spar } x \mid x_r \mid x_1 \mid \text{Skip} \bullet \\ \text{inpB}?z_1 \rightarrow \text{int}?z_2 \rightarrow z_1 > z_2 \,\&\, \text{out}!(z_1 - x_r) \rightarrow \text{Skip} \end{array} \right) \end{array} \right) \end{array} \right)$$

The second parallel action has write control over no variables, so we write the assignment to the empty list of variables as Skip. □

In this work, from the semantics of the new **spar** construct, we only need the transition rules that allow silent independent evolutions of the parallel actions. The rule that considers evolution of the first parallel action is presented below.

$$(c \mid s; \; \text{end} \, v, y \models A_1) \xrightarrow{\epsilon} (c_3 \mid s_3 \models A_3)$$

$$\left(\begin{array}{l} c \mid s \\ \models \\ \left(\begin{array}{c} (\text{spar} \, v \mid x \mid y \mid x_1 := z_1 \bullet A_1) \\ \llbracket cs \rrbracket \\ (\text{spar} \, v \mid y \mid x \mid x_2 := z_2 \bullet A_2) \end{array} \right) \end{array} \right) \xrightarrow{\epsilon} \left(\begin{array}{l} c \mid s_3 \wedge s; \; \text{end} \, x \\ \models \\ \left(\begin{array}{c} (\text{spar} \, v \mid x \mid y \mid x_1 := z_1 \bullet A_3) \\ \llbracket cs \rrbracket \\ (\text{spar} \, v \mid y \mid x \mid x_2 := z_2 \bullet A_2) \end{array} \right) \end{array} \right) \tag{13}$$

The action A_1 is evaluated in the state s after the original global variables v and the local variables y of A_2 are undeclared. The updated state of the parallelism is characterised by the conjunction of the state s_3 reached by A_1, with the original state s, after the local variables x of A_1 are eliminated. It is important to observe that the input variables of s_3 and s; $\text{end} \, x$ are the same, but their sets of output variables are disjoint, so that conjunction captures the effect of the parallelism. This is akin to the construct for parallelism of designs considered in [18].

Going back to the specification-oriented transition system, independent evolution of the left-hand parallel action A_1 is covered by the following rule. A similar rule caters for evolution of A_2. Like in the operational semantics, the state for A_1 is the global state s, with the global variables v and the local variables y of A_2 undeclared. To compose the new state we conjoin the after state s_3 of A_1, with the original state s followed by the undeclaration of y.

Variables declared in the scope of A_1, as flagged by the label 1, are made global, and so they need to be mentioned in the set of variables under the control of A_1 in both parallel actions. Similarly, if the scope of a variable is closed, then it needs to be removed from the set of variables under the control of A_1.

$$\frac{(c \mid s; \; \text{end} \, v, y \models A_1) \overset{1}{\Longrightarrow}_L (c_3 \mid s_3 \models A_3) \quad \text{chan} \, 1 = \epsilon \vee \text{chan} \, 1 \notin cs}{}$$

$$(c \mid s \models (\text{spar} \, v \mid x \mid y \mid x_1 := z_1 \bullet A_1) \llbracket \, cs \, \rrbracket (\text{spar} \, v \mid y \mid x \mid x_2 := z_2 \bullet A_2))$$

$$\overset{1}{\Longrightarrow}_L$$

$$\left(\begin{array}{l} c_3 \mid s_3 \wedge s; \; \text{end} \, x \\ \models \\ \left(\begin{array}{c} (\text{spar} \, v \mid x \upharpoonright (end \, 1), (var \, 1) \mid y \mid x_1 := z_1 \bullet A_3) \\ \llbracket cs \rrbracket \\ (\text{spar} \, v \mid y \mid x \upharpoonright (end \, 1), (var \, 1) \mid x_2 := z_2 \bullet A_2) \end{array} \right) \end{array} \right) \tag{14}$$

The function $end \, 1$ gives the variables whose scope are closed in the label 1. For example, $end(\text{end} \, x) = x$. The function $var \, 1$, on the other hand, gives the variables declared in 1. For example, $var(\text{var} \, x) = x$ and $var(d?x) = x$. Both end and var are syntactic functions that can be defined by induction on the structure of the actions used in labels in the obvious way. The syntactic function $x \upharpoonright y$ removes from the list of variables x the variables in the list y.

Example 12. Proceeding with the previous example, we have the following sequence of transitions if the left-hand action evolves first.

$\overset{\text{inpA?y}}{\Longrightarrow}$ [Rules (7) and (14)]

$$\left(\begin{array}{l} w_0 \in \mathbb{Z} \wedge w_1 = 2 \wedge w_2 \in \mathbb{Z} \mid x := w_1;\ var\, x_1, x_r := x, x;\ var\, y := w_2 \\ \models \\ \left(\begin{array}{c} (\text{spar } x \mid x_1, y \mid x_r \mid x := x_1 \bullet (\text{let } y \bullet \text{int!}y \rightarrow \text{out!}(y - x_1) \rightarrow \text{Skip})) \\ \llbracket \{\!| \text{ int } |\!\} \rrbracket \\ \left(\begin{array}{c} \text{spar } x \mid x_r \mid x_1, y \mid \text{Skip} \bullet \\ \text{inpB?}z_1 \rightarrow \text{int?}z_2 \rightarrow z_1 > z_2\ \&\ \text{out!}(z_1 - x_r) \rightarrow \text{Skip} \end{array}\right) \end{array}\right) \end{array}\right)$$

Above and in what follows, for conciseness, instead of the text actually generated by the application of the transition rules to describe the new state, we give a semantically equivalent, but simpler, description.

$\overset{\text{inpB?}z_1}{\Longrightarrow}$ [Rule (7) and Rule similar to (14)]

$$\left(\begin{array}{l} w_0 \in \mathbb{Z} \wedge w_1 = 2 \wedge w_2 \in \mathbb{Z} \wedge w_3 \in \mathbb{Z} \\ \mid x := w_1;\ var\, x_1, x_r := x, x;\ var\, y := w_2;\ var\, z_1 := w_3 \\ \models \\ \left(\begin{array}{c} (\text{spar } x \mid x_1, y \mid x_r, z_1 \mid x := x_1 \bullet (\text{let } y \bullet \text{int!}y \rightarrow \text{out!}(y - x_1) \rightarrow \text{Skip})) \\ \llbracket \{\!| \text{ int } |\!\} \rrbracket \\ \left(\begin{array}{c} \text{spar } x \mid x_r, z_1 \mid x_1, y \mid \text{Skip} \bullet \\ (\text{let } z_1 \bullet \text{int?}z_2 \rightarrow z_1 > z_2\ \&\ \text{out!}(z_1 - x_r) \rightarrow \text{Skip}) \end{array}\right) \end{array}\right) \end{array}\right)$$

□

The rule for synchronisation of an input d?a with an output d!e is as follows.

$$(c \mid s;\ end\, v, y \models A_1) \overset{(g_1, d?a, LA_1)}{\Longrightarrow}_L (c_3 \mid s_3 \models A_3)$$

$$(c \mid s;\ end\, v, x \models A_2) \overset{(g_2, d!e, LA_2)}{\Longrightarrow}_L (c_4 \mid s_4 \models A_4)$$

$$d \in cs \quad c_3 \wedge c_4 \wedge \exists w_0 \bullet (s_3;\ (w_0 = x)) \Leftrightarrow (s_4;\ (w_0 = e))$$

$$(c \mid s \models (\text{spar } v \mid x \mid y \mid x_1 := z_1 \bullet A_1) \llbracket cs \rrbracket (\text{spar } v \mid y \mid x \mid x_2 := z_2 \bullet A_2))$$

$\overset{(g_1 \wedge g_2, d!e, var\, a := e;\ LA_1;\ LA_2)}{\Longrightarrow}_L$

$$\left(\begin{array}{l} c_3 \wedge c_4 \wedge \exists w_0 \bullet (s_3;\ (w_0 = x)) \Leftrightarrow (s_4;\ (w_0 = e)) \mid s_3 \wedge s_4 \wedge s;\ end\, x, y \\ \models \\ \left(\begin{array}{c} (\text{spar } v \mid x \upharpoonright (end\, LA_1), a, (var\, LA_1) \mid y \upharpoonright (end\, LA_2), (var\, LA_2) \mid x_1 := z_1 \bullet A_3) \\ \llbracket cs \rrbracket \\ (\text{spar } v \mid y \upharpoonright (end\, LA_2), (var\, LA_2) \mid x \upharpoonright (end\, LA_1), a, (var\, LA_1) \mid x_2 := z_1 \bullet A_4) \end{array}\right) \end{array}\right)$$

(15)

For the parallelism to progress, both guards in the labels have to be satisfied jointly. As a result of the parallelism, we actually have an output d!e: this is what is observed by the environment of the parallelism. In addition, the input variable a is declared, and its value is initialized to that of e.

The constraint $\exists\, w_0 \bullet s_3;\ (w_0 = x) \Leftrightarrow s_4;\ (w_0 = e)$ requires that there is a value w_0 that is both the value of a in the after state s_3 of A_1, and the value of e in the after state s_4 of A_2. In fact, the value of the expression could be taken in the original state s but an output does not change the state.

The new state is the conjunction of the after states s_3 and s_4 of the parallel actions, and the original state s where the local versions x and y of the original global variables are all undeclared. This is necessary because neither s_3 nor s_4 includes the original global variables. On the other hand, in s; end x, y, these are the only output variables in scope. So, the conjunction is between predicates with the same input variables, but disjoint sets of output variables.

As for the previous transition rule, variables declared or undeclared, as stated in the labels, are recorded in the appropriate sets of variables of the parallel actions. These include the implicit declaration of the input variable a, and the variables declared or undeclared in the actions LA_1 and LA_2 of the labels.

We omit the similar rules for synchronisation of an output and an input, two inputs, or two outputs. For two inputs d?a and d?b, one of the input variables a is implicitly declared by the input event, and the other b is declared explicitly, and initialised to a. In the case of two outputs d!e and d!f, there are no variable declarations. The output value is that of e, and the guard guarantees that e = f.

Example 13. Proceeding with our example, we have the synchronisation.

$$\xrightarrow{(\mathrm{int}!y, \mathrm{var}\, z_2 := y)} \qquad [\text{Rules (6), (10), (7), and similar to (15)}]$$

$$\left(\begin{array}{l} w_0 \in \mathbb{Z} \wedge w_1 = 2 \wedge w_2 \in \mathbb{Z} \wedge w_3 \in \mathbb{Z} \wedge w_4 = w_2 \wedge w_5 \in \mathbb{Z} \wedge w_2 = w_5 \\ \mid x := w_1;\ \mathrm{var}\, x_1, x_r := x, x;\ \mathrm{var}\, y, z_1, z_2 := w_2, w_3, w_5 \\ \models \\ \left(\begin{array}{c} (\mathrm{spar}\ x \mid x_1, y \mid x_r, z_1, z_2 \mid x := x_1 \bullet (\mathrm{let}\ y \bullet \mathrm{out}!(y - x_1) \to \mathrm{Skip})) \\ [\![\{\!\mid \mathrm{int}\!\mid\}]\!] \\ \left(\begin{array}{c} \mathrm{spar}\ x \mid x_r, z_1, z_2 \mid x_1, y \mid \mathrm{Skip}\ \bullet \\ (\mathrm{let}\ z_1, z_2 \bullet z_1 > z_2\ \&\ \mathrm{out}!(z_1 - x_r) \to \mathrm{Skip}) \end{array}\right) \end{array}\right) \end{array}\right)$$

Again, the parallel actions can both evolve independently. We consider below one order of evolution: the first action evolves first.

$$\xrightarrow{\mathrm{out}!(y - x_1)} \qquad [\text{Rules (6), (10), and (14)}]$$

$$\left(\begin{array}{l} \left(\begin{array}{l} w_0 \in \mathbb{Z} \wedge w_1 = 2 \wedge w_2 \in \mathbb{Z} \wedge w_3 \in \mathbb{Z} \wedge \\ w_4 = w_2 \wedge w_5 \in \mathbb{Z} \wedge w_2 = w_5 \wedge w_6 = w_2 - w_1 \end{array}\right) \\ \mid x := w_1;\ \mathrm{var}\, x_1, x_r := x, x;\ \mathrm{var}\, y, z_1, z_2 := w_2, w_3, w_5 \\ \models \\ \left(\begin{array}{c} (\mathrm{spar}\ x \mid x_1, y \mid x_r, z_1, z_2 \mid x := x_1 \bullet (\mathrm{let}\ y \bullet \mathrm{Skip})) \\ [\![\{\!\mid \mathrm{int}\!\mid\}]\!] \\ \left(\begin{array}{c} \mathrm{spar}\ x \mid x_r, z_1, z_2 \mid x_1, y \mid \mathrm{Skip}\ \bullet \\ (\mathrm{let}\ z_1, z_2 \bullet z_1 > z_2\ \&\ \mathrm{out}!(z_1 - x_r) \to \mathrm{Skip}) \end{array}\right) \end{array}\right) \end{array}\right)$$

$$\overset{z_1 \ge z_2}{\Longrightarrow} \qquad \qquad \text{[Rules (5), (10), and similar to (14)]}$$

$$
\left(
\begin{array}{l}
\left(
\begin{array}{l}
w_0 \in \mathbb{Z} \wedge w_1 = 2 \wedge w_2 \in \mathbb{Z} \wedge w_3 \in \mathbb{Z} \wedge \\
w_4 = w_2 \wedge w_5 \in \mathbb{Z} \wedge w_2 = w_5 \wedge w_6 = w_2 - w_1 \wedge w_3 > w_5
\end{array}
\right) \\
\mid x := w_1; \; \text{var}\, x_1, x_r := x, x; \; \text{var}\, y, z_1, z_2 := w_2, w_3, w_5 \\
\models \\
\left(
\begin{array}{c}
(\text{spar}\, x \mid x_1, y \mid x_r, z_1, z_2 \mid x := x_1 \bullet (\text{let}\, y \bullet \text{Skip})) \\
[\![\{\, \text{int}\, \}]\!] \\
\left(
\begin{array}{l}
\text{spar}\, x \mid x_r, z_1, z_2 \mid x_1, y \mid \text{Skip} \bullet \\
\quad (\text{let}\, z_1, z_2 \bullet \text{out}!(z_1 - x_r) \to \text{Skip})
\end{array}
\right)
\end{array}
\right)
\end{array}
\right)
$$

$$\overset{\text{out}!(z_1 - x_r)}{\Longrightarrow} \qquad \qquad \text{[Rules (6), (10), and similar to (14)]}$$

$$
\left(
\begin{array}{l}
\left(
\begin{array}{l}
w_0 \in \mathbb{Z} \wedge w_1 = 2 \wedge w_2 \in \mathbb{Z} \wedge w_3 \in \mathbb{Z} \wedge \\
w_4 = w_2 \wedge w_5 \in \mathbb{Z} \wedge w_2 = w_5 \wedge w_6 = w_2 - w_1 \wedge w_3 > w_5 \wedge w_7 = w_3 - w_1
\end{array}
\right) \\
\mid x := w_1; \; \text{var}\, x_1, x_r := x, x; \; \text{var}\, y, z_1, z_2 := w_2, w_3, w_5 \\
\models \\
\left(
\begin{array}{c}
(\text{spar}\, x \mid x_1, y \mid x_r, z_1, z_2 \mid x := x_1 \bullet (\text{let}\, y \bullet \text{Skip})) \\
[\![\{\, \text{int}\, \}]\!] \\
(\text{spar}\, x \mid x_r, z_1, z_2 \mid x_1, y \mid \text{Skip} \bullet (\text{let}\, z_1, z_2 \bullet \text{Skip}))
\end{array}
\right)
\end{array}
\right)
$$

$$\overset{\text{end}\, y}{\Longrightarrow} \qquad \qquad \text{[Rules (10) and (14)]}$$

$$
\left(
\begin{array}{l}
\left(
\begin{array}{l}
w_0 \in \mathbb{Z} \wedge w_1 = 2 \wedge w_2 \in \mathbb{Z} \wedge w_3 \in \mathbb{Z} \wedge \\
w_4 = w_2 \wedge w_5 \in \mathbb{Z} \wedge w_2 = w_5 \wedge w_6 = w_2 - w_1 \wedge w_3 > w_5 \wedge w_7 = w_3 - w_1
\end{array}
\right) \\
\mid x := w_1; \; \text{var}\, x_1, x_r := x, x; \; \text{var}\, y, z_1, z_2 := w_2, w_3, w_5; \; \text{end}\, y \\
\models \\
\left(
\begin{array}{c}
(\text{spar}\, x \mid x_1 \mid x_r, z_1, z_2 \mid x := x_1 \bullet \text{Skip}) \\
[\![\{\, \text{int}\, \}]\!] \\
(\text{spar}\, x \mid x_r, z_1, z_2 \mid x_1 \mid \text{Skip} \bullet (\text{let}\, z_1, z_2 \bullet \text{Skip}))
\end{array}
\right)
\end{array}
\right)
$$

$$\overset{\text{end}\, z_1, z_2}{\Longrightarrow} \qquad \qquad \text{[Rules (10) and similar to (14)]}$$

$$
\left(
\begin{array}{l}
\left(
\begin{array}{l}
w_0 \in \mathbb{Z} \wedge w_1 = 2 \wedge w_2 \in \mathbb{Z} \wedge w_3 \in \mathbb{Z} \wedge \\
w_4 = w_2 \wedge w_5 \in \mathbb{Z} \wedge w_2 = w_5 \wedge w_6 = w_2 - w_1 \wedge w_3 > w_5 \wedge w_7 = w_3 - w_1
\end{array}
\right) \\
\mid \left(
\begin{array}{l}
x := w_1; \; \text{var}\, x_1, x_r := x, x; \\
\text{var}\, y, z_1, z_2 := w_2, w_3, w_5; \; \text{end}\, y; \; \text{end}\, z_1, z_2
\end{array}
\right) \\
\models \\
(\text{spar}\, x \mid x_1 \mid x_r \mid x := x_1 \bullet \text{Skip}) [\![\{\, \text{int}\, \}]\!] (\text{spar}\, x \mid x_r \mid x_1 \mid \text{Skip} \bullet \text{Skip})
\end{array}
\right)
$$

$$\qquad \qquad \qquad \qquad \qquad \qquad \qquad \qquad \qquad \qquad \qquad \qquad \square$$

The rule that applies when both parallel actions terminate is as follows. The label records the changes to the state.

$$\dfrac{c}{\begin{pmatrix} c \mid s \\ \models \\ \left(\dfrac{(\text{spar } v \mid x, z_1 \mid y, z_2 \mid x_1 := z_1 \bullet \text{Skip})}{\llbracket cs \rrbracket} \right) \\ (\text{spar } v \mid y, z_2 \mid x, z_1 \mid x_2 := z_2 \bullet \text{Skip}) \end{pmatrix}} \tag{16}$$

$$\xrightarrow{x_1, x_2 := z_1, z_2;\ \text{end } x, z_1, y, z_2}_{L}$$

$$(c \mid s;\ x_1, x_2 := z_1, z_2;\ \text{end } x, z_1, y, z_2 \models \text{Skip})$$

In the final state of the parallelism, the local versions x and y of the global variables are undeclared after they are used to update the global variables.

Example 14. We can now conclude our running example.

$$\xrightarrow{x := x_1;\ \text{end } x_1, x_r} \qquad\qquad [\text{Rule (16)}]$$

$$\left(\begin{array}{l} \left(\begin{array}{l} w_0 \in \mathbb{Z} \wedge w_1 = 2 \wedge w_2 \in \mathbb{Z} \wedge w_3 \in \mathbb{Z} \wedge \\ w_4 = w_2 \wedge w_5 \in \mathbb{Z} \wedge w_2 = w_5 \wedge w_6 = w_2 - w_1 \wedge w_3 > w_5 \wedge w_7 = w_3 - w_1 \end{array} \right) \\ \mid \left(\begin{array}{l} x := w_1;\ \text{var } x_1, x_r := x, x; \\ \text{var } y, z_1, z_2 := w_2, w_3, w_5;\ \text{end } y;\ \text{end } z_1, z_2;\ x := x_1;\ \text{end } x_1, x_r \end{array} \right) \\ \models \\ \text{Skip} \end{array} \right)$$

It is not difficult to prove that the final state of the parallelism is equivalent to $x := w_1$; its alphabet includes only x (and x').   □

The rules for external choice are not given here.

Hiding. There are two rules for hiding. The first allows evolution of the action to which the hiding is applied to lead to evolution of the hiding. This occurs when the evolution is not via a communication through a hidden channel.

$$\dfrac{(c_1 \mid s_1 \models A_1) \xRightarrow{1}_{L} (c_2 \mid s_2 \models A_2) \quad \text{chan } 1 \notin cs}{(c_1 \mid s_1 \models A_1 \setminus cs) \xRightarrow{1}_{L} (c_2 \mid s_2 \models A_2 \setminus cs)} \tag{17}$$

The second rule is for when the communication is through a hidden channel. In this case, the communication disappears. The evolution, therefore, is only possible if the guard is not **True** and the action is not **Skip**. In this case, we do not have the possibility of introducing a silent transition.

$$\dfrac{(c_1 \mid s_1 \models A_1) \xRightarrow{(g, e, A)}_{L} (c_2 \mid s_2 \models A_2)}{(g \neq \text{True} \vee A \neq \text{Skip}) \wedge (\text{chan } e = \epsilon \vee \text{chan } e \in cs)} \tag{18}$$
$$(c_1 \mid s_1 \models A_1 \setminus cs) \xRightarrow{(g, \epsilon, A)}_{L} (c_2 \mid s_2 \models A_2 \setminus cs)$$

Transitions of the operational semantics that are truly silent in the sense of the $\Longrightarrow_L$ relation, so that they do not entail any guards, communications, or state changes, are considered in the next section.

3.3 Silent Transitions

As already explained, the specification-oriented transition system has no silent transitions. In the previous section, we have defined a transition relation $\Longrightarrow_L$ which indeed has no silent transitions, but is not defined for some configurations for which there is a transition in the operational semantics. For instance, in Example 7, the second transition and a few others are transitions of the operational semantics. There are no corresponding transitions for $\Longrightarrow_L$.

We proceed with the definition of the specification-oriented transition system by introducing a new transition relation $(c_1 \mid s_1 \models A_1) \overset{(g,e,A)}{\Longrightarrow}_{SR} (c_2 \mid s_2 \models A_2)$. It associates a configuration $(c_1 \mid s_1 \models A_1)$ to a configuration $(c_2 \mid s_2 \models A_2)$ if, by starting from $(c_1 \mid s_1 \models A_1)$, following a transition from $\Longrightarrow_L$, and then as many silent transitions $\overset{\epsilon}{\longrightarrow}$ as possible, we reach $(c_2 \mid s_2 \models A_2)$.

By considering as many silent transitions as possible, we ensure that a configuration $(c_1 \mid s_1 \models A_1)$ is related only to those configurations $(c_2 \mid s_2 \models A_2)$ that can be reached after as much internal progress as possible has been made. For testing, extra transitions that represent partial internal progress are of no value. They would give rise to useless tests, and are avoided here.

To define the new relation $(c_1 \mid s_1 \models A_1) \overset{(g,e,A)}{\Longrightarrow}_{SR} (c_2 \mid s_2 \models A_2)$, we consider first the transitive closure $\longrightarrow^{\epsilon*}$ of the transition relation $\longrightarrow$ of the operational semantics when restricted to silent transitions with no corresponding transition in $\Longrightarrow_L$. It is defined by the two transition rules in the sequel.

$$\frac{(c_1 \mid s_1 \models A_1) \overset{\epsilon}{\longrightarrow} (c_2 \mid s_2 \models A_2) \quad (c_1 \mid s_1 \models A_1) \not\Rightarrow_L (c_2 \mid s_2 \models A_2)}{(c_1 \mid s_1 \models A_1) \longrightarrow^{\epsilon*} (c_2 \mid s_2 \models A_2)} \tag{19}$$

In the above rule, we write $(c_1 \mid s_1 \models A_1) \not\Rightarrow_L (c_2 \mid s_2 \models A_2)$ as an abbreviation for $\neg \exists 1 \bullet (c_1 \mid s_1 \models A_1) \overset{1}{\Longrightarrow}_L (c_2 \mid s_2 \models A_2)$. We require that there is no specification-oriented transition from $(c_1 \mid s_1 \models A_1)$ to $(c_2 \mid s_2 \models A_2)$ because many of the silent transitions of the operational semantics correspond to (non-silent) transitions of the specification-oriented system. For instance, the transitions for assignment are silent in the operational semantics, but not in the specification-oriented system. What we want is to ignore transitions that genuinely provide no information is terms of guards, events, or action execution. Examples are the transitions for internal choice (see Rules (11) in Appendix A).

The second transition rule allows the composition of silent transitions.

$$\frac{(c_1 \mid s_1 \models A_1) \longrightarrow^{\epsilon*} (c_2 \mid s_2 \models A_2)}{(c_2 \mid s_2 \models A_2) \overset{\epsilon}{\longrightarrow} (c_3 \mid s_3 \models A_3) \quad (c_2 \mid s_2 \models A_2) \not\Rightarrow_L (c_3 \mid s_3 \models A_3)}{(c_1 \mid s_1 \models A_1) \longrightarrow^{\epsilon*} (c_3 \mid s_3 \models A_3)} \tag{20}$$

We again check that the transitions composed are truly silent.

Example 15. In the context of our example action E, we have the following.

$$
\left(
\begin{array}{l}
w_0 \in \mathbb{Z} \wedge w_1 \in \mathbb{Z} \wedge w_2 = 2 \mid x, y := w_2, w_1 \\
\models \\
\mathrm{Skip};\; (y > x \;\&\; \mathrm{out}!(y - x) \to \mathrm{Skip} \sqcap \mathrm{inp}?z \to \mathrm{Stop});\; x := y
\end{array}
\right)
$$

$$\longrightarrow^{\epsilon*}$$

$$
\left(
\begin{array}{l}
w_0 \in \mathbb{Z} \wedge w_1 \in \mathbb{Z} \wedge w_2 = 2 \mid x, y := w_2, w_1 \\
\models \\
(y > x \;\&\; \mathrm{out}!(y - x) \to \mathrm{Skip});\; x := y
\end{array}
\right)
$$

This corresponds to choosing the first action of the internal choice. For a choice of the second action, we have the transition below.

$$
\left(
\begin{array}{l}
w_0 \in \mathbb{Z} \wedge w_1 \in \mathbb{Z} \wedge w_2 = 2 \mid x, y := w_2, w_1 \\
\models \\
\mathrm{Skip};\; (y > x \;\&\; \mathrm{out}!(y - x) \to \mathrm{Skip} \sqcap \mathrm{inp}?z \to \mathrm{Stop});\; x := y
\end{array}
\right)
$$

$$\longrightarrow^{\epsilon*}$$

$$
\left(
\begin{array}{l}
w_0 \in \mathbb{Z} \wedge w_1 \in \mathbb{Z} \wedge w_2 = 2 \mid x, y := w_2, w_1 \\
\models \\
(\mathrm{inp}?z \to \mathrm{Stop});\; x := y
\end{array}
\right)
$$

We also have the transition below.

$$
\left(
\begin{array}{l}
w_0 \in \mathbb{Z} \wedge w_1 \in \mathbb{Z} \wedge w_2 = 2 \wedge w_1 > w_2 \wedge w_3 = w_1 - w_2 \mid x, y := w_2, w_1 \\
\models \\
\mathrm{Skip};\; x := y
\end{array}
\right)
$$

$$\longrightarrow^{\epsilon*}$$

$$
\left(
\begin{array}{l}
w_0 \in \mathbb{Z} \wedge w_1 \in \mathbb{Z} \wedge w_2 = 2 \wedge w_1 > w_2 \wedge w_3 = w_1 - w_2 \mid x, y := w_2, w_1 \\
\models \\
x := y
\end{array}
\right)
$$

This corresponds to a single silent transition of the operational semantics.   □

The new relation $(c_1 \mid s_1 \models A_1) \stackrel{(g,e,A)}{\Longrightarrow}_{SR} (c_2 \mid s_2 \models A_2)$ is defined below.

$$
\frac{(c_1 \mid s_1 \models A_1) \stackrel{1}{\Longrightarrow}_L (c_2 \mid s_2 \models A_2) \quad}{(c_1 \mid s_1 \models A_1) \stackrel{1}{\Longrightarrow}_{SR} (c_3 \mid s_3 \models A_3)}
\frac{(c_2 \mid s_2 \models A_2) \longrightarrow^{\epsilon*} (c_3 \mid s_3 \models A_3) \quad (c_3 \mid s_3 \models A_3) \nrightarrow^{\epsilon*}}{}
\tag{21}
$$

We write $(c_1 \mid s_1 \models A_1) \nrightarrow^{\epsilon*}$ when $(c_1 \mid s_1 \models A_1)$ is a stuck configuration with respect to $\longrightarrow^{\epsilon*}$, that is, when $\neg \; \exists c_2, s_2, A_2 \bullet (c_1 \mid s_1 \models A_1) \longrightarrow^{\epsilon*} (c_2 \mid s_2 \models A_2)$.

Since the configurations of the specification-oriented transition system are the same as those of the *Circus* operational semantics, we can combine their transition relations in a simple way. This has already been indicated in Example 7, where we consider the two transition relations for a single example.

It is possible that a $\Longrightarrow_L$ transition is followed by no $\longrightarrow^{\epsilon*}$ transitions. In this case the $\Longrightarrow_L$ transition corresponds to a $\Longrightarrow_{SR}$ transition.

$$\frac{(c_1 \mid s_1 \models A_1) \overset{1}{\Longrightarrow}_L (c_2 \mid s_2 \models A_2) \quad (c_2 \mid s_2 \models A_2) \not\longrightarrow^{\epsilon*}}{(c_1 \mid s_1 \models A_1) \overset{1}{\Longrightarrow}_{SR} (c_2 \mid s_2 \models A_2)} \tag{22}$$

Example 16. Following from Examples 7 and 15, we can use the rules above to justify the following transitions for our example action E. Again, we present separately the two paths arising from the internal choice.

$(w_0 \in \mathbb{Z} \wedge w_1 \in \mathbb{Z} \mid x, y := w_0, w_1 \models E)$

$\overset{x:=2}{\Longrightarrow}_{SR}$

$\begin{pmatrix} w_0 \in \mathbb{Z} \wedge w_1 \in \mathbb{Z} \wedge w_2 = 2 \mid x, y := w_2, w_1 \\ \models \\ (y > x \,\&\, \text{out}!(y - x) \rightarrow \text{Skip}); \; x := y \end{pmatrix}$

$\overset{y>x}{\Longrightarrow}_{SR}$

$\begin{pmatrix} w_0 \in \mathbb{Z} \wedge w_1 \in \mathbb{Z} \wedge w_2 = 2 \wedge w_1 > w_2 \mid x, y := w_2, w_1 \\ \models \\ (\text{out}!(y - x) \rightarrow \text{Skip}); \; x := y \end{pmatrix}$

$\overset{\text{out}!(y-x)}{\Longrightarrow}_{SR}$

$\begin{pmatrix} w_0 \in \mathbb{Z} \wedge w_1 \in \mathbb{Z} \wedge w_2 = 2 \wedge w_1 > w_2 \wedge w_3 = w_1 - w_2 \mid x, y := w_2, w_1 \\ \models \\ x := y \end{pmatrix}$

$\overset{x:=y}{\Longrightarrow}_{SR}$

$\begin{pmatrix} w_0 \in \mathbb{Z} \wedge w_1 \in \mathbb{Z} \wedge w_2 = 2 \wedge w_1 > w_2 \wedge w_3 = w_1 - w_2 \wedge w_4 = w_2 \mid x, y := w_4, w_1 \\ \models \\ \text{Skip} \end{pmatrix}$

For the second option of the internal choice, we proceed as follows.

$(w_0 \in \mathbb{Z} \wedge w_1 \in \mathbb{Z} \mid x, y := w_0, w_1 \models E)$

$\overset{x:=2}{\Longrightarrow}_{SR}$

$\begin{pmatrix} w_0 \in \mathbb{Z} \wedge w_1 \in \mathbb{Z} \wedge w_2 = 2 \mid x, y := w_2, w_1 \\ \models \\ (\text{inp}?z \rightarrow \text{Stop}); \; x := y \end{pmatrix}$

$\overset{\text{inp}?z}{\Longrightarrow}_{SR}$

$\begin{pmatrix} w_0 \in \mathbb{Z} \wedge w_1 \in \mathbb{Z} \wedge w_2 = 2 \wedge w_3 \in \mathbb{Z} \mid x, y := w_2, w_1; \; \text{var}\, z := w_3 \\ \models \\ (\text{let}\, z \bullet \text{Stop}); \; x := y \end{pmatrix}$

From here, we cannot proceed once again.   □

If the behaviour of an action as described by the operational semantics starts with (truly) silent transitions, then $\Longrightarrow_{SR}$ cannot give a complete account of its execution, because it does not consider leading silent transitions.

Example 17. We consider the transitions below.

$$(w_0 \in \mathbb{Z} \wedge w_1 \in \mathbb{Z} \mid x, y := w_0, w_1 \models (x := 0 \sqcap x := 1; \ y := 1) \sqcap x := 1)$$

$$\longrightarrow$$

$$(w_0 \in \mathbb{Z} \wedge w_1 \in \mathbb{Z} \mid x, y := w_0, w_1 \models x := 0 \sqcap x := 1; \ y := 1)$$

$$\longrightarrow$$

$$(w_0 \in \mathbb{Z} \wedge w_1 \in \mathbb{Z} \mid x, y := w_0, w_1 \models x := 1; \ y := 1)$$

$$\overset{x:=1}{\Longrightarrow}_L \qquad\qquad\qquad\qquad\qquad\qquad \text{[Rules (11) and (4)]}$$

$$(w_0 \in \mathbb{Z} \wedge w_1 \in \mathbb{Z} \wedge w_2 = 1 \mid x, y := w_2, w_1 \models \mathbf{Skip}; \ y := 1)$$

$$\longrightarrow$$

$$(w_0 \in \mathbb{Z} \wedge w_1 \in \mathbb{Z} \wedge w_2 = 1 \mid x, y := w_2, w_1 \models y := 1)$$

$$\overset{y:=1}{\Longrightarrow}_L \qquad\qquad\qquad\qquad\qquad\qquad\quad \text{[Rule (4)]}$$

$$(w_0 \in \mathbb{Z} \wedge w_1 \in \mathbb{Z} \wedge w_2 = 1 \wedge w_3 = 1 \mid x, y := w_2, w_3 \models \mathbf{Skip})$$

This justifies the following.

$$(w_0 \in \mathbb{Z} \wedge w_1 \in \mathbb{Z} \mid x, y := w_0, w_1 \models (x := 0 \sqcap x := 1; \ y := 1) \sqcap x := 1)$$

$$\longrightarrow$$

$$(w_0 \in \mathbb{Z} \wedge w_1 \in \mathbb{Z} \mid x, y := w_0, w_1 \models x := 0 \sqcap x := 1; \ y := 1)$$

$$\longrightarrow$$

$$(w_0 \in \mathbb{Z} \wedge w_1 \in \mathbb{Z} \mid x, y := w_0, w_1 \models x := 1; \ y := 1)$$

$$\overset{x:=1}{\Longrightarrow}_{SR} \qquad\qquad\qquad\qquad\qquad \text{[Rules (21) and (19)]}$$

$$(w_0 \in \mathbb{Z} \wedge w_1 \in \mathbb{Z} \wedge w_2 = 1 \mid x, y := w_2, w_1 \models y := 1)$$

$$\overset{y:=1}{\Longrightarrow}_{SR} \qquad\qquad\qquad\qquad\qquad\qquad \text{[Rule (22)]}$$

$$(w_0 \in \mathbb{Z} \wedge w_1 \in \mathbb{Z} \wedge w_2 = 1 \wedge w_3 = 1 \mid x, y := w_2, w_3 \models \mathbf{Skip})$$

We cannot, however, relate the initial configuration to any other configuration using $\Longrightarrow_{SR}$.   □

We define a new transition rule that allows initial silent transitions.

$$\frac{(c_1 \mid s_1 \models A_1) \longrightarrow^{\epsilon*} (c_2 \mid s_2 \models A_2) \quad (c_2 \mid s_2 \models A_2) \overset{1}{\Longrightarrow}_{SR} (c_3 \mid s_3 \models A_3)}{(c_1 \mid s_1 \models A_1) \overset{1}{\Longrightarrow}_{SR} (c_3 \mid s_3 \models A_3)} \qquad (23)$$

Example 18. Now, with Rule (23), we can proceed with Example 17 to infer the following transitions.

$$(w_0 \in \mathbb{Z} \wedge w_1 \in \mathbb{Z} \mid x, y := w_0, w_1 \models (x := 0 \sqcap x := 1; \ y := 1) \sqcap x := 1)$$

$$\overset{x:=1}{\Longrightarrow}_{SR} \qquad\qquad\qquad\qquad\qquad \text{[Rules (23),(21) and (19)]}$$
$$(w_0 \in \mathbb{Z} \wedge w_1 \in \mathbb{Z} \wedge w_2 = 1 \mid x, y := w_2, w_1 \models y := 1)$$
$$\overset{y:=1}{\Longrightarrow}_{SR} \qquad\qquad\qquad\qquad\qquad\qquad \text{[Rule (22)]}$$
$$(w_0 \in \mathbb{Z} \wedge w_1 \in \mathbb{Z} \wedge w_2 = 1 \wedge w_3 = 1 \mid x, y := w_2, w_3 \models Skip)$$

Once the starting configuration is defined, we have a unique $\Longrightarrow_{SR}$ transition. $\square$

3.4 Composing Labels

Transitions with labels without an event cannot be (easily) observed during the execution of a system in a testing experiment. A well known solution for this issue of observability is the use of characterising traces, which identify the current state of an SUT. We, however, want to minimise the number of such transitions, and therefore we compose transitions whenever possible.

The possibility of combination of transitions is characterised by the syntactic function $\oplus$ that combines labels; it is defined below.

$$(g, e, A_1) \oplus A_2 = (g, e, A_1;\ A_2)$$

An action can lead to a change of state, so when there is an action (different from $Skip$) in a label, we cannot move forward any of the later guards or events. Therefore, we can only compose (g, e, A_1) with a label A_2.

A guard potentially blocks an associated event, so if there is a guard (different from $True$) and associated event in an label, we cannot move forward any later guards. Additionally, we do not combine two labels that have events (different from ϵ). Each transition should correspond to at most one observable event. So, (g_2, e, A) can only be composed with a previous label if it has only a guard g_1.

$$g_1 \oplus (g_2, e, A) = (g_1 \wedge g_2, e, A)$$

In conclusion, the domain of $\oplus$ includes exactly the pairs of labels where either the second label contains only an action, or the first label contains only a guard.

To define a system whose transitions are maximal in terms of label composition as defined by $\oplus$, we first consider a transitive closure for $\Longrightarrow_{SR}$ based on label composition. Afterwards, we define the definitive specification-oriented relation $\Longrightarrow$ as that for which no further label compositions are possible.

We define closure of $\Longrightarrow_{SR}$ in the standard way. The first rule allows a single $\Longrightarrow_{SR}$ transition to be included in the closure.

$$\frac{(c_1 \mid s_1 \models A_1) \overset{1}{\Longrightarrow}_{SR} (c_2 \mid s_2 \models A_2)}{(c_1 \mid s_1 \models A_1) \overset{1}{\Longrightarrow}^*_{SR} (c_2 \mid s_2 \models A_2)} \qquad (24)$$

The second rule allows proper composition when there are two consecutive transitions with labels that can be combined according to $\oplus$.

$$\frac{(c_1 \mid s_1 \models A_1) \overset{l_1}{\Longrightarrow}{}^*_{SR} (c_2 \mid s_2 \models A_2) \quad (c_2 \mid s_2 \models A_2) \overset{l_2}{\Longrightarrow}_{SR} (c_3 \mid s_3 \models A_3) \quad (l_1, l_2) \in \mathrm{dom} \oplus}{(c_1 \mid s_1 \models A_1) \overset{l_1 \oplus l_2}{\Longrightarrow}{}^*_{SR} (c_3 \mid s_3 \models A_3)} \quad (25)$$

Our last rule defines that a $\Longrightarrow$ transition exists when there is a corresponding $\Longrightarrow^*_{SR}$, and it is (right) maximal, in the sense that there is no further $\Longrightarrow_{SR}$ transition from the target configuration.

$$\frac{(c_1 \mid s_1 \models A_1) \overset{1}{\Longrightarrow}{}^*_{SR} (c_2 \mid s_2 \models A_2) \quad (c_2 \mid s_2 \models A_2) \not\Longrightarrow_{SR}}{(c_1 \mid s_1 \models A_1) \overset{1}{\Longrightarrow} (c_2 \mid s_2 \models A_2)} \quad (26)$$

We use $(c_1 \mid s_1 \models A_1) \not\Longrightarrow_{SR}$ as an abbreviation for

$$\neg \ \exists c_2, s_2, A_2, 1 \bullet (c_1 \mid s_1 \models A_1) \overset{1}{\Longrightarrow}_{SR} (c_2 \mid s_2 \models A_2)$$

Example 19. Following from Example 16, we can use the rules above to justify the following transitions for our example action E. Again, we present separately the two paths arising from the internal choice.

$(w_0 \in \mathbb{Z} \land w_1 \in \mathbb{Z} \mid x, y := w_0, w_1 \models E)$

$\overset{x:=2}{\Longrightarrow}$

$\begin{pmatrix} w_0 \in \mathbb{Z} \land w_1 \in \mathbb{Z} \land w_2 = 2 \mid x, y := w_2, w_1 \\ \models \\ (y > x \ \& \ \mathrm{out}!(y - x) \rightarrow \mathrm{Skip}); \ x := y \end{pmatrix}$

$\overset{(y>x, \mathrm{out}!(y-x), x:=y)}{\Longrightarrow}$

$\begin{pmatrix} w_0 \in \mathbb{Z} \land w_1 \in \mathbb{Z} \land w_2 = 2 \land w_1 > w_2 \land w_3 = w_1 - w_2 \land w_4 = w_2 \mid x, y := w_4, w_1 \\ \models \\ \mathrm{Skip} \end{pmatrix}$

For the second option of the internal choice, we do not have opportunities for composition.

$(w_0 \in \mathbb{Z} \land w_1 \in \mathbb{Z} \mid x, y := w_0, w_1 \models E)$

$\overset{x:=2}{\Longrightarrow}$

$\begin{pmatrix} w_0 \in \mathbb{Z} \land w_1 \in \mathbb{Z} \land w_2 = 2 \mid x, y := w_2, w_1 \\ \models \\ (\mathrm{inp}?z \rightarrow \mathrm{Stop}); \ x := y \end{pmatrix}$

$\overset{\mathrm{inp}?z}{\Longrightarrow}$

$$
\left(
\begin{array}{l}
\mathtt{w_0} \in \mathbb{Z} \land \mathtt{w_1} \in \mathbb{Z} \land \mathtt{w_2} = 2 \land \mathtt{w_3} \in \mathbb{Z} \mid \mathtt{x, y} := \mathtt{w_2, w_1}; \; \mathtt{var\, z} := \mathtt{w_3} \\
\models \\
(\mathtt{let\ z} \bullet \mathtt{Stop}); \; \mathtt{x} := \mathtt{y}
\end{array}
\right)
$$

From here, we cannot proceed once again.   □

All the transition relations above can be defined in the UTP *Circus* theory, so that the soundness of the transitions rules that we have defined can be formally justified. Before discussing soundness, however, we illustrate how the new transition system can be useful in practical testing techniques.

4   Test-Selection Criteria Based on the New Transition System: Examples

We perceive two approaches for selection of finite test sets from a *Circus* specification. The first defines subsets of the exhaustive test sets as defined in [6] (see Section 2.3), and the second is guided by the text of the *Circus* specification. The first one is directly based on the operational semantics of *Circus*. The second one is the main motivation for the definition of the specification-oriented transition system presented above. This is what we consider in the sequel.

The selection approaches based on the structure of the tests in the exhaustive test set does not take into account the structure of the specification and the internal state changes that may occur during some unlabelled transitions of the operational semantics. The symbolic exhaustive test sets cover by construction the constrained symbolic traces of the specification. Introducing selection criteria among the constrained symbolic traces to characterise a finite subset has the merit of simplicity and of closeness to the underlying semantic model of *Circus*. However, it is the coverage of this model that is considered, and the coverage of the original specification is not taken into account.

For instance, coming back to action E of Example 1, we can note that there is no mention of the variable x and of its definition in the constrained symbolic traces. Thus, a selection criteria based on such traces cannot take into account the coverage of, for example, variable definitions and their uses.

It is the same when an operation specified by a Z schema is used in the specification: from Rule (3) of the operational semantics (see Appendix A), we can see that the associated symbolic traces does not mention the operation, and it is impossible to know which case has been covered or not by a symbolic test. Since the labels of the specification-oriented transition system contain parts of the text of the specification and record changes of state (see, for instance, Rules (3) and (4) in Section 3.2), it becomes possible to select traces (of the specification-oriented transition system, with these new labels) on the basis of the structure of the specification. For illustration, we sketch how we can use the new transition system to define data-flow-oriented test selection methods.

In the early nineties, some approaches have been proposed for generating test cases from specifications written in languages including processes interactions and data types, such as Full LOTOS, SDL, or more generally EFSM (Extended Finite State Machines). Several of these works have considered data-flow-oriented selection criteria [34,30,31,27] like we do here.

Briefly, data-flow coverage criteria were originally developed for sequential imperative languages, with the coverage of definition-use associations as motivation [13]. In a data-flow graph, a definition-use association is a triple $\langle d, u, v \rangle$ where d is a node in which the variable v is defined, u is a node in which the value of v is used, and there is a definition-clear path with respect to v from d to u. The strongest data-flow criterion, all definition-use paths, requires that, for each variable, every definition-clear path (with at most one iteration by loop) is executed by a test. In order to reduce the number of paths required, weaker strategies such as all-definitions and all-uses have been defined.

When using these criteria, is is assumed that the data-flow graph has unique start and end nodes, and that there is no data-flow anomaly, that is, every path from the start node to a use of v passes through a node with a definition of v. Thus data-flow analysis is required both for checking the absence of anomalies and constructing the set of definition-use associations. (Such analysis always provide an over-approximation of data-flow dependencies due to feasibility issues).

The transposition of these criteria to the specification-oriented transition system of *Circus* requires a few adjustments. Since the relevant information is carried by the labels of the transitions, the definition-use associations are defined as triples of two transitions and one variable. In the first transition label, the variable is defined by an assignment, or an input, or its declaration, or a Z operation where it is an output, or a specification statement in which it is in the frame. In the second transition label, it is used in a guard, or in the right-hand side of an assignment, or in an output, or in a Z operation where it is an input, or in a specification statement where it is used without decoration (in the pre or postcondition). The notion of trace is used instead of path.

Example 20. In the case of our example action E, we have a definition-use association for x whose first component is the following transition.

$$(w_0 \in \mathbb{Z} \land w_1 \in \mathbb{Z} \mid x, y := w_0, w_1 \models x := 2)$$

$$\stackrel{x:=2}{\Longrightarrow}$$

$$(w_0 \in \mathbb{Z} \land w_1 \in \mathbb{Z} \land w_2 = 2 \mid x, y := w_2, w_1 \models Skip)$$

Indeed, x is defined in the label of this transition by an assignment. The second transition of the association is as follows.

$$\left(\begin{array}{l} w_0 \in \mathbb{Z} \land w_1 \in \mathbb{Z} \land w_2 = 2 \mid x, y := w_2, w_1 \\ \models \\ (y > x \,\&\, out!(y - x) \to Skip); \; x := y \end{array} \right)$$

$$\stackrel{(y>x, out!(y-x), x:=y)}{\Longrightarrow}$$

$$\left(\begin{array}{l} w_0 \in \mathbb{Z} \land w_1 \in \mathbb{Z} \land w_2 = 2 \land w_1 > w_2 \land w_3 = w_1 - w_2 \land w_4 = w_2 \mid x, y := w_4, w_1 \\ \models \\ Skip \end{array} \right)$$

The variable x is used (twice) in this second transition, and there is an empty trace between the two transitions that is obviously definition clear with respect to x. The third component of the association is just x itself. □

Since the association in the above example is the only definition-use association for x in the simple action E, it means that it is sufficient to cover its two transitions to satisfy the criterion "all definition-use traces" for x. We note that the second definition of x in this example, namely $x := y$, does not need to be covered. It comes from the fact that it is not associated to any use. It is not a problem: since it has no effect, it would be useless to test it.

Example 21. Among the definition-use associations of action PA in Example 2, with respect to the local variable x_l corresponding to the program variable x, there is one whose first transition is as follows (*cf.* Examples 11 and 14).

$$
\begin{pmatrix}
w_0 \in \mathbb{Z} \wedge w_1 = 2 \mid x := w_1 \\
\models \\
\begin{pmatrix}
(inpA?y \rightarrow int!y \rightarrow out!(y - x) \rightarrow Skip) \\
\llbracket \{x\} \mid \{\!| int |\!\} \mid \{\} \rrbracket \\
(inpB?z_1 \rightarrow int?z_2 \rightarrow z_1 > z_2 \& out!(z_1 - x) \rightarrow Skip)
\end{pmatrix}
\end{pmatrix}
$$

$\xRightarrow{var\ x_1, x_r := x, x}$

$$
\begin{pmatrix}
w_0 \in \mathbb{Z} \wedge w_1 = 2 \mid x := w_1; \ var\, x_1, x_r := x, x \\
\models \\
\begin{pmatrix}
(spar\ x \mid x_1 \mid x_r \mid x := x_1 \bullet inpA?y \rightarrow int!y \rightarrow out!(y - x_1) \rightarrow Skip) \\
\llbracket \{\!| int |\!\} \rrbracket \\
\begin{pmatrix}
spar\ x \mid x_r \mid x_1 \mid Skip \bullet \\
inpB?z_1 \rightarrow int?z_2 \rightarrow z_1 > z_2 \& out!(z_1 - x_r) \rightarrow Skip
\end{pmatrix}
\end{pmatrix}
\end{pmatrix}
$$

The second transition is as follows.

$$
\begin{pmatrix}
\begin{pmatrix}
w_0 \in \mathbb{Z} \wedge w_1 = 2 \wedge w_2 \in \mathbb{Z} \wedge w_3 \in \mathbb{Z} \wedge \\
w_4 = w_2 \wedge w_5 \in \mathbb{Z} \wedge w_2 = w_5 \wedge w_6 = w_2 - w_1 \wedge w_3 > w_5 \wedge w_7 = w_3 - w_1
\end{pmatrix} \\
\mid
\begin{pmatrix}
x := w_1; \ var\, x_1, x_r := x, x; \\
var\, y, z_1, z_2 := w_2, w_3, w_5; \ end\, y; \ end\, z_1, z_2
\end{pmatrix} \\
\models \\
(spar\ x \mid x_1 \mid x_r \mid x := x_1 \bullet Skip) \llbracket \{\!| int |\!\} \rrbracket (spar\ x \mid x_r \mid x_1 \mid Skip \bullet Skip)
\end{pmatrix}
$$

$\xRightarrow{x := x_1; \ end\, x_1, x_r}$

$$
\begin{pmatrix}
\begin{pmatrix}
w_0 \in \mathbb{Z} \wedge w_1 = 2 \wedge w_2 \in \mathbb{Z} \wedge w_3 \in \mathbb{Z} \wedge \\
w_4 = w_2 \wedge w_5 \in \mathbb{Z} \wedge w_2 = w_5 \wedge w_6 = w_2 - w_1 \wedge w_3 > w_5 \wedge w_7 = w_3 - w_1
\end{pmatrix} \\
\mid
\begin{pmatrix}
x := w_1; \ var\, x_1, x_r := x, x; \\
var\, y, z_1, z_2 := w_2, w_3, w_5; \ end\, y; \ end\, z_1, z_2; \ x := x_1; \ end\, x_1, x_r
\end{pmatrix} \\
\models \\
Skip
\end{pmatrix}
$$

The third component is, of course, x_l. □

The definition-use association above forces, if the selection criterion used is "all definition-use traces" for x_l, the coverage all the interleavings of the parallel actions. In the case where the weaker criterion "all definitions" is used, following the pattern in [13], one interleaving only is required.

There are various conditions for applying data-flow testing methods to sequential programs that must be revisited for applying them to *Circus*. The existence of a unique end node can be relaxed using the observation in [26] that, in a reactive program, reaching again a start node is analogous to reaching the end node of a sequential program. Following variants of this principle, some algorithms for symbolic analysis of control dependencies are given in [26,19] and used for data-flow analysis when there are several or no end nodes.

Data-flow analysis in presence of concurrency has been studied intensively. Of special interest in the context of *Circus* is the work in [19] for IOSTS (Input-Output Symbolic Transition Systems), where the main difference to *Circus* is that the state is not hidden, and there are no shared variables between concurrent processes. Another work of interest is the slicing algorithm for Promela in [21], where both shared variables and communications are taken into account.

5   Soundness

In the UTP, the transition rules of an operational semantics can be defined as theorems of the theory that characterises the corresponding relational model. For that, we define the transition relation in terms of the constructs of the theory (and refinement). This establishes the soundness of the operational semantics. It has been carried out for designs and CSP [18], and for *Circus* [36].

For the *Circus* operational semantics, it is defined that the transition relation $(c_1 \mid s_1 \models A_1) \overset{\epsilon}{\longrightarrow} (c_2 \mid s_2 \models A_2)$ holds if (a) there exists a valuation of the symbolic variables used in c_1 and c_2 such that c_1 and c_2 hold, and (b) for every such valuation, execution of A_1 in the state s_1 is refined by the execution of A_2 in s_2 [36]. By requiring that c_1 and c_2 hold, we avoid configurations with unsatisfiable state specifications. Refinement is required, not equality, since a transition reflects one, among the possibly many, available steps in the execution of A_1. As an example, we have the Rules 11 for internal choice in Appendix A: each transition captures just one of the possible choices.

For a labelled transition $(c_1 \mid s_1 \models A_1) \overset{d.w_0}{\longrightarrow} (c_2 \mid s_2 \models A_2)$, it is required that execution of A_1 in s_1 is refined by an external choice between $d.w_0 \rightarrow A_2$ in the state s_2, and A_1 itself in the state s_1. This establishes that $d.w_0 \rightarrow A_2$ (in s_2) is one of the possible behaviours of A_1. The external choice captures the fact that $d.w_0$ may or may not be available, as the choice may be taken away by other behaviours of A_1. For example, if A_1 may also terminate, make some internal progress, or provide another external choice, these are all taken into account.

For the new specification-oriented transition system, we define the transition relations in terms of the constructs of the original UTP *Circus* theory, and also the $\longrightarrow$ relation of the operational semantics. For example, in the new transition system, we do not want to relate configurations that cannot be related by the

Circus operational semantics. As already explained, it is not the objective of the new system to introduce transitions, but to remove and to annotate.

The definition for a transition $(c_1 \mid s_1 \models A_1) \overset{(g,e,A)}{\Longrightarrow}_L (c_2 \mid s_2 \models A_2)$ requires

(a) $g \neq \text{True}$, or $e \neq \epsilon$, or $A \neq \text{Skip}$.

(b) if e is a communication over a channel d, there is a symbolic variable w_0 such that $(c_1 \mid s_1 \models A_1) \overset{d.w_0}{\longrightarrow} (c_2 \mid s_2 \models A_2)$;

(c) if e is ϵ, then $(c_1 \mid s_1 \models A_1) \overset{\epsilon}{\longrightarrow} (c_2 \mid s_2 \models A_2)$ holds;

(d) for all valuations of the symbolic variables that satisfy c_1 and c_2, the following properties hold:

   (d1) A_1 in s_1 is refined by the external choice between A_1 in s_1 itself, and $(g \mathbin{\&} e \to A; A_2)$ also in s_1; and, finally

   (d2) $g \mathbin{\&} \mathbf{var}\, var(e); A$ in s_1 is refined by the state s_2 guarded by g in the state s_1.

With (a), we guarantee that there are no silent transitions. The inequalities there are all syntactic, and this trivially holds for all transitions in Section 3.2. With (b) and (c), we check that, for all valuations that satisfy the constraints, there is a corresponding transition of the operational semantics. The condition (d1) is similar to that used in the definition of labelled transitions of the operational semantics, which was explained above. The difference is that instead of considering the prefixing in the new state s_2, we use the label to construct the new state for A_2. That s_2 is indeed the appropriate next state is guaranteed by (d2), which requires that guarding A with g and declaring any variable implicitly declared by e is refined by s_2, guarded by g, all in s_1. If e is ϵ, then $var(e)$ is ϵ itself. We define that, in this case, the variable declaration is Skip, and so can be omitted.

In establishing the soundness of the transition rules, we also need to show that s_2 is a total assignment. In most cases, this is trivial. We leave a complete account of the soundness of our transition rules for another paper.

6 Conclusions and Future Work

In this paper, we have presented a novel transition system for a state-rich process algebra, *Circus*. Its existing operational semantics takes forwards the UTP ideas for an operational semantics for CSP by using symbolic variables to capture nondeterminism in the state. It is the basis of a testing theory for *Circus*. What we now present is an alternative characterisation of the evolutions of the *Circus* models that records information about the way in which data is defined and used. It is what we call a specification-oriented transition system for *Circus*.

We have briefly discussed how this new transition system can be used to specify selection criteria based on the use of data. Once the traces of the new transition system are selected, they are mapped to traces of the operational semantics, and in this way to tests for traces refinement and *conf*.

We have also sketched the soundness argument of the transition system. It is based on the UTP theory for *Circus*. A detailed account is going to be the subject of another paper.

In the new transition system, we still do not record in labels the internal and external choices, or parallelisms. They are recorded, of course, in the actions of the configurations. We, therefore, based solely on traces, cannot have coverage criteria that requires, for instance, covering all actions in a parallelism. For that, we will need to take into account the actions in the configurations themselves. Internal choice is covered by the use of acceptance sets in tests for *conf*.

A first piece of future work is related to completeness. We need to prove that we have the appropriate number of transitions to cater for all possible behaviours. This can be achieved by taking the transition rules as the definition of the transition relation, and recovering the denotational semantics using them. The technique applied in the UTP requires us to use the transition relation to define a semantic function that associates programs to relations of the UTP *Circus* theory. If we can prove that the relations are those defined in the denotational semantics, we have characterised the way in which concepts of the operational and denotational semantics are related in a complete and consistent way.

In the case of the our specification-based transition system, we have restricted ourselves to divergence-free processes. The completeness result, therefore, necessarily has to be qualified. The specification-oriented system is not proposed as a replacement for the *Circus* operational semantics. For $\Longrightarrow_L$, proof of completeness can rely on the corresponding result for the operational semantics.

The most exciting plans that we have for the future, however, are the implementation of the new transition system (using a theorem prover), and the definition and application of a variety of selection criteria.

Acknowledgments

We are grateful to the Université de Paris-Sud and the Royal Academy of Engineering for their financial support of our collaboration. We would like to thank Shamim Ripon, Jim Woodcock, and Frank Zeyda for their valuable comments on the work reported here, and on a draft version of this paper.

References

1. Bernot, G., Gaudel, M.-C., Marre, B.: Software testing based on formal specifications: a theory and a tool. Software Engineering Journal 6(6), 387–405 (1991)
2. Bougé, L., Choquet, N., Fribourg, L., Gaudel, M.-C.: Test set generation from algebraic specifications using logic programming. Journal of Systems and Software 6(4), 343–360 (1986)
3. Brinksma, E.: A theory for the derivation of tests. In: Protocol Specification, testing and Verification VIII, pp. 63–74. North-Holland, Amsterdam (1988)
4. Butterfield, A., Sherif, A., Woodcock, J.C.P.: Slotted Circus: A UTP-family of reactive theories. In: Davies, J., Gibbons, J. (eds.) IFM 2007. LNCS, vol. 4591, pp. 75–97. Springer, Heidelberg (2007)
5. Cavalcanti, A.L.C., Gaudel, M.-C.: Testing for Refinement in CSP. In: Butler, M., Hinchey, M.G., Larrondo-Petrie, M.M. (eds.) ICFEM 2007. LNCS, vol. 4789, pp. 151–170. Springer, Heidelberg (2007)

6. Cavalcanti, A.L.C., Gaudel, M.-C.: Testing for Refinement in Circus – Extended version. Technical report, University of York (2009), www-users.cs.york.ac.uk/~alcc/CG09.pdf

7. Cavalcanti, A.L.C., Gaudel, M.-C.: A note on traces refinement and the *conf* relation in the Unifying Theories of Programming. In: Butterfield, A. (ed.) UTP 2008. LNCS, vol. 5713, pp. 42–61. Springer, Heidelberg (2010)

8. Cavalcanti, A.L.C., Sampaio, A.C.A., Woodcock, J.C.P.: Unifying Classes and Processes. Software and System Modelling 4(3), 277–296 (2005)

9. Cavalcanti, A.L.C., Woodcock, J.C.P.: A Tutorial Introduction to CSP in Unifying Theories of Programming. In: Cavalcanti, A., Sampaio, A., Woodcock, J. (eds.) PSSE 2004. LNCS, vol. 3167, pp. 220–268. Springer, Heidelberg (2006)

10. Chow, T.S.: Testing Software Design Modeled by Finite-State Machines. IEEE Transactions on Software Engineering SE-4(3), 178–187 (1978)

11. Dick, J., Faivre, A.: Automating the generation and sequencing of test cases from model-based specifications. In: Larsen, P.G., Woodcock, J.C.P. (eds.) FME 1993. LNCS, vol. 670, pp. 268–284. Springer, Heidelberg (1993)

12. Dijkstra, E.W.: A Discipline of Programming. Prentice-Hall, Englewood Cliffs (1976)

13. Frankl, P.G., Weyuker, E.J.: An applicable family of data-flow testing criteria. IEEE Transactions on Software Engineering 14(10), 1483–1498 (1988)

14. Gannon, J., McMullin, P., Hamlet, R.: Data abstraction implementation, specification and testing. ACM Transactions on Programming Languages and Systems 3(3), 211–223 (1981)

15. Gaudel, M.-C.: Testing can be formal, too. In: Mosses, P.D., Schwartzbach, M.I., Nielsen, M. (eds.) CAAP 1995, FASE 1995, and TAPSOFT 1995. LNCS, vol. 915, pp. 82–96. Springer, Heidelberg (1995)

16. Harwood, W., Cavalcanti, A.L.C., Woodcock, J.C.P.: A Theory of Pointers for the UTP. In: Fitzgerald, J.S., Haxthausen, A.E., Yenigun, H. (eds.) ICTAC 2008. LNCS, vol. 5160, pp. 141–155. Springer, Heidelberg (2008)

17. Hierons, R.M., Kim, T.H., Ural, H.: On the testability of SDL specifications. Computer Networks 44(5), 681–700 (2004)

18. Hoare, C.A.R., Jifeng, H.: Unifying Theories of Programming. Prentice-Hall, Englewood Cliffs (1998)

19. Labbé, S., Gallois, J.-P.: Slicing communicating automata specifications: polynomial algorithms for model reduction. Formal Aspects of Computing 20(6), 563–595 (2008)

20. Lee, D., Yannakakis, M.: Principles and methods of testing finite state machines - A survey. Proceedings of the IEEE 84, 1090–1126 (1996)

21. Millett, L.I., Teitelbaum, T.: Issues in slicing PROMELA and its applications to model checking, protocol understanding, and simulation. Software Tools for Technology Transfer 2(4), 343–349 (2000)

22. Morgan, C.C.: Programming from Specifications, 2nd edn. Prentice-Hall, Englewood Cliffs (1994)

23. Oliveira, M.V.M.: Formal Derivation of State-Rich Reactive Programs Using Circus. PhD thesis, University of York (2006)

24. Oliveira, M.V.M., Cavalcanti, A.L.C., Woodcock, J.C.P.: Unifying Theories in ProofPowerZ. Formal Aspects of Computing (online first) (2007), doi:10.1007/s00165-007-0044-5

25. Oliveira, M.V.M., Cavalcanti, A.L.C., Woodcock, J.C.P.: A UTP Semantics for Circus. Formal Aspects of Computing 21(1-2), 3–32 (2009)

26. Ranganath, V.P., Amtoft, T., Banerjee, A., Hatcliff, J., Dwyer, M.B.: A new foundation for control dependence and slicing for modern program structures. ACM Transactions on Programming Languages and Systems 29(5), 27 (2007)
27. Robinson-Mallett, C., Hierons, R.M., Poore, J., Liggesmeyer, P.: Using communication coverage criteria and partial model generation to assist software integration testing. Software Quality Control 16(2), 185–211 (2008)
28. Roscoe, A.W.: The Theory and Practice of Concurrency. Prentice-Hall Series in Computer Science. Prentice-Hall, Englewood Cliffs (1998)
29. Santos, T.L.V.L., Cavalcanti, A.L.C., Sampaio, A.C.A.: Object Orientation in the UTP. In: Dunne, S., Stoddart, B. (eds.) UTP 2006. LNCS, vol. 4010, pp. 18–37. Springer, Heidelberg (2006)
30. Schoot, H.V.D., Ural, H.: Data flow oriented test selection for LOTOS. Computer Networks and ISDN Systems 27(7) (1993)
31. Schoot, H.V.D., Ural, H.: Data flow analysis of system specifications in LOTOS. International Journal of Software Engineering and Knowledge Engineering 7, 43–68 (1997)
32. Sherif, A., Cavalcanti, A.L.C., Jifeng, H., Sampaio, A.C.A.: A process algebraic framework for specification and validation of real-time systems. Formal Aspects of Computing 22(7), 153–191 (2009) (online first)
33. Tang, X., Woodcock, J.C.P.: Travelling Processes. In: Kozen, D., Shankland, C. (eds.) MPC 2004. LNCS, vol. 3125, pp. 381–399. Springer, Heidelberg (2004)
34. Tripathy, P., Sarikaya, B.: Test Generation from LOTOS Specifications. IEEE Transactions on Computers 40(4), 543–552 (1991)
35. Woodcock, J.C.P., Cavalcanti, A.L.C.: A Tutorial Introduction to Designs in Unifying Theories of Programming. In: Boiten, E.A., Derrick, J., Smith, G. (eds.) IFM 2004. LNCS, vol. 2999, pp. 40–66. Springer, Heidelberg (2004); Invited tutorial
36. Woodcock, J.C.P., Cavalcanti, A.L.C., Gaudel, M.-C., Freitas, L.J.S.: Operational Semantics for **Circus**. Formal Aspects of Computing (to appear)
37. Woodcock, J.C.P., Davies, J.: Using Z—Specification, Refinement, and Proof. Prentice-Hall, Englewood Cliffs (1996)

A   Operational Semantics: Table of Selected Transition Rules

$$\frac{c \wedge (\mathtt{s};\ p) \wedge (\exists v' \bullet \mathtt{s};\ \mathtt{Q})}{(c \mid \mathtt{s} \models p \vdash \mathtt{Q}) \xrightarrow{\epsilon} (c \wedge (\mathtt{s};\ \mathtt{Q}\,[w_0/v']) \mid \mathtt{s};\ v := w_0 \models \mathtt{Skip})} \quad v' = out\alpha s \qquad (1)$$

$$\frac{c}{(c \mid \mathtt{s} \models v := e) \xrightarrow{\epsilon} (c \wedge (\mathtt{s};\ w_0 = e) \mid \mathtt{s};\ v := w_0 \models \mathtt{Skip})} \qquad (2)$$

$$\frac{c \wedge (s;\ \mathbf{pre}\ Op)}{(c \mid \mathtt{s} \models \mathtt{Op}) \xrightarrow{\epsilon} (c \wedge (\mathtt{s};\ \mathtt{Op}\,[w_0/v']) \mid \mathtt{s};\ v := w_0 \models \mathtt{Skip})} \quad v' = out\alpha s \qquad (3)$$

$$\frac{c}{(c \mid \mathtt{s} \models d!e \to A) \xrightarrow{d!w_0} (c \wedge (\mathtt{s};\ w_0 = e) \mid \mathtt{s} \models A)} \qquad (4)$$

$$\frac{c \wedge T \neq \varnothing \qquad x \notin \alpha s}{(c \mid s \models d?x : T \to A) \xrightarrow{d?w_0} (c \wedge w_0 \in T \mid s; \ var\,x := w_0 \models let\,x \bullet A)} \tag{5}$$

$$\frac{c \wedge T \neq \varnothing \qquad x \notin \alpha s}{(c \mid s \models var\,x : T \bullet A) \xrightarrow{\epsilon} (c \wedge w_0 \in T \mid s; \ var\,x := w_0 \models let\,x \bullet A)} \tag{6}$$

$$\frac{(c_1 \mid s_1 \models A_1) \xrightarrow{1} (c_2 \mid s_2 \models A_2)}{(c_1 \mid s_1 \models let\,x \bullet A_1) \xrightarrow{1} (c_2 \mid s_2 \models let\,x \bullet A_2)} \tag{7}$$

$$\frac{c}{(c \mid s \models let\,x \bullet Skip) \xrightarrow{\epsilon} (c \mid s; \ end\,x \models Skip)} \tag{8}$$

$$\frac{(c_1 \mid s_1 \models A_1) \xrightarrow{1} (c_2 \mid s_2 \models A_2)}{(c_1 \mid s_1 \models A_1; \ B) \xrightarrow{1} (c_2 \mid s_2 \models A_2; \ B)} \tag{9}$$

$$\frac{c}{(c \mid s \models Skip; \ A) \xrightarrow{\epsilon} (c \mid s \models A)} \tag{10}$$

$$\frac{c}{(c \mid s \models A_1 \sqcap A_2) \xrightarrow{\epsilon} (c \mid s \models A_1)} \qquad \frac{c}{(c \mid s \models A_1 \sqcap A_2) \xrightarrow{\epsilon} (c \mid s \models A_2)} \tag{11}$$

$$\frac{c \wedge (s; \ g)}{(c \mid s \models g \,\&\, A) \xrightarrow{\epsilon} (c \wedge (s; \ g) \mid s \models A)} \tag{12}$$

$$\frac{c}{(c \mid s \models A_1 [\![x_1 \mid cs \mid x_2]\!] A_2) \xrightarrow{\epsilon} \left(\begin{array}{c} c \mid s \\ \models \\ (par\,s \mid x_1 \bullet A_1) [\![cs]\!] (par\,s \mid x_2 \bullet A_2) \end{array} \right)} \tag{13}$$

$$\frac{c}{\left(\begin{array}{c} c \mid s \\ \models \\ \left(\begin{array}{c} (par\,s_1 \mid x_1 \bullet Skip) \\ [\![cs]\!] \\ (par\,s_2 \mid x_2 \bullet Skip) \end{array} \right) \end{array} \right) \xrightarrow{\epsilon} (c \mid (\exists x_2' \bullet s_1) \wedge (\exists x_1' \bullet s_2) \models Skip)} \tag{14}$$

$$\frac{(c \mid s_1 \models A_1) \xrightarrow{1} (c_3 \mid s_3 \models A_3) \quad 1 = \epsilon \vee chan\,1 \notin cs}{\left(\begin{array}{c} c \mid s \\ \models \\ \left(\begin{array}{c} (par\,s_1 \mid x_1 \bullet A_1) \\ [\![cs]\!] \\ (par\,s_2 \mid x_2 \bullet A_2) \end{array} \right) \end{array} \right) \xrightarrow{1} \left(\begin{array}{c} c_3 \mid s \\ \models \\ \left(\begin{array}{c} (par\,s_3 \mid x_1 \bullet A_3) \\ [\![cs]\!] \\ (par\,s_2 \mid x_2 \bullet A_2) \end{array} \right) \end{array} \right)} \tag{15}$$

$$\dfrac{(\mathtt{c} \mid \mathtt{s_2} \models \mathtt{A_2}) \xrightarrow{\;1\;} (\mathtt{c_3} \mid \mathtt{s_3} \models \mathtt{A_3}) \quad 1 = \epsilon \vee \mathrm{chan}\,1 \notin cs}{\begin{pmatrix} \mathtt{c} \mid \mathtt{s} \\ \models \\ \begin{pmatrix} (\mathtt{par}\ \mathtt{s_1} \mid \mathtt{x_1} \bullet \mathtt{A_1}) \\ [\![\mathtt{cs}]\!] \\ (\mathtt{par}\ \mathtt{s_2} \mid \mathtt{x_2} \bullet \mathtt{A_2}) \end{pmatrix} \end{pmatrix} \xrightarrow{\;1\;} \begin{pmatrix} \mathtt{c_3} \mid \mathtt{s} \\ \models \\ \begin{pmatrix} (\mathtt{par}\ \mathtt{s_1} \mid \mathtt{x_1} \bullet \mathtt{A_1}) \\ [\![\mathtt{cs}]\!] \\ (\mathtt{par}\ \mathtt{s_3} \mid \mathtt{x_2} \bullet \mathtt{A_3}) \end{pmatrix} \end{pmatrix}} \tag{16}$$

$$\dfrac{\begin{pmatrix} (\mathtt{c} \mid \mathtt{s_1} \models \mathtt{A_1}) \xrightarrow{d?w_1} (\mathtt{c_3} \mid \mathtt{s_3} \models \mathtt{A_3}) \ \wedge\ (\mathtt{c} \mid \mathtt{s_2} \models \mathtt{A_2}) \xrightarrow{d!w_2} (\mathtt{c_4} \mid \mathtt{s_4} \models \mathtt{A_4}) \\ \vee \\ (\mathtt{c} \mid \mathtt{s_1} \models \mathtt{A_1}) \xrightarrow{d!w_1} (\mathtt{c_3} \mid \mathtt{s_3} \models \mathtt{A_3}) \ \wedge\ (\mathtt{c} \mid \mathtt{s_2} \models \mathtt{A_2}) \xrightarrow{d?w_2} (\mathtt{c_4} \mid \mathtt{s_4} \models \mathtt{A_4}) \\ \vee \\ (\mathtt{c} \mid \mathtt{s_1} \models \mathtt{A_1}) \xrightarrow{d!w_1} (\mathtt{c_3} \mid \mathtt{s_3} \models \mathtt{A_3}) \ \wedge\ (\mathtt{c} \mid \mathtt{s_2} \models \mathtt{A_2}) \xrightarrow{d!w_2} (\mathtt{c_4} \mid \mathtt{s_4} \models \mathtt{A_4}) \end{pmatrix}}{} \tag{17}$$

$$\dfrac{\mathbf{d} \in cs \quad c_3 \wedge c_4 \wedge w_1 = w_2}{\begin{pmatrix} \mathtt{c} \mid \mathtt{s} \\ \models \\ \begin{pmatrix} (\mathtt{par}\ \mathtt{s_1} \mid \mathtt{x_1} \bullet \mathtt{A_1}) \\ [\![\mathtt{cs}]\!] \\ (\mathtt{par}\ \mathtt{s_2} \mid \mathtt{x_2} \bullet \mathtt{A_2}) \end{pmatrix} \end{pmatrix} \xrightarrow{d!w_2} \begin{pmatrix} c_3 \wedge c_4 \wedge \mathtt{w_1} = \mathtt{w_2} \mid \mathtt{s} \\ \models \\ \begin{pmatrix} (\mathtt{par}\ \mathtt{s_3} \mid \mathtt{x_1} \bullet \mathtt{A_3}) \\ [\![\mathtt{cs}]\!] \\ (\mathtt{par}\ \mathtt{s_4} \mid \mathtt{x_2} \bullet \mathtt{A_4}) \end{pmatrix} \end{pmatrix}}$$

$$\dfrac{(\mathtt{c} \mid \mathtt{s_1} \models \mathtt{A_1}) \xrightarrow{d?w_1} (\mathtt{c_3} \mid \mathtt{s_3} \models \mathtt{A_3}) \quad (\mathtt{c} \mid \mathtt{s_2} \models \mathtt{A_2}) \xrightarrow{d?w_2} (\mathtt{c_4} \mid \mathtt{s_4} \models \mathtt{A_4}) \quad \mathbf{d} \in cs \quad c_3 \wedge c_4 \wedge w_1 = w_2}{\begin{pmatrix} \mathtt{c} \mid \mathtt{s} \\ \models \\ \begin{pmatrix} (\mathtt{par}\ \mathtt{s_1} \mid \mathtt{x_1} \bullet \mathtt{A_1}) \\ [\![\mathtt{cs}]\!] \\ (\mathtt{par}\ \mathtt{s_2} \mid \mathtt{x_2} \bullet \mathtt{A_2}) \end{pmatrix} \end{pmatrix} \xrightarrow{d?w_2} \begin{pmatrix} c_3 \wedge c_4 \wedge \mathtt{w_1} = \mathtt{w_2} \mid \mathtt{s} \\ \models \\ \begin{pmatrix} (\mathtt{par}\ \mathtt{s_3} \mid \mathtt{x_1} \bullet \mathtt{A_3}) \\ [\![\mathtt{cs}]\!] \\ (\mathtt{par}\ \mathtt{s_4} \mid \mathtt{x_2} \bullet \mathtt{A_4}) \end{pmatrix} \end{pmatrix}} \tag{18}$$

$$\dfrac{(\mathtt{c_1} \mid \mathtt{s_1} \models \mathtt{A_1}) \xrightarrow{\;1\;} (\mathtt{c_2} \mid \mathtt{s_2} \models \mathtt{A_2}) \quad 1 \neq \epsilon \quad \mathrm{chan}\,1 \notin cs}{(\mathtt{c_1} \mid \mathtt{s_1} \models \mathtt{A_1} \setminus \mathtt{cs}) \xrightarrow{\;1\;} (\mathtt{c_2} \mid \mathtt{s_2} \models \mathtt{A_2} \setminus \mathtt{cs})} \tag{19}$$

$$\dfrac{(\mathtt{c_1} \mid \mathtt{s_1} \models \mathtt{A_1}) \xrightarrow{\;1\;} (\mathtt{c_2} \mid \mathtt{s_2} \models \mathtt{A_2}) \quad 1 = \epsilon \vee \mathrm{chan}\,1 \in cs}{(\mathtt{c_1} \mid \mathtt{s_1} \models \mathtt{A_1} \setminus \mathtt{cs}) \xrightarrow{\;\epsilon\;} (\mathtt{c_2} \mid \mathtt{s_2} \models \mathtt{A_2} \setminus \mathtt{cs})} \tag{20}$$

$$\dfrac{c}{(\mathtt{c} \mid \mathtt{s} \models \mathtt{Skip} \setminus \mathtt{cs}) \xrightarrow{\;\epsilon\;} (\mathtt{c} \mid \mathtt{s} \models \mathtt{Skip})} \tag{21}$$

UTP and Sustainability

Yifeng Chen[1] and Jeff W. Sanders[2,*]

[1] Peking University, Beijing
[2] UNU-IIST, Macao

Abstract. Hoare and He's approach to unifying theories of programming, UTP, is a dozen years old. In spite of the importance of its ideas, UTP does not seem to be attracting due interest. The purpose of this article is to discuss why that is the case, and to consider UTP's destiny. To do so it analyses the nature of UTP, focusing primarily on unification, and makes suggestions to expand its use.

1 Preamble

The history of science is a maze of roads not taken; of ideas not pursued. You can't drift in style from Shanghai to Beijing in a Zeppelin. Nor do you explain the evolution of the Panda using Lamarckism. The Theremin has not replaced the Stadivarius. Your laptop bears little resemblance to Babbage's difference engine. Those analogue computers, the astrolabe, slide rule and Bush's differential analyser, have all been interred in a graveyard for nondigital devices. And wither quantum computing?[1]

It is interesting to speculate on the reasons for lack of success. They may be social: too much has already been invested in alternatives (the world has overlooked *nonstandard calculus*, in spite of its capturing the Leibnizian intuition of infinitesimals and boasting a first-year textbook [20]). Or the reasons may be commercial: a more powerful competitor has its own alternative or an alternative offers better profitability (VHS quickly dominated Betamax [40]). Of course most often the reasons are simply scientific (perpetual motion machines, the geocentric solar system (or was it universe?) and phlogiston).

Science evolves by following pathways at the expense of those neglected, for whatever reasons. Seldom does a choice between paths have the opportunity to be weighed up publicly.

Is UTP a dead-end? The purpose of this paper is to reflect on and promote discussion of just that question. The importunate reader might skip Section 2, in which the problem confronting UTP is considered; Section 3, in which UTP is 'kick started'; Section 4, in which alternative UTP projects are considered; and instead move straight to the Conclusions.

---

[*] The first author was partially supported by the China HGJ Significant Project 2009ZX01036-001-002-4, and the second author by the Macao Science and Technology Development Fund, under the PEARL project grant number 041/2007/A3.
[1] The reader is invited to a complementary parlour game: list ever-more insignificant things which nonetheless prevail. Let's start with '*lorem ipsum*'.

S. Qin (Ed.): UTP 2010, LNCS 6445, pp. 46–73, 2010.

2   UTP at the Crossroads

2.1   The Evidence

UTP is struggling. It seems that the previous two conferences (UTP2006 in Durham [9] and UTP2008 in Dublin) required considerable organisational skill on the parts of Steve Dunne and Andrew Butterfield respectively. Recall the difficulty attracting interest in the present event, despite Shengchao Qin's best efforts. And witness the continued poor acceptance rate for papers. How many Ph.D. theses has UTP supported? Are there case studies that make non-specialists want to use it? Are there special conference tracks that have the effect of incorporating UTP into the wider community?

For comparison, think of the manner in which Z [12,38] became established: the early case study of IBM's CICS [18]; the large number of M.Sc. and Ph.D. theses (from Oxford alone); its integration into the wider community of Formal Methods and the blossoming of case studies; tool support and its adoption by industry; organisation of user-group meetings (which owe much to Jonathan Bowen); expansion and re-use (for instance object-Z [8]); and the proliferation of courses and books. A similar story could be told for the theories VDM, CSP, CCS, …

It is now a dozen years since the UTP textbook [17] was published. Since Z started with a whimper rather than a bang, comparison is difficult; perhaps for Z a similar time would have elapsed by the mid 90s. By then it appeared stronger and to be expanding *much* more rapidly than UTP does now. Surely the time has come to reflect on the situation.

Let's start, well, at the beginning. What might be expected of theories of programming? Why seek to unify them? Finally, how might unification be expected to go?

2.2   Theories of Programming

Once upon a time, in the early days of ALGOL, a theory of programming consisted of the syntax of a programming language, an advance that has been accorded the name BNF for John Bachus and Peter Nauer. That 'theory' helped programmers who, at a time when new programming languages were appearing fast, furious and in a wide range of styles, could otherwise learn a new language only by following examples.

But compiler writers required more: a semantics by which to validate and compare their products. At first, semantic descriptions were informal. The case of ALGOL 60 provoked the transition to formality: its reports [30,3] of 1960 and 1963 in natural language were (inevitably?) criticised as being ambiguous [21]. The variety of semantic approaches was evident from the start: an axiomatic semantics was given to Pascal [14] in 1971; an operational style was used for PL/I [23] in 1971 and ALGOL 68 [39] in 1975; and denotational semantics was demonstrated on ALGOL-like languages [25] by 1976. A theory of programming consisted, by the mid 1970's, of a language's syntax accompanied by a semantic description. It seems fair to say that the unfortunate divergence between programming and theoretical computer science dates from this time.

During the first half of the 1970's programmers, now in the rôle of humble software engineers, required yet more from a theory of programming. Support was required for *system engineering*: for verification against a more asbtract specification of a design that was either posited, or obtained by incremental development in a manner supporting the top-down approach of engineering

$$Spec = Design_0 \sqsubseteq Design_1 \sqsubseteq \ldots \sqsubseteq Design_n = Impl$$

(including algorithmic refinements over the same state space, and refinements over distinct spaces by data representation). The important feature of the 'domain of discourse' is that it be powerful enough to express specifications, code, and the combinations that arise at intermediate levels of design. The semantic model is thus required to span various levels of abstraction and to be founded on a (reflexive and) transitive notion of refinement.

That approach has since retained its importance because it enables:

- a design to be verified against a specification (without an understanding of conformance, what does a specification mean?);
- abstract interpretation and model checking, firstly of the abstract model and secondly of the property being checked against it;
- comprehension of a system incrementally, by layers of successively finer detail; that approach has been traditionally used qualitatively to describe complex software (for example operating systems [22]), and now is able to be interpreted quantitatively;
- stepwise system derivation, of the kind begun by Dijkstra in the 1970's for simple programs but now extended to systems, through all layers of abstraction using laws and machine assistance;
- comprehension of new behaviours (like concurrency, probability and time) when intuition alone is too risky as a basis for programming;
- program analysis of the usual kinds: data-flow, constraint-based, abstract interpretation, type systems and effect systems [32].

This time theoreticians took longer to respond, though the first step was immediate. In 1975 Dijkstra provided the predicate transformer model [7], then at just one level of abstration and without explicit use of laws or the refinement relation $\sqsubseteq$. Over the next fifteen years the concepts Dijkstra had introduced for code were extended to the more general commands appropriate for software engineering (unbounded nondeterminism, angelic choice and unenabled commands ('miracles') [31,28,1,29], and data refinement [35]) and studied in both the predicate-transformer and binary-relation models [15]. The result was, by 1990, what two decades later is still recognised as a 'theory of programming':

1. a semantic domain $(\mathcal{X}, \sqsubseteq)$, incorporating a partial order representing refinement

2. a mapping ⟦ · ⟧ from the syntactically-defined 'programming' language to the semantic domain $\mathcal{X}$
3. accompanying laws that are sound (and ideally complete) with respect to the semantic model.

2.3 Unification

But whilst theoretical support for such theories of programming is satisfactory, applications remain scant. Examples include: functional programming languages [27] (cartesian-closed categories); the guarded-command language [15] (predicate transformers or binary relations); process algebras CSP [37] (failures and divergences) and CCS [26] (transition trees); and receptive-process theory (for use in asynchronous devices) [19] (failures and divergences).

The difficulty is that, as new features are incorporated, the complexity increases due to the interaction between the new feature and (potentially) *each* existing feature. The incorporation of probability with nondeterminism [24] is certainly a success; but occam [36] has been of limited success semantically, due to interactions between state, nondeterminism and synchronisation.

Fortunately in many paradigms of computation, a new feature interacts in a severely circumscribed manner with previous features. So there is hope that a satisfactory theory can be obtained incrementally, by adding new features gradually to existing theory.

That, of course, is what is meant by *unification* in UTP, and why the approach is so vitally important. Without it there seems little chance of providing a patently correct, comprehensible, semantics for something like occam which combines, as already observed, various features that interact nontrivially. Without it that list of successes seems destined to remain short. But using it, one might hope to describe occam, for example, in layers that correspond to sequential programs, nondeterministic programs, reactive programs, and finally occam processes. Indeed that has been one of the principle motivations for UTP, and a measure by which its success can be judged.

To demonstrate its utility, a unification of theories of programming ought to explicate further pressing paradigms of computation. Examples include

 – service computing
 – real time
 – object orientation (including mutable objects)
 – component-based systems
 – adaptivity and other self-* system properties
 – hybrid and cyberphysical systems
 – machine learning
 – quantum computation
 – game-theoretic semantics
 – hardware systems
 – biologically-inspired systems.

If the unifying approach *is* as important as has just been reasoned from a scientific viewpoint, why has it not been more widely adopted in a dozen years?

2.4   The Three-Chapter Problem

It has been observed that many students of UTP do not progress past Chapter 3 of Hoare and He's eleven-chapter text [17]. The implication is that by being exposed to only the first thirty percent of the book (85 pages of 282), their view of UTP is dominated by relations, predicates and the healthiness conditions **Hi**, for $1 \leq \mathbf{i} \leq 4$. Indeed there does seem to be evidence, amongst students and even researchers, for the accuracy of this harsh claim.

Can the 'three-chapter problem' be related to our lack of progress in unifying theories? Can that in turn be part of the reason behind the limited adoption of UTP? Since there seems little hope of systematic progress in the area of providing theories of contemporary programming without use of unification, some investigation seems required.

2.5   What Might Might Be Expected of Unification?

It has been argued in Section 2.2 that a theory of 'programming' consists of a semantic domain (partially ordered), an interpretation of the language in that domain and a collection of sound laws for the language constructs. The purpose of this section is, in view of the UTP programme having seemingly stalled, to consider afresh what might be expected from unification.

The expectation is that, by viewing theories hierarchically, a simple theory $\mathcal{A}$ is to be embedded in a more complex $\mathcal{C}$ in a manner that enables $\mathcal{A}$'s semantics to be imported. So the semantics of the more complex $\mathcal{C}$, as far as it concerns just the features it shares with the simple language $\mathcal{A}$, has already been provided in $\mathcal{A}$; only features unique to $\mathcal{C}$ (lying outside the range of the embedding) need now be considered. The theory of $\mathcal{C}$ has been unified with that of $\mathcal{A}$ *via* the embedding. Examples will be familiar to UTP *aficionados*; several are considered in Section 3.

The partial order $\sqsubseteq$ of each theory captures conformance. As usual there are operators corresponding to its *infimum*, $\sqcap$, and *supremum*, $\sqcup$. The former arises from abstraction, or information hiding, *via* local blocks and it is preserved by the embedding ε—as is required for lifting a semantics that includes $\sqcap$— iff for any family $\mathcal{E}$ (empty, nonempty and finite, or infinite) in the abstract domain $\mathcal{A}$,

$$\varepsilon.\sqcap\mathcal{E} \; = \; \sqcap\{\varepsilon.E \mid E \in \mathcal{E}\}. \tag{1}$$

That condition is equivalent to ε being the embedding in an embedding-projection pair (ε, π) known as a *Galois connection* and defined by the equivalence

$$\varepsilon.a \sqsubseteq_{\mathcal{C}} c \; \equiv \; a \sqsubseteq_{\mathcal{A}} \pi.c. \tag{2}$$

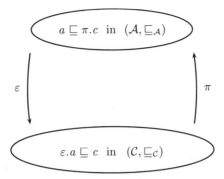

Fig. 1. A Galois embedding $gc(\varepsilon, \pi; \mathcal{A}, \mathcal{C})$ relates abstract and concrete theories

The case in which ε is injective embeds $\mathcal{A}$ in $\mathcal{C}$ and so forms the basis of the hierarchical approach. Then the connection is called a *Galois embedding*; see Figure 1.

So Galois connections and embeddings must be expected to play a central rôle in unifying theories. Moreover, in lifting semantics to a more detailed level, the embedding ε must preserve further combinators. For instance preservation of sequential composition,

$$\varepsilon.(r \, \fatsemi \, s) \;=\; \varepsilon.r \, \fatsemi \, \varepsilon.s \,,$$

enables ε to be used to lift the behaviour of a sequential composition from one level to the next in the hierarchy. Similarly for the other combinators, including recursion (and hence) iteration. That way, laws in $\mathcal{A}$ are *re-used* in $\mathcal{C}$: a major benefit of unifying theories.

It will then be important to characterise the lifted space $ran.\varepsilon$ as a subset of $\mathcal{C}$ and furthermore to determine—if possible—the manner in which it generates $\mathcal{C}$. For that determines the $\mathcal{C}$-semantics in terms of the $\mathcal{A}$-semantics.

But now we find ourselves firmly in Chapter 4, without having mentioned predicates or healthiness conditions. How can that be? From our present viewpoint, predicates merely form the basis of certain models (predicate transformers, for example!); and healthiness conditions are merely used in defining domains. Suddenly both have disappeared from the centre of the stage on which we expect unification to be performed.

Is it possible that there is an alternative entry to UTP which starts from Galois connections—Chapter 4—instead of Chapter 3? If so, how does it go and what then is the importance of Chapter 3? Perhaps by following it the 'three-chapter problem' might be avoided.

3   A Fresh Start

3.1   Computability: Theory $\mathcal{P}$

The theory of Computer Science began in the 1930s with the various models, by Hilbert, Turing, Kleene, Church, Markov *et al.*, of the concept of a *computation*

abort	nontermination
$x := e$	assignment, with expression e
P **if** b **else** Q	conditional
$P \, \fatsemi \, Q$	sequential composition
$\mu.F$	recursion

Fig. 2. Syntax for the space *Predet* of predeterministic programs. Assignment is assumed to be predeterministic and recursion to be with respect to a continuous function.

(or of recursiveness). By modelling a 'mechanism', mathematicians had for the first time to model the possibility of nontermination. Today such computations are called *predeterministic* because from any initial state they are either nonterminating or deterministic, and written using syntax like that of Figure 2. The set of all predeterministic programs over state space X is written $Predet(X)$.

Our intention is that sequential composition be associative with identity the assignment **skip** (which changes no variable). More interestingly, if a nonterminating program precedes or follows another program the result remains nonterminating:

$$\mathbf{abort} \, \fatsemi \, P \;=\; \mathbf{abort} \;=\; P \, \fatsemi \, \mathbf{abort} \,. \tag{3}$$

Of course recursion includes iteration as tail recursion.

The time-honoured model [5] for $Predet(X)$ consists of partial functions on X, with refinement as extension; it is denoted $\mathcal{P}(X)$:

$$\mathcal{P}(X) \;:=\; (X \nrightarrow X, \supseteq) \,.$$

It is a domain[2] with least element the empty partial function, $\{\,\}$, with maximal elements the total functions and with compact elements the partial functions having finite domains. The semantic mapping is given in Figure 3. Both its well-definedness, and soundness of the laws, are routine.

By starting with the 'historical' theory $\mathcal{P}(X)$, explicit consideration of healthiness conditions has been avoided: predeterminism is captured enitrely by the type $X \nrightarrow X$.

3.2   An Alternative: Theory $\mathcal{Q}$

A popular alternative, in view of models soon to come, is to replace the partial functions with total functions whose range includes a 'virtual' element for non-termination. Thus each partial function is made total on X by mapping each element outside its domain to the virtual element $\bot$. Furthermore, for the new

---

[2] By 'domain' here is meant a complete partial order in which each element is the supremum of its compact approximations. Recall that an element k is *compact* iff any directed set $\mathcal{E}$ that exceeds it contains an element which does so: if $k \sqsubseteq \sqcup \mathcal{E}$ then $\exists e : \mathcal{E} \cdot k \sqsubseteq e$. In the case of partial functions, the domain conditions mean: $\forall f : \mathcal{P} \cdot f = \cap \{ k : \mathcal{P} \mid \#(dom.k) < \infty \wedge k \sqsubseteq f \}$. Indeed without loss of generality there k ranges over singleton partial functions: $\#(dom.k) = 1$.

$$[\textbf{abort}]_{\mathcal{P}} \;:=\; \{\,\}$$
$$[x := e]_{\mathcal{P}} \;:=\; \lambda\,x : X \cdot e$$
$$[P \textbf{ if } b \textbf{ else } Q]_{\mathcal{P}} \;:=\; \lambda\,x : X \cdot [P]_{\mathcal{P}}.x \textbf{ if } b.x \textbf{ else } [Q]_{\mathcal{P}}.x$$
$$[P \, \mathbin{;} \, Q]_{\mathcal{P}} \;:=\; [Q]_{\mathcal{P}} \circ [P]_{\mathcal{P}}$$
$$[\mu.F]_{\mathcal{P}} \;:=\; \cup\{\,f : \mathcal{P}(X) \mid F.f \subseteq f\,\}$$

Fig. 3. The $\mathcal{P}$ semantics of predeterministic programs, in which program P is denoted by a partial function $[P]_{\mathcal{P}}$ and variable x is used for both its argument and the state of the program. Recursion is the least fixed point of F, as given by the first recursion theorem of Kleene (for instance [5], Theorem 10.3.1).

model to be closed under sequential composition, it must be 'homogeneous': the virtual state $\bot$ must also belong to the domain. Let

$$X_{\bot} \;:=\; X \cup \{\bot\}\,.$$

Now for the left zero law in (3) to hold, it suffices for each denotation f of a program to be *strict* (with the flat ordering on $X_{\bot}$):

$$f.\bot = \bot\,.$$

For the right zero law in (3) to hold, it suffices for f also to be *up-closed* at that bottom element. Such relational behaviour is most easily captured by defining, for a function $f : X \to X$, its '(relational) strict and up-closed extension to $X_{\bot}$' by

$$(f)_{\bot} \;:=\; f \cup \{\bot\} \times X_{\bot}$$

(an idea that is extended from functions f to relations in Section 3.3).

Writing $pre.f$ for the set of elements of X not mapped by the extension f to $\bot$,

$$pre.f \;:=\; \{\,x : X \mid f.x \neq \bot\,\}\,,$$

in order for ε to be isotone, the partial order of conformance must translate in the new model to:

$$f \sqsubseteq f' \;:=\; (f \restriction pre.f = f' \restriction pre.f)\,.$$

Thus

$$\mathcal{Q}(X) \;:=\; (\{(f)_{\bot} \mid \exists f : X \to X\}, \sqsubseteq)\,,$$

and the translation function is

$$\varepsilon : \mathcal{P}(X) \to \mathcal{Q}(X)$$
$$\varepsilon.f \;:=\; f \cup \{\,(x,\bot) \mid x \in X_{\bot} \setminus dom.f\,\}\,.$$

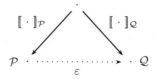

Fig. 4. Using ε to translate the semantics of predeterministic programs from $\mathcal{P}$ to $\mathcal{Q}$

$$
\begin{aligned}
[\![\mathbf{abort}]\!]_{\mathcal{Q}} &= \lambda x : X \cdot \bot \\
[\![x := e]\!]_{\mathcal{Q}} &= \varepsilon.(\lambda x : X \cdot e) \\
[\![P \ \mathbf{if} \ b \ \mathbf{else} \ Q]\!]_{\mathcal{Q}} &= \lambda x : X \cdot [\![P]\!]_{\mathcal{Q}}.x \ \mathbf{if} \ b.x \ \mathbf{else} \ [\![Q]\!]_{\mathcal{Q}}.x \\
[\![P \ \mathring{,} \ Q]\!]_{\mathcal{Q}} &= [\![Q]\!]_{\mathcal{Q}} \circ [\![P]\!]_{\mathcal{Q}} \\
[\![\mu.F]\!]_{\mathcal{Q}} &= \sqcup \{ f : \mathcal{Q}(X) \mid F.f \sqsubseteq f \}
\end{aligned}
$$

Fig. 5. The $\mathcal{Q}$ semantics of predeterministic programs, inferred from the $\mathcal{P}$ semantics (Figure 3) using the technique of Figure 4

Theorem 1.   The translation function $\varepsilon : \mathcal{P}(X) \rightarrow \mathcal{Q}(X)$

1. is an isotone bijection so that in particular $ran.\varepsilon$ is the carrier of $\mathcal{Q}(X)$;
2. ensures that the domain $\mathcal{Q}(X)$ has least element the constant function $\bot$, maximal elements the functions f with $pre.f = X$ and compact elements the functions f with $pre.f$ finite;
3. preserves total functions (*i.e.* assignment): if f is total then $(\varepsilon.f) \restriction X = f$;
4. preserves composition: $\varepsilon.(f \circ g) = (\varepsilon.f) \circ (\varepsilon.g)$.

Now the $\mathcal{Q}$ semantics of *Predet* is obtained by translating the $\mathcal{P}$ semantics with the embedding ε as indicated in Figure 4. Theorem 1 ensures accuracy of the result and preservation of the laws; the result is given in Figure 5.

It is worth emphasising that the semantics is not defined anew, but translated by ε from $\mathcal{P}$. For example

$[\![\mathbf{abort} \ \mathring{,} \ P]\!]_{\mathcal{Q}}$

$=$ definition of $\mathcal{Q}$ semantics, Figure 4

$\varepsilon.[\![\mathbf{abort} \ \mathring{,} \ P]\!]_{\mathcal{P}}$

$=$ law of $\mathcal{P}$ semantics

$\varepsilon.[\![\mathbf{abort}]\!]_{\mathcal{P}}$

$=$ definition of $\mathcal{Q}$ semantics again

$[\![\mathbf{abort}]\!]_{\mathcal{Q}}$.

3.3   Nondeterminism: Theory $\mathcal{D}$

Nondeterminism arises for several reasons. Firstly, it might simply be inherent in functionality being specified: locate x in an array (where x may occur more than once); find a minimum spanning tree (where there may be several), a shortest path, a Hamiltonian circuit, ... Secondly, it might be the result of abstracting the mechanism determining a choice made at a lower level of abstraction: a random-number generator whose seed and mechanism of generation are concealed. Thirdly, it might be assumed in order to ensure that reasoning is local: a choice determined by testing a global variable might be assumed to be a nondeterministic choice in order to avoid global reasoning.

Predeterministic programs are extended to be finitely[3] nondeterministic by augmenting the language *Predet* with a binary combinator for *nondeterministic choice*:

$$P \sqcap Q \,.$$

The set of such programs over state space X is written $Prog(X)$ and the relationship of conformance still written $\sqsubseteq$. Its connection with nondeterminism is, as already observed,

$$P \sqsubseteq P' \;\equiv\; P \sqcap P' = P \,.$$

Important laws involving programs and nondeterminism include:

$$P \sqcap \textbf{abort} \;=\; \textbf{abort} \tag{4}$$
$$(P \sqcap Q) \,\fatsemi\, R \;=\; (P \,\fatsemi\, R) \sqcap (Q \,\fatsemi\, R) \tag{5}$$
$$P \,\fatsemi\, (Q \sqcap R) \;=\; (P \,\fatsemi\, Q) \sqcap (P \,\fatsemi\, R) \,. \tag{6}$$

The first characterises the Dijkstra-Hoare approach: in order to guarantee entirely correct implementations, a theory must ensure that the (nondeterministic) possibility of an error is identified with certain error. In (5) the demonic choice responsible for the nondeterminism is made first on both sides, which are therefore indistinguishable. Law (6) is more subtle because the choice is made first on the right, but on the left only after P; nonetheless, the two programs are expected to have identical behaviour (because P on the left-hand side is a program and not a more general kind of computation (like angelic choice) able to offers behaviour which the later demonic choice can exploit).

What is the relationship between $Prog(X)$ and $Predet(X)$, *i.e.* between programs and predeterministic programs? The following law 'quantifies' the relationship by expressing each program as the (not necessarily finitely) nondeterministic combination of its predeterministic refinements.

$$\forall P : Prog(X) \cdot P \;=\; \sqcap\{\, Q : Predet(X) \mid P \sqsubseteq Q \,\} \tag{7}$$

A 'dual' law, extended from predeterministic programs to programs and hence analogous to the 'domain law' in Footnote 2, expresses each program (and so in particular, each predeterministic program) as the supremum of the compact programs (defined in that footnote, and to be characterised semantically in Theorem 2) it refines:

---

[3] More precisely, the nondeterministic choice is now considered of any nonempty finite set of programs. That is equivalent to the nondeterministic choice of two programs, by induction and the laws of associativity, idempotence and commutativity of binary nondeterministic choice.

$$\forall\, Q : Prog(X) \cdot Q \;=\; \bigsqcup\{\, K : Prog(X) \mid K \sqsubseteq Q,\ K \text{ compact}\,\}. \qquad (8)$$

A compelling model of nondeterministic programs [15] consists of allowing the elements of the model $\mathcal{Q}(X)$ to be multivalued, since $\mathcal{Q}(X)$ already captures nontermination with the value $\bot$, and now would capture nondeterminism as multi-valueness of a relation. Then the partial order of conformance, 'at least as deterministic as', between such relations would be containment (as sets)

$$r \sqsubseteq s \;\equiv\; r \supseteq s .$$

Let us determine the healthiness conditions on such a relation r on $X_\bot$, using the same method as for $\mathcal{Q}(X)$. For the right zero law to hold in (3), it suffices for r to be total on X, as were the elements of $\mathcal{Q}(X)$

$$\forall\, x : X \cdot \exists\, x' : X_\bot \cdot x\, r\, x'. \qquad (9)$$

For the left zero law, again it suffices for r to map $\bot$ to all of $X_\bot$.

In order for **abort** to be minimum in the refinement ordering of containment, Law (4), it suffices for

$$x\, r\, \bot \;\Rightarrow\; \forall\, x' : X_\bot \cdot x\, r\, x'.$$

Finally in order for the least upper bound, or intersection, of a chain of healthy relations again to be healthy, as required for recursion, it suffices for the image of each state to be *finitary*: to be either all of $X_\bot$ or nonempty and finite

$$\{\, x' : X_\bot \mid x\, r\, x'\,\} \neq X_\bot \;\Rightarrow\; 0 < \#\{\, x' : X_\bot \mid x\, r\, x'\,\} < \infty. \qquad (10)$$

Evidently being nonempty supersedes totality (9).

Those conditions can be abbreviated using the notation $X \leftrightarrow X$ for the type of all relations on X and $r.(\!| x |\!)$ for the relational image of r at x

$$r.(\!| x |\!) \;:=\; \{\, x' : X_\bot \mid x\, r\, x'\,\}.$$

That model is called $\mathcal{D}(X)$, and has ordering $\supseteq$ and carrier set

$$\left\{\, r : X_\bot \leftrightarrow X_\bot \ \middle|\ \left(\begin{array}{l} \bot\, r\, \bot \\ \forall\, x : X_\bot \cdot \left(\begin{array}{l} x\, r\, \bot \;\Rightarrow\; r.(\!| x |\!) = X_\bot \\ r.(\!| x |\!) \neq X_\bot \;\Rightarrow\; 0 < \#r.(\!| x |\!) < \infty \end{array} \right) \end{array} \right) \right\}.$$

There is a Galois connection from the model $\mathcal{Q}(X)$ for predeterministic programs to the model $\mathcal{D}(X)$, whose embedding is

$$\varepsilon : \mathcal{Q}(X) \to \mathcal{D}(X)$$
$$\varepsilon.f \;:=\; f \cup (X_\bot \setminus pre.f) \times X_\bot . \qquad (11)$$

In other words,

$$x\, (\varepsilon.f)\, x' \;\equiv\; (\, x \in pre.f \;\Rightarrow\; f.x = x'\,).$$

Its adjoint $\pi.r$ denotes the largest partial function in r which 'accounts for all of r's results at its arguments'. It may be thought of as the largest partial function which approximates, in $\mathcal{Q}(X)$, total relation r. Indeed that is the form for π expected by adjunction:

$$\pi.r \;=\; \cup\{f:\mathcal{Q}(X) \mid \varepsilon.f \supseteq r\}.$$

Then:

Theorem 2.   The function $\varepsilon : \mathcal{Q}(X) \to \mathcal{D}(X)$

1. is an injection that preserves arbitrary suprema from $\mathcal{Q}(X)$ under $\sqsubseteq$ to $\mathcal{D}(X)$ under $\supseteq$: more generally, Definition (11) of ε makes sense if its argument is merely a relation, and then for *any* subset F of the carrier of $\mathcal{Q}(X)$ (not just those having a well-defined supremum $\sqcup F \in \mathcal{Q}(X)$),

$$\varepsilon.\cup F \;=\; \cap\{\varepsilon.f \mid f \in F\};$$

2. has adjoint $\pi : \mathcal{D}(X) \to \mathcal{Q}(X)$, thus $gc(\varepsilon, \pi; \mathcal{Q}(X), \mathcal{D}(X))$, where

$$\pi.r \;=\; \{(x,y) : r \mid y \neq \bot \;\wedge\; \forall x' \neq \bot \cdot x\,r\,x' \Rightarrow x' = y\} \qquad (12)$$

which is $(\supseteq, \sqsubseteq)$-continuous: if R is a $\supseteq$-directed subset of $\mathcal{D}(X)$ then

$$\pi.\cap R \;=\; \sqcup\{\pi.r \mid r \in R\}; \qquad (13)$$

3. has range which generates $\mathcal{D}(X)$ under nonempty finite unions:

$$\mathcal{D}(X) \;=\; \{\cup F \mid F \subseteq ran.\varepsilon \text{ is nonempty and finite}\};$$

4. ensures that the domain $\mathcal{D}(X)$ has least element the universal relation on $X_\bot$, maximal elements the (total) functions and compact elements the relations r with $pre.r$ finite (extending Definition (4) from functions to relations); thus each $r : \mathcal{D}$ is the supremum of compact elements which it refines (a fact which is weaker than 3 since each compact element of $\mathcal{D}$ is a nonempty finite union of elements of ran ε);

5. preserves sequential composition: $\varepsilon.(\mathrm{id}_X) = (\mathrm{id}_X)_\bot$ and $\varepsilon.(f \circ g) \;=\; (\varepsilon.g)\,\mathring{,}\,(\varepsilon.f)$.

It is convenient to define an embedding from relations on X to those on $X_\bot$ to capture that part of the healthiness conditions relating to initial virtual state:

$$(\cdot)_\bot : (X \leftrightarrow X) \to (X_\bot \leftrightarrow X_\bot)$$
$$(r)_\bot \;=\; r \cup \{\bot\}\times X_\bot .$$

Since $(\cdot)_\bot$ preserves arbitrary intersections (though only nonempty unions) it is Galois from $(X \leftrightarrow X, \supseteq)$ to $(X_\bot \leftrightarrow X_\bot, \supseteq)$. Its adjoint is restriction to X:

$$\pi : (X_\bot \leftrightarrow X_\bot) \to (X \leftrightarrow X)$$
$$\pi.s \;:=\; s \cap (X \times X),$$

$$
\begin{aligned}
[\![\textbf{abort}]\!]_\mathcal{D} &= X_\perp \times X_\perp \\
[\![x := e]\!]_\mathcal{D} &= (\lambda\, x : X \cdot e)_\perp \\
[\![P\ \textbf{if}\ b\ \textbf{else}\ Q]\!]_\mathcal{D} &= \{\, (x, x') \mid x[\![P]\!]_\mathcal{D} x' \ \text{if}\ b.x\ \text{else}\ x[\![Q]\!]_\mathcal{D} x' \,\} \\
[\![P \,\fatsemi\, Q]\!]_\mathcal{D} &= [\![P]\!]_\mathcal{D} \,\fatsemi\, [\![Q]\!]_\mathcal{D} \\
[\![\mu.F]\!]_\mathcal{D} &= \cap\{\, d : \mathcal{D}(X) \mid F.d \supseteq d \,\} \\
[\![P \sqcap Q]\!]_\mathcal{D} &= [\![P]\!]_\mathcal{D} \cup [\![Q]\!]_\mathcal{D}
\end{aligned}
$$

Fig. 6. Important properties of the relational semantics for *Prog*. Function F is monotone on $\mathcal{D}$

a projection that preserves arbitrary intersections (as well as arbitrary unions as expected from the basic property of Galois connections) and is surjective. The embedding $(\cdot)_\perp$ is injective (as expected from properties of Galois connections) and preserves sequential composition:

$$
(r \,\fatsemi\, s)_\perp \ = \ (r)_\perp \,\fatsemi\, (s)_\perp . \tag{14}
$$

The semantic space $\mathcal{D}(X)$ is comprehensively more complex than $\mathcal{P}(X)$. Our task, then, is to define the semantics of $Prog(X)$ in $\mathcal{D}(X)$ in such a way that the simplicity of the $\mathcal{P}(X)$ semantics is not obscured. That is achieved—of course— by lifting with ε *via* $\mathcal{Q}(X)$.

For each $P : Prog(X)$ its relational semantics $[\![P]\!]_\mathcal{D}$ is defined by Law (7) using union for nondeterministic choice and the lifting (Figure 4), under the Galois connection of Theorem 2, of the $\mathcal{Q}$ semantics of P's predeterministic refinements:

$$
[\![P]\!]_\mathcal{D} \ = \ \cup\{\, \varepsilon.[\![Q]\!]_\mathcal{P} \mid Q \in Predet(X) \ \wedge\ P \sqsubseteq Q \,\}. \tag{15}
$$

In particular, if P is itself predeterministic then

$$
[\![P]\!]_\mathcal{D} \ = \ \varepsilon.[\![P]\!]_\mathcal{Q}.
$$

For example **skip**, because it is deterministic, has semantics

$[\![\textbf{skip}]\!]_\mathcal{D}$

$=$ definition of $\mathcal{D}$ semantics

$\varepsilon.[\![\textbf{skip}]\!]_\mathcal{Q}$

$=$ $\mathcal{Q}$ semantics with **skip** abbreviating $(x := x)$

$\varepsilon.(\lambda\, x : X \cdot x)$

$=$ definition of ε

$(\lambda\, x : X \cdot x)_\perp .$

A similar argument works for **abort**; as does the fact that $[\![\textbf{abort}]\!]_\mathcal{Q}$ is the least element of $\mathcal{Q}(X)$ and ε preserves minima (a basic property of Galois connections).

Thus the $\mathcal{D}$ semantics of $Prog(X)$ is defined by lifting on $Predet(X)$ and otherwise by union. Now the properties, that before were a matter of definition in the $\mathcal{P}$ semantics of Figure 3, are simply inferred, though with a little more work than for the $\mathcal{Q}$ semantics as inferred in Figure 5; see Figure 6.

Consider, for example, sequential composition. The proof relies on predeterministic computations whose $\mathcal{P}$ semantics consists of a singleton partial function (recall Footnote 2); thus the computation terminates from just a single state. Writing $Predet_1(X)$ for the set of such computations, for $P, P' : Prog(X)$,

$\llbracket P \,\mathring{,}\, P' \rrbracket_{\mathcal{D}}$

$=$ (15)

$\cup\{\, \varepsilon.[R]_{\mathcal{Q}} \mid R \in Predet(X) \land P \,\mathring{,}\, P' \sqsubseteq R \,\}$

$=$ Footnote 2 and set theory

$\cup\{\, \varepsilon.[R]_{\mathcal{Q}} \mid R \in Predet_1(X) \land P \,\mathring{,}\, P' \sqsubseteq R \,\}$

$=$ property of $Predet_1(X)$

$\cup\{\, \varepsilon.\llbracket R \rrbracket_{\mathcal{Q}} \mid \exists\, Q, Q' \in Predet_1(X) \land P \sqsubseteq Q \land P' \sqsubseteq Q' \land R = Q \,\mathring{,}\, Q' \,\}$

$=$ 1-point law

$\cup\{\, \varepsilon.\llbracket Q \,\mathring{,}\, Q' \rrbracket_{\mathcal{Q}} \mid Q, Q' \in Predet_1(X) \land P \sqsubseteq Q \land P' \sqsubseteq Q' \,\}$

$=$ ε preserves sequential composition (Theorem 2, Part 5)

$\cup\{\, \varepsilon.\llbracket Q \rrbracket_{\mathcal{Q}} \,\mathring{,}\, \varepsilon.\llbracket Q' \rrbracket_{\mathcal{Q}} \mid Q, Q' \in Predet_1(X) \land P \sqsubseteq Q \land P' \sqsubseteq Q' \,\}$

$=$ set theory

$\cup\{\, \varepsilon.\llbracket Q \rrbracket_{\mathcal{Q}} \mid Q \in Predet_1(X) \land P \sqsubseteq Q \,\} \,\mathring{,}\,$
$\cup\{\, \varepsilon.\llbracket Q' \rrbracket_{\mathcal{Q}} \mid Q' \in Predet_1(X) \land P' \sqsubseteq Q' \,\}$

$=$ Footnote 2 again

$\cup\{\, \varepsilon.\llbracket Q \rrbracket_{\mathcal{Q}} \mid Q \in Predet(X) \land P \sqsubseteq Q \,\} \,\mathring{,}\,$
$\cup\{\, \varepsilon.\llbracket Q' \rrbracket_{\mathcal{Q}} \mid Q' \in Predet(X) \land P' \sqsubseteq Q' \,\}$

$=$ (15)

$\llbracket P \rrbracket_{\mathcal{D}} \,\mathring{,}\, \llbracket P' \rrbracket_{\mathcal{D}}$.

The case of nondeterminism is similar using instead (in the third step) the property that, for $Q : Predet_1(X)$,

$$P \sqcap P' \sqsubseteq Q \;\equiv\; P \sqsubseteq Q \lor P' \sqsubseteq Q .$$

The proofs of Laws (4) to (6) are immediate from basic set theory.

There is an alternative to this approach to the semantics of $Prog(X)$ based on Law (7) with $\cup$ for nondeterminism. It assigns semantics by structural induction on $P : Prog(X)$, 'building in' Equation (15) at each step. But then Law (7) must be checked and so the amount of work is equivalent. The former approach has been chosen because it seems to extend better to more complex domains, like probabilistic domains.

In summary, a Galois connection has been used to lift the $\mathcal{Q}$ semantics, and laws, to $\mathcal{D}$.

3.4 Angelic Choice: Theory $\mathcal{T}$

Just as Software Engineering brought to light (demonic) nondeterminism, so the formal development process discussed in Section 2.2 revealed the utility of

<table>
</table>

magic	the command that is never enabled
$\sqcap\mathcal{F}$	nondeterminstic choice over $\mathcal{F}$
$\sqcup\mathcal{F}$	angelic choice over $\mathcal{F}$

Fig. 7. Syntax completing the space $Comm(X)$ of commands over state space X: the unenabled command, and arbitrary nondeterministic and angelic choices. $\mathcal{F}$ is an arbitrary set of commands.

'partially enabled' computations and 'angelic' choice. We call such computations, which extend programs, *commands*.

An example of a partially-enabled command is choice of an element from a set which happens to be empty; computation cannot be started—is not enabled—in a manner that is dual to a computation that fails to terminate. This situation arises when a procedure for choosing an element from a set is used in a context which ensures the set is nonempty; but when developed 'in isolation', the empty case must also be considered.

Angelic choice is simply supremum $\sqcup$, the dual of nondeterminism $\sqcap$. A simple example is provided by the angelic choice of two consistent commands. The first, R, chooses x nondeterministically between 0 and 1 whilst the second, S, chooses nondeterministically between 1 and 2. Their angelic choice $R \sqcup S$ is the weakest program stronger than both: $x := 1$.

If R and S had not been consistent in that example then their angelic choice, their supremum, would not have been a program. The supremum of an inconsistent set of commands is a command (though not a program) that is never enabled. Notation for the command that is never enabled and for angelic choice are introduced in Figure 7, as is our last ingredient of command space: arbitrary (rather than just binary) nondeterminism. The set of commands on X is written $Comm(X)$. As usual, the relation of conformance is $\sqsubseteq$, satisfying (4). Of course equivalently:

$$P \sqsubseteq P' \;\equiv\; P \sqcup P' = P'.$$

With the extension from programs to commands, the previous laws must be revisited for correctness. Law (5) remains valid: the nondeterministic choice is made initially on both sides and so the demon resolving the nondeterminism, confronted with the same choices, produces the same behaviours. But for just that reason its partner (6) does not remain valid, and must be weakened: for $R, S, T : Comm(X)$,

$$R \,\fatsemi\, (S \sqcap T) \;\sqsubseteq\; (R \,\fatsemi\, S) \sqcap (R \,\fatsemi\, T). \tag{16}$$

Refinement there must of course hold by monotonicity. But equality may fail since the demon (having memory but not prescience), has more choices the later it acts. There are thus fewer choices on the right and so fewer behaviours than on the left. The choices coincide if execution of R results in no angelic choice by which the demon might profit: if R is free of angelic choice.

Important laws involving the new combinators include:

$$R \sqcup \mathbf{magic} \; = \; \mathbf{magic} \tag{17}$$

$$\mathbf{magic} \, \mathring{,} \, R \; = \; \mathbf{magic} \tag{18}$$

$$(R \sqcup S) \, \mathring{,} \, T \; = \; (R \, \mathring{,} \, T) \sqcup (S \, \mathring{,} \, T) \tag{19}$$

$$R \, \mathring{,} \, (S \sqcup T) \; \sqsupseteq \; (R \, \mathring{,} \, S) \sqcup (R \, \mathring{,} \, T). \tag{20}$$

The first, (17), says that **magic** is indeed dual to **abort** and so is the greatest (or 'most refined') command (and thus equals the empty angelic choice $\sqcap\{\,\}$). The second says that an unenabled command cannot be enabled by any sequential successor (even **abort**). In (19) the choice is made initially on both sides so, reasoning as above (with the angel in place of the demon), equality holds. But (20) is dual to (16): on the right the angel acts early and—having prescience but not memory—has more choices and so produces more behaviours; alternatively, the refinement follows by monotonicity. The choices coincide if execution of R results in no nondeterministic choices by which the angel might profit: if R is predeterministic.

The relationship between commands and programs is given by the law analogous to (8) (evidently the analogue of (7) fails): for any command R

$$R \; = \; \sqcup\{\, P : Prog(X) \mid P \sqsubseteq R \,\}. \tag{21}$$

In fact the domain property holds: without loss of generality, program P can be assumed to be compact.

In the relational model $\mathcal{D}(X)$, angelic choice must be intersection and partial enabledness must therefore be captured by partial-ness of a relation. But that means the healthiness condition of totality, (9), no longer holds. Because nondeterminism is now arbitrary, the finitary condition (10) also fails (at both ends of the inequality, in view of lack of totality). Thus all that remains is strictness and upclosure. The extension to $\mathcal{D}(X)$ consisting of relations satisfying just strictness and upclosure, but with the same criterion of conformance, is called $\mathcal{R}(X)$.

The space $\mathcal{R}(X)$ is a domain and a complete lattice with same least element as $\mathcal{D}(X)$ but greatest element $(\{\,\})_{\perp}$ and compact elements the cofinite 'subsets' of $X_{\perp} \times X_{\perp}$. Moreover it is a Boolean algebra under the complement $r \mapsto (X_{\perp} \times X_{\perp} \setminus r)_{\perp}$. However the natural embedding of $\mathcal{D}(X)$ in $\mathcal{R}(X)$ is not Galois. Otherwise its adjoint π would map the greatest element in $\mathcal{R}(X)$ to a greatest element of $\mathcal{D}(X)$; but no such element exists.[4]

Nonetheless the injection of $\mathcal{D}(X)$ in $\mathcal{R}(X)$ does generate $\mathcal{R}(X)$ under arbitrary intersections, reflecting Law (21) (recall that from Theorem 2 nonempty finite unions were used to generate $\mathcal{D}(X)$ from $\mathcal{Q}(X)$, reflecting Law (7)). Thus the carrier set of $\mathcal{R}(X)$ equals

$$\{\cap F \mid F \subseteq \mathcal{D}(X)\}.$$

---

[4] Since the natural embedding from $\mathcal{D}(X)$ to $\mathcal{R}(X)$ preserves arbitrary unions, why is it not Galois by adjunction? Because suprema in $\mathcal{R}(X)$ (arbitrary unions) are not the same as suprema in $\mathcal{D}(X)$; consider for example the empty union.

$$[\textbf{magic}]_{\mathcal{R}} := (\{\,\})_{\perp}$$
$$[\sqcap\mathcal{F}]_{\mathcal{R}} := \cup\{\,[P]_{\mathcal{R}} \mid P \in \mathcal{F}\,\}$$
$$[\sqcup\mathcal{F}]_{\mathcal{R}} := \cap\{\,[P]_{\mathcal{R}} \mid P \in \mathcal{F}\,\}$$

Fig. 8. Relational semantics for $Comm(X)$; this augments the extension of the semantics in Equation (15) from $\mathcal{D}$ to $\mathcal{R}$ using the natural embedding

The relational semantics of $Comm(X)$ may be thought of—like the semantics for $Prog$—as follows.

1. Firstly, the $\mathcal{R}$ semantics equals the $\mathcal{D}$ semantics for commands that are code (like **skip**). In other words the $\mathcal{R}$ semantics *extends* the $\mathcal{D}$ semantics.
2. Secondly, the $\mathcal{R}$ semantics is inferred from the $\mathcal{D}$ semantics by extending the combinators of code to commands (as in the case of sequential composition, or even arbitrary nondeterministic choice, on $Prog$ from $Predet$). This is possible because the natural embedding preserves those combinators.
3. Thirdly, it is defined for the (new) combinator of angelic choice by edict, to be intersection.

Thus the $\mathcal{R}$ semantics of $Comm$ is provided by Equation (15) (thus extended) and Figure 8 (which also includes arbitrary nondeterminism and its empty case, **magic**).

The proofs of Laws (17), (18) and (20) are now straightforward using basic set theory. For example, for Law (20),

$[P \,\fatsemi\, (Q \sqcup R)]_{\mathcal{R}}$

$=$ $\mathcal{R}$ semantics of $\sqcup$ and $\fatsemi$ from Figure 8

$[P]_{\mathcal{R}} \,\fatsemi\, ([Q]_{\mathcal{R}} \cap [R]_{\mathcal{R}})$

$\subseteq$ set theory

$([P]_{\mathcal{R}} \,\fatsemi\, [Q]_{\mathcal{R}}) \cap ([P]_{\mathcal{R}} \,\fatsemi\, [R]_{\mathcal{R}})$

$=$ $\mathcal{R}$ semantics of $\fatsemi$ and $\sqcup$ again

$[(P \,\fatsemi\, Q) \sqcup (P \,\fatsemi\, R)]_{\mathcal{R}}$.

Moreover equality holds in the middle step if, pointwise, the relation $[P]_{\mathcal{R}}$ either maps to $\perp$ (and hence to all of $X_{\perp}$) or is single valued: as required, the command P is predeterministic.

Unfortunately, for Identity (19) the analogous argument establishes only $\sqsupseteq$, unless relation $[R]_{\mathcal{R}}$ is a total function; in other words, command R is deterministic. Furthermore in Law (16) equality always holds (the existential quantification of $\fatsemi$ distributing the $\cup$ of nondeterminism). It is inferred that the relational model $\mathcal{R}(X)$ does not fully capture angelic behaviour.

Thus stretching the relational model $\mathcal{R}(X)$ from programs to commands reveals deficiencies. The situation is analogous to the introduction of nondeterminism: the model $\mathcal{P}(X)$ was simply not expressive enough and so was extended to $\mathcal{D}(X)$. Now with the introduction of angelic choice, the relational model is in turn not expressive enough and must be extended.

Again, a more detailed model is needed. One possibility is the 'binary mul-tirelation' model [33] of Rewitzky. Instead the *premier* model of sequential se-mantics, Dijkstra's predicate-transformer model, is chosen.

The *predicate-transformer* model (Dijkstra [7]) views each command as trans-forming postconditions (predicates on final states) to preconditions (predicates on initial states). For command P, the operational interpretation of its trans-former semantics $[\![P]\!]_\mathcal{T}$ is: for any postcondition q and any initial state x

$[\![P]\!]_\mathcal{T}.q.x$ holds iff P terminates from x in a state satisfying q.

Of course that is sufficient to motivate a formal definition of the semantics. But our interest here lies in reusing the relational semantics to infer the transformer semantics, as far as that is possible.

Let $(pred.X, \leq)$ denote the space of all predicates (*i.e.* conditions) on X par-tially ordered by implication. The *predicate-transformer* model, $\mathcal{T}(X)$, of com-mands consists of those predicate transformers $t : pred.X \rightarrow pred.X$ that are *monotone*

$$q \leq q' \;\Rightarrow\; t.q \leq t.q',$$

ordered under the lifting of the ordering on predicates

$$t \leq t' \;:=\; \forall\, q : pred.X \cdot t.q \leq t'.q.$$

Then $\mathcal{T}(X)$ is a domain and complete lattice with least and greatest elements the constant functions *false* and *true* respectively. Its compact elements are the transformers t for which there is a finite subset $F \subseteq X$ such that

$$\forall\, q : pred.X \cdot t.q \;=\; \vee\{\, q.x \mid x \in F \,\}. \tag{22}$$

The space $\mathcal{T}(X)$ is endowed with an involution (see Back and von Wright [2])

$$t^*.q \;:=\; \neg t.\neg q$$

that preserves sequential composition but exchanges nondeterministic with an-gelic choice, enabledness with termination and **magic** with **abort**.

The embedding from relations $\mathcal{R}(X)$ to transformers $\mathcal{T}(X)$ is traditionally called the *weakest precondition*

$$wp : \mathcal{R}(X) \rightarrow \mathcal{T}(X)$$
$$wp.r.q.x \;:=\; \forall\, x' : X_\perp \cdot x\, r\, x' \;\Rightarrow\; (x' \neq \perp \wedge q.x').$$

It is Galois, but with orders reversed. Writing $(\mathcal{A}, \leq)^\sim$ for $(\mathcal{A}, \geq)$,

Theorem 3.   The function $wp : \mathcal{R}(X) \rightarrow \mathcal{T}(X)$

1. is an injection that preserves arbitrary suprema from $\mathcal{R}^\sim$ to $\mathcal{T}^\sim$: for any subset $R \subseteq \mathcal{R}$,

$$wp. \cup R \;=\; \wedge\{\, wp.r \mid r \in R \,\}; \tag{23}$$

2. has adjoint the *relational projection, rp* $: \mathcal{T}(X) \rightarrow \mathcal{R}(X)$ completing a Galois connection: $gc(wp, rp; \mathcal{R}^\sim, \mathcal{T}^\sim)$, where

$$x\,(rp.t)\,x' \;\; := \;\; x = \bot \;\vee\; \forall q : pred.X \cdot t.q.x \Rightarrow q.x' \qquad (24)$$

which of course preserves infima: for any subset T of the carrier of $\mathcal{T}(X)$,

$$rp.\vee T \;=\; \cap\{\, rp.t \mid t \in T \,\} \qquad (25)$$

but moreover preserves suprema:

$$rp.\wedge T \;=\; \cup\{\, rp.t \mid t \in T \,\}\,; \qquad (26)$$

3. satisfies merely

$$wp.(r \cap s) \;\geq\; (wp.r) \vee (wp.s) \qquad (27)$$

rather than equality (in contrast to the identities (23), (25) and (26));
4. has range *ran.wp* consisting of the conjunctive transformers,

$$t \in ran.wp \;\; \equiv \;\; \forall q, q' : pred.X \cdot t.(q \wedge q') = t.q \wedge t.q'\,, \qquad (28)$$

and that generates the carrier of $\mathcal{T}(X)$ under angelic choice:[5]

$$\mathcal{T}(X) \;=\; \{\, \vee F \mid F \subseteq ran.wp \,\}\,; \qquad (29)$$

5. ensures that the domain $\mathcal{T}(X)^\sim$ has least element the constant function $\lambda q : pred.X \cdot true$, greatest element the constant function $\lambda q : pred.X \cdot false$ and with compact elements the transformers analogous (because of the reversal of orders) to those described in (22);
6. preserves sequential composition: $wp.(\text{id}_X)_\bot = \text{id}_{pred.X}$ and $wp.(r \,\fatsemi\, s) = (wp.r) \circ (wp.s)$, as does its adjoint rp in the reverse direction.

As expected from adjunction, the projection $rp.t$ defined by (24) is the largest relation that approximates t under wp.

The semantic space $\mathcal{T}(X)$ appears deceptively simple although the manner of expressing a computation is radically different from that in relations. Naturally a Galois connection is used to bridge the gap!

The Galois connection can be used to lift much of the relational semantics to transformers following our standard approach. As usual for Galois connections, it maps the least element $(\{\,\})_\bot$ in $\mathcal{R}(X)^\sim$ to the least element, the constant transformer *true*, in $\mathcal{T}(X)^\sim$ thus providing the semantics of **magic**. For sequential composition,

---

[5] The space $\mathcal{T}(X)$ is also generated by the composition of wp with its involution [2]— $\forall t \cdot \exists u, v : ran.wp \cdot t = u^* \circ v$—but that fact appears less useful here because the transformer involution is not the lifting of an involution on relations [34].

$$\begin{aligned}
\llbracket \mathbf{abort} \rrbracket_T &:= \mathit{false} \\
\llbracket \mathbf{magic} \rrbracket_T &:= \mathit{true} \\
\llbracket x := e \rrbracket_T &:= \lambda\, q : pred.X \cdot q[e/x] \\
\llbracket P \ \mathbf{if}\ b\ \mathbf{else}\ Q \rrbracket_T &:= \llbracket P \rrbracket_T \ \mathbf{if}\ b\ \mathbf{else}\ \llbracket Q \rrbracket_T \\
\llbracket P \,\fatsemi\, Q \rrbracket_T &:= \llbracket P \rrbracket_T \circ \llbracket Q \rrbracket_T \\
\llbracket \mu.F \rrbracket_T &:= \vee\{\, t : T(X) \mid F.t \le t \,\} \\
\llbracket \sqcap \mathcal{F} \rrbracket_T &:= \wedge\{\, \llbracket P \rrbracket_T \mid P \in \mathcal{F} \,\} \\
\llbracket \sqcup \mathcal{F} \rrbracket_T &:= \vee\{\, \llbracket P \rrbracket_T \mid P \in \mathcal{F} \,\}
\end{aligned}$$

Fig. 9. Transformer semantics for commands, inferred from Figure 8 using the *wp* Galois connection

$$\llbracket P \,\fatsemi\, Q \rrbracket_T$$
$=$ definition of T semantics

$$wp.\llbracket P \,\fatsemi\, Q \rrbracket_R$$
$=$ definition of R semantics, Equation (15) and Figure 8

$$wp.(\llbracket P \rrbracket_R \,\fatsemi\, \llbracket Q \rrbracket_R)$$
$=$ property of *wp*, Theorem 3.6

$$(wp.\llbracket P \rrbracket_R) \circ (wp.\llbracket Q \rrbracket_R)$$
$=$ definition of T semantics again

$$\llbracket P \rrbracket_T \circ \llbracket Q \rrbracket_T\ .$$

It maps arbitrary unions in $R(X)$ to arbitrary conjunctions in $T(X)$, by (23), thus providing the semantics of arbitrary nondeterminism. But the lack of equality in (27) means that *wp* can not be used to lift angelic choice from $R(X)$ to $T(X)$. That must simply be defined to be disjunction. The resulting transformer semantics is given in Figure 9.

The proofs of Laws (17), (18) and (19) are now straightforward using elementary logic. For Law (20),

$$\llbracket P \,\fatsemi\, (Q \sqcup R) \rrbracket_T$$
$=$ T semantics of $\sqcup$ and $\fatsemi$ from Figure 9

$$\llbracket P \rrbracket_T \circ (\llbracket Q \rrbracket_T \vee \llbracket R \rrbracket_T)$$
$\ge$ monotonicity

$$(\llbracket P \rrbracket_T \circ \llbracket Q \rrbracket_T) \vee (\llbracket P \rrbracket_T \circ \llbracket R \rrbracket_T)$$
$=$ T semantics of $\fatsemi$ and $\sqcup$ again

$$\llbracket (P \,\fatsemi\, Q) \sqcup (P \,\fatsemi\, R) \rrbracket_T\ .$$

Moreover equality holds in the middle step if the transformer $\llbracket P \rrbracket_T$ is disjunctive; in other words, the command P is predeterministic.

3.5 Refinement Calculus

For theoretical purposes a computation is conveniently described as a single predicate; a form familiar to this audience is $(p \wedge ok) \Rightarrow (P \wedge ok')$. Similarly for the purposes of specification; a familiar form is the body of a Z specification [38]. But for development towards code, it is more convenient to reveal the *precondition*, or predicate from which termination is assured. That idea, first promoted by VDL [4], is incorporated into the 'refinement calculus' [28], the main focus of [17]'s Chapter 3.

A *specification statement*

$$x : [p, P]$$

consists of a *frame* x of variables (a list containing all those that may change), *precondition*, p, a predicate whose free variables denote the initial state of the computation and which represents the states from which termination is certain, and a *postcondition*, P, a binary predicate in initial and final states which specifies the computation when it terminates. Enabledness is captured by feasibility: those initial states from which termination in a final state is possible

$$p[x_0/x] \ \Rightarrow \ \exists\, x \cdot P(x_0, x)$$

(the substitution of x_0 for x in the precondition is a technicality required by the decision to use x as free variable in p).

The semantics of a specification statement is given (see, for example, [28]) as a predicate transformer

$$\varepsilon.(x : [p, P]).q \ := \ p \wedge (\forall\, x \cdot P \Rightarrow q)[x/x_0]\,,$$

and the ordering on specification statements is that inherited from $\mathcal{T}$. So, since ε is in fact surjective, specification statements are 'the same' as $\mathcal{T}$. Finally, having gained experience of unification and the benefits it affords, our path has returned to the context of [17]'s Chapter 3.

3.6   Chapter 3 Revisited

It may now be appreciated that, from the viewpoint of unification, [17]'s Chapter 3 contains two unifications, performed almost effortlessly because they occur within the same, predicative, model [13]. To proceed in reverse order, a model of 'feasible specification statements' is defined as the subspace of single predicates satsifying all four healthiness conditions **H1** $\wedge$ **H2** $\wedge$ **H3** $\wedge$ **H4**. A model of 'not-necessarily-feasible specification statements' is defined by just the first three: **H1** $\wedge$ **H2** $\wedge$ **H3**. And the general space of *designs*, of use whenever enabledness, ok, and termination, ok', are observable, is defined by just the first two **H1** $\wedge$ **H2**.

Following the approach of the present paper, the original model of specification statements as predicate transformers [28] is adopted, and Galois connections are defined to relate to those other models. Chapter 3 is highly elegant in making those connections actually injections. It does so by using a predicative semantics with implication for refinement, using single-predicates (compared with the p and P in the previous section) and moreover by establishing an isomorphism

between certain laws and healthiness conditions on the semantic space of predicates, which it then captured by closure operators. Little wonder, perhaps, that
the reader may be distracted from the task of unification.

Indeed most of that is subservient to the primary concern of unification. What
is the further benefit of ensuring that a model has that particular form? Of
primary importance is unification of new paradigms of computation and the
use of the unifying framework to simplify reasoning about realistic case studies.
Surely that kind of endeavour is of secondary importance and may even look
precious from outside the tight-knit UTP community.

That is why starting from Chapter 4 has been advocated, and only later
returning to Chapter 3 to see the special nature of the relational/predicative
injections.

4   Unifying Further

The field of program semantics is specialised and any single approach to it,
like UTP, even more so. Much of our hope for UTP must therefore lie in further
applications of unification and the techniques UTP provides, outside the confines
of program semantics. What for programming languages was *semantics* is now
thought of as *behaviour*.

The best examples are the complex systems currently preoccupying us: hybrid
systems like cyberphysical systems and those from biology and finance. Can the
hierarchical approach be used to describe them incrementally in such a way
that desirable properties 'accumulate'? That would make accessible 'closed form'
analysis, to complement simulation and model checking which appear to be the
sole techniques used at present.

The theories provided for incremental development, as summarised at the end
of Section 2.2, are founded on a *uniform* domain $\mathcal{X}$ of discourse. A typical example is provided by the refinement calculus, which makes explicit the types
of all variables appearing in the development. Thus when a development step
involves a data refinement, both abstract and concrete spaces are included in
$\mathcal{X}$. But data refinement is a special kind of increment which by definition pro-
hibits observation of information encapsulated in the concrete data type, which
is instead accessed only using the same operations as the abstract type.

In the setting of complex systems it may well be impractical to conceive the
domain $\mathcal{X}$ *ab initio*. Instead, the complexity of the system may be revealed incrementally by successive Galois connections, following the approach of unification.

Here is an example from hardware design.

4.1   Beyond Programming

The Boolean model of signal values provides a satisfactory account of hardware
devices at one level of abstraction. Unfortunately it is quite abstract so, for
realistic design, simulations (typically in HSPICE) based on lower-level models
are required. One of the difficulties is in unifying the detailed model with the
Boolean model. This seems like an ideal test for the UTP approach.

$$[\![pow]\!]_{\mathcal{B}} := out$$

$$[\![ntran]\!]_{\mathcal{B}} := g \Rightarrow (s = d)$$

$$[\![pow]\!]_{\mathcal{H}} := [\![pow]\!]_{\mathcal{B}} \wedge \delta out$$

$$= out \wedge \delta out$$

$$[\![ntran]\!]_{\mathcal{H}} := \left(\begin{matrix} [\![ntran]\!]_{\mathcal{B}} \\ g \wedge \delta g \wedge (\neg s \vee \neg d) \end{matrix} \Rightarrow (\delta s = \delta d) \right)$$

Fig. 10. Two devices, power and an n-type transistor, seen in two semantic models: the Boolean model $\mathcal{B}$ and the driven model $\mathcal{H}$

For example in the Boolean model, a wire connected to power by a p-type transistor is accurately modelled as being high if the gate of the transistor is low. But if the p-type transistor is replaced by an n-type transistor, the Boolean model predicts the same result, which is wrong: the wire is only weakly high, a result not able to be expressed in the model (but which is fatal because a chain of such transistors successively reduces the signal until it is not merely weakly high, but low).

A further observation—of 'drive'—needs to be incorporated in the model. This has been achieved elegantly by Hoare [16]. Each device is modelled first at the Boolean level (as is standard) but then at the driven level (this is new) and properties of the models ensure that the first is unified in the second. In fact both are embedded in predicates and the second extends the first, in the style of Chapter 3. Again, the situation is as in Figure 4, with the language being that of devices, $\mathcal{P}$ the Boolean model and $\mathcal{Q}$ the driven model.

The *Boolean model* is given by the set of predicates whose free variables are wire names from some set say W and whose ordering is equivalence (since implication is too weak for the usual reason)

$$\mathcal{B}(W) := (pre.W, =)$$

For example the device *pow* which connects output *out* to power is modelled by the predicate $out = true$. An n-type transistor *ntran* with gate g, source s and drain d is modelled by the predicate which states that if the gate is high then source and drain equilibrate. See Figure 10.

In the 'driven model' an extra Boolean observable δw is included for each wire w in the Boolean model, representing whether or not that wire is driven to its value. For example the output of power is always driven and so its description in the driven model is its Boolean description conjoined with $\delta out = true$. The driven description of the n-type transistor consists of its Boolean description conjoined with a predicate relating drive of wires to their values: if the gate is driven high and either source or drain is low then when they equilibrate, as is guaranteed from the Boolean description, they are equi-driven. See Figure 10.

Thus the *driven model* extends the Boolean model by also containing a predicate whose free variables are both the wires and their δ version. Its order conjoins the Boolean order with the assurance that the driven predicate Δ' of the finer device is stronger than that, Δ, of the coarser:

$$\mathcal{H}(W) := (pre.\,W \times pre.(W \cup \delta W), \preceq)$$

where

$$(B, \Delta) \preceq (B', \Delta') := \begin{pmatrix} B = B' \\ \Delta' \Rightarrow \Delta \end{pmatrix}.$$

Those examples suffice to confirm the example of weak signals mentioned above. But our concern here is with the unification. The Boolean model $\mathcal{B}$ is embedded in the driven model $\mathcal{H}$ by *injection*; and the ordering of $\mathcal{H}$ is stronger than that of $\mathcal{B}$. Thus the embedding is universally $\wedge$-junctive and the models are related by a Galois embedding.

Suppose it is required to model greater device detail. For example capacitance may be modelled as persistence of drive—say after a cycle's delay. That is captured by a third model, the capacitive model, in which the driven model is embedded. If, again, it is necessary to reason about time in more detail, a fourth model could be defined in which one cycle is replaced by a clock, so that a signal value and its single-cycle delay are replaced by a signal with values at discrete times. And so on. The state information required in more detailed models may be much more detailed than that of the abstract models (just Booleans, in this case), but nonetheless the relationship is mediated by Galois connections.

The case being made is that the techniques developed in UTP stretch far beyond theories of programming. They may be advantageously used to model, and reason about, complex systems.

4.2 The Philosopher's Stone?

When will the UTP approach, of unification, not be helpful? When the incremental approach fails: when each feature is coupled so tightly with the others that the full behaviour cannot be 'teased out' into strands enabling it to be understood by approximation.

Consider a physical example. The n-body problem [6] requires the determination of the motion of n bodies, given their momenta at one instant and assuming Newtonian interactions. Specification of the problem is easy, by differential equation; the challenge lies in finding the solution. The problem is difficult because it must take into account all possible interactions between the bodies. There seems to be no scope for unification unless approximation is allowed. In Physics, approximation is a natural step to take because small changes in the momenta of the bodies lead to small changes in the solution. So one can imagine progressively more accurate solutions. In the case of discrete systems that kind of approximation is of little use (how do you approximate a bit?), and any method must instead approximate complexity *exactly* at each level of abstraction, through a series of abstractions. In that sense unification is our version of approximation in Physics. In the n-body it seems unachievable.

In the terms of Computer Science, the n-body problem is a distributed system in which each process interacts with each other. That, then, is going to be difficult to analyse incrementally unless there is some very special structure to the interactions. But if a process interacts with only a small number of others (for example its nearest neighbours, if they are distributed spatially) then unification might be expected.

5   Conclusion

Systems are inherently complicated. Since detail cannot ultimately be avoided, theories must be as simple as possible. In the areas of traditional engineering, where relationships between observables are assumed to be differentiable, approximation by simpler behaviours which approximate closely that of the real system, provides a successful method. It has been argued that unification, describing complex behaviour exactly at varying levels of abstraction, is the equivalent for the discrete systems of Computer Science.

In studying a complex system the first stage, then, must be to study its abstractions (ignore real time, the hybrid nature of the system and so on). But then must come a stage in which detail is restored. Then unification is our only technique. We conclude that every effort must therefore be made to sustain the theory of unification, UTP.

Unification might be appreciated as one of two 'orthogonal' techniques. That of *modularisation* structures descriptions at a given level of abstraction. *Unification* structures complexity incrementally across levels of abstraction. The former is reasonably well understood, is still being productively pursued at the research level (information hiding), and is the foundation of almost all Software Engineering. The UTP community appears to be guardians of the latter.

A single case study of the incremental approach has been presented, moving from predeterministic (*i.e.* computable) computations through finitely nondeterministic programs to angelic and arbitrary nondeterministic commands. The journey could readily have been continued to include probabilistic computations and even quantum computations (to go in just one direction). At most of the increments the semantic intuition and laws have been able to be lifted by Galois connections. Where that has not been the case, valuable insight has been provided by the property that fails (for example failure of wp to map intersections to disjunctions).

Though founded on unification, UTP offers further delightful distractions along the way. Many of them are compressed in to Chapter 3, and so the case has been made that, in teaching, attention be gently deflected to Chapter 4, then its predecessor viewed in context. Perhaps 'relational semantics' is not as important as might be thought from Chapter 3. As has just been seen in Section 3, it is not at all *required* for unification.

It has been suggested that unification offers a way of analysing complex systems, not just theories of programming. Indeed it has been claimed that only by diversifying from program semantics will the techniques of UTP be properly and widely appreciated. It would be very persuasive were the method to be used on complex systems currently being analysed by simulation or model checking, like hybrid systems arising from cyberphysical, biological or financial study. But within the confines of program semantics, it would be interesting to unify the standard models with more recent models, like the game theoretic model.

Many important topics have been overlooked in this paper. Just two are: the use of Galois connections for *calculation* by use of 'trading'; and data refinement in the domain of discourse and seen in terms of a Galois connection.

What, then, lies in store for UTP? It has been argued that the approach it takes, and the techniques it provides for unifying theories, are scientifically indispensible. But it has also been acknowledged that important ideas wither. Is UTP becoming a road less travelled, destined for obsolescence? The former appears to be true; the latter may be up to us. It seems obvious that (unless it is rediscovered) the approach will die without serious action: more courses might be taught, promoting unification; more students be engaged in MSc. and PhD. degrees based on UTP; more unification be performed, mastering new paradigms, making non-specialists want to use the method—good opportunities are provided by hybrid, cyberphysical and biological systems; and an undue amount of effort not be spent on second-order concerns. Otherwise, UTP will be as familiar in 20 years' time as are Zeppelins, Theremins and the slide rule.

What we call the beginning is often the end
And to make an end is to make a beginning.
The end is where we start from.

. . .

We shall not cease from exploration
And the end of all our exploring
Will be to arrive where we started
And know the place for the first time.

Little Gidding [10]

References

1. Back, R.-J.R., von Wright, J.: Refinement calculus, Part I: Sequential nondeterministic programs. In: de Bakker, J.W., de Roever, W.-P., Rozenberg, G. (eds.) REX 1989. LNCS, vol. 430, pp. 42–66. Springer, Heidelberg (1989)

2. Back, R.-J.R., von Wright, J.: Duality in specification languages: a lattice-theoretical approach. Acta Informatica 27(7), 583–625 (1990)

3. Backus, J.W., et al. (eds.): Revised report on the algorithm language ALGOL 60; CACM, 6(1), 1–17 (1963) (Supplement by M. Woodger, 18–20)

4. Bjørner, D., Jones, C.B.: The Vienna Development Method: The Meta-Language. LNCS, vol. 61. Springer, Heidelberg (1978)

5. Cutland, N.J.: Computability: An Introduction to Recursive Function Theory. Cambridge University Press, Cambridge (1980)

6. Diacu, F.: The solution of the n-body problem. The Mathematical Intelligencer 18, 66–70 (1996)

7. Dijkstra, E.W.: Guarded commands, nondeterminacy and formal derivation of programs. Communications of the ACM 18, 453–457 (1975)
8. Duke, R., Rose, G.: Formal Object-Oriented Specification Using Object-Z. Macmillan Press, Basingstoke (2000)
9. Dunne, S., Stoddart, W. (eds.): UTP 2006. LNCS, vol. 4010, pp. 123–140. Springer, Heidelberg (2006)
10. Eliot, T.S.: Four Quartets. Harcourt, Inc., New York (1943)
11. Gardiner, P.H.B., Martin, C.E., de Moor, O.: An algebraic construction of predicate transformers. In: Bird, R.S., Woodcock, J.C.P., Morgan, C.C. (eds.) MPC 1992. LNCS, vol. 669, pp. 100–121. Springer, Heidelberg (1993)
12. Hayes, I.J. (ed.): Specification Case Studies. Prentice-Hall International, Englewood Cliffs (1987)
13. Hehner, E.C.R.: Predicative programming, parts I and II. Communications of the ACM 27(2), 134–151 (1984)
14. Hoare, C.A.R., Wirth, N.: An axiomatic definition of the programming language Pascal. Acta Informatica 2(4), 335–355 (1973)
15. Hoare, C.A.R., et al.: The laws of programming. Communications of the ACM 30(8), 672–686 (1987)
16. Hoare, C.A.R.: A theory for the derivation of combinational C-MOS circuit designs. Theoretical Computer Science 90(1), 235–251 (1991)
17. Hoare, C.A.R., He, J.: Unifying Theories of Programming. Prentice Hall, Englewood Cliffs (1998)
18. Houston, I., King, S.: CICS project report: Experiences and results from the use of Z in IBM. VDM Europe 1, 588–596 (1991)
19. Josephs, M.B.: Receptive process theory. Acta Informatica 29(1), 17–31 (1992)
20. Jerome Keisler, H.: Elementary Calculus: An Infinitesimal Approach, 2nd edn. Prindle, Weber and Schmidt (1986)
21. Knuth, D.E.: The remaining troublespots in ALGOL 60. Communications of the ACM 10(10), 611–617 (1967)
22. Lister, A.M.: Fundamentals of Operating Systems, 2nd edn. Macmillan, Basingstoke (1979)
23. Lucas, P., Walk, K.: On the formal description of PL/I. In: Halpern, M.I., Shaw, C.J. (eds.) Annual Review in Automatic Programming, vol. 6, pp. 105–182. Pergamon Press, Oxford (1971)
24. McIver, A.K., Morgan, C.C.: Abstraction, Refinement and Proof for Probabilistic Systems. Springer, Heidelberg (2005)
25. Milne, R., Strachey, C.: A Theory of Programming Language Semantics. Chapman and Hall, Boca Raton (1976)
26. Milner, R.: Communication and Concurrency. Prentice Hall, Englewood Cliffs (1989)
27. Mitchell, J.C.: Foundations for Programming Languages. MIT Press, Cambridge (1996)
28. Morgan, C.C.: Programming from Specifications, 1st edn. Prentice-Hall International, Englewood Cliffs (1990)
29. Morris, J.M.: A theoretical basis for stepwise refinement and the programming calculus. Science of Computer Programming 9(3), 287–306 (1987)
30. Nauer, P. (ed.): Report on the algorithmic language ALGOL 60. Communications of the ACM 6, 299–314 (1960)
31. Nelson, G.: A generalisation of Dijkstra's calculus. ACM Transactions on Programming Language and Systems 11(4), 517–561 (1989)

32. Nielsen, F., Nielsen, H.R., Hankin, C.: Principles of Program Analysis. Springer, Heidelberg (2005)
33. Rewitzky, I.M.: Binary Multirelations. In: de Swart, H., Orłowska, E., Schmidt, G., Roubens, M. (eds.) TARSKI 2003. LNCS, vol. 2929, pp. 256–271. Springer, Heidelberg (2003)
34. Rewitzky, I.M., Sanders, J.W.: Involutions on relational program calculi. Scientific Annals of Computer Science 18, 129–171 (2008)
35. de Roever, W.-P., Engelhardt, K.: Data Refinement: Model-Oriented Proof Methods and their Comparison. Cambridge Tracts in Theoretical Computer Science. Cambridge University Press, Cambridge (1998)
36. Roscoe, A.W., Hoare, C.A.R.: The laws of **occam** programming. Theoretical Computer Science 60(2), 177–229 (1988)
37. Roscoe, A.W.: The Theory and Practice of Concurrency. Prentice-Hall, Englewood Cliffs (1998)
38. Spivey, J.M.: The Z Notation: A Reference Manual, 2nd edn. Prentice-Hall International, Englewood Cliffs (1992)
39. van Wijngaarden, A., et al.: Revised report on the algorithmic language ALGOL 68. Acta Informatica 5, 1–236 (1975)
40. Wikipedia on the competition between VHS and Betamax, http://en.wikipedia.org/wiki/Videotape_format_war

A Probabilistic BPEL-Like Language

He Jifeng

Shanghai Key Laboratory of Trustworthy Computing
East China Normal University, China

Abstract. Exception and failure are the typical phenomena of the execution of long-running transactions. To capture the random features of internet-based computing, this paper investigates a BPEL-like language which is enriched with probabilistic choice operator. We extend the standard design model [12] with the new healthiness conditions to accommodate the coordination and compensation mechanisms of the language.

1   Introduction

The aim of the web services is to achieve the universal interoperability between different web-based applications. Coordination and compensation mechanisms are vital in handling exception and failure which occur during the execution of a long-running transaction.

In recent years, in order to describe the infrastructure for carrying out long-running transactions, various business modelling languages have been introduced, such as XLANG, WSFL, BPEL4WS (BPEL) and StAC [22,13,7,6]. This paper is an attempt at taking a step forward to gain some perspectives on the random features of long-running transactions. The language examined in this paper is an extension of the BPEL language with the following features:

1. It contains a probabilistic choice operator to describe the random feature of the web-services whose behaviours rely on the status of the environment. The probabilistic choice operator acts as a refinement of the nondeterministic choice operator. In discussion of distributive laws of sequential composition, we explore the substantial difference between these two choice operators.
2. The language is armed with the exception handling and compensation mechanism to improve the robustness of the programs.
3. The language provides a family of coordination operators in support of design of highly dependable programs.

The model we adopt for our language enriches the design calculus with the following ingredients:

1. Besides the logical variables ok and ok' used in the design calculus to specify the termination status of a program, the model we build for our BPEL-like language presents new logical variables to describe the rollback and failure status of transactions.

S. Qin (Ed.): UTP 2010, LNCS 6445, pp. 74–100, 2010.

2. Corresponding to the additional left zeroes of the sequential composition, we put forward new healthiness conditions for our programs.
3. We adopt the notion of final distribution to replace the final state used in the design calculus to characterise the random feature of the outcome of a web-service.
4. To capture algebraic properties of the probabilistic and nondeterministic choices we impose convex-closed property on final distributions of our programs.

In summary, our novel contributions include

– A BPEL-like language equipped with the exception handling and compensation mechanisms
– A family of coordination operators for improvement of design of highly dependable programs
– A probabilistic model to handle exception and program failure.

2   Probabilistic Program Syntax

The language examined in this paper extends the Guarded Command Language [8] by including the probabilistic choice operator, compensation operator and coordination operator. The abstract syntax of the programming language is given below.

$$
\begin{array}{lll}
P ::= & \bot & \text{abort} \\
& \texttt{fail} & \text{failure} \\
& \texttt{throw} & \text{exception} \\
& \texttt{skip} & \text{empty command} \\
& x := e & \text{assignment} \\
& P \lhd b \rhd P & \text{conditional} \\
& P \, [\![r]\!] \, P & \text{probabilistic choice} \\
& P \sqcap P & \text{Nondeterministic choice} \\
& P \, \texttt{caughtby} \, P & \text{exception handling} \\
& P \, \texttt{cpens} \, P & \text{compensation} \\
& P \, \texttt{else} \, P & \text{coordination operator} \\
& P \, \texttt{seq} \, P & \text{sequential composition} \\
& (\mu X \bullet P(X)) & \text{recursion}
\end{array}
$$

where

– `fail` halts with indication of the failure of the execution.
– Let $0 \le r \le 1$. $P[\![r]\!]Q$ makes a choice between programs P and Q with probabilities r and $1 - r$ respectively.
– $P \, \texttt{caughtby} \, Q$ runs program P first. If its execution throws an exception case, then Q will be invoked to handle that exception.
– $P \, \texttt{cpens} \, Q$ runs P as its primary task. Q is invoked only when the execution of P fails.
– $P \, \texttt{else} \, Q$ behaves like P if its execution succeeds. Otherwise it will fire Q on the same initial state as P.

In the following sections, we will abbreviate the entire list of program variables $(x, y, .., z)$ by the simple vector variable v.

3 A Probabilistic Model

In this section we work towards a precise characterisation of the class of *designs* [12] that can handle new programming features such as program failure, coordination and compensation.

3.1 State

To equip a language with exception handling mechanism, it is necessary to record the cases when a program throws an exception. We add a new logical variable $eflag$ (standing for error-flag) to the standard design model for the description of the current status of a program:

- $eflag' = false$ indicates it terminates successfully.
- $eflag' = true$ indicates it is forced to halt due to an exception case during its execution.

To deal with the compensation mechanism we are required to figure out the cases when a program decides to rollback its execution. By adopting the technique used in handling the exception cases we introduce another logical variable $forward$ to describe the status of the execution of a program:

- $forward' = true$ indicates successful termination of the execution of the forward activity of a program. In this case, its sequential successor will go ahead with the initial state set up by the program.
- $forward' = false$ indicates it decides to undo the effect caused by the execution. In this case, the corresponding compensation module will be invoked.

As a result, the enriched state space S used in later discussion has the type

$$(Var \rightarrow Val) \times (\{eflag\} \rightarrow Bool) \times (\{forward\} \rightarrow Bool)$$

3.2 Final Distribution

We extend our standard states to probabilistic states by replacing the final state with a final *distribution* over S.

Definition (Probabilistic distribution)

A final distribution is a total function from S into the closed interval of reals $[0, 1]$. We define

$$\textbf{PROB} \quad =_{df} \quad S \rightarrow [0, 1]$$

where each member of **PROB** is a discrete function on the countable set S.

We insist further that for any member prob of **PROB** the probabilities must NOT exceed 1:

$$\Sigma_{s \in S} \, \mathtt{prob}(s) \; \leq \; 1 \, .$$

For any subset X of S we define

$$\mathtt{prob}(X) \quad =_{df} \quad \Sigma_{s \in X} \, \mathtt{prob}(s) \, .$$

We use the notation **0** to denote the zero distribution, and define

$$\mathtt{prob}_1 \leq \mathtt{prob}_2 \quad =_{df} \quad \forall s \in S \bullet (\mathtt{prob}_1(s) \leq \mathtt{prob}_2(s))$$

For any $\mathtt{prob} \in$ **PROB** we have

$$\mathbf{0} \leq \mathtt{prob}$$

For any $s \in S$ we introduce its corresponding point-distribution η_s:

$$\eta_s(t) \;=_{df}\; \begin{cases} 1 & \text{if } t = s \\ 0 & \text{otherwise} \end{cases}$$

This paper identifies a probabilistic program as a predicate which relates initial states to final distributions, and inherits the refinement relation defined in [12]: probabilistic programs as follows:

$$P \sqsupseteq Q \;=_{df}\; \forall s \in S, \, \mathtt{prob}' \in \mathbf{PROB} \bullet (P(s, \mathtt{prob}') \Rightarrow Q(s, \mathtt{prob}'))$$

3.3 Healthiness Condition

A subclass of predicates may be defined in a variety of ways. Sometimes it is done by a syntactic property. Sometimes the definition requires satisfaction of a particular collection of algebraic laws. In general, the most useful definitions are these that are given in many different forms, together with a proof that all of them are equivalent. This section will put forward additional healthiness conditions to capture such a subclass of designs.

The introduction of error states has implication for sequential composition: all the exception cases of program P are of course also the exception cases of $P; Q$. Rather than change the definition of sequential composition given in [12], we enforce this rule by means a healthiness condition: if the program Q is asked to start in an exception case of its predecessor, it leaves the state unchanged

$$(\mathbf{Req}_1) \; Q \;=\; II \lhd eflag \rhd Q$$

when the command II adopts the following definition

$$II \;=_{df}\; \mathtt{prob}' = \eta_s$$

where s denotes all the variables in the alphabet of Q.

A predicate is $\mathbf{Req}_1$-healthy if it satisfies the healthiness condition $\mathbf{Req}_1$. Define

$$\mathcal{H}_1(Q) \;=_{df}\; (II \lhd eflag \rhd Q)$$

Clearly $\mathcal{H}_1$ is idempotent,

$$\mathcal{H}_1^2 = \mathcal{H}_1$$

As a result, Q is **Req$_1$** healthy if and only if Q lies in the range of $\mathcal{H}_1$.

When a program starts to rollback the execution, its sequential successor becomes void in the sense that it must keep silent when invoked in the state where $forward = false$:

(**Req$_2$**) $Q = II \triangleleft \neg forward \triangleright Q$

This condition can be identified by the idempotent mapping

$$\mathcal{H}_2(Q) =_{df} II \triangleleft \neg forward \triangleright Q$$

in the sense that a program meets **Req$_2$** iff it is a fixed point of $\mathcal{H}_2$

Probabilistic choice is introduced to make a choice between its two components with certain probabilities. Because this choice is made internally, it is impossible to distinguish Q from $Q \llbracket r \rrbracket Q$ by comparing their external behaviours. Therefore, we require all programs Q must meet the following convex-closure property:

(**Req$_3$**) $Q = Q \llbracket\,\rrbracket Q$

where

$$P \llbracket\,\rrbracket Q =_{df} \exists prob_1, prob_2 : \mathbf{PROB}, \exists r : [0, 1] \bullet$$

$$P[prob_1/prob'] \wedge Q[prob_2/prob'] \wedge$$

$$prob' = r \times prob_1 + (1 - r) \times prob_2$$

(**Req$_3$**) is identified by the following idempotent mapping

$$\mathcal{H}_3(Q) =_{df} Q \llbracket\,\rrbracket Q$$

Our probabilistic model adopts the same refinement ordering as the standard state model. Taking the ordering among final distributions into account, we require that every probabilistic program must satisfy following healthiness condition:

(**Req$_4$**) $Q = Q ; (prob \leq prob')$

where ; stands for the relational composition.

This healthiness condition is characterised by the idempotent mapping

$$\mathcal{H}_4(Q) =_{df} Q ; (prob \leq prob')$$

Lemma 3.1 (Commutativity)
$\mathcal{H}_i \circ \mathcal{H}_j = \mathcal{H}_j \circ \mathcal{H}_i$ for all i and j.

Proof

$(\mathcal{H}_1 \circ \mathcal{H}_3)(P)$	{Def of $\mathcal{H}_3$}
$= \mathcal{H}_1(P \llbracket\,\rrbracket P)$	{Def of $\mathcal{H}_1$}
$= II \triangleleft eflag \triangleright (P \llbracket\,\rrbracket P)$	{$II \llbracket\,\rrbracket II = II$}
$= \mathcal{H}_1(P) \llbracket\,\rrbracket \mathcal{H}_1(P)$	{Def of $\mathcal{H}_3$}
$= (\mathcal{H}_3 \circ \mathcal{H}_1)(P)$	

$(\mathcal{H}_1 \circ \mathcal{H}_4)(P)$ {Def of $\mathcal{H}_4$}

$= \mathcal{H}_1(P \,;\, (\mathbf{prob} \leq \mathbf{prob}'))$ {Def of $\mathcal{H}_1$}

$= II \lhd eflag \rhd (P \,;\, (\mathbf{prob} \leq \mathbf{prob}'))$ {$II \,;\, (\mathbf{prob} \leq \mathbf{prob}') = II$}

$= \mathcal{H}_1(P) \,;\, (\mathbf{prob} \leq \mathbf{prob}')$ {Def of $\mathcal{H}_4$}

$= (\mathcal{H}_4 \circ \mathcal{H}_1)(P)$

$(\mathcal{H}_4 \circ \mathcal{H}_3)(P)$

{Def of $\mathcal{H}_3$ and $\mathcal{H}_4$}

$= (P \,\lbrack\!\lbrack\, P) \,;\, (\mathbf{prob} \leq \mathbf{prob}')$

{Def of $\lbrack\!\lbrack$}

$= \exists r : [0,\,1], \mathbf{prob}_1, \mathbf{prob}_2 : \mathbf{PROB} \bullet$

$P[\mathbf{prob}_1/\mathbf{prob}'] \wedge P[\mathbf{prob}_2/\mathbf{prob}'] \wedge$

$\mathbf{prob}' \geq (r \times \mathbf{prob}_1 + (1-r) \times \mathbf{prob}_2)$

{Let $X =_{df} 1 - \Sigma_t \mathbf{prob}_1(t)$, and $Y =_{df} 1 - \Sigma_t \mathbf{prob}_2(t)$}

{and $\Delta(s) =_{df} \mathbf{prob}'(s) - (r \times \mathbf{prob}_1(s) + (1-r) \times \mathbf{prob}_2(s))$}

$\Rightarrow \exists r : [0,\,1], \mathbf{prob}_1, \mathbf{prob}_2, \mathbf{prob}_3, \mathbf{prob}_4 : \mathbf{PROB} \bullet$

$P[\mathbf{prob}_1/\mathbf{prob}'] \wedge P[\mathbf{prob}_2/\mathbf{prob}'] \wedge$

$\mathbf{prob}_3 = \mathbf{prob}_1 + \lambda t \bullet (X \times \Delta(t))/(r \times X + (1-r) \times Y) \wedge$

$\mathbf{prob}_4 = \mathbf{prob}_2 + \lambda t \bullet (Y \times \Delta(t))/(r \times X + (1-r) \times Y) \wedge$

$\mathbf{prob}' = (r \times \mathbf{prob}_3 + (1-r) \times \mathbf{prob}_4)$

{Def of $\mathcal{H}_3$ and $\mathcal{H}_4$}

$\Rightarrow (\mathcal{H}_3 \circ \mathcal{H}_4)(P)$

{Def of $\mathcal{H}_3$ and $\mathcal{H}_4$}

$= \exists r : [0,\,1], \mathbf{prob}_1, \mathbf{prob}_2, \mathbf{prob}_3, \mathbf{prob}_4 : \mathbf{PROB} \bullet$

$P[\mathbf{prob}_1/\mathbf{prob}'] \wedge P[\mathbf{prob}_2/\mathbf{prob}'] \wedge$

$\mathbf{prob}_3 \geq \mathbf{prob}_1 \wedge \mathbf{prob}_4 \geq \mathbf{prob}_2 \wedge$

$\mathbf{prob}' = (r \times \mathbf{prob}_3 + (1-r) \times \mathbf{prob}_4)$

{Calculation}

$\Rightarrow \exists r : [0,\,1], \mathbf{prob}_1, \mathbf{prob}_2, : \mathbf{PROB} \bullet$

$P[\mathbf{prob}_1/\mathbf{prob}'] \wedge P[\mathbf{prob}_2/\mathbf{prob}'] \wedge$

$\mathbf{prob}' \geq (r \times \mathbf{prob}_1 + (1-r) \times \mathbf{prob}_2)$

{Def of $\mathcal{H}_3$ and $\mathcal{H}_4$}

$= (\mathcal{H}_4 \circ \mathcal{H}_3)(P)$

Theorem 3.2
Healthy predicates form a complete lattice with respect the refinement ordering $\sqsubseteq$. **Proof** Define

$$\mathcal{H} =_{df} \mathcal{H}_1 \cdot \mathcal{H}_2 \cdot \mathcal{H}_3 \cdot \mathcal{H}_4$$

Clearly $\mathcal{H}$ is a monotonic mapping. From Lemma 3.1 we conclude it is also idempotent. It follows that a predicate P meets the healthiness conditions $\mathbf{Req}_1$–$\mathbf{Req}_4$ if and only if it is a fixed point of $\mathcal{H}$. The conclusion follows from Tarski's fixed point theorem [21].

In the following sections, we will confine ourselves to healthy predicates only.

4   Probabilistic Semantics

This section provides a probabilistic semantics to our language. Each program will be defined as a healthy predicate.

4.1   Primitive Commands

The behaviour of the chaotic program $\perp$ is totally unpredictable

$$\perp =_{df} \mathcal{H}(\mathbf{true})$$

The execution of `skip` leaves program variables intact.

$$\texttt{skip} =_{df} II$$

The execution of `fail` rollbacks the execution.

$$\texttt{fail} =_{df} \mathcal{H}_1(\mathbf{prob}' = \eta_{s[false/forward]})$$

An exception case arises from the execution of `throw`

$$\texttt{throw} =_{df} \mathcal{H}_2(\mathbf{prob}' = \eta_{s[true/eflag]})$$

4.2   Probabilistic Choice

Let P and Q be programs, and r a real satisfying $0 \le r \le 1$. Probabilistic choice $P[r]Q$ selects P and Q with probabilities r and $1 - r$ respectively.

$$P[r]Q =_{df} \exists \mathbf{prob}_1, \mathbf{prob}_2 : \mathbf{PROB} \bullet P[\mathbf{prob}_1/\mathbf{prob}'] \wedge Q[\mathbf{prob}_2/\mathbf{prob}'] \wedge$$

$$\mathbf{prob}' = r \times \mathbf{prob}_1 + (1 - r) \times \mathbf{prob}_2$$

Healthy predicates are closed under probabilistic choice operator:

Lemma 4.2

$$\mathcal{H}(P)[r]\mathcal{H}(Q) = \mathcal{H}(P[r]Q)$$

Proof

$\mathcal{H}_3(P[\![r]\!]Q)$

{Def of $\mathcal{H}_3$}

$=\ \exists \text{prob}_1,\ \text{prob}_2\ \text{prob}_3,\ \text{prob}_4 : \mathbf{PROB},\ \exists p : [0,1]\bullet$

$P[\text{prob}_1/\text{prob}'] \wedge Q[\text{prob}_2/\text{prob}'] \wedge P[\text{prob}_3/\text{prob}'] \wedge Q[\text{prob}_4/\text{prob}'] \wedge$

$\text{prob}' = p \times (r \times \text{prob}_1 + (1-r)\text{prob}_2) +$

$\qquad\qquad (1-p) \times (r \times \text{prob}_3 + (1-r) \times \text{prob}_4)$

{$\mathcal{H}_3(P) = P$ and $\mathcal{H}_3(Q) = Q$}

$\Rightarrow\ \exists \text{prob}_1,\ \text{prob}_2,\ \text{prob}_3,\ \text{prob}_4,\ \text{prob}_P,\ \text{prob}_Q : \mathbf{PROB},\ \exists p : [0,1]\bullet$

$\text{prob}_P\ =\ p \times \text{prob}_1 + (1-p) \times \text{prob}_3 \wedge$

$\text{prob}_Q\ =\ p \times \text{prob}_2 + (1-p) \times \text{prob}_4 \wedge$

$P[\text{prob}_P/\text{prob}'] \wedge Q[\text{prob}_Q/\text{prob}'] \wedge \text{prob}' = r \times \text{prob}_P + (1-r) \times \text{prob}_Q$

{Def of $[\![]\!]$}

$=\ P[\![r]\!]Q$

{$X \sqsupseteq \mathcal{H}_3(X)$}

$\Rightarrow\ \mathcal{H}_3(P[\![r]\!]Q)$

$\mathcal{H}_4(P[\![r]\!]Q)$

{Def of $\mathcal{H}_4$}

$=\ \exists \text{prob}_1,\ \text{prob}_2 : \mathbf{PROB} \bullet P[\text{prob}_1/\text{prob}'] \wedge Q[\text{prob}_2/\text{prob}'] \wedge$

$\text{prob}' \geq (r \times \text{prob}_1 + (1-r) \times \text{prob}_2)$

{Let $X =_{df} (1 - \Sigma_t \text{prob}_1(t))$ and $Y =_{df} (1 - \Sigma_t \text{prob}_2(t))$}

{and $\Delta(s) =_{df} \text{prob}'(s) - (r \times \text{prob}_1(s) + (1-r) \times \text{prob}_2(s))$}

$\Rightarrow\ \exists \text{prob}_1,\ \text{prob}_2,\ \text{prob}_3,\ \text{prob}_4 : \mathbf{PROB}\bullet$

$P[\text{prob}_1/\text{prob}'] \wedge Q[\text{prob}_2/\text{prob}'] \wedge$

$\text{prob}_3\ =\ \text{prob}_1 + \lambda s \bullet (X \times \Delta(s))/(r \times X + (1-r) \times Y) \wedge$

$\text{prob}_4\ =\ \text{prob}_2 + \lambda s \bullet (Y \times \Delta(s))/(r \times X + (1-r) \times Y) \wedge$

$\text{prob}'\ =\ (r \times \text{prob}_1 + (1-r) \times \text{prob}_2)$

{$\mathcal{H}_4(P) = P,\ \mathcal{H}_4(Q) = Q$}

$\Rightarrow\ P[\![r]\!]Q$

{$X \Rightarrow \mathcal{H}_4(X)$}

$\Rightarrow\ \mathcal{H}_4(P[\![r]\!]Q)$

Probabilistic choice is symmetric, associative and idempotent.

Theorem 4.1

(1) $P\,[r]\,Q \;=\; Q\,[1-r]\,P$

(2) $P\,[1]\,Q \;=\; P$

(3) $P\,[r]\,P \;=\; P$

(4) $(P\,[p]\,Q)\,[q]\,R \;=\; P\,[(p\times q)]\,(Q\,[r]\,R)$

where $r =_{df} (q - p\times q)/(1 - \ominus p\times q)$,

and $1\ominus p =_{df} (1-p) \lhd 0\leq p < 1 \rhd 1$

Proof (1) and (2) follow from the definition of probabilistic choice. (3) comes from the healthiness condition **Req$_3$**. We are going to prove the conclusion (4):

$(P[p]Q)[q]R$

{Def of $[p]$}

$= \exists \mathbf{prob}_P, \mathbf{prob}_Q, \mathbf{prob}_R : \mathbf{PROB}\bullet$

$\quad P[\mathbf{prob}_P/\mathbf{prob}'] \wedge Q[\mathbf{prob}_Q/\mathbf{prob}'] \wedge R[\mathbf{prob}_R/\mathbf{prob}']\wedge$

$\quad \mathbf{prob}' = q\times(p\times\mathbf{prob}_P + (1-p)\times\mathbf{prob}_Q) + (1-q)\times\mathbf{prob}_R$

$\quad$ {Def of r}

$= \exists \mathbf{prob}_P, \mathbf{prob}_Q, \mathbf{prob}_R : \mathbf{PROB}\bullet$

$\quad P[\mathbf{prob}_P/\mathbf{prob}'] \wedge Q[\mathbf{prob}_Q/\mathbf{prob}'] \wedge R[\mathbf{prob}_R/\mathbf{prob}']\wedge$

$\quad \mathbf{prob}' = (p\times q)\times\mathbf{prob}_P + (1-p\times q)\times(r\times\mathbf{prob}_Q + (1-r)\times\mathbf{prob}_R)$

$\quad$ {Def of $[r]$}

$= P\,[p\times q]\,(Q[r]R)$

4.3   Nondeterministic Choice

Let P and Q be programs. $P \sqcap Q$ selects P and Q with arbitrary probability

$$P \sqcap Q \;=_{df}\; (P\,[\!]\,Q)$$

Healthy functions are closed under nondeterministic choice operator:

Lemma 4.3

$\mathcal{H}(P) \sqcap \mathcal{H}(Q) \;=\; \mathcal{H}(P \sqcap Q)$

Proof. From Lemma 3.1.

Nondeterministic choice is symmetric, associative and idempotent.

Theorem 4.2

(1) $P \sqcap Q \;=\; Q \sqcap P$

(2) $P \sqcap (Q \sqcap R) \;=\; (P \sqcap Q) \sqcap R$

(3) $P \sqcap P \;=\; P$

Proof. From Theorem 4.1, and the fact that

$$P \,[\!]\, Q \;=\; \exists r : [0,\,1] \bullet (P[\![r]\!]Q)$$

4.4   Conditional

Let P and Q be programs, and let b be a Boolean expression. $P \lhd b \rhd Q$ selects P and Q according to the value of b at the initial state. If the evaluation of b fails, then the conditional choice will throw an exception case.

$$P \lhd b \rhd Q \;=_{df}\; \mathcal{D}(b) \wedge (b \wedge P \vee \neg b \wedge Q) \vee \neg \mathcal{D}(b) \wedge \texttt{throw}$$

where $\mathcal{D}b$ is true in just those circumstances in which the evaluation of e will yield a value properly [?]. For example

$$\mathcal{D}17 =_{df} true$$

$$\mathcal{D}(e + f) =_{df} \mathcal{D}e \wedge \mathcal{D}f$$

$$\mathcal{D}(e/f) =_{df} \mathcal{D}e \wedge \mathcal{D}f \wedge (f \neq 0)$$

$$\mathcal{D}(e \lhd b \rhd f) =_{df} (b \Rightarrow \mathcal{D}e) \wedge (\neg b \Rightarrow \mathcal{D}f)$$
$$\text{provided that } \mathcal{D}b \equiv true$$

An expression e is well-defined if $\mathcal{D}e \equiv true$. For example

$$e \lhd \mathcal{D}e \rhd x$$

is well-defined.

Healthy predicates are closed under conditional choice operator.

Lemma 4.4

$$\mathcal{H}(P) \lhd b \rhd \mathcal{H}(Q) \;=\; \mathcal{H}(P \lhd b \rhd Q)$$

Proof

$\qquad \mathcal{H}_4(P \lhd b \rhd Q)$

$\qquad \{\text{Def of } \mathcal{H}_4\}$

$= \quad (P \lhd b \rhd Q); (\texttt{prob} \lhd \texttt{prob}')$

$\qquad \{; \text{ distributes over } \vee \text{ and } \mathcal{H}_4(\texttt{throw}) = \texttt{throw}\}$

$= \quad (P; (\texttt{prob} \leq \texttt{prob}')) \lhd b \rhd (Q; (\texttt{prob} \leq \texttt{prob}'))$

$\qquad \{\text{Def of } \mathcal{H}_4\}$

$= \quad \mathcal{H}_4(P) \lhd b \rhd \mathcal{H}_4(Q)$

Conditional choice enjoys the same properties as its counterpart in the Guarded Command Language. Furthermore, it distributes through probabilistic choice.

Theorem 4.3

(1) $(P[\![r]\!]Q) \triangleleft b \triangleright R \;=\; (P \triangleleft b \triangleright R)[\![r]\!](Q \triangleleft b \triangleright R)$

(2) $P[\![r]\!](Q \triangleleft b \triangleright R) \;=\; (P[\![r]\!]Q) \triangleleft b \triangleright (P[\![r]\!]R)$ if b is well-defined.

Proof

$(2)\, P[\![r]\!](Q \triangleleft b \triangleright R)$ {Def of $[\![]\!]$}

$= \exists \mathbf{prob}_1, \mathbf{prob}_2 : \mathbf{PROB} \bullet$
   $P[\mathbf{prob}_1/\mathbf{prob'}] \wedge (Q \triangleleft b \triangleright R)[\mathbf{prob}_2/\mathbf{prob'}] \wedge$
   $\mathbf{prob'} = (r \times \mathbf{prob}_1 + (1 - r) \times \mathbf{prob}_2)$ {Def of $\triangleleft b \triangleright$}

$= \exists \mathbf{prob}_1, \mathbf{prob}_2 : \mathbf{PROB} \bullet P[\mathbf{prob}_1/\mathbf{prob'}] \wedge$
   $(b \wedge Q[\mathbf{prob}_2/\mathbf{prob'}] \vee \neg b \wedge R[\mathbf{prob}_2/\mathbf{prob'}]) \wedge$
   $\mathbf{prob'} = (r \times \mathbf{prob}_1 + (1 - r) \times \mathbf{prob}_2)$ {Predicate calculus}

$= b \wedge (P[\![r]\!]Q) \vee \neg b \wedge (P[\![r]\!]R)$ {b is well-defined}

$= (P[\![r]\!]Q) \triangleleft b \triangleright (P[\![r]\!]R)$

4.5   Assignment

The execution of $x := e$ assigns the value of e to variable x if e can be successfully evaluated. Otherwise it behaves like `throw`

$$(x := e) \;=_{df}\; \mathcal{H}(\mathbf{prob'} = \eta_{s[e/x]}) \triangleleft \mathcal{D}e \triangleright \texttt{throw}$$

Lemma 4.5

$x := e$ is a healthy predicate.

Proof. From Lemma 4.4.

An assignment $x := e$ is **total** if the expression e is well-defined. In the following sections we will confine ourselves to total assignments because an assignment $x := e$ can always be converted to a conditional with total assignment as its component.

Theorem 4.4

$x := e \;=\; (x := (e \triangleleft \mathcal{D}e \triangleright x)) \triangleleft \mathcal{D}e \triangleright \texttt{throw}$

4.6   Sequential Composition

For sequential composition we follow the Kleisli-triple approach to semantics of programming languages [18], introducing a function ↑ to deal with sequential composition, which maps a binary relation $P(s, \text{prob}')$ to a 'lifted' relation ($\uparrow P$)($\text{prob}, \text{prob}'$)

Definition 4.1 (Kleisli lifting)

$$\uparrow P =_{df} \exists G : (S \rightarrow \textbf{PROB}), \forall s : S \bullet P(s, G(s))) \; \wedge$$

$$\text{prob}' = \Sigma_{t \in S}(\text{prob}(t) \times G(t))$$

From the facts that $\Sigma_{s \in S}\text{prob}(s) \leq 1$ and that for all $t \in S$ we have $G(t) \in$ **PROB** we conclude that

$$\Sigma_{s \in S}(\Sigma_{t \in S}(\text{prob}(t) \times G(t)(s))) \leq 1$$

Lemma 4.6

Let α and β be nonnegative reals satisfying $0 < (\alpha + \beta) \leq 1$. Then

$\uparrow P(\text{prob}_1, \text{prob}'_1) \wedge \uparrow P(\text{prob}_2, \text{prob}'_2) \Rightarrow$

$\uparrow P((\alpha \times \text{prob}_1 + \beta \times \text{prob}_1), \; (\alpha \times \text{prob}'_1 + \beta \times \text{prob}'_2))$

Proof. Define

$$r_1(t) =_{df} \begin{cases} (\alpha \times \text{prob}_1(t))/(\alpha \times \text{prob}_1(t) + \beta \times \text{prob}_2(t)) \\ \qquad\qquad (\alpha \times \text{prob}_1(t) + \beta \times \text{prob}_2(t)) > 0 \\ 0 \qquad\qquad \text{otherwise} \end{cases}$$

$$r_2(t) =_{df} \begin{cases} (\beta \times \text{prob}_2(t))/(\alpha \times \text{prob}_1(t) + \beta \times \text{prob}_2(t)) \\ \qquad\qquad (\alpha \times \text{prob}_1(t) + \beta \times \text{prob}_2(t)) > 0 \\ 0 \qquad\qquad \text{otherwise} \end{cases}$$

$\quad LHS$ \hfill {Def of $\uparrow$}

$\Rightarrow \; \exists G, H : (S \rightarrow \textbf{PROB}), \forall s : S \bullet (P(s, G(s)) \wedge P(s, H(s))) \wedge$

$\quad \text{prob}'_1 = \Sigma_t(\text{prob}_1 \times G(t)) \wedge \text{prob}'_2 = \Sigma_t(\text{prob}_2 \times H(t))$ \hfill {**Req₃**}

$\Rightarrow \; \exists G, H : (S \rightarrow \textbf{PROB}),$

$\quad \forall s : S \bullet P(s, r1(s) \times G(s) + r2(s) \times H(s)) \wedge$

$\quad \alpha \times \text{prob}'_1 + \beta \times \text{prob}'_2 =$

$\quad \Sigma_t(\alpha \times \text{prob}_1(t) + \beta \times \text{prob}_2(t)) \times (r_1(t) \times G(t) + r_2(t) \times H(t))$ {Def of $\uparrow$}

$\Rightarrow \; RHS$

Lemma 4.7

(1) $\uparrow (P\,;\,(\text{prob} \leq \text{prob}'))\,;\,(\text{prob} \leq \text{prob}') \; = \; \uparrow P\,;\,(\text{prob} \leq \text{prob}')$

(2) $\text{skip};\uparrow P \; = \; P$

(3) $\uparrow (P \,;\, \uparrow Q) \;=\; (\uparrow P) \,;\, (\uparrow Q)$

(4) $(\text{prob} \le \text{prob}') \,;\, \uparrow P \,;\, (\text{prob} \le \text{prob}') \;=\; \uparrow P \,;\, (\text{prob} \le \text{prob}')$

Proof

(1) LHS

   {Def of $\uparrow$}

$= \exists G : S \to \textbf{PROB}, \forall s : S \bullet (P \,;\, (\text{prob} \le \text{prob}'))(s,\, G(s)) \wedge$

   $\text{prob}' \ge \Sigma_t(\text{prob}(t) \times G(t))$

   {Def of relational composition}

$\Rightarrow \exists H, G : S \to \textbf{PROB}, \forall s : S \bullet (P(s,\, H(s)) \wedge H(s) \le G(s)) \wedge$

   $\text{prob}' \ge \Sigma_t(\text{prob}(l) \times G(t))$

   {calculation}

$\Rightarrow \exists H : S \to \textbf{PROB}, \forall s : S \bullet P(s,\, H(s)) \wedge$

   $\text{prob}' \ge \Sigma_t(\text{prob}(t) \times H(t))$

   {Def of $\uparrow$}

$= RHS$

   {$\uparrow$ is monotonic}

$\Rightarrow LHS$

(2) $\text{skip} \,;\, \uparrow P$ {Def of skip}

$= \uparrow P[\eta_s/\text{prob}]$ {Def of $\uparrow$}

$= \exists G : (S \to \textbf{PROB}), \forall t : S \bullet P(t,\, G(t)) \wedge$

   $\text{prob}' = \Sigma_{t \in S}(\eta_s(t) \times G(t))$ {Def of η_s}

$= \exists G : (S \to \textbf{PROB}) \bullet P(s,\, G(s)) \wedge \text{prob}' = G(s)$ {predicate calculus}

$= P$

(3) LHS

   {Def of $\uparrow$}

$= \exists G : (S \to \textbf{PROB}), \forall s : S \bullet (P \,;\, \uparrow Q)(s,\, G(s)) \wedge$

   $\text{prob}' = \Sigma_t(\text{prob}(t) \times G(t))$

   {Def of $(P \,;\, \uparrow Q)$}

$= \exists H, G : (S \to \textbf{PROB}), \forall s : S \bullet P(s,\, H(s)) \wedge$

   $\uparrow Q(H(s),\, G(s)) \wedge \text{prob}' = \Sigma_t(\text{prob}(t) \times G(t))$

   {Def of $\uparrow$}

$\Rightarrow \exists G, H : (S \rightarrow \mathbf{PROB}) \bullet \uparrow P(\mathtt{prob}, \Sigma_t(\mathtt{prob}(t) \times H(t))) \wedge$

$\quad \forall s : S \bullet \uparrow Q(H(s), G(s)) \wedge \mathtt{prob}' = \Sigma_t(\mathtt{prob}(t) \times G(t))$

$\quad \{\text{Lemma 4.6}\}$

$\Rightarrow \exists H : (S \rightarrow \mathbf{PROB}) \bullet \uparrow P(\mathtt{prob}, \Sigma_t(\mathtt{prob}(t) \times H(t))) \wedge$

$\quad \uparrow Q(\Sigma_t(\mathtt{prob}(t) \times H(t)), \mathtt{prob}')$

$\quad \{\text{Def of ; }\}$

$\Rightarrow RHS$

$\quad \{\text{Def of ; }\}$

$\Rightarrow \exists m : \mathbf{PROB} \bullet \uparrow P(\mathtt{prob}, m) \wedge \uparrow Q(m, \mathtt{prob}')$

$\quad \{\text{Def of } \uparrow\}$

$\Rightarrow \exists G : (S \rightarrow \mathbf{PROB}) \bullet \forall s : S \bullet P(s, G(s)) \wedge m = \Sigma_t(\mathtt{prob}(t) \times G(t)) \wedge$

$\quad \exists H : (S \rightarrow \mathbf{PROB}), \forall s : S \bullet Q(s, H(s)) \wedge \mathtt{prob}' = \Sigma_s(m(s) \times H(s))$

$\quad \{\text{Calculation}\}$

$\Rightarrow \exists G, H : (S \rightarrow \mathbf{PROB}) \bullet P(s, G_(s)) \wedge Q(s, H(s)) \wedge$

$\quad \mathtt{prob}' = \Sigma_t(\mathtt{prob}(t) \times (\Sigma_s(G(t)(s) \times H(s))))$

$\quad \{\text{Lemma 4.6}\}$

$\Rightarrow \exists G, H : (S \rightarrow \mathbf{PROB}) \bullet \forall s : S \bullet (P(s, G(s)) \wedge$

$\quad \uparrow Q(G(s), \Sigma_t(G(s)(t) \times H(t)))) \wedge \mathtt{prob}' = \Sigma_t(\mathtt{prob}(t) \times (\Sigma_s(G(t)(s) \times H(s))))$

$\quad \{\text{Let } K(s) = \Sigma_t(G(s)(t) \times H(t))\}$

$\Rightarrow \exists K : (S \rightarrow \mathbf{PROB}), \forall s : S \bullet (P; \uparrow Q)(s, K(s)) \wedge \mathtt{prob}' = \Sigma_t(\mathtt{prob}(t) \times K(t))$

$\quad \{\text{Def of } \uparrow\}$

$\Rightarrow LHS$

(4) LHS ⟨right⟩{Def of $\uparrow$}

$= \exists G : (S \rightarrow \mathbf{PROB}), \exists m : \mathbf{PROB}, \forall s : S \bullet P(s, G(s)) \wedge$

$\quad (m \geq \mathtt{prob}) \wedge \mathtt{prob}' \geq \Sigma_t(m(t) \times G(t))$ ⟨right⟩{predicate calculus}

$\Rightarrow \exists G : (S \rightarrow \mathbf{PROB}), \forall s : S \bullet P(s, G(s)) \wedge$

$\quad (\mathtt{prob}' \geq \Sigma_t(\mathtt{prob}(t) \times G(t))$ ⟨right⟩{Def of $\uparrow$}

$= RHS$ ⟨right⟩{; is monotonic}

$\Rightarrow LHS$

We define

$$P \ \mathbf{seq} \ Q \ =_{df} \ P; \uparrow Q; (\mathtt{prob} \leq \mathtt{prob}')$$

Lemma 4.8

Healthy predicates are closed under sequential composition.

Because sequential composition adopts a new definition, we are obliged to reestablish its well-known properties.

Theorem 4.5

(1) skip seq $P = P = P$ seq skip

(2) P seq $(Q$ seq $R) = (P$ seq $Q)$ seq R

Proof

$$
\begin{aligned}
&(1)\ \text{skip seq}\ P && \{\text{Def of seq}\}\\
&= \text{skip};\uparrow P;(\text{prob} \leq \text{prob}') && \{\text{Lemma 4.7.(2)}\}\\
&= P;(\text{prob} \leq \text{prob}') && \{\mathcal{H}_3(P) = P\}\\
&= P && \{\mathcal{H}_3(P) = P\}\\
&= P;(\text{prob} \leq \text{prob}') && \{\uparrow \text{skip} = (\text{prob} = \text{prob}')\}\\
&= P;\uparrow \text{skip};(\text{prob} \leq \text{prob}') && \{\text{Def of seq}\}\\
&= P\ \text{seq skip}
\end{aligned}
$$

$$
\begin{aligned}
&(2)\quad LHS && \{\text{Def of seq}\}\\
&=\quad P;\uparrow (Q;\uparrow R;(\text{prob} \leq \text{prob}'));(\text{prob} \leq \text{prob}') && \{\text{Lemma 4.7(1), (3)}\}\\
&=\quad P;\uparrow Q;\uparrow R;(\text{prob} \leq \text{prob}') && \{\text{Lemma 4.7(4)}\}\\
&=\quad P;\uparrow Q;(\text{prob} \leq \text{prob}');\uparrow R;(\text{prob} \leq \text{prob}') && \{\text{Def of seq}\}\\
&=\quad (P\ \text{seq}\ Q)\ \text{seq}\ R
\end{aligned}
$$

$\bot$, fail and throw all act as left zeroes of sequential composition

Theorem 4.6

(1) fail seq $P = $ fail

(2) throw seq $P = $ throw

(3) $\bot$ seq $P = \bot$

Sequential composition distributes backward over conditional, nondeterministic and probabilistic choices.

Theorem 4.7

(1) $(P \triangleleft b \triangleright Q)$ seq $R = (P\ \text{seq}\ R) \triangleleft b \triangleright (Q\ \text{seq}\ R)$

(2) $(P\,[\![r]\!]\,Q)$ seq $R = (P\ \text{seq}\ R)[\![r]\!](Q\ \text{seq}\ R)$

(3) $(P \sqcap Q)$ seq $R = (P\ \text{seq}\ R) \sqcap (Q\ \text{seq}\ R)$

(4) $x := e;(P[\![r]\!]Q) = (x := e;P)[\![r]\!](cx := e;Q)$

(5) $x := e;(P \sqcap Q) = (x := e;P) \sqcap (x := e;Q)$

Proof

(1) $(P \triangleleft b \triangleright Q)$ seq R

    {Def of conditional}

$= (\mathcal{D}(b) \wedge b \wedge P \vee \mathcal{D}(b) \wedge \neg b \wedge Q \vee \neg \mathcal{D}(b) \wedge \mathtt{throw}) \,; \uparrow R\,; (\mathtt{prob} \leq \mathtt{prob}')$

    {; distributes over disjunction}

$= \mathcal{D}(b) \wedge b \wedge (P \,; \uparrow R\,; (\mathtt{prob} \leq \mathtt{prob}')) \vee$

    $\mathcal{D}(b) \wedge \neg b \wedge (Q \,; \uparrow R\,; (\mathtt{prob} \leq \mathtt{prob}')) \vee$

    $\neg \mathcal{D}(b) \wedge (\mathtt{throw}\,; \uparrow R\,; (\mathtt{prob} \leq \mathtt{prob}'))$

    {Theorem 4.6(2)}

$= \mathcal{D}(b) \wedge b \wedge (P \text{ seq } R) \vee \mathcal{D}(b) \wedge \neg b \wedge (Q \text{ seq } R) \neg \mathcal{D}(b) \wedge \mathtt{throw}$

    {Def of conditional}

$= (P \text{ seq } R) \triangleleft b \triangleright (Q \text{ seq } R)$

(2) $(P[\![r]\!]Q)$ seq R

    {Def of $[\![]\!]$}

$= \exists \mathtt{prob}_1, \mathtt{prob}_2 : \mathbf{PROB},\ \exists G : (S \to \mathbf{PROB}) \bullet$

    $\forall s : S \bullet R(s, G(s)) \wedge P[\mathtt{prob}_1/\mathtt{prob}'] \wedge Q[\mathtt{prob}_2/\mathtt{prob}'] \wedge$

    $\mathtt{prob}' \geq \Sigma_t((r \times \mathtt{prob}_1(t) + (1 - r) \times \mathtt{prob}_2(t)) \times G(t))$

    {Calculation}

$\Rightarrow \exists \mathtt{prob}_1, \mathtt{prob}_2, \mathtt{prob}_3, \mathtt{prob}_4 : \mathbf{PROB},\ \exists G : (S \to \mathbf{PROB}) \bullet$

    $\forall s : S \bullet R(s, G(s)) \wedge P[\mathtt{prob}_1/\mathtt{prob}'] \wedge Q[\mathtt{prob}_2/\mathtt{prob}'] \wedge$

    $\mathtt{prob}_3 = \Sigma_t(\mathtt{prob}_1(t) \times G(t)) \wedge \mathtt{prob}_4 = \Sigma_t(\mathtt{prob}_2(t) \times G(t)) \wedge$

    $\mathtt{prob}' \geq (r \times \mathtt{prob}_3 + (1 - r) \times \mathtt{prob}_4)$

    {Def of seq}

$\Rightarrow ((P \text{ seq } R)[\![r]\!](Q \text{ seq } R))\,; (\mathtt{prob} \leq \mathtt{prob}')$

    {Lemma 4.2}

$= (P \text{ seq } R)[\![r]\!](Q \text{ seq } R)$

    {Def of seq}

$= \exists \mathtt{prob}_1, \mathtt{prob}_2, \mathtt{prob}_3, \mathtt{prob}_4 : \mathbf{PROB},\ \exists G_1, G_2 : (S \to \mathbf{PROB}) \bullet$

    $P[\mathtt{prob}_1/\mathtt{prob}'] \wedge \forall s : S \bullet R(s, G_1(s)) \wedge$

    $Q[\mathtt{prob}_2/\mathtt{prob}'] \wedge \forall s : S \bullet R(s, G_2(s)) \wedge$

    $\mathtt{prob}_3 \geq \Sigma_t(\mathtt{prob}_1(t) \times G_1(t)) \wedge \mathtt{prob}_4 \geq \Sigma_t(\mathtt{prob}_2(t) \times G_2(t)) \wedge$

    $\mathtt{prob}' = (r \times \mathtt{prob}_3 + (1 - r) \times \mathtt{prob}_4)$

    {Calculation}

$\Rightarrow \exists \text{prob}_1, \text{prob}_2 : \textbf{PROB}, \exists G_1, G_2 : (S \rightarrow \textbf{PROB})\bullet$

$\quad P[\text{prob}_1/\text{prob}'] \wedge \forall s : S \bullet R(s, G_1(s)) \wedge$

$\quad Q[\text{prob}_2/\text{prob}'] \wedge \forall s : S \bullet R(s, G_2(s)) \wedge$

$\quad \text{prob}' \geq (r \times \Sigma_t(\text{prob}_1(t) \times G_1(t)) + (1 - r) \times \Sigma_t(\text{prob}_2(t) \times G_2(t)))$

$\quad \{\text{Let } W(s) =_{df} (r \times \text{prob}_1(s) + (1 - r) \times \text{prob}_2(s))\}$

$\Rightarrow \exists \text{prob}_1, \text{prob}_2 : \textbf{PROB}, \exists G_1, G_2, G : (S \rightarrow \textbf{PROB})\bullet$

$\quad P[\text{prob}_1/\text{prob}'] \wedge \forall s : S \bullet R(s, G_1(s)) \wedge$

$\quad Q[\text{prob}_2/\text{prob}'] \wedge \forall s : S \bullet R(s, G_2(s)) \wedge$

$\quad \forall s : S \bullet (W(s) = 0 \wedge G(s) = (r \times G_1(s) + (1 - r) \times G_2(s) \vee$

$\quad W(s) > 0 \wedge G(s) = (r \times \text{prob}_1(s) \times G_1(s) + (1 - r) \times \text{prob}_2(s) \times G_2(s))/W(s) \wedge$

$\quad \text{prob}' \geq \Sigma_t(r \times \text{prob}_1(t) + (1 - r) \times \text{prob}_2(t)) \times G(t)$

$\quad \{\mathcal{H}_3(R) = R\}$

$\Rightarrow \exists \text{prob}_1, \text{prob}_2 : \textbf{PROB}, \exists G : (S \rightarrow \textbf{PROB})\bullet$

$\quad P[\text{prob}_1/\text{prob}'] \wedge Q[\text{prob}_2/\text{prob}'] \wedge \forall s : S \bullet R(s, G(s)) \wedge$

$\quad \text{prob}' \geq \Sigma_t(r \times \text{prob}_1(t) + (1 - r) \times \text{prob}_2(t)) \times G(t)$

$\quad \{\text{Def of } [\![r]\!] \text{ and } \textbf{seq}\}$

$\Rightarrow (P[\![r]\!]Q) \textbf{ seq } R$

(5) RHS {Def of $\textbf{seq}$}

$= \exists r : [0, 1], \text{prob}_1, \text{prob}_2, \text{prob}_3, \text{prob}_4 : \textbf{PROB}\bullet$

$\quad P[s[e/x], \text{prob}_1/s, \text{prob}'] \wedge Q[s[e/x], \text{prob}_2/s, \text{prob}'] \wedge$

$\quad \text{prob}_3 \geq \text{prob}_1 \wedge Prob_4 \geq \text{prob}_2 \wedge$

$\quad \text{prob}' = r \times \text{prob}_3 + (1 - r) \times \text{prob}_4$ {calculation}

$\Rightarrow \exists r : [0, 1], \text{prob}_1, \text{prob}_2 : \textbf{PROB}\bullet$

$\quad P[s[e/x], \text{prob}_1/s, \text{prob}'] \wedge Q[s[e/x], \text{prob}_2/s, \text{prob}'] \wedge$

$\quad \text{prob}' \geq r \times \text{prob}_1 + (1 - r) \times \text{prob}_2$ {Def of $\textbf{seq}$}

$\Rightarrow LHS$

$= \exists G : S \rightarrow \textbf{PROB} \bullet \forall s : S \bullet (P \sqcap Q)(s, G(s)) \wedge$

$\quad \text{prob}' \geq \Sigma_{t \in S}\eta_{s[e/x]}(t) \times G(t)$ {Def of η_s}

$= \exists \text{prob} : \textbf{PROB} \bullet (P \sqcap Q)[s[e/x], \text{prob}/s, \text{prob}'] \wedge$

$\quad \text{prob}' \geq \text{prob}$ {Def of $\sqcap$}

$= \exists r : [0, 1], \exists \text{prob}_1, \text{prob}_2 : \textbf{PROB}\bullet$

$\quad P[s[e/x], \text{prob}_1/s, \text{prob}'] \wedge Q[s[e/x], \text{prob}_2/s, \text{prob}'] \wedge$

$\quad \text{prob}' \geq (r \times \text{prob}_1 + (1 - r) \times \text{prob}_2)$ {Def of $\textbf{seq}$}

$\Rightarrow RHS$

4.7   Exception Handling

Let P and Q be programs. The notation P `caughtby` Q represents a program which runs P first. If its execution throws an exception case then Q is invoked to handle that case.

$$P \text{ caughtby } Q =_{df} \mathcal{H}_{1,2}(P \text{ seq } \phi(Q))$$

where $\mathcal{H}_{1,2} =_{df} (\mathcal{H}_1 \circ \mathcal{H}_2)$

and $\phi(Q) =_{df} \text{skip} \lhd \neg eflag \rhd Q[false, true/eflag, forward]$

Lemma 4.9

Healthy predicates are closed under the exception handling operator.

Lemma 4.10

$\phi(P) \text{ seq } \phi(Q) = \phi(P \text{ seq } \phi(Q))$

$\qquad \phi(P) \text{ seq } \phi(Q)$

$\qquad \{\text{Def of seq}\}$

$= \phi(P) ; \uparrow \phi(Q) ; (\text{prob} \le \text{prob}')$

$\qquad \{\text{Def of } \phi\}$

$= (\text{skip} \lhd \neg eflag \rhd P[false, true/eflag, forward]);$

$\qquad \uparrow \phi(Q) ; (\text{prob} \le \text{prob}')$

$\qquad \{; \text{ distributes over conditional}\}$

$= (\text{skip}; (\uparrow \phi(Q)); (\text{prob} \le \text{prob}')) \lhd \neg eflag \rhd$

$\quad (P[false, true/eflag, forward] ; \uparrow \phi(Q) ; (\text{prob} \le \text{prob}'))$

$\qquad \{\text{Lemma 4.7(2)}\}$

$= \phi(Q) \lhd \neg eflag \rhd (P[false, true/eflag, forward] \text{ seq } \phi(Q))$

$\qquad \{\text{Def of } \phi\}$

$= \text{skip} \lhd \neg eflag \rhd (P[false, true/eflag, forward] \text{ seq } \phi(Q))$

$\qquad \{\text{Def of } \phi\}$

$= \phi(P \text{ seq } \phi(Q))$

Theorem 4.8

(1) P `caughtby` $(Q$ `caughtby` $R) = (P$ `caughtby` $Q)$ `caughtby` R

(2) $(\text{throw caughtby } Q) = Q = (Q \text{ caughtby throw})$

(3) $P \text{ caughtby } Q = P$ if $P \in \{\bot, \texttt{fail}, (v := e)\}$

(4) $(P \lhd b \rhd Q) \text{ caughtby } R = (P \text{ caughtby } R) \lhd b \rhd (Q \text{ caughtby } R)$

provided that b is well-defined.

(5) $(P \llbracket r \rrbracket Q)$ caughtby $R = (P$ caughtby $R) \llbracket r \rrbracket (Q$ caughtby $R)$

(6) $(P \sqcap Q)$ caughtby $R = (P$ caughtby $R) \sqcap (Q$ caughtby $R)$

Proof

(1) LHS {Def of caughtby}

$= \mathcal{H}_{1,2}(\mathcal{H}_{1,2}(P$ seq $\phi(Q))$ seq $\phi(R))$ {Def of $\mathcal{H}_{1,2}$}

$= \mathcal{H}_{1,2}(P$ seq $\phi(Q)$ seq $\phi(R))$ {Lemma 4.10}

$= \mathcal{H}_{1,2}(P$ seq $\phi(Q$ seq $\phi(R)))$ $\{\phi(S) = \phi(\mathcal{H}_{1,2}(S))\}$

$= \mathcal{H}_{1,2}(P$ seq $\phi(\mathcal{H}_{1,2}(Q$ seq $\phi(R))))$ {Def of caughtby}

$= \mathcal{H}_{1,2}(P$ seq $\phi(Q$ caught $-$ by $R))$ {Def of caughtby}

$= RHS$

(3) LHS {Def of caughtby}

$= \mathcal{H}_{1,2}((P \lhd b \rhd Q)$ seq $\phi(R))$ {Theorem 4.7(1) and $\mathcal{D}(b) = true$}

$= \mathcal{H}_{1,2}((P$ seq $\phi(R)) \lhd (Q$ seq $\phi(R)))$ {$\mathcal{H}_{1,2}$ distributes over $\lhd b \rhd$}

$= RHS$

4.8 Compensation

Let P and Q be programs. The program P cpens Q runs P first. If its execution fails, then Q is invoked as its compensation.

$$P \text{ cpens } Q =_{df} \mathcal{H}_{1,2}(P \text{ seq } \psi(Q))$$

where $\psi(Q) =_{df}$ (skip $\lhd forward \lor eflag \rhd Q[true/forward]$)

Lemma 4.11

Healthy predicates are closed under compensation operator.

Theorem 4.9

(1) P cpens $(Q$ cpens $R) = (P$ cpens $Q)$ cpens R

(2) P cpens $Q = P$ if $P \in \{$throw, $\perp, (v := e)\}$

(3) $($fail cpens $Q) = Q = (Q$ cpens fail$)$

(4) $(P \lhd b \rhd Q)$ cpens $R = (P$ cpens $R) \lhd b \rhd (Q$ cpens $R)$

(5) $(P\llbracket r \rrbracket Q)$ cpens $R = (P$ cpens $R)\llbracket r \rrbracket(Q$ cpens $R)$

(6) $(P \sqcap Q)$ cpens $R = (P$ cpens $R) \sqcap (Q$ cpens $R)$

(7) $(v := e$ seq $P)$ cpens $Q = (v := e)$ seq $(P$ cpens $Q)$

Proof

(3) Q cpens fail   {Def of cpens}

$= \mathcal{H}_{1,2}(Q \text{ seq } \psi(\text{fail}))$ {Def of seq}

$= \mathcal{H}_{1,2}(\exists prob : \textbf{PROB}, \exists G : (S \rightarrow \textbf{PROB}),$

   $\forall t : S \bullet \psi(\text{fail})(t, G(t)) \wedge Q[\text{prob}/\text{prob}'] \wedge$

   $\text{prob}' \geq \Sigma_t(\text{prob}(t) \times G(t)))$ {Calculation}

$= \mathcal{H}_{1,2}(\exists prob : \textbf{PROB}, \exists G : (S \rightarrow \textbf{PROB}),$

   $\forall t : S \bullet \psi(\text{fail})(t, G(t)) \wedge Q[\text{prob}/\text{prob}'] \wedge$

   $\text{prob}' \geq \Sigma_{t.forward=true}(\text{prob}(t) \times G(t)) +$

   $\Sigma_{t.forward=false} \times G(t))$ {Def of $\psi(\text{fail})$}

$= \mathcal{H}_{1,2}(\exists prob : \textbf{PROB}, \exists G : (S \rightarrow \textbf{PROB}),$

   $\forall t : S \bullet \psi(\text{fail})(t, G(t)) \wedge Q[\text{prob}/\text{prob}'] \wedge$

   $\text{prob}' \geq \Sigma_{t.forward=true}(\text{prob}(t) \times \eta_t) + \Sigma_{t.forward=false} \times \eta_t)$ {Calculation}

$= \mathcal{H}_{1,2}(\exists prob : \textbf{PROB} \bullet Q[\text{prob}/\text{prob}'] \wedge$

   $\text{prob}' \geq \text{prob})$ {Q is healthy}

$= Q$ {Q is healthy}

$= \mathcal{H}_{1,2}(Q; (\text{prob} \leq \text{prob}'))$ {Def of fail}

$= \mathcal{H}_{1,2}(Q; \uparrow \psi(Q); (\text{prob} \leq \text{prob}'))$ {Def of cpens}

$= $ fail cpens Q

4.9 Coordination

Let P and Q be programs. The program P else Q behaves like P if its execution succeeds. Otherwise it behaves like Q.

$$P \text{ else } Q =_{df} \exists \text{prob}_1, \text{prob}_2 : \textbf{PROB} \bullet P[\text{prob}_1/\text{prob}'] \wedge Q[\text{prob}_2/\text{prob}'] \wedge$$

$$\text{prob}' \geq \{forward = true\} \lhd \text{prob}_1 +$$

$$\text{prob}_1(forward = false) \times \text{prob}_2$$

where $X \lhd f$ denotes the result of restricting the domain of function f to the set X.

Lemma 4.12

Healthy predicates are closed under the coordination operator.

Proof

$\mathcal{H}_3(P \text{ else } Q)$

$\{\text{Def of else and } \mathcal{H}_3\}$

$= \exists \text{prob}_1, \text{prob}_2, \text{prob}_3, \text{prob}_4, \text{prob}_5, \text{prob}_6 : \textbf{PROB}\bullet$

$P[\text{prob}_1/\text{prob}'] \wedge Q[\text{prob}_2/\text{prob}'] \wedge P[\text{prob}_4/\text{prob}'] \wedge Q[\text{prob}_5/\text{prob}'] \wedge$

$\text{prob}_3 \geq \{forward = true\} \lhd \text{prob}_1 + \text{prob}_1(forward = false) \lhd \text{prob}_2 \wedge$

$\text{prob}_6 \geq \{forward = true\} \lhd \text{prob}_4 + \text{prob}_4(forward = false) \lhd \text{prob}_5 \wedge$

$\exists r : [0, 1] \bullet \text{prob}' = (r \times \text{prob}_3 + (1 - r) \times \text{prob}_6)$

$\{\text{Let } W =_{df} r \times \text{prob}_1(foward = false) + (1 - r) \times \text{prob}_4(forward = false)\}$

$\Rightarrow \exists r : [0, 1], \exists \text{prob}_1, \text{prob}_2, \text{prob}_4, \text{prob}_5 : \textbf{PROB}\bullet$

$P[\text{prob}_1/\text{prob}'] \wedge Q[\text{prob}_2/\text{prob}'] \wedge P[\text{prob}_4/\text{prob}'] \wedge Q[\text{prob}_5/\text{prob}'] \wedge$

$\text{prob}' \geq \{forward = true\} \lhd (r \times \text{prob}_1 + (1 - r) \times \text{prob}_4) +$

$W \times (r \times \text{prob}_1(forward = false) \times \text{prob}_2/W +$

$(1 - r) \times \text{prob}_2(forward(forward = false) \times \text{prob}_4)/W)$

$\{\mathcal{H}_3(P) = P \text{ and } \mathcal{H}_3(Q) = Q\}$

$\Rightarrow P \text{ else } Q$

$\{X \sqsupseteq \mathcal{H}_3(X)\}$

$\Rightarrow \mathcal{H}_3(P \text{ else } Q)$

Theorem 4.10

(1) $P \text{ else } (Q \text{ else } R) = (P \text{ else } Q) \text{ else } R$

(2) $P \text{ else } Q = P \text{ if } P \in \{\bot, (v := e), (v := e; \textbf{throw})\}$

(3) $(x := e \text{ } \textbf{fail}) \text{ else } Q = Q$

(4) $(P \lhd b \rhd Q) \text{ else } R = (P \text{ else } R) \lhd b \rhd (Q \text{ else } R)$

(5) $(P[r]Q) \text{ else } R = (P \text{ else } R)[r](Q \text{ else } R)$

(6) $(P \sqcap Q) \text{ else } R = (P \text{ else } R) \sqcap (Q \text{ else } R)$

Proof

(1) *LHS* $\{\text{Def of else}\}$

$= \exists \text{prob}_1, \text{prob}_2, \text{prob}_3, \text{prob}_4 : \textbf{PROB}\bullet$

$P[\text{prob}_1/\text{prob}'] \wedge Q[\text{prob}_3/\text{prob}'] \wedge R[\text{prob}_4/\text{prob}'] \wedge$

$\text{prob}' \geq \{forward = true\} \lhd \text{prob}_1 +$

$\text{prob}_1(forward = false) \times \text{prob}_2 \wedge$

$\text{prob}_2 \geq \{forward = true\} \lhd \text{prob}_3 +$

$\text{prob}_3(forward = false) \times \text{prob}_4$ $\{\text{Calculation}\}$

$\Rightarrow \exists \text{prob}_1, \text{prob}_3, \text{prob}_4 \bullet$

$P[\text{prob}_1/\text{prob}'] \wedge Q[\text{prob}_3/\text{prob}'] \wedge R[\text{prob}_4/\text{prob}'] \wedge$

$\text{prob}' \geq \{forward = true\} \lhd \text{prob}_1 +$

$\text{prob}_1(forward = false) \times (\{forward = true\} \triangle \} \text{prob}_3 +$

$\text{prob}_1(forwatd = false) \times \text{prob}_3(forward = false) \times \text{prob}_4$ {Calculation}

$= \exists \text{prob}_1, \text{prob}_3, \text{prob}_4, \text{prob}_5 \bullet$

$P[\text{prob}_1/\text{prob}'] \wedge Q[\text{prob}_3/\text{prob}'] \wedge R[\text{prob}_4/\text{prob}'] \wedge$

$\text{prob}' \geq \{forward = true\} \lhd \text{prob}_5 +$

$\text{prob}_5(forward = false) \times \text{prob}_4 \wedge$

$\text{prob}_5 = \{forward = true\} \lhd \text{prob}_1 +$

$\text{prob}_3(forward = false) \times \text{prob}_3$ {Def of else}

$\Rightarrow RHS$ {Def of else}

$= \exists \text{prob}_1, \text{prob}_3, \text{prob}_4, \text{prob}_5 : \textbf{PROB} \bullet$

$P[\text{prob}_1/\text{prob}'] \wedge Q[\text{prob}_3/\text{prob}'] \wedge R[\text{prob}_4/\text{prob}'] \wedge$

$\text{prob}' \geq \{forward = true\} \lhd \text{prob}_5 +$

$\text{prob}_5(forward = false) \times \text{prob}_4 \wedge$

$\text{prob}_5 \geq \{forward = true\} \lhd \text{prob}_1 +$

$\text{prob}_1(forward = false) \times \text{prob}_5$ {Calculation}

$\Rightarrow \exists \text{prob}_1, \text{prob}_3, \text{prob}_4 : \textbf{PROB} \bullet$

$P[\text{prob}_1/\text{prob}'] \wedge Q[\text{prob}_3/\text{prob}'] \wedge R[\text{prob}_4/\text{prob}'] \wedge$

$\text{prob}' \geq \{forward = true\} \lhd \text{prob}_1 +$

$\text{prob}_1(forward = false) \times (\{forward = true\} \lhd \text{prob}_3) +$

$(\text{prob}_1(forward = false) \times \text{prob}_3(forward = false)) \times \text{prob}_4$ {calculation}

$= \exists \text{prob}_1, \text{prob}_2, \text{prob}_3, \text{prob}_4 : \textbf{PROB} \bullet$

$P[\text{prob}_1/\text{prob}'] \wedge Q[\text{prob}_3/\text{prob}'] \wedge R[\text{prob}_4/\text{prob}'] \wedge$

$\text{prob}_2 = \{forward = true\} \lhd \text{prob}_3 +$

$\text{prob}_3(forward = false) \times \text{prob}_4 \wedge$

$\text{prob}' \geq \{forward = true\} \lhd \text{prob}_1 +$

$\text{prob}_1(forward = false) \times \text{prob}_2$ {Def of else}

$\Rightarrow LHS$

4.10   Normal Form

Let $\{ r_i \mid 1 \leq i \leq n \}$ be a set of positive reals satisfying

$$\Sigma_i r_i \leq 1$$

Let $\{P_i \mid 1 \leq i \leq n\}$ be a set of programs. We define the generalised probabilistic choice as follows:

$$\textbf{pchoice}(r_1 \& P_1, ..., r_n \& P_n) \ =_{df}$$

$$\begin{pmatrix} P_1[r_1]\textbf{pchoice}(r_2/(1 - r_1)\&P_2, ..., r_n/(1 - r_1)\&P_n) \ r_1 < 1 \\ P_1 \hspace{8cm} r_1 = 1 \end{pmatrix}$$

$$\textbf{pchoice}() \ =_{df} \ \bot$$

Let $\{b_i \mid 1 \leq i \leq n\}$ be a set of well-defined boolean guards satisfying

$$b_i \wedge b_j \ = \ false$$

As usual we define the alternation construct

$$\textbf{if}(b_1 \rightarrow P_1, ..., b_n \rightarrow P_n)\textbf{fi} \ =_{df} \ \bigvee_i (b_i \wedge P_i) \vee \bigwedge_i \neg b_i \wedge \bot$$

The normal form we adopt for our language is an alternation of the form:

$$\textbf{if} \begin{pmatrix} b_1 \rightarrow \textbf{pchoice}(p_1 \& P_1, ... p_m \& P_m), \\ ...... \\ b_k \rightarrow \textbf{pchoice}(q_1 \& Q_1, ... q_n \& Q_n) \end{pmatrix} \textbf{fi},$$

where P_i and Q_j have the form

$$R_1 \sqcap ... \sqcap R_n$$

where all R_k lie in the following set

$$\{v := e, \ (v := e; \texttt{fail}), \ (v := e; \texttt{throw})\}$$

where the expression e is well-defined.

Theorem 4.11

All finite program can be reduced to a normal form.

5   Link with the Original Design Model

This section explores the link between the model of Section 2 with the original design model given in [12].

For any design P and **Req**-healthy design Q we define

$$\mathcal{F}(P) =_{df} \mathcal{H}(P; \texttt{success})$$

$$\mathcal{G}(Q) =_{df} Q[true, \ false/forward, \ eflag]; (forward \wedge \neg eflag)_\bot$$

Theorem 5.1

$\mathcal{F}$ and $\mathcal{G}$ form a Galois connection:

(1) $\mathcal{G}(\mathcal{F}(P)) = P$

(2) $\mathcal{F}(\mathcal{G}(Q)) \sqsubseteq Q$

Proof. $\mathcal{G}(\mathcal{F}(P))$ {Def of $\mathcal{F}$ and $\mathcal{G}$}

$= \quad P; \mathsf{success}; (true \vdash (v' = v)) \lhd forward \land \neg eflag \rhd \bot)$

                                                                {Def of $\mathsf{success}$}

$= \quad P; (true \vdash (v' = v))$ {unit law of ; }

$= \quad P$

$\quad \mathcal{F}(\mathcal{G}(Q))$ {Def of $\mathcal{F}$ and $\mathcal{G}$}

$= \quad \mathcal{H}(Q[true, \neg false/forward, eflag];$

$\quad\quad (true \vdash (v' = v) \lhd forward \land \neg eflag \rhd \bot); \mathsf{success})$

                          {Def of $\mathcal{H}$, $(P \lhd b \rhd Q); R = (P; R) \lhd b \rhd (Q; R)$}

$= \quad Q; (\mathsf{success} \lhd forward \land \neg eflag \rhd \bot)$ {Def of sucess}

$= \quad Q; ((true \vdash (v' = v \land forwared' = forward \land eflag' = eflag))$

$\quad\quad \lhd forward \land \neg eflag \rhd \bot)$ {$\bot \sqsubseteq D$}

$\sqsubseteq \quad Q; (true \vdash (v' = v \land forwared' = forward \land eflag' = eflag))$

                                                                {unit law of ; }

$= \quad Q$

$\mathcal{F}$ is a homomorphism.

Theorem 5.2

(1) $\mathcal{F}(true \vdash (v' = v)) = \mathsf{skip}$

(2) $\mathcal{F}(true \vdash (x' = e \land y' = y \land z' = z)) = (x := e)$

provided that e is well-defined.

(3) $\mathcal{F}(true) = \bot$

(4) $\mathcal{F}(P1 \sqcap P2) = \mathcal{F}(P1) \sqcap \mathcal{F}(P2)$

(5) $\mathcal{F}(P1 \lhd b \rhd P2) = \mathcal{F}(P1) \lhd b \rhd \mathcal{F}(P2)$

provided that b is well-defined.

(6) $\mathcal{F}(P1; P2) = \mathcal{F}(P1); \mathcal{F}(P2)$

(7) $\mathcal{F}(b * P) = b *_{\mathcal{H}} \mathcal{F}(P)$

Proof

(6) $\mathcal{F}(P1; P2)$ {Def of $\mathcal{F}$}

$= \mathcal{H}(P1; P2; \text{success})$ {$\text{success}; P2; \text{success} =$

$P2; \text{success}$}

$= \mathcal{H}((P1; \text{success}; P2; \text{success}))$ {$(forward \wedge \neg eflag)^{\top}; \text{success}; Q =$

$(forward \wedge \neg eflag)^{\top}; \text{success}; \mathcal{H}(Q)$}

$= \mathcal{H}((P1; \text{success}); \mathcal{H}(P2; \text{success}))$ {Theorem 2.4}

$= \mathcal{H}(P1; \text{success}); \mathcal{H}(P2; \text{success})$ {Def of $\mathcal{F}$}

$= \mathcal{F}(P1) \,;\, \mathcal{F}(P2)$

(7) LHS {fixed point theorem}

$= \mathcal{F}((P; b * P) \lhd b \rhd (true \vdash (v' = v)))$ {Conclusion (1), (5), (6)}

$= (\mathcal{F}(P); LHS) \lhd b \rhd \text{skip}$

which implies that $LHS \sqsupseteq RHS$

$\mathcal{G}(RHS)$ {fixed point theorem}

$= \mathcal{G}((\mathcal{F}(P); RHS) \lhd b \rhd \text{skip})$ {$\mathcal{G}$ distributes over $\lhd b \rhd$}

$= \mathcal{G}(\mathcal{F}(P); RHS) \lhd b \rhd \mathcal{G}(\text{skip})$ {Def of $\mathcal{G}$}

$= (\mathcal{F}(P)[true, false/forward, eflag]; RHS;$

$(foward \wedge \neg eflag)_{\perp}) \lhd b \rhd (true \vdash (v' = v))$ {Def of $\mathcal{F}$}

$= (P; \text{success}; RHS;$

$(forward \wedge \neg eflag)_{\perp}) \lhd b \rhd (true \vdash (v' = v))$ {Def of **success**}

$= (P; RHS[true, false/forward, eflag];$

$(forward \wedge \neg eflag)_{\perp}) \lhd b \rhd (true \vdash (v' = v))$ {Def of $\mathcal{G}$}

$= (P; \mathcal{G}(RHS)) \lhd b \rhd (true \vdash (v' = v))$

which implies

$\mathcal{G}(RHS) \sqsupseteq (b * P)$ {$\mathcal{F}$ is monotonic}

$\Rightarrow \mathcal{F}(\mathcal{G}(RHS)) \sqsupseteq LHS$ {Theorem 5.1(2)}

$\Rightarrow RHS \sqsupseteq LHS$

6   Conclusion

This paper presents a design model for compensable programs. We add new logical variables $eflag$ and $forward$ to the standard design model to deal with the features of exception and failures. As a result, we put forward new healthiness conditions **Req₁** and **Req₂** to characterise those designs which can be used to specify the dynamic behaviour of compensable programs.

    This paper treats an assignment $x := e$ as a conditional (Theorem 4.1). After it is shown that `throw` is a new left zero of sequential composition, we are allowed to use the algebraic laws established for the conventional imperative language in [12] to convert finite programs to normal form. This shows that the model of Section 2 is really a conservative extension of the original design model in [12] in the sense that it preserves the algebraic laws of the Guarded Command Language.

Acknowledgement. This work was supported by the Open Fund of the State Key Laboratory of Software Development Environment under Grant No. SKLSDE-2009KF-2-05, Beijing University of Aeronautics and Astronautics, and by the National Basic Research Program of China under Grant No. 2005CB321904, National Natural Science Foundation of China under Grant No. 90718004, and Shanghai Leading Academic Discipline Project B412.

References

1. Abadi, M., Gordon, A.D.: A calculus for cryptographic protocols: The spi calculus. Information and Computation 148(1), 1–70 (1999)
2. Bhargavan, K., Fournet, C., Gordon, A.D.: A Semantics for Web Service Authentication. Theoretical Computer Science 340(1), 102–153 (2005)
3. Bruni, R., Montanari, H.C., Montannari, U.: Theoretical foundation for compensation in flow composition languages. In: Proc. POPL 2005, 32nd ACM SIGPLAN-SIGACT Symposium on Principle of Programming Languages, pp. 209–220. ACM, New York (2004)
4. Bruni, R., Ferrari, G.L., Melgratti, H.C., Montanari, U., Strollo, D., Tuosto, E.: From Theory to Practice in Transactional Composition of Web Services. In: Bravetti, M., Kloul, L., Zavattaro, G. (eds.) EPEW/WS-EM 2005. LNCS, vol. 3670, pp. 272–286. Springer, Heidelberg (2005)
5. Bulter, M.J., Ferreria, C.: A process compensation language. In: Grieskamp, W., Santen, T., Stoddart, B. (eds.) IFM 2000. LNCS, vol. 1945, pp. 61–76. Springer, Heidelberg (2000)
6. Bulter, M.J., Ferreria, C.: An Operational Semantics for StAC: a Lanuage for Modelling Long-Running Business Transactions. In: De Nicola, R., Ferrari, G.-L., Meredith, G. (eds.) COORDINATION 2004. LNCS, vol. 2949, pp. 87–104. Springer, Heidelberg (2004)
7. Curbera, F., Goland, Y., Klein, J., Leymann, F., Roller, D., Satish Thatte, M., Weerawarana, S.: Business Process Execution Language for Web Service (2003), http://www.siebei.com/bpel
8. Dijkstra, E.W.: A Discipline of Programming. Prentice Hall, Englewood Cliffs (1976)
9. Gordon, A.D., Pucella, R.: Validating a Web Service Security Abstraction by Typing. Formal Aspect of Computing 17(3), 277–318 (2005)
10. Jifeng, H., Huibiao, Z., Geguang, P.: A model for BPEL-like languages. Frontiers of Computer Science in China 1(1), 9–20 (2007)
11. Jifeng, H.: Compensable Programs. In: Jones, C.B., Liu, Z., Woodcock, J. (eds.) Formal Methods and Hybrid Real-Time Systems. LNCS, vol. 4700, pp. 349–363. Springer, Heidelberg (2007)
12. Hoare, C.A.R., Jifeng, H.: Unifying theories of programming. Prentice Hall, Englewood Cliffs (1998)

13. Leymann, F.: Web Service Flow Language (WSFL1.0). IBM (2001)
14. Laneve, C., Zavattaro, G.: Web-pi at work. In: De Nicola, R., Sangiorgi, D. (eds.) TGC 2005. LNCS, vol. 3705, pp. 182–194. Springer, Heidelberg (2005)
15. Jing, L., Jifeng, H., Geguang, P., Huibiao, Z.: Towards the Semantics for Web Services Choreography Description Language. In: Liu, Z., He, J. (eds.) ICFEM 2006. LNCS, vol. 4260, pp. 246–263. Springer, Heidelberg (2006)
16. Lucchi, R., Mazzara, M.: A Pi-calculus based semantics for WS-BPEL. Journal of Logic and Algebraic Programming 70(1), 96–118 (2007)
17. Milner, R.: Communication and Mobile System: the π-calculus. Cambridge University Press, Cambridge (1999)
18. Morris, J.M.: Non-deterministic expressions and predicate transformers. Information Processing Letters 61, 241–246 (1997)
19. Geguang, P., Huibiao, Z., Zongyan, Q., Shuling, W., Xiangpeng, Z., Jifeng, H.: Theoretical Foundation of Scope-based Compensation Flow Language for Web Service. In: Ning, P., Qing, S., Li, N. (eds.) ICICS 2006. LNCS, vol. 4307, pp. 251–266. Springer, Heidelberg (2006)
20. Zongyan, Q., Shuling, W., Geguang, P., Xiangpeng, Z.: Semantics of BPEL4WS-Like Fault and Compensation Handling. In: Fitzgerald, J.S., Hayes, I.J., Tarlecki, A. (eds.) FM 2005. LNCS, vol. 3582, pp. 350–365. Springer, Heidelberg (2005)
21. Tarski, A.: A lattice-theoretical fixpoint theorem and its applications. Pacific Journal of Mathematics 5, 285–309 (1955)
22. Thatte, S.: XLANG: Web Service for Business Process Design. Microsoft, Redmond (2001)

On Modelling User Observations in the UTP

Michael J. Banks and Jeremy L. Jacob

Department of Computer Science, University of York, UK
{Michael.Banks,Jeremy.Jacob}@cs.york.ac.uk

Abstract. This paper presents an approach for modelling interactions between users and systems in the *Unifying Theories of Programming*. Working in the predicate calculus, we outline generic techniques for calculating a user's observations of a system and, in turn, for identifying the information that a user can deduce about the system's behaviour from those observations. To demonstrate how this approach can be applied in practical software development, we propose some alternative refinement relations that offer greater flexibility than classical refinement by utilising knowledge of the observational abilities of users.

Keywords: UTP, multi-user systems, co-operating and independent refinement, information flow, distributed testing.

1 Introduction

This paper is concerned with software systems whose purpose is to provide a range of services to multiple end-users. This class of *multi-user* systems encompasses a large range of software products, from operating systems and database software to telecommunications networks and cloud computing services.

A multi-user system consists of a central server that receives requests from multiple users (clients) and delivers service in response to those requests. Naturally, the system may offer different services to different users. It is usual to provide each user with its own private interface to the system, to ensure that the system can distinguish between its users and to ensure that users do not interfere with each other's interactions with the system. These interfaces impose a structure on the system's environment and allow the system's designers to model the interactions that users can perform with the system.

When working in process algebras such as CSP, it is usual to model the users of a system as individual processes operating in parallel with a process representing the system [1]. By analysing the synchronisations between the system and the user processes, this approach may be used to verify that a system specification delivers the functionality expected by its users. However, this approach is suitable only for reasoning about systems expressed in the same semantic domain in which the user processes are formulated. This may be problematic if the designers of a system wish to analyse its interactions with users in a more concrete description of the system (such as a program), or a system description that consists of

S. Qin (Ed.): UTP 2010, LNCS 6445, pp. 101–119, 2010.

multiple components expressed in different formalisms. In such circumstances, it may be necessary to adopt a more general approach for reasoning about the interactions between a system and its users.

Our main contribution in this paper is a systematic approach for formally modelling the interactions between users and systems in Hoare and He's Unifying Theories of Programming (UTP) [2]. This approach fits seamlessly within the predicate semantics of the UTP; it can, therefore, be integrated with existing UTP theories to support the analysis of multi-user systems that are specified in languages with a UTP semantics.

This paper is structured as follows. Section 2 provides an overview of the UTP. Section 3 formalises two distinct classes of observations of multi-user systems and introduces our approach for modelling the abilities of users to observe a system's execution. Building on this approach, Section 4 presents a method for calculating the space of observations that individual users can make of a system. This method is extended to the UTP theory of designs in Section 5 and applied to a byte register in Section 6 as a simple worked example.

To demonstrate how our approach can be advantageous in formal software development, Section 7 describes some alternative notions of refinement that are based on the observational abilities of users. These refinement relations offer system designers the ability to carry out refinement steps that do not compromise the system's functionality from the perspective of its users, but which are nevertheless forbidden by classical refinement.

In Section 8, we survey some areas of research addressing multi-user systems in a formal setting and discuss the relevance of our approach to those areas. Finally, we present our conclusions and outline some topics for future work.

2   Unifying Theories of Programming

The semantic model of the UTP is the alphabetised relational calculus. In the UTP, specifications and programs alike are expressed as predicates over an alphabet (set) of observational variables. The purpose of the observational variables is to record all of the information about a program's behaviour that is visible to the program's environment whenever an observation of the program is made.

In the UTP theory of relations, a program operation is expressed as a predicate that relates initial observations of the program state to the corresponding observations of the program state taken after (or during) the execution of the operation. The observational variables representing intermediate observations of a program state are decorated with a prime, to distinguish them from the (undecorated) observational variables of the initial program state.

Central to the UTP is the refinement ordering between predicates, which is characterised by implication: [2]

$$S \sqsubseteq T \triangleq [\, T \Rightarrow S \,] \tag{1}$$

where the square brackets denote universal quantification over all free variables. Hence, $S \sqsubseteq T$ asserts that every observation of T is a possible observation of S.

The UTP is best known as a framework for giving a denotational semantics to various programming paradigms and the features of programming languages. However, the UTP also features a powerful standalone notation for reasoning about program correctness. We adopt the UTP in this capacity as the framework in which we cast our approach for reasoning about multi-user systems.

3 Preliminaries

3.1 System-Level and Interface-Level Observations

We model an observation of a UTP predicate S as a predicate that associates each observational variable in S's alphabet with a single value. For instance, the predicate $x = 42 \land y = 99$ records a possible observation of the predicate $x > 0 \land y > x$. We distinguish between two separate classes of observations:

- A *system-level* observation records the entirety of the information about the behaviour of a system (expressed as a predicate) that may be acquired by monitoring the whole of the system's environment.
- An *interface-level* observation records the information that a specified user acquires when it observes a system's behaviour through its interface. Hence, each interface-level observation is a *projection* of a system-level observation.

While a system-level observation provides all the information about a system's behaviour that is visible to the environment, an interface-level observation provides only a subset of that information. Throughout this paper, we assume that a user's observation of a system provides the only source of information about the execution of the system that is available to the user. Hence, a user can neither inspect the internal state of the system directly, nor can it monitor the aspects of the system's behaviour that are not visible through its interface. Unless stated otherwise, we require that users are isolated from each other and do not share their observations of the system with other users.

Following the UTP notational conventions, we denote the list of undashed variables $s_1, \ldots, s_i$ of a system-level observation by s and the corresponding list of dashed variables by s'. Likewise, we denote the lists $u_1, \ldots, u_j$ and $u'_1, \ldots, u'_j$ of variables of an interface-level observation by u and u' respectively. In keeping with our assumption that system-level variables are hidden from users, we enforce the condition that the sets of variables in s and u (and s' and u') are disjoint.

3.2 Views

A user's interface to a system is modelled by a predicate known as a *view*. A view defines the mapping between interface-level observational variables and system-level observational variables. Thus, a view determines which aspects of each system-level observation are relayed to the user associated with that view.

Example 1. Suppose x and y are observational variables of an arbitrary system-level predicate. Consider the following views:

$$A \triangleq x_A = x \wedge y_A = y$$

$$B \triangleq z_B = \max(x, y)$$

$$C \triangleq x_C = x \wedge (z_C = 0 \lhd x < y \rhd z_C = 1)$$

View A provides a user with complete knowledge of the values of x and y, since they are a function of the interface-level observational variables x_A and y_A. View B provides a user with the value of the larger of x and y, but no indication of whether $x < y$, $x = y$ or $x > y$. View C provides the value of x, but offers only partial information about y's value in relation to x's value.

When dealing with multiple views, each representing a different interface to a system, we require that each view's set of interface-level observational variables is disjoint from those of the other views. (All of the views listed in Example 1 are pairwise disjoint.)

Definition 1 (Disjoint views). *A pair of views $V_1(s, u_1)$ and $V_2(s, u_2)$ are said to be disjoint if and only if $u_1 \cap u_2 = \emptyset$.*

3.3   Healthiness Conditions for Views

To ensure that all views represent a viable mapping between system-level and interface-level observations, it is necessary to impose some constraints on the structure of views. We capture the space of viable views by defining two healthiness conditions **VH1** and **VH2**.

Definition 2 (VH1). *A view $V(s, u)$ is **VH1**-healthy if and only if, for every system-level observation over the variables in s and s', there is a complementary interface-level observation over the variables in u and u' that satisfies V:*

$$\textbf{VH1}(V) \quad \textit{iff} \quad \forall\, s, s' \bullet \exists\, u, u' \bullet V \tag{2}$$

The purpose of **VH1** is to ensure that a view maps each system-level observation to at least one interface-level observation. It follows that predicates such as $x = y$, $x > 0$ and **false** are not **VH1**-healthy views, because they restrict the domain of x.

While **VH1** insists that a view describes a total mapping from system-level to interface-level observations, it does not require that mapping to be functional — i.e. each system-level observation maps to exactly one interface-level observation — although this will often be the case for views in practice. Moreover, **VH1** does not place any restrictions on whether an interface-level observation maps to zero, one or multiple system-level observations.

It is possible to write a "time-travelling" **VH1**-healthy predicate where the values of the initial (undashed) interface-level observational variables depend upon the values of the intermediate (dashed) system-level observational variables. Such a predicate cannot correspond to a user's interface of a system in reality, since an intermediate observation of a system state can only be made once a system has started, whereas an initial observation describes the system state before execution commences.

Another class of undesirable **VH1**-healthy predicates are those featuring dependencies between the initial and intermediate system-level variables (such as $x' = x + 1$), or the initial and intermediate interface-level variables. These predicates impose functional requirements on the structure of systems and therefore should not be considered to be views. We exclude these predicates — along with the aforementioned "time-travelling" predicates — from the space of views by defining a second healthiness condition **VH2**.

Definition 3 (VH2). *A view $V(s, u)$ is **VH2**-healthy if and only if it places no dependencies between s and s', u and u', or s' and u:*

$$\textbf{VH2}(V) \quad iff \quad ((\exists\, s, u \bullet V) \wedge (\exists\, s', u \bullet V) \wedge (\exists\, s', u' \bullet V)) = V \quad (3)$$

We say that a view that satisfies both **VH1** and **VH2** is **VH**-healthy. All of the views in Example 1 are **VH**-healthy, as are all the views that we consider in the following sections.

The following lemma states that the view obtained by taking the conjunction of disjoint **VH**-healthy views is itself a **VH**-healthy view, which gives at least as much information about a system's behaviour as each view individually.

Lemma 1 (Conjunction of VH-healthy views). *If $V_1(s, u_1)$ and $V_2(s, u_2)$ are disjoint **VH**-healthy views over the same set of system-level observational variables s, then $(V_1 \wedge V_2)(s, u_1 \cup u_2)$ is also **VH**-healthy.*

4 Relating Users and Systems

In this section, we define predicate transformers for calculating the aspects of a system's behaviour that are visible to a user through a specified view and, given an interface-level observation of the system, the information that a user can deduce about the system's behaviour.

4.1 Calculating Interface-Level Predicates

Given a system-level predicate S and a view V, it is possible to derive a predicate that encodes the space of all interface-level observations that can be made of S when viewed through V. We define a predicate transformer **P** (for "project") to calculate this predicate.

Definition 4 (P predicate transformer). *The interface-level predicate obtained by substituting $V(s, u)$ into a predicate $S(s)$ is given by:*

$$\textbf{P}(V, S) \triangleq \exists\, s, s' \bullet V \wedge S \quad (4)$$

The predicate $\mathbf{P}(V, S)$ is the image of S as viewed through V; in other words, $\mathbf{P}(V, S)$ is satisfied by exactly those interface-level observations that can be made by viewing S through V. Notice that applying $\mathbf{P}(V)$ to S hides the system-level observational variables in S.

Example 2. Consider the system-level predicate $E \triangleq x + y = 10$, where $x, y \in \mathbb{N}$. For the views listed in Example 1, the projections of E are:

$$\mathbf{P}(A, E) = x_A + y_A = 10$$
$$\mathbf{P}(B, E) = z_B \geq 5 \wedge z_B \leq 10$$
$$\mathbf{P}(C, E) = (z_C = 0 \wedge x_C \geq 0 \wedge x_C \leq 4) \vee (z_C = 1 \wedge x_C \geq 5 \wedge x_C \leq 10)$$

A view can be regarded as a special kind of linking predicate between two data types, where system-level observational variables are instances of the concrete data type, and interface-level observational variables are instances of the abstract data type. It follows that applying $\mathbf{P}(V)$ to a predicate S may be interpreted as performing data refinement on S *in reverse*, because concrete (system-level) observations are replaced by abstract (interface-level) observations. This suggests that existing techniques for reasoning about data refinement can be applied to identify results concerning the application of $\mathbf{P}(V)$ to predicates. Moreover, the application of views to translate from system-level to interface-level models of systems is related to *abstract interpretation* [3].

We now present some properties of $\mathbf{P}$ that we use later in the paper.

Lemma 2 ($\mathbf{P}$ is order-preserving). *Provided that S and T are predicates defined over the same space of system-level observational variables as V:*

$$S \sqsubseteq T \Rightarrow \mathbf{P}(V, S) \sqsubseteq \mathbf{P}(V, T) \tag{5}$$

If a view V is divided into two parts V_1 and V_2, such that $V = (V_1 \wedge V_2)$ and V_1 and V_2 are disjoint, then the interface-level predicate $\mathbf{P}(V_1, S) \wedge \mathbf{P}(V_2, S)$ that is generated by projecting S through V_1 and V_2 separately is satisfied by a (potentially) larger space of observations than $\mathbf{P}(V, S)$ itself. We generalise this result to an arbitrary number of views in Lemma 3.

Lemma 3 (Splitting V may weaken $\mathbf{P}(V)$). *When $V_1, \ldots, V_n$ are pairwise disjoint views over the same space of system-level observational variables:*

$$\mathbf{P}\left(\left(\bigwedge_{i \in 1..n} V_i\right), S\right) \Rightarrow \bigwedge_{i \in 1..n} \mathbf{P}(V_i, S) \tag{6}$$

4.2   Calculating System-Level Predicates

Given an interface-level predicate U formed by projecting a system-level predicate S through view V, it is possible to recover some (if not all) knowledge of the definition of S by substituting V back into U. We formalise this process by defining another predicate transformer $\mathbf{R}$ (for "retract").

Definition 5 (R predicate transformer). *The system-level predicate obtained by substituting $V(s, u)$ into an interface-level predicate $U(u)$ is given by:*

$$\mathbf{R}(V, U) \triangleq \forall\, u, u' \bullet V \Rightarrow U \qquad (7)$$

$\mathbf{R}(V, U)$ recovers the weakest system-level predicate T such that the projection of each system-level observation of T through V matches an interface-level observation of U, and each observation of U corresponds to an observation of T projected through V. It follows from $\mathbf{R}$'s definition that $[\, V \wedge T \Rightarrow U\,]$ [2].

The $\mathbf{P}$ and $\mathbf{R}$ predicate transformers are not inverses of each other, since a view need not define a one-to-one correspondence between system-level and interface-level observations. They do, however, form a Galois connection between system-level and interface-level predicates under the refinement ordering.

Theorem 1 (P and R form a Galois connection). *The $\mathbf{P}$ and $\mathbf{R}$ predicate transformers form a Galois connection (axiality) between the spaces of system-level and interface-level predicates linked by a given view. Thus:*

$$U \sqsubseteq \mathbf{P}(V, S) \quad \text{if and only if} \quad \mathbf{R}(V, U) \sqsubseteq S \qquad (8)$$

Corollary 1. *By substituting $\mathbf{P}(V, S)$ in place of U in Theorem 1, we obtain:*

$$\mathbf{R}(V, \mathbf{P}(V, S)) \sqsubseteq S \qquad (9)$$

Corollary 1 implies that every system-level observation of S is also a system-level observation of $\mathbf{R}(V, \mathbf{P}(V, S))$. This conforms to the intuition that applying $\mathbf{P}(V)$ to a system-level predicate S may discard information about the observations permitted by S, which cannot be recovered by applying $\mathbf{R}(V)$ to $\mathbf{P}(V, S)$.

Example 3. Continuing from Example 2, the system-level predicates recovered by applying $\mathbf{R}(V)$ to each interface-level projection of E are as follows:

$$\mathbf{R}(A, \mathbf{P}(A, E)) = x + y = 10$$
$$\mathbf{R}(B, \mathbf{P}(B, E)) = \max(x, y) \geq 5 \wedge \max(x, y) \leq 10$$
$$\mathbf{R}(C, \mathbf{P}(C, E)) = (x \geq 0 \wedge x \leq 4 \lhd x < y \rhd x \geq 5 \wedge x \leq 10)$$

Observe that $\mathbf{R}(A, \mathbf{P}(A, E)) = E$, because view A preserves the values of x and y in x_A and y_A. However, both $\mathbf{R}(B, \mathbf{P}(B, E))$ and $\mathbf{R}(C, \mathbf{P}(C, E))$ are weaker predicates than E, because information about the exact values of x and y is discarded when $\mathbf{P}(B)$ and $\mathbf{P}(C)$ are applied to E.

4.3   Observations and Deductions

Users can acquire knowledge about a system's behaviour in two ways: by observation and by deduction. While we assume users can only observe a system's behaviour through an interface supplied by the system, there may be nothing to prevent a user from possessing *a priori* knowledge of the design of the system or its interface. Hence, if a user has knowledge of the system's implementation then, given a projection of a system-level observation through its view, the user may apply this knowledge to rule out potential system-level observations that are incompatible with its own observation and thereby deduce more detailed information about the system behaviour.

When ϕ is an interface-level observation of a predicate S viewed through V, the predicate describing all system-level observations of S that are compatible with ϕ is given by $\mathbf{R}(V, \phi) \wedge S$. Thus, a user that knows the definition of S can deduce more (but not necessarily all) information about the system-level observation of S than it can from $\mathbf{R}(V, \phi)$ alone. In turn, if a user at V has knowledge of the structure of another user's view W, then the user can infer all observations of S through W that are compatible with its own observation ϕ by calculating $\mathbf{P}(W, (\mathbf{R}(V, \phi) \wedge S))$.

We note in passing that, at the level of a system's implementation, a user's interface will exhibit physical and temporal characteristics (such as fluctuations in responsiveness) that are not modelled at the abstract level of a view. By monitoring these properties of its interface, a user may be able to deduce greater knowledge about the internal state of the system than can be calculated from its interface-level observation of the system alone.

5   Reasoning about Multi-User Designs

The UTP theory of designs represents the space of terminating programs with precondition (assumption) P and postcondition (commitment) Q: [2]

$$P \vdash Q \ \triangleq \ ok \wedge P \Rightarrow ok' \wedge Q \tag{10}$$

The Boolean variables ok and ok' facilitate reasoning about termination: ok records that the program has started and ok' signifies that the program has terminated. Thus, if the program is started in an initial state that satisfies P, then the program is guaranteed to terminate in a final state satisfying Q.

We interpret a design as a system that starts in an initial state consisting of inputs from users and terminates in a final state that yields outputs to users. It is reasonable to expect that users can identify when a system has started and when it has terminated. Since system-level variables are not directly visible to users (Section 3.1), it is necessary to extend the alphabet of a view V by introducing new interface-level observational variables ok_V and ok'_V corresponding to ok and ok'. We require that V guarantees that $ok_V = ok$ and $ok'_V = ok'$. This requirement is encoded by the **OK** healthiness condition.

Definition 6 (OK and VHD). *A view $V(s, u)$ is **OK**-healthy if and only if $V = \mathbf{OK}(V)$ holds:*

$$\mathbf{OK}(V) \ \triangleq \ V \wedge ok_V = ok \wedge ok'_V = ok' \tag{11}$$

*We say a view is **VHD**-healthy if it is both **VH**-healthy and **OK**-healthy.*

Since designs are defined in terms of ok and ok', we generalise the definition of a design by substituting ok_V and ok'_V in place of ok and ok'. Definition 7 introduces a shorthand for interface-level projections of designs.

Definition 7 (Interface-level design). *Provided V denotes a view:*

$$P \vdash_V Q \triangleq ok_V \wedge P \Rightarrow ok'_V \wedge Q \tag{12}$$

The **P** predicate transformer can be applied to a **VHD**-healthy view V and a design to obtain an interface-level design that expresses the interface-level projection of the behaviour of the design.

Lemma 4 (P and designs). *Whenever V is **VHD**-healthy, then $\mathbf{P}(V, P \vdash Q)$ can always be written in the form of an interface-level design:*

$$\mathbf{P}(V, P \vdash Q) = (\forall s, s' \bullet V \Rightarrow P) \vdash_V \mathbf{P}(V, Q) \tag{13}$$

The precondition of $\mathbf{P}(V, P \vdash Q)$ is the weakest condition over interface-level observations that is sufficient to ensure that, whenever ϕ is an interface-level observation that satisfies that precondition, then *all* system-level observations compatible with ϕ satisfy P. Therefore, if a user's initial observation of $P \vdash Q$ (projected through V) satisfies the precondition of $\mathbf{P}(V, P \vdash Q)$, then the user is guaranteed that P is satisfied. It follows that if the precondition of $\mathbf{P}(V, P \vdash Q)$ is satisfied, then Q will hold upon the termination of $P \vdash Q$, as will the interface-level projection $\mathbf{P}(V, Q)$ of Q.

If no projection of the initial system-level observational variables through V provides sufficient information about the initial system-level observational variables to guarantee that P holds, then the precondition of $\mathbf{P}(V, P \vdash Q)$ collapses to **false** and so nothing is guaranteed about the final observation of $\mathbf{P}(V, P \vdash Q)$.

6   Worked Example: A Byte Register

We now consider the application of the theory developed in the previous sections to a simple multi-user system. The purpose of this example is to demonstrate how the specification and design of multi-user systems may be guided by calculating the interface-level observations of a system and identifying the information that users can deduce from these observations.

Our example focuses on a register capable of storing a single byte. We model the register's value by an integer variable x with domain $0..255$. The register also features a Boolean variable y that indicates numeric overflow when set.

Consider an operation that doubles the value stored in x, provided that the initial value of x lies in the range $0..127$ and the overflow bit is not set. We model this operation as a UTP design as follows:

$$DBL \triangleq x \in 0..127 \wedge y = 0 \vdash x' = 2x \wedge y' = 0$$

Suppose that two users can observe the register: the first user (with view H) can observe the values of the higher four bits of the value of x, and the second user (with view L) can observe the lower four bits of x. The overflow bit y is visible to both users. The views of these users are given by:

$$H \triangleq \mathbf{OK} \left(x_H = \left\lfloor \frac{x}{16} \right\rfloor \wedge x'_H = \left\lfloor \frac{x'}{16} \right\rfloor \wedge y_H = y \wedge y'_H = y' \right)$$

$$L \triangleq \mathbf{OK} \left(x_L = x \bmod 16 \wedge x'_L = x' \bmod 16 \wedge y_L = y \wedge y'_L = y' \right)$$

Effectively, the H view masks out the lower four bits of the register from the first user's observations, while the L view hides the higher four bits from the second user. Both of these views are **VHD**-healthy.

We now investigate the projections of DBL's behaviour through H and L. The calculation of $\mathbf{P}(H, DBL)$ is simplified by applying Lemma 4:

$$\mathbf{P}(H, DBL) = \begin{pmatrix} \forall\, x, y, x', y' \bullet H \Rightarrow x \in 0..127 \wedge y = 0 \\ \vdash_H \\ \exists\, x, y, x', y' \bullet H \wedge x' = 2x \wedge y' = 0 \end{pmatrix}$$

$$= x_H \in 0..7 \wedge y_H = 0 \vdash_H (x'_H = 2x_H \vee x'_H = 2x_H + 1) \wedge y'_H = 0$$

$\mathbf{P}(H, DBL)$ indicates that a user at H can only be certain that DBL's precondition is satisfied when $x_H \in 0..7$, since any other value of x_H corresponds to a value of x that violates the precondition of DBL.

Assuming the precondition of DBL holds, the value of the fifth most significant bit of x determines whether $x'_H = 2x_H$ or $x'_H = 2x_H + 1$. However, since this bit cannot be observed by a user at H, that user can only be certain of the value of x'_H once the operation is complete.

It is instructive to consider what can be observed of DBL through L:

$$\mathbf{P}(L, DBL) = \begin{pmatrix} \forall\, x, y, x', y' \bullet L \Rightarrow x \in 0..127 \wedge y = 0 \\ \vdash_L \\ \exists\, x, y, x', y' \bullet L \wedge x' = 2x \wedge y' = 0 \end{pmatrix}$$

$$= \mathbf{false} \vdash_L x'_L = 2x_L \bmod 16 \wedge y'_L = 0$$

$$= \mathbf{true}$$

Since an observation at L provides no information regarding the upper four bits of x, a user at L cannot determine in any circumstances whether the precondition of DBL is satisfied. Thus, from the perspective of L, nothing can be guaranteed about DBL's behaviour, as is reflected by the outcome of the calculation above.

Depending on the context in which the register is used, this limitation may be unacceptable. Hence, we relax the precondition of DBL to cover all values of x that can be stored by the register and, when $x \geq 128$, to assign an arbitrary value from the range $0..255$ to x' and set y' to 1:

$$DBL2 \triangleq x \in 0..255 \wedge y = 0 \vdash \begin{pmatrix} x' = 2x \wedge y' = 0 \\ \triangleleft\ x \in 0..127\ \triangleright \\ x' \in 0..255 \wedge y' = 1 \end{pmatrix}$$

Observe that $DBL \sqsubseteq DBL2$, because the postcondition of $DBL2$ reduces to the postcondition of DBL when the precondition of DBL is satisfied.

The interface-level observations of $DBL2$ through L are given by:

$$\mathbf{P}\,(L, DBL2) = x_L \in 0..15 \land y_L = 0 \vdash \left(\begin{array}{c} x'_L = (2x_L) \bmod 16 \land y'_L = 0 \\ \lhd\ x_L \in 0..7\ \rhd \\ x'_L \in 0..15 \land y'_L = 1 \end{array} \right)$$

After the $DBL2$ operation completes, the user at L can determine if the double operation was successful by checking that $y'_L = 0$.

One may now proceed to refine $DBL2$ to the implementation level. Of course, if one carries out data refinement on the variables of $DBL2$ (such as replacing x with eight Boolean variables to represent the bits of the register), then the corresponding data refinements must also be made to the H and L views.

7   Refinement of Multi-User Systems

$S \sqsubseteq T$ mandates that every system-level observation of T is a system-level observation of S. This condition is sufficient to ensure that a concrete design T satisfies all the functionality properties of its abstract predecessor S. However, this condition is sometimes too strong for stepwise developments of multi-user systems, since it forbids some classes of reasonable refinement steps that do not impair functionality. This point is illustrated by the following example.

Example 4. Consider an operation on the aforementioned register that doubles the lower four bits of x and the upper four bits of x in isolation:

$$INDBL2 \triangleq x \in 0..255 \land y = 0 \vdash \left(\begin{array}{c} x' \bmod 16 = (2x) \bmod 16 \\ \land \left(\begin{array}{c} \lfloor \frac{x'}{16} \rfloor = (2\lfloor \frac{x}{16} \rfloor) \land y' = 0 \\ \lhd\ x \in 0..127\ \rhd \\ x' \in 0..255 \land y' = 1 \end{array} \right) \end{array} \right)$$

Notice that $DBL2 \not\sqsubseteq INDBL2$, because when $x \in 0..127 \land y = 0$, $INDBL2$ always sets the fourth most significant bit of x' to 0 regardless of the value of the fifth most significant bit of x, unlike $DBL2$. However, the users at H and L cannot individually tell $INDBL2$ apart from $DBL2$, since each interface-level observation of $INDBL2$ matches an interface-level observation of $DBL2$.

The proposed transition from $DBL2$ to $INDBL2$ indicates that, when developing a multi-user system, it may be more appropriate (in some cases) to carry out refinement w.r.t. the interface-level observations of the system, rather than the system-level observations of the system as a whole.

7.1   Interface-Level Refinement

This section outlines some alternative notions of refinement that are defined in terms of the interface-level observations of systems, instead of system-level observations. These refinement relations are more flexible than the classical notion of refinement, because they allow particular refinement steps to introduce new behaviours into a system in a controlled manner, while preserving the correctness of the system from the perspective of its users.

First, we introduce an notion of refinement which we call *user refinement*. We say that T is a user refinement of S w.r.t. a view V if and only if every interface-level observation of T made through V corresponds to an observation of S made through V. Intuitively, user refinement allows new system-level observations to be added to a predicate, provided that no interface-level observations are introduced to the projection of the predicate through V.

Definition 8 (User refinement). *For a given view V, T is a user refinement of S — denoted by $S \sqsubseteq_V T$ — if and only if:*

$$S \sqsubseteq_V T \triangleq \mathbf{P}(V, S) \sqsubseteq \mathbf{P}(V, T) \tag{14}$$

It follows from Lemma 2 that $S \sqsubseteq T$ implies $S \sqsubseteq_V T$. Unlike $\sqsubseteq$, $\sqsubseteq_V$ is not a partial order in the general case, although it is always a pre-order.

7.2   Co-operating and Independent Refinement

Jacob [4,5] proposed two notions of refinement — known as *co-operating refinement* and *independent refinement* — intended for application in the development of multi-user systems.

Co-operating refinement allows users to exchange their observations of a system after its execution has terminated. Hence, the users may potentially reconstruct more information about the system behaviour than they could obtain from their individual observations alone.

Independent refinement assumes users cannot communicate with each other; instead, the only information that each user can obtain about the behaviour of a system is their own interface-level observation of the system.

We express co-operating and independent refinement in the UTP by extending the definition of user refinement to a set of disjoint views $\mathcal{W}$ (representing multiple users) in different ways.

Definition 9 (Co-operating and independent refinement). *Co-operating and independent refinement generalise $\sqsubseteq$ as follows:*

$$S \sqsubseteq_{\mathcal{W}}^{co} T \triangleq S \sqsubseteq_{\bigwedge \mathcal{W}} T \tag{15}$$

$$S \sqsubseteq_{\mathcal{W}}^{ind} T \triangleq \bigwedge_{V \in \mathcal{W}} S \sqsubseteq_V T \tag{16}$$

As with $\sqsubseteq_V$, the $\sqsubseteq_{\mathcal{W}}^{co}$ and $\sqsubseteq_{\mathcal{W}}^{ind}$ orderings are pre-orders but not partial orders [4]. When $\mathcal{W}$ contains only a single view V, the $\sqsubseteq_{\mathcal{W}}^{co}$ and $\sqsubseteq_{\mathcal{W}}^{ind}$ relations reduce to the definition of $\sqsubseteq_V$.

Theorem 2 (Ordering on refinement relations). *Standard refinement is a stronger ordering than co-operating refinement which, in turn, is a stronger ordering than independent refinement:*

$$S \sqsubseteq T \;\Rightarrow\; S \sqsubseteq_{\mathcal{W}}^{co} T \tag{17}$$

$$S \sqsubseteq_{\mathcal{W}}^{co} T \;\Rightarrow\; S \sqsubseteq_{\mathcal{W}}^{ind} T \tag{18}$$

As established by Theorem 2, co-operating and independent refinement are weaker than the conventional definition of refinement, because they allow non-determinism to be *added* to a specification, so long as no new interface-level observations of the specification are possible. However, these notions of refinement are strong enough to preserve the functionality inherent in a system's specification from the perspectives of the users of the system.

Example 5. Returning to Example 4, it is the case that $DBL2 \sqsubseteq_{\{H,L\}}^{ind} INDBL2$, since $DBL2 \sqsubseteq_H INDBL2$ and $DBL2 \sqsubseteq_L INDBL2$ both hold. This means that $INDBL2$ can safely substitute for $DBL2$, provided that the users at H and L are unable to communicate with each other. However, we do not have $DBL2 \sqsubseteq_{\{H,L\}}^{co} INDBL2$, because if the users at H and L combine their observations, they can identify behaviours of $INDBL2$ that are not behaviours of $DBL2$.

Relaxing the notion of refinement to co-operating or independent refinement provides an extra degree of flexibility when making design choices for a system. In particular, $INDBL2$ allows the users at H and L to access separate registers without needing to keep those registers synchronised, which means that an implementation of $INDBL2$ may provide each user with their own local instance of the register. More generally, these refinement relations offer the opportunity to distribute a system's workload across multiple processors, provided the refined system produces the same results to its users.

A spectrum of refinement relations may be constructed from the $\sqsubseteq^{co}$ relation. A set of views $\mathcal{W}$ may be partitioned into subsets $\mathcal{W}_1, \ldots, \mathcal{W}_n$ to represent groups of users, whereby users associated with views in the same group may co-operate but users associated with views in different groups are isolated from each other. Thus, a multi-user refinement relation which accounts for the boundaries separating these users is given by:

$$S \sqsubseteq_{\mathcal{W}}^{grp} T \;\triangleq\; S \sqsubseteq_{\mathcal{W}_1}^{co} T \wedge \ldots \wedge S \sqsubseteq_{\mathcal{W}_n}^{co} T \tag{19}$$

The notion of co-operating refinement may also be applicable in the development of distributed systems composed of multiple interacting components. For instance, it may be desirable to replace one component Z of the system with another component Z'. This replacement can be carried out with the assurance that other components of the system are not affected by the change, if it can be shown that $Z \sqsubseteq_{\mathcal{W}}^{co} Z'$ holds, where $\mathcal{W}$ is the set of views representing the channels through which the other components interact with Z. The replacement is justified because these other components cannot distinguish Z' from Z by their interactions with Z', even if they share information about those interactions with each other.

7.3   Reasoning about Information Flow

An important topic in theoretical studies of computer security is to measure the information that a low-level (unprivileged) user of a system can learn about the activities of other high-level users by observing the system. If the high-level interactions are associated with sensitive or intrinsically valuable data, then it is imperative that the low-level user is unable to deduce confidential information about this data by monitoring the system's execution [6].

In Section 4.3, we described how one user can deduce information about the observations of another user. We are now able to define an ordering for comparing systems according to the amount of information about high-level observations that can "flow" to a low-level user.

Definition 10 (Security ordering). *Let H and L denote the (disjoint) views of a high-level user and a low-level user respectively. Then, a system T provides no more information flow from H to L than a system S if and only if:*

$$S \preceq_L^H T \triangleq S \sqsubseteq_L T \wedge (\mathbf{P}(L \wedge H, T) \sqsubseteq \mathbf{P}(L \wedge H, S) \wedge \mathbf{P}(L, T)) \qquad (20)$$

The $\preceq_L^H$ relation encodes a *security ordering* on predicates [5,7]. The first condition ensures that, from the perspective of a low-level user at L, every observation of T is an observation of S. The second condition requires that, for every observation ϕ of T viewed through L, the set of H observations of S that are compatible with ϕ is a subset of the H observations of T compatible with ϕ. These conditions together guarantee that the low-level user can deduce no more information about the activities at H from an observation of T as it can from the equivalent observation of S. Hence, if $S \preceq_L^H T$ holds, then we say that T provides no more information flow about activities at H to the low-level user as does S. (Of course, this assertion applies only so far as the semantic model of S and T, as it excludes from consideration factors such as the probability distribution or the timing characteristics of system behaviours.)

8   Related Work

Our approach for reasoning about multi-user systems in the UTP opens up several new avenues of investigation. We briefly review two areas of research in which we believe our approach is particularly relevant.

Information Flow Security. A multitude of techniques for measuring and restricting information flow within systems — to guarantee the secrecy of confidential data — have been defined within frameworks based on trace semantics [5,8,9,10]. In these frameworks, a user's observation is given by applying a projection function to the system trace. Our notion of a view is a generalisation of these projection functions, because a view may cover other observational variables besides the trace variables, such as the variables recording the refusal set associated with a trace (when working in the UTP theory of reactive designs.)

Refining a specification may introduce new paths of information flow into the specification, thus enabling a low-level user to deduce more detailed information about the activities of a high-level user and potentially violating security requirements [7]. Various techniques have been proposed to resolve this problem, such as ensuring that the system appears deterministic from the low-level user's viewpoint [11] or strengthening the definition of refinement to preserve information flow security properties [12]. The refinement relation obtained by intersecting the $\sqsubseteq$ and $\preceq$ orderings is an example of the latter approach, but it may be too strong a refinement relation for practical use. It is perhaps more appropriate to employ a weaker notion of refinement (such as co-operating or independent refinement) together with the $\preceq$ ordering in the development of multi-user systems where information security is a priority.

Distributed Testing. When testing distributed systems, it is customary to place an isolated tester (user) at each interface of the system. For the results of test runs to be useful, it should be possible to combine the observations of multiple testers in order to reconstruct the exact trace of a system. However, if testers are physically separated and no global clock is present, then it may be difficult (or impossible) to rule out alternative behaviours of the system.

Recent work has identified conditions under which tests of distributed systems (modelled as finite state machines) can be designed and controlled to ensure that the exact system behaviour can always be identified, without requiring testers to synchronise their actions externally of the system under test [13,14]. This problem can be stated using our terminology as follows: for every set of interface-level observations $\{\phi_1, \ldots, \phi_n\}$ of a system S projected through views $V_1, \ldots V_n$, there must exist a unique system-level observation Φ of S such that $\mathbf{P}(V_i, \Phi) = \phi_i$ for each $i \in 1..n$.

9   Conclusions

We have presented an approach for studying multi-user systems in the UTP. We have described how the observational abilities of users can be modelled as UTP predicates (views) and have identified predicate transformers for calculating the projection of a system's behaviour to its users. The novelty of our approach is that, by codifying these concepts in the UTP explicitly, we obtain a semantically appealing method for reasoning about specifications of multi-user systems across the spectrum of UTP theories.

We have also investigated some alternative notions of refinement that are based on what users can deduce about the system's behaviour from their observations. These refinement relations afford the implementer of a system greater flexibility in making particular design decisions that would be prohibited by classical refinement.

The emphasis of this paper is on generality. Our approach is sufficiently abstract to be used in combination with a variety of UTP theories; for instance, we have demonstrated its application within the theory of designs in Section 5.

Moreover, our definitions of co-operating and independent refinement are not tied to the semantics of particular UTP theories. Indeed, these refinement relations may potentially be applied in practice to the stepwise development of multi-user systems, wherever the observational abilities of users are known.

A drawback of our approach is that applying the **P** and **R** predicate transformers can be tedious and error-prone if carried out manually, because a view may define a complex relation between interface-level and system-level observational variables. With the emergence of tool support for the UTP, there is potential for overcoming this difficulty by mechanising our approach. This would enable some of the techniques described in this paper — such as reasoning about information flow between users, or verifying co-operating or independent refinements over systems — to be carried out with machine assistance.

The focus of our current research is to integrate our approach with the UTP semantics of the *Circus* formalism [15], in order to reason about the observational abilities of users of systems modelled in *Circus*. We envisage the work presented in this paper will provide the foundations for a comprehensive platform for analysing *Circus* systems from the perspective of their users.

Acknowledgements

Michael Banks is supported by a UK Engineering and Physical Sciences Research Council DTA studentship.

We are grateful to Ana Cavalcanti, Frank Zeyda and the anonymous referees for offering insightful comments on this paper, and to Chris Poskitt for proofreading. We also thank Jim Woodcock and the members of the Programming Languages and Systems research group at York for their feedback on an seminar talk on the ideas described in this paper, which helped us to clarify our ideas and to simplify the presentation of technical details.

References

1. Roscoe, A.W.: The Theory and Practice of Concurrency. Prentice Hall PTR, Upper Saddle River (1997)
2. Hoare, C.A.R., He, J.: Unifying Theories of Programming. Prentice Hall International Series in Computer Science. Prentice Hall Inc., Englewood Cliffs (1998)
3. Cousot, P., Cousot, R.: Abstract interpretation: a unified lattice model for static analysis of programs by construction or approximation of fixpoints. In: POPL 1977: Proceedings of the 4th ACM SIGACT-SIGPLAN Symposium on Principles of Programming Languages, pp. 238–252. ACM, New York (1977)
4. Jacob, J.L.: Refinement of shared systems. In: McDermid, J.A. (ed.) The Theory and Practice of Refinement: Approaches to the Development of Large-Scale Software Systems, pp. 27–36. Butterworths, London (1989)
5. Jacob, J.L.: Basic theorems about security. Journal of Computer Security 1(4), 385–411 (1992)
6. Denning, D.E.: Cryptography and Data Security. Addison-Wesley Longman Publishing Company, Inc., Boston (1982)

7. Jacob, J.L.: On the derivation of secure components. In: Proceedings of the 1989 IEEE Symposium on Security and Privacy, pp. 242–247. IEEE Computer Society, Los Alamitos (1989)
8. McLean, J.: A general theory of composition for trace sets closed under selective interleaving functions. In: Proceedings of the 1994 IEEE Symposium on Security and Privacy, pp. 79–93 (1994)
9. Mantel, H.: A Uniform Framework for the Formal Specification and Verification of Information Flow Security. PhD thesis, Universität Saarbrücken (July 2003)
10. Seehusen, F., Stølen, K.: Information flow security, abstraction and composition. IET Information Security 3(1), 9–33 (2009)
11. Roscoe, A.W., Woodcock, J.C.P., Wulf, L.: Non-interference through determinism. In: Gollmann, D. (ed.) ESORICS 1994. LNCS, vol. 875, pp. 33–53. Springer, Heidelberg (1994)
12. Morgan, C.: The shadow knows: Refinement and security in sequential programs. Science of Computer Programming 74(8), 629–653 (2009)
13. Chen, J., Hierons, R.M., Ural, H.: Conditions for resolving observability problems in distributed testing. In: de Frutos-Escrig, D., Núñez, M. (eds.) FORTE 2004. LNCS, vol. 3235, pp. 229–242. Springer, Heidelberg (2004)
14. Chen, J., Hierons, R.M., Ural, H.: Overcoming observability problems in distributed test architectures. Information Processing Letters 98(5), 177–182 (2006)
15. Oliveira, M., Cavalcanti, A., Woodcock, J.: A UTP semantics for Circus. Formal Aspects of Computing 21(1), 3–32 (2009)

A   Proofs

Lemma 1

Proof. We assume that V_1 and V_2 are **VH**-healthy individually. To prove that $V_1 \wedge V_2$ is **VH**-healthy, it is sufficient to show that $V_1 \wedge V_2$ is **VH1**-healthy and **VH2**-healthy separately.

$$\textbf{VH1}(V_1) \wedge \textbf{VH1}(V_2)$$
$$\Leftrightarrow \quad \langle \text{ definition of } \textbf{VH1} \rangle$$
$$(\forall s, s' \bullet \exists u_1, u_1' \bullet V_1) \wedge (\forall s, s' \bullet \exists u_2, u_2' \bullet V_2)$$
$$\Leftrightarrow \quad \langle \text{ predicate calculus } \rangle$$
$$\forall s, s' \bullet (\exists u_1, u_1' \bullet V_1) \wedge (\exists u_2, u_2' \bullet V_2)$$
$$\Leftrightarrow \quad \langle \text{ assumption: } V_1 \text{ and } V_2 \text{ are disjoint } \rangle$$
$$\forall s, s' \bullet \exists u_1, u_1', u_2, u_2' \bullet V_1 \wedge V_2$$
$$\Leftrightarrow \quad \langle \text{ definition of } \textbf{VH1} \rangle$$
$$\textbf{VH1}(V_1 \wedge V_2)$$

The proof that $V_1 \wedge V_2$ is **VH2**-healthy follows similarly.   □

Lemma 2

$$S \sqsubseteq T \Rightarrow \mathbf{P}(V, S) \sqsubseteq \mathbf{P}(V, T)$$

Proof

> $S \sqsubseteq T$
>
> $\Leftrightarrow$ ⟨ definition of $\sqsubseteq$ ⟩
>
> $[\forall s, s' \bullet T \Rightarrow S]$
>
> $\Rightarrow$ ⟨ predicate calculus ⟩
>
> $[\forall s, s' \bullet (V \wedge T) \Rightarrow (V \wedge S)]$
>
> $\Rightarrow$ ⟨ predicate calculus ⟩
>
> $[(\exists s, s' \bullet V \wedge T) \Rightarrow (\forall s, s' \bullet V \wedge S)]$
>
> $\Rightarrow$ ⟨ predicate calculus ⟩
>
> $[(\exists s, s' \bullet V \wedge T) \Rightarrow (\exists s, s' \bullet V \wedge S)]$
>
> $\Leftrightarrow$ ⟨ definition of $\mathbf{P}$ ⟩
>
> $[\mathbf{P}(V, T) \Rightarrow \mathbf{P}(V, S)]$
>
> $\Leftrightarrow$ ⟨ definition of $\sqsubseteq$ ⟩
>
> $\mathbf{P}(V, S) \sqsubseteq \mathbf{P}(V, T)$ $\square$

Lemma 3

$$\mathbf{P}\left(\left(\bigwedge_{i \in 1..n} V_i\right), S\right) \Rightarrow \bigwedge_{i \in 1..n} \mathbf{P}(V_i, S)$$

Proof

> $\mathbf{P}\left(\left(\bigwedge_{i \in 1..n} V_i\right), S\right)$
>
> $\Leftrightarrow$ ⟨ definition of $\mathbf{P}$ ⟩
>
> $\exists s, s' \bullet \left(\bigwedge_{i \in 1..n} V_i\right) \wedge S$
>
> $\Rightarrow$ ⟨ predicate calculus ⟩
>
> $\bigwedge_{i \in 1..n} \exists s, s' \bullet V_i \wedge S$
>
> $\Leftrightarrow$ ⟨ definition of $\mathbf{P}$ ⟩
>
> $\bigwedge_{i \in 1..n} \mathbf{P}(V_i, S)$ $\square$

Theorem 1

$$U \sqsubseteq \mathbf{P}(V, S) \Leftrightarrow \mathbf{R}(V, U) \sqsubseteq S$$

Proof

> $U \sqsubseteq \mathbf{P}(V, S)$
>
> $\Leftrightarrow$ ⟨ definition of $\sqsubseteq$ and $\mathbf{P}$ ⟩
>
> $[(\exists s, s' \bullet V \wedge S) \Rightarrow U]$

$\Leftrightarrow$ $\langle$ predicate calculus $\rangle$

$[\,(\forall\, s, s' \bullet \neg\, V \vee \neg\, S) \vee U\,]$

$\Leftrightarrow$ $\langle$ s, s' not free in U and s, s' covered by universal closure $\rangle$

$[\,\neg\, V \vee \neg\, S \vee U\,]$

$\Leftrightarrow$ $\langle$ u, u' not free in S and u, u' covered by universal closure $\rangle$

$[\,\neg\, S \vee (\forall\, u, u' \bullet \neg\, V \vee U)\,]$

$\Leftrightarrow$ $\langle$ predicate calculus $\rangle$

$[\, S \Rightarrow (\forall\, u, u' \bullet V \Rightarrow U)\,]$

$\Leftrightarrow$ $\langle$ definition of $\sqsubseteq$ and $\mathbf{R}$ $\rangle$

$\mathbf{R}\,(V, U) \sqsubseteq S$ $\square$

Lemma 4

$\mathbf{P}\,(V, P \vdash Q) = (\forall\, s, s' \bullet V \Rightarrow P) \vdash_V \mathbf{P}\,(V, Q)$

Proof

$\mathbf{P}\,(V, P \vdash Q)$

$\Leftrightarrow$ $\langle$ definition of $\mathbf{P}$ and $\vdash$ $\rangle$

$\exists\, s, s' \bullet V \wedge (ok \wedge P \Rightarrow ok' \wedge Q)$

$\Leftrightarrow$ $\langle$ unfold implication $\rangle$

$\exists\, s, s' \bullet V \wedge (\neg\, ok \vee \neg\, P \vee (ok' \wedge Q))$

$\Leftrightarrow$ $\langle$ distributivity, twice $\rangle$

$(\exists\, s, s' \bullet V \wedge (\neg\, ok \vee \neg\, P)) \vee (\exists\, s, s' \bullet ok' \wedge V \wedge Q)$

$\Leftrightarrow$ $\langle$ V is $\mathbf{VHD}$-healthy $\rangle$

$(\neg\, ok_V \vee \exists\, s, s' \bullet V \wedge \neg\, P) \vee (ok'_V \wedge \exists\, s, s' \bullet V \wedge Q)$

$\Leftrightarrow$ $\langle$ de Morgan, twice $\rangle$

$\neg\, (ok_V \wedge \forall\, s, s' \bullet \neg\, (V \wedge \neg\, P)) \vee (ok'_V \wedge \exists\, s, s' \bullet V \wedge Q)$

$\Leftrightarrow$ $\langle$ predicate calculus $\rangle$

$(ok_V \wedge (\forall\, s, s' \bullet V \Rightarrow P)) \Rightarrow (ok'_V \wedge \exists\, s, s' \bullet V \wedge Q)$

$\Leftrightarrow$ $\langle$ definition of $\mathbf{P}$ and $\vdash_V$ $\rangle$

$(\forall\, s, s' \bullet V \Rightarrow P) \vdash_V \mathbf{P}\,(V, Q)$ $\square$

Theorem 2

Proof. Equation 17 is a consequence of Lemma 2 and Definition 8. Equation 18 follows from Lemma 3. $\square$

Unifying Theories of Confidentiality

Michael J. Banks and Jeremy L. Jacob

Department of Computer Science, University of York, UK
{Michael.Banks,Jeremy.Jacob}@cs.york.ac.uk

Abstract. This paper presents a framework for reasoning about the security of confidential data within software systems. A novelty is that we
use Hoare and He's *Unifying Theories of Programming* (UTP) to do so
and derive advantage from this choice. We identify how information flow
between users can be modelled in the UTP and devise conditions for verifying that system designs may not leak secret information to untrusted
users. We also investigate how these conditions can be combined with
existing notions of refinement to produce refinement relations suitable
for deriving secure implementations of systems.

Keywords: UTP, computer security, information flow, confidentiality
properties, confidentiality-preserving refinement, MAKS.

1 Introduction

When designing a computer system that stores or manipulates confidential data,
it is vital to define a security policy for this data and to obtain reliable assurances
that the system never discloses this data to untrusted users in violation of the
security policy. In software engineering, a security policy is usually implemented
by combining access control mechanisms with user authentication schemes and
cryptographic measures [1]. However, access control does not restrict how data
can be manipulated once it has been released to users, so it cannot prevent
confidential data from propagating indirectly to low-level users [2].

A radically different approach to computer security is to specify constraints
on the *information flow* between a system and its users. We say that information
flows from a high-level user ($\mathcal{H}$) to a low-level user ($\mathcal{L}$) whenever $\mathcal{L}$'s observations
of a system are perturbed by the activities performed by $\mathcal{H}$. To ensure that a
system does not leak sensitive or valuable data to $\mathcal{L}$, it is necessary to design
the system with built-in restrictions on information flow [1]. These constraints
are known as *confidentiality properties*, since they codify an upper limit on the
flow of information about $\mathcal{H}$ activities classed as confidential to $\mathcal{L}$. Confidentiality properties specify *what* information must not be disclosed to $\mathcal{L}$, but unlike
models of access control, they allow the designers of a system to decide *how* that
information should be protected.

The confidentiality property known as *noninterference* [3] mandates that $\mathcal{H}$'s
actions must have no effect on $\mathcal{L}$'s observations of the system; effectively, $\mathcal{L}$
cannot determine whether or not $\mathcal{H}$ has interacted with the system at all. It

S. Qin (Ed.): UTP 2010, LNCS 6445, pp. 120–136, 2010.

follows that a system satisfying noninterference cannot disclose confidential information to $\mathcal{L}$. However, noninterference is too strong a requirement for many kinds of software products, because it is often necessary for $\mathcal{H}$ to communicate some kinds of data to $\mathcal{L}$. We contend that software developers should be able to specify custom confidentiality properties that are tailored to the intricacies of the system domain, rather than choosing from a limited range of ready-made noninterference-like confidentiality properties.

The central topic of this paper is a novel encoding of confidentiality properties in Hoare and He's Unifying Theories of Programming (UTP) [4]. Our encoding is inspired by Mantel's *Modular Assembly Kit for Security Properties* (MAKS) [5,6]. The MAKS is designed for expressing a wide range of confidentiality properties in the security literature in a uniform trace-based style. We generalise the foundations of the MAKS to the UTP, which allows us to define a class of confidentiality properties in a predicate style across the spectrum of existing UTP theories. Moreover, these predicates can be applied to verify that a software specification (written in a language with a UTP semantics) satisfies a given confidentiality property by means of formal proof.

This paper is structured as follows. We provide an overview of the UTP in Section 2. In Section 3, we describe the foundations of our approach for modelling the observations of users in the UTP. This approach provides the basis of our encoding of confidentiality properties in the UTP, which we present in Section 4. We investigate how refinement can be extended to accommodate confidentiality properties in Section 5. We examine the relationship between our work and existing techniques for applying confidentiality properties in rigorous software developments in Section 6 and summarise our work in Section 7.

2   Unifying Theories of Programming

The UTP provides an abstract framework for modelling the denotational semantics of a wide range of programming paradigms and the features of programming languages [4]. The UTP features a powerful standalone notation for specifying the behaviour of systems and reasoning about program correctness.

The mathematical foundation of the UTP is the alphabetised relational calculus. In the UTP, specifications and program constructs alike are expressed as predicates over an alphabet (a set) of observational variables. The observational variables in a predicate record all of the information about a program's execution that is visible when an observation of the program is made. These variables are grouped into two classes: by convention, undashed variables $(x, y, \ldots)$ record the initial observation of the program state taken before execution commences, while dashed variables $(x', y', \ldots)$ record an intermediate observation of the program state taken during (or after) the program's execution [4].

Example 1 gives a UTP specification of a simple system that we use later.

Example 1. Consider a simple guessing game played by two users Laurel ($\mathcal{L}$) and Hardy ($\mathcal{H}$). $\mathcal{H}$ chooses a number $n \in 0..9$, which is concealed from $\mathcal{L}$. $\mathcal{L}$ makes a guess g of the value of n. $\mathcal{L}$ is informed whether its guess was correct or greater or smaller than n by setting t to 0, a positive value or a negative value respectively.

We model all acceptable runs of the game by defining a UTP predicate G_0:

$$G_0 \triangleq n \in 0..9 \land (g = n \Rightarrow t = 0) \land (g > n \Rightarrow t > 0) \land (g < n \Rightarrow t < 0) \quad (1)$$

While G_0 represents the game as seen by the environment as a whole, we expect that $\mathcal{L}$ is unable to observe the value of n. However, this expectation is not recorded in G_0. If we wish to reason about $\mathcal{L}$'s observations of G_0, we need to define a mapping from G_0's behaviours to the aspects of G_0 visible to $\mathcal{L}$.

3   Modelling User Observations

This section outlines a UTP approach for modelling the observational abilities of users. We cover this approach in greater depth elsewhere [7]; here, we present only the details that are essential for studying information flow in the UTP.

Observations. An observation of a UTP predicate S is any predicate that maps each variable in S's alphabet to a single value, such that S is satisfied by that mapping. (For example, $n = 3 \land g = 7 \land t = 42$ is a valid observation of G_0.)

Given a predicate S representing a system, we distinguish between two classes of observations of S. A *system-level* observation of S describes the behaviour of S in its entirety. The list of undashed variables $(s_1, \ldots, s_i)$ of a system-level observation is denoted by s and the corresponding list of dashed variables by s'. Whenever Φ is a system-level observation of S, we have:

$$(\exists_1 s, s' \bullet \Phi) \land [\Phi \Rightarrow S] \quad (2)$$

The first condition requires that Φ is satisfied by exactly one valuation of the system-level variables in S's alphabet. The second condition states that Φ is an actual observation of S.

It is often reasonable to expect that individual users cannot observe all of a system's behaviour; rather, each user is provided with an interface to the system, through which it can observe some elements of the system's behaviour. We say that a user's observation of a system is an *interface-level* observation. To record interface-level observations, we introduce separate lists of interface-level observational variables $u = (u_1, \ldots, u_j)$ and $u' = (u'_1, \ldots, u'_j)$, which must be disjoint from s and s'.

Views. A view is a predicate that formalises a user's interface to a system by defining a total relation from system-level observations to interface-level observations[1]. The interface-level observational variables in a view's alphabet are decorated with the view's identifier: for example, x_V refers to an interface-level variable associated with view V, whereas x refers to a system-level variable.

---

[1] The theory presented in Section 4 is unchanged if views are required to be functional. However, by relaxing this requirement, we allow for the possibility that a user's interface gives a non-deterministic (noisy) representation of a system's behaviour.

Given a system-level observation Φ and a view V, the set of interface-level observations corresponding to Φ is given by calculating the image of Φ as projected through V. A view should not restrict the domains of the system-level observational variables in any way; that is, predicates such as $x < y$, $x' = 0$ and **false** are not views. Moreover, we exclude "time-travelling" predicates such as $x_V = x'$ (which demands a user with view V can observe the value of x' *before* it is computed) from the space of views. (These constraints on views may be formalised in the UTP as healthiness conditions [7].)

Example 2. Returning to Example 1, we may expect that $\mathcal{H}$ can observe the values of all variables in G_0's alphabet, but the value of n is hidden from $\mathcal{L}$. The observational abilities of $\mathcal{L}$ and $\mathcal{H}$ are modelled by the following views:

$$L \triangleq g_L = g \wedge t_L = t \tag{3}$$

$$H \triangleq g_H = g \wedge n_H = n \wedge t_H = t \tag{4}$$

The view H gives $\mathcal{H}$ total information about the state of G_0. The view L allows $\mathcal{L}$ to observe its own guess and the outcome of that guess, but it does not directly reveal the value of n to $\mathcal{L}$.

We insist that views associated with different users are *interface-disjoint*; that is to say, they share no interface-level observational variables.

Calculating Interface-Level Predicates. Given a system-level predicate S and a view V, we can derive a predicate that encodes the space of all interface-level observations that can be made of S when viewed through V. We define a predicate transformer **P** (for "project") to calculate this interface-level predicate:

$$\mathbf{P}(V, S) \triangleq \exists s, s' \bullet V \wedge S \tag{5}$$

The predicate $\mathbf{P}(V, S)$ is the image of S as projected through V. Hence, $\mathbf{P}(V, S)$ is satisfied by exactly those interface-level observations that can be made by monitoring the behaviour of S through V.

Given two interface-disjoint views $V_1(s_1, u_1)$ and $V_2(s_2, u_2)$ of the same system (i.e. $s_1 = s_2$), the view $V_1 \wedge V_2$ represents the combination of the interfaces corresponding to V_1 and V_2. Hence, $\mathbf{P}(V_1 \wedge V_2, S)$ is a predicate with alphabet $u_1 \cup u_2$ describing the relation between interface-level observations of S as made through V_1 and V_2.

Example 3. Applying $\mathbf{P}(L \wedge H)$ to G_0 yields the predicate:

$$\mathbf{P}(L \wedge H, G_0) = \exists g, n, t \bullet \left(\begin{array}{c} g_L = g \wedge t_L = t \\ \wedge\, g_H = g \wedge n_H = n \wedge t_H = t \end{array} \right) \wedge G_0$$

$$= \left(\begin{array}{l} n_H \in 0..9 \wedge g_L = g_H \wedge t_L = t_H \\ \wedge\, (g_H = n_H \Rightarrow t_L = 0) \\ \wedge\, (g_H > n_H \Rightarrow t_L > 0) \wedge (g_H < n_H \Rightarrow t_L < 0) \end{array} \right) \tag{6}$$

This predicate represents all compatible $\mathcal{H}$- and $\mathcal{L}$-observations of G_0.

4   Encoding Confidentiality Properties

When designing a system S, we may wish to prevent $\mathcal{L}$ from acquiring information about confidential features of $\mathcal{H}$'s interactions with S. Hence, our goals are to specify which aspects of $\mathcal{H}$'s observations of S are classed as confidential and to verify that $\mathcal{L}$ cannot use its observations of S to deduce information about those aspects.

In the worst case, $\mathcal{L}$ may possess complete knowledge of the implementation of S and the structure of its own view and that of $\mathcal{H}$. Hence, for each observation ϕ that $\mathcal{L}$ can make of S, $\mathcal{L}$ can deduce the set of $\mathcal{H}$ observations consistent with ϕ. The predicate that encodes this subset of $\mathcal{H}$ observations is given by:

$$\Omega_L^H (S, \phi) \triangleq \exists\, u_L, u_L' \bullet \mathbf{P} (L \wedge H, S) \wedge \phi \qquad (7)$$

(Quantifying over u_L and u_L' hides $\mathcal{L}$'s observational variables, leaving a predicate over $\mathcal{H}$'s observational variables.) From $\mathcal{L}$'s perspective, the $\mathcal{H}$-observations encoded by $\Omega_L^H (S, \phi)$ are *indistinguishable*; that is, $\mathcal{L}$ is unable to identify which of those observations corresponds to $\mathcal{H}$'s actual observation of S.

For S to be considered secure, $\mathcal{L}$ must not be able to deduce confidential information about $\mathcal{H}$ for any observation of S that it can make. Following the MAKS approach [5,6], we encode this requirement in terms of two parameters:

- The *restriction* R is a predicate over $\mathcal{H}$'s observational variables (u_H, u_H') that represents the space of $\mathcal{H}$ observations featuring confidential activities. A $\mathcal{H}$ observation is classed as confidential if and only if it features in R.
- The *closure requirement* Q is a predicate that relates confidential $\mathcal{H}$ observations (in R) to alternative $\mathcal{H}$ observations that are not classed as confidential. Whenever Q relates a confidential activity ψ to a non-confidential activity $\widetilde{\psi}$ such that ψ and $\widetilde{\psi}$ are indistinguishable to $\mathcal{L}$, we say that $\widetilde{\psi}$ represents a *cover story* for ψ. The presence of $\widetilde{\psi}$ in a system ensures that if $\mathcal{H}$ performs ψ, then $\mathcal{L}$ is unable to deduce whether ψ (rather than $\widetilde{\psi}$) has occurred.

The cover stories in Q are encoded over a renaming $(\widetilde{u_H}, \widetilde{u_H'})$ of the variables in u_H and u_H', in order to distinguish between confidential $\mathcal{H}$ activities and non-confidential cover stories. We assume that the domain and co-domain of the relation encoded by Q are disjoint, so that no cover story observations are themselves classed as confidential.

We are now ready to present a formal definition of the space of properties that we call confidentiality properties.

Definition 1 (Confidentiality property). *A confidentiality property is a tuple of the form* $\pi = \langle H, L, R, Q \rangle$, *where H and L denote the views of $\mathcal{H}$ and $\mathcal{L}$, R is a restriction and Q a closure requirement over H.*

We do not claim that all confidentiality properties described in the literature can be expressed as a $\langle H, L, R, Q \rangle$ tuple (or a combination of such tuples). Nevertheless, Mantel has demonstrated that many confidentiality properties can indeed be encoded as combinations of pairs of restrictions and closure requirements, assuming a trace-based semantic model for observations [5,6].

Of course, the purchaser of a system may wish to specify particular confidentiality requirements that the system implementation must satisfy. These requirements may be encoded by defining a custom confidentiality property, as we illustrate in the following example.

Example 4. Suppose that the operator of the system G_0 (described in Example 1) insists that $\mathcal{L}$ cannot identify the exact value of n if it guesses incorrectly. We define a confidentiality property $\pi_G = \langle H, L, R_G, Q_G \rangle$ to express this requirement, where R_G and Q_G are as follows:

$$R_G \triangleq g_H \neq n_H \tag{8}$$

$$Q_G \triangleq \widetilde{g_H} = g_H \wedge \widetilde{n_H} \neq n_H \wedge \widetilde{t_H} = t_H \tag{9}$$

R_G indicates the confidentiality property applies only to those system-level observations in G_0 where $\mathcal{L}$'s guess is incorrect. Q_G mandates that, for each such observation, there exists another observation in G_0 with a different value of n but the same values for g and t. Hence, Q_G requires that, when R_G is fulfilled, information giving the exact value of n does not flow to $\mathcal{L}$.

A confidentiality property can be strengthened by weakening R (i.e. making more $\mathcal{H}$ activities confidential) or by strengthening Q (i.e. removing acceptable cover stories). The weakest confidentiality property $\perp$ is obtained when $R = \mathbf{false}$ (i.e. no $\mathcal{H}$ activities are confidential). Likewise, the strongest confidentiality property $\top$ arises when $R = \mathbf{true}$ and $Q = \mathbf{false}$.

The predicate that relates $\mathcal{H}$ observations of S that are classed as confidential to $\mathcal{L}$ observations of S is given by:

$$\mathbf{P}\,(L \wedge H, S) \wedge R \tag{10}$$

Let ϕ denote a $\mathcal{L}$ observation and ψ denote a confidential $\mathcal{H}$ observation, where ϕ and ψ together satisfy Equation 10. To ensure that $\mathcal{L}$ cannot deduce that ψ has occurred with certainty, Q must relate ψ to a cover story $\widetilde{\psi}$ such that $\widetilde{\psi}$ is a valid $\mathcal{H}$ observation of S consistent with ϕ. Formally:

$$\phi \wedge \psi \Rightarrow \exists\, \widetilde{u_H}, \widetilde{u'_H} \bullet \mathbf{P}\left(L \wedge \widetilde{H}, S\right) \wedge Q \tag{11}$$

$\widetilde{H}$ denotes the view H where each variable in u_H and u'_H is renamed to its counterpart in $\widetilde{u_H}$ and $\widetilde{u'_H}$. Following Mantel [5,6], we combine Equation 10 and Equation 11 to obtain a "schema" for confidentiality properties in the UTP, which we present in Definition 2.

Definition 2 (Confidentiality property schema). *We say a system S satisfies a confidentiality property* $\pi = \langle H, L, R, Q \rangle$ *if and only if* $\mathbf{C}(\pi, S)$ *holds:*

$$\mathbf{C}(\pi, S) \triangleq \left[\mathbf{P}\,(L \wedge H, S) \wedge R \Rightarrow \left(\exists\, \widetilde{u_H}, \widetilde{u'_H} \bullet \mathbf{P}\left(L \wedge \widetilde{H}, S\right) \wedge Q \right) \right] \tag{12}$$

Hence, a system satisfies a confidentiality property if and only if the system permits only those information flows from $\mathcal{H}$ to $\mathcal{L}$ which are acceptable to the property. It follows from Definition 2 that the weakest property $\bot$ is satisfied by all systems, but that no implementable system specification can satisfy $\top$.

Example 5. We can determine whether G_0 satisfies π_G by calculating the constituent predicates of **C** corresponding to R_G and Q_G:

$$
\mathbf{P}\left(L \wedge H, G_0\right) \wedge R_G = \left(
\begin{array}{l}
n_H \in 0..9 \wedge g_L = g_H \wedge t_L = t_H \\
\wedge\ g_H \neq n_H \wedge (g_H > n_H \Rightarrow t_L > 0) \\
\wedge\ (g_H < n_H \Rightarrow t_L < 0)
\end{array}
\right) \tag{13}
$$

$$
\begin{array}{l}
\exists \widetilde{u_H}, \widetilde{u'_H} \bullet \\
\mathbf{P}\left(L \wedge \widetilde{H}, G_0\right) \wedge Q_G
\end{array}
=
\left(
\begin{array}{l}
g_L = g_H \wedge t_L = t_H \\
\wedge\ \exists \widetilde{n_H} \bullet
\left(
\begin{array}{l}
\widetilde{n_H} \in 0..9 \wedge \widetilde{n_H} \neq n_H \\
\wedge\ (g_H = \widetilde{n_H} \Rightarrow t_L = 0) \\
\wedge\ (g_H > \widetilde{n_H} \Rightarrow t_L > 0) \\
\wedge\ (g_H < \widetilde{n_H} \Rightarrow t_L < 0)
\end{array}
\right)
\end{array}
\right) \tag{14}
$$

When $g_L = g_H = 1 \wedge n_H = 0 \wedge t_H = t_L \wedge t_H > 0$, Equation 13 is satisfied but Equation 14 is not. In this scenario, $\mathcal{L}$ observes (guesses) $g_L = 1$ and learns from t_L that $g_L > n$. Since $n_H \in 0..9$, $\mathcal{L}$ can deduce from its observation of g_L and t_L that $n_H = 0$. (A similar situation arises when $n_H = 9$ and $g_L = 8$.) It follows that Equation 13 does not imply Equation 14 in all circumstances, and so we conclude that G_0 does not satisfy π_G.

The discrepancy between G_0 and π_G may be resolved by relaxing R_G to exclude system-level observations where $n_H = 0$ or $n_H = 9$. Hence, we define a weaker confidentiality property $\pi'_G = \langle H, L, R'_G, Q_G \rangle$, where:

$$
R'_G \triangleq g_H \neq n_H \wedge n_H \neq 0 \wedge n_H \neq 9 \tag{15}
$$

Of course, the discrepancy could be resolved by weakening G_0: for instance, by using t to indicate only whether the guess was correct or incorrect.

This example highlights an important trade-off between functionality and security requirements in software development. While confidentiality properties place an upper bound on information flow to $\mathcal{L}$, functionality requirements may be interpreted as placing a *lower* bound on information flow to $\mathcal{L}$. Should these bounds conflict (as in our example), then no system could ever satisfy both kinds of requirements and so these requirements should be re-evaluated before proceeding with the design of a system.

5   Confidentiality-Preserving Refinement

A system specification is *refined* (improved) by adding implementation details to the specification to remove non-determinism. In the UTP, the classical notion of refinement is characterised by implication between predicates: [4]

$$
S \sqsubseteq T \triangleq [\,T \Rightarrow S\,] \tag{16}
$$

$S \sqsubseteq T$ holds if and only if every system-level observation of T is a (possible) system-level observation of S. A significant feature of the UTP is that the notion of refinement is the same across the various UTP theories [4].

Refinement guarantees that a program satisfies all the functionality properties in its specification. Unfortunately, the $\sqsubseteq$ relation is not strong enough to preserve confidentiality properties in specifications, since it may introduce new conduits of information flow to low-level users [8,9]. This result can be established in our framework by appealing to the following lemma (from [7]).

Lemma 1 (P is order-preserving). *If $S \sqsubseteq T$ holds, then every pair of $\mathcal{L}$ and $\mathcal{H}$ observations of T must correspond to a pair of $\mathcal{L}$ and $\mathcal{H}$ observations of S:*

$$S \sqsubseteq T \;\Rightarrow\; \mathbf{P}\,(L \wedge H, S) \sqsubseteq \mathbf{P}\,(L \wedge H, T) \tag{17}$$

Lemma 1 indicates that whenever $S \sqsubseteq T$ holds, then for each $\mathcal{L}$ observation ϕ of T, the set of $\mathcal{H}$ observations of T consistent with ϕ is a subset of the $\mathcal{H}$ observations of S consistent with ϕ. Hence, $\mathcal{L}$ can deduce at least as much knowledge of $\mathcal{H}$'s activities by observing T as it can deduce by observing S. In turn, T may violate confidentiality properties that S satisfies, if T does not provide all of the cover stories that S provides. In the absence of these cover stories from T, $\mathcal{L}$ can deduce extra knowledge about $\mathcal{H}$'s activities that may enable it to establish that a certain confidential $\mathcal{H}$ activity has taken place. Hence, $S \sqsubseteq T$ is not sufficient to guarantee that T satisfies any given confidentiality property that S satisfies.

Example 6. The guessing game of Example 1 may be implemented as follows:

$$G_1 \;\triangleq\; n \in 0..9 \wedge t = g - n \tag{18}$$

While $G_0 \sqsubseteq G_1$ holds, it is clear that G_1 is less secure than G_0, since the values of g and t allow $\mathcal{L}$ to deduce the exact value of n in G_1. Indeed, G_1 violates the confidentiality property π'_G from Example 5, whereas G_0 satisfies this property.

When a system specification incorporates confidentiality properties, it is desirable for refinement steps to uphold these properties, to save the effort of re-verifying each confidentiality property after each refinement step and the expense of carrying out refinement steps that reach insecure system designs. In this section, we demonstrate how notions of refinement can be strengthened to preserve confidentiality properties of the form $\pi = \langle H, L, R, Q \rangle$.

A *confidentiality ordering* is a pre-order over the space of systems [10]. We define a confidentiality ordering $\preceq_\pi$ — parameterised by the encoding of confidentiality properties presented in Section 4 — to relate predicates according to what $\mathcal{L}$ can deduce about $\mathcal{H}$'s confidential activities as specified by π. [2]

---

[2] The confidentiality ordering presented here is conceptually related to Jacob's security ordering [7,10]. However, the orderings are different in their details: the security ordering is concerned only with what $\mathcal{L}$ can deduce about $\mathcal{H}$'s activities and does not discriminate between confidential and non-confidential activities.

Definition 3 (Confidentiality ordering). *Let* $\pi = \langle H, L, R, Q \rangle$. *T provides no more information about $\mathcal{H}$-observations in R to $\mathcal{L}$ than does S if and only if:*

$$S \preceq_\pi T \triangleq S \lesssim_\pi T \wedge S \trianglelefteq_\pi T \tag{19}$$

holds, where $\lesssim_\pi$ and $\trianglelefteq_\pi$ are defined as follows:

$$S \lesssim_\pi T \triangleq \mathbf{P}(L \wedge H, S) \sqsubseteq \mathbf{P}(L \wedge H, T) \wedge R \tag{20}$$

$$S \trianglelefteq_\pi T \triangleq \mathbf{P}\left(L \wedge \tilde{H}, T\right) \sqsubseteq \mathbf{P}(L \wedge H, T) \wedge R \wedge \mathbf{P}\left(L \wedge \tilde{H}, S\right) \wedge Q \tag{21}$$

$S \lesssim_\pi T$ mandates that every confidential $\mathcal{H}$ observation ψ present in T must also be present in S and, moreover, all $\mathcal{L}$ observations of T consistent with ψ must also be present in S. $S \trianglelefteq_\pi T$ requires that, for every $\mathcal{H}$ activity ψ in T classed as confidential by R, all of the cover stories related to ψ by Q that are present in S must also be present in T. When both of these conditions are satisfied, T provides no more information flow about $\mathcal{H}$'s confidential activities to $\mathcal{L}$ than S; in other words, $\mathcal{L}$ can deduce no more confidential information from any observation of T than it can deduce by observing S.

(Note that T may provide more information flow from $\mathcal{H}$ to $\mathcal{L}$ than S without violating π, so long as for each confidential $\mathcal{H}$ observation ψ in T, there is at least one cover story compatible with ψ also in T.)

Lemma 2 formalises the relationship between confidentiality properties and the confidentiality ordering.

Lemma 2 (π is closed under $\preceq_\pi$). *Whenever S satisfies the confidentiality property π and $S \preceq_\pi T$ holds, then T also satisfies π.*

It follows from Lemma 2 that a refinement relation that preserves π may be constructed as the least upper bound of the $\sqsubseteq$ and $\preceq_\pi$ orderings:

$$S \sqsubseteq_\pi^{cp} T \triangleq S \sqsubseteq T \wedge S \preceq_\pi T \tag{22}$$

Since $S \sqsubseteq T$ implies $S \lesssim_\pi T$ (by Lemma 1), it is sufficient to prove that $S \sqsubseteq T$ and $S \trianglelefteq_\pi T$ hold in order to establish that $S \preceq_\pi T$ holds. Hence, we can simplify the definition of $\sqsubseteq_\pi^{cp}$ as follows:

$$S \sqsubseteq_\pi^{cp} T = S \sqsubseteq T \wedge S \trianglelefteq_\pi T \tag{23}$$

Corollary 1 ($\sqsubseteq^{cp}$ preserves confidentiality properties). *Lemma 2 implies that, if $S \sqsubseteq_\pi^{cp} T$ holds and S satisfies π, then T also satisfies π.*

Example 7. An alternative implementation of the guessing game is:

$$G_2 \triangleq n \in 0..9 \wedge (g = n \Rightarrow t = 0) \wedge (g > n \Rightarrow t = 1) \wedge (g < n \Rightarrow t = -1) \tag{24}$$

We have $G_0 \sqsubseteq G_2$ and $G_0 \preceq_{\pi'_G} G_2$, so it follows that $G_0 \sqsubseteq_{\pi'_G}^{cp} G_2$. From Corollary 1, we can conclude that G_2 preserves π'_G.

Lemma 3 (Ordering of $\preceq_\pi$ and $\sqsubseteq$). *The $\preceq_\pi$ and $\sqsubseteq$ orderings are neither monotonic nor anti-monotonic w.r.t. each other.*

Lemma 3 suggests that, during a stepwise system development that employs the $\sqsubseteq_\pi^{cp}$ refinement relation, one may reach a system design where no useful refinement steps can be made without violating the $\preceq_\pi$ ordering (for instance, by removing cover stories from the design without also removing all confidential observations related to those cover stories). Since no progress towards a correct implementation of the specification can be made from such a design, the system's designers must either weaken π, or backtrack to an earlier design in their development and try a different series of refinement steps. This potential for costly backtracking suggests that the $\sqsubseteq_\pi^{cp}$ refinement relation may be impractical for developing software by stepwise refinement.

It is usually assumed that all behaviours of a system are distinguishable by its environment; hence, no new behaviours can be added to a system design without violating the system's specification. However, if a system is known to operate in an environment consisting of multiple users (each with limited observational abilities) then we may relax the definition of refinement by allowing certain system-level observations to be *added* to a system design without compromising its functionality, so long as these observations do not induce new interface-level observations. Given a set of interface-disjoint views $\mathcal{W}$ representing a group of users, we say T is a *co-operating refinement* of S (w.r.t. $\mathcal{W}$) [11] if, for all sets of observations of T that can be made through the views in $\mathcal{W}$, these observations can be combined in order to reconstruct at least one system-level observation of T that is present in S. Intuitively, co-operating refinement ensures the users represented by $\mathcal{W}$ are collectively unable to detect that T possesses any behaviour not present in S.

Co-operating refinement can be expressed in the UTP in terms of $\sqsubseteq$ and the **P** predicate transformer, as shown in Definition 4 [7].

Definition 4 (Co-operating refinement). *T is a co-operating refinement of S w.r.t. a set of views $\mathcal{W}$ if and only if, for every system-level observation Φ of T, the projections of Φ through each view in $\mathcal{W}$ are matched by the projections of a system-level observation of S through each view:*

$$S \sqsubseteq_{\mathcal{W}}^{co} T \triangleq \mathbf{P}\left(\bigwedge \mathcal{W}, S\right) \sqsubseteq \mathbf{P}\left(\bigwedge \mathcal{W}, T\right) \tag{25}$$

Corollary 2 ($\sqsubseteq_{\mathcal{W}}^{co}$ is weaker than $\sqsubseteq$). *It follows from Lemma 1 that, for all sets $\mathcal{W}$ of interface-disjoint views, $S \sqsubseteq T$ guarantees $S \sqsubseteq_{\mathcal{W}}^{co} T$ [7,11].*

While co-operating refinement is not as strong as classical refinement, it is strong enough to preserve the inherent functionality in a system's specification from the perspective of the system's groups of users. Furthermore, co-operating refinement provides the designers of a system with extra flexibility to execute some kinds of useful refinement steps that are not permitted by classical refinement, such as distributing a system across independent processors [7,11]. We postulate that this ability to add new behaviours to system designs (in a controlled manner) can help to overcome the difficulties encountered when developing a system to satisfy a given confidentiality property by stepwise refinement.

When defining a co-operating refinement relation for a group of users, we assume that users in the group can communicate with each other (but not with users outside the group). It follows that, by exchanging their observations, a group of low-level users may therefore be able to deduce more information about high-level activities than they could deduce from their individual observations alone. Hence, when reasoning about confidentiality properties in the setting of co-operating refinement, we represent a group of low-level users $\mathcal{LS}$ as a single user with observational abilities equivalent to those of all the users in $\mathcal{LS}$ combined.

Suppose that Z is a system that interacts with a single high-level user (with view H_Z) and a group of communicating low-level users associated with a set LS_Z of (interface-disjoint) views. Using co-operating refinement in place of $\sqsubseteq$, we can obtain a refinement relation that preserves the confidentiality property $\pi_Z = \langle H_Z, \bigwedge LS_Z, R_Z, Q_Z \rangle$ for this system:

$$S \sqsubseteq_{\pi_Z}^{co/cp} T \triangleq S \sqsubseteq_{\{H_Z\}}^{co} T \wedge S \sqsubseteq_{LS_Z}^{co} T \wedge S \preceq_{\pi_Z} T \qquad (26)$$

A potential advantage of $\sqsubseteq_\pi^{co/cp}$ over $\sqsubseteq_\pi^{cp}$ is that all the terms of $\sqsubseteq_\pi^{co/cp}$ are expressed with the **P** predicate transformer, which may simplify the task of verifying that $\sqsubseteq_\pi^{co/cp}$ holds between system designs. It is also unnecessary to redefine the R and Q components of π when dealing with multiple low-level users, since R and Q refer exclusively to high-level observations.

Corollary 3 ($\sqsubseteq^{co/cp}$ preserves confidentiality properties). *Whenever S satisfies the confidentiality property $\pi = \langle H, \bigwedge LS, R, Q \rangle$ and $S \sqsubseteq_\pi^{co/cp} T$ holds, then T also satisfies π.*

A family of confidentiality-preserving refinement relations can be constructed from $\sqsubseteq^{co/cp}$. If a system is required to satisfy a set of confidentiality properties Π, then a suitable refinement relation for that system can be constructed by taking the least upper bound of the $\sqsubseteq_\pi^{co/cp}$ relations for each $\pi \in \Pi$. Furthermore, if the users of a system are partitioned into a set of isolated groups — such that high-level users are not placed in the same group as low-level users — then a suitable refinement relation can be calculated by combining $\sqsubseteq^{co/cp}$ relations for each group and each confidentiality property that the system must satisfy.

6   Related Work

Frameworks. Several semantic frameworks (including the MAKS) for expressing a range of confidentiality properties in a uniform manner have been proposed in the security literature [5,6,9,10,12,13,14]. The objective of these frameworks is to consolidate the existing definitions of noninterference-like properties in the literature, in order to evaluate and compare these properties systematically and to enable new confidentiality properties to be defined rigorously.

In these frameworks, a system's semantics is taken to be a set of traces. This emphasis on a trace semantics contrasts with the UTP approach, in which systems are represented by predicates within a UTP theory. By abstracting away from a trace semantics, our framework avoids the need to translate a system specification (with a UTP semantics) to a set of traces. However, our framework does not differentiate between inputs and outputs of systems, which is a prerequisite for expressing many noninterference-like properties. In order to capture such properties, it would be necessary to extend our framework with notation for modelling inputs and outputs separately or, alternatively, to interpret undashed UTP variables as inputs and dashed variables as outputs.

In contrast to noninterference-like properties, we do not regard all $\mathcal{H}$ activities as (equally) confidential. We also expect that $\mathcal{L}$ can deduce some aspects of $\mathcal{H}$'s observations legitimately and seek only to constrain $\mathcal{L}$ from deducing the occurrence of a subset of $\mathcal{H}$ activities. Moreover, we argue that confidentiality properties weaker than noninterference fit more closely with software development in practice. For example, noninterference from $\mathcal{H}$ to $\mathcal{L}$ is too strong a requirement for the guessing game, where the functionality of the game dictates that $\mathcal{L}$'s observation of the outcome of its guess must be influenced by $\mathcal{H}$.

To date, the most complete framework for expressing noninterference-like confidentiality properties is Mantel's MAKS [5,6]. The MAKS defines a collection of "basic security predicates" (BSPs) to express a variety of transformations on the high-level components of system traces, capturing low-level users' uncertainty about high-level inputs and outputs. These BSPs can be combined to express many (but not all) of the noninterference-like confidentiality properties defined in the literature. Since our definition of confidentiality properties is based on the schema form of these BSPs, we may select predicates to model restrictions and closure requirements encoding the range of BSPs within a UTP theory with a trace semantics. This implies that existing noninterference-like properties that are expressible in the MAKS can be re-expressed using our framework within a UTP theory that distinguishes input events from output events.

Refinement. Most notions of confidentiality-preserving refinement in the literature are realised in two ways: by limiting the space of confidentiality properties to those that are closed under classical refinement, or by strengthening the refinement relation to ensure it preserves confidentiality properties in specifications. To ensure that confidentiality properties are not unreasonably strong, the first approach often necessitates a means for distinguishing between two kinds of nondeterminism — namely, under-specification (which can be removed safely) and unpredictability (which restricts information flow from $\mathcal{H}$ to $\mathcal{L}$ and so should not be removed) — in specifications [15]. However, many specification languages (and UTP theories) lack facilities for modelling non-determinism intended to provide unpredictability separately from under-specification. Thus, it is unclear how the first approach can be applied to a UTP theory without extending the semantics of that theory to distinguish between these kinds of non-determinism explicitly. We have instead focused on the second approach for confidentiality-preserving refinement by applying the confidentiality ordering, to avoid specialising our framework to particular UTP theories.

Seehusen and Stølen [13,14] have proposed a (MAKS-like) framework for integrating confidentiality properties into stepwise software development processes. In their framework, a system specification is formalised as a set of *obligations* (trace sets); a system satisfies a specification if it contains at least one trace from each obligation in the specification. Intuitively, the obligations ensure that a system's implementation provides a minimum level of unpredictability about the system's behaviour from a low-level perspective. Hence, obligations are closely related to our notion of cover stories. Seehusen and Stølen use obligations to facilitate a novel approach to confidentiality-preserving refinement, which parallels our own: while refinement may remove some traces from a system design, the refined system must still fulfil each obligation in the specification.

A recent and significant development is Morgan's *shadow semantics* [16,17], which builds on the refinement calculus for sequential programs [18]. In this semantics, $\mathcal{L}$ (the adversary) is assumed to be able to monitor how demonic non-determinism is resolved at each program step. This novel device allows the "shadow set" of possible values of a high-level variable that are consistent with $\mathcal{L}$'s observations to itself be modelled at the semantic level. A program is secure if the shadow set never reveals the value of the high-level variable to $\mathcal{L}$ (even when $\mathcal{L}$ monitors the control flow); and refinement is "ignorance-preserving" if it does not decrease the shadow set associated with any confidential variable. This notion of refinement (like our own) ensures that $\mathcal{L}$ can never deduce any more information regarding confidential data from an implementation of a system as it could from the corresponding specification.

Our approach towards confidentiality-preserving refinement also has links to work by Alur et al. [19]. In this work, the refinement of a labelled transition system is expected to preserve $\mathcal{L}$'s inability to deduce whether system runs satisfy a specified set of properties on secret variables. Alur et al. also describe how this refinement relation maps to standard simulation-based proof techniques, which (we conjecture) may be useful for discharging the proof obligations associated with our own confidentiality-preserving refinement relations.

Compositionality. An important topic in the study of information flow security is the compositionality of system designs, as a means of developing secure systems in a modular fashion. Given a collection of sub-systems $S_1, \ldots, S_N$ which individually satisfy a confidentiality property π, it is desirable that the system obtained by composing $S_1, \ldots, S_N$ together will also satisfy π. However, this is not generally the case for operators such as parallel composition, because the composite system may feature confidential activities but lack the cover stories that are permitted by its components. Mantel has identified a collection of formal conditions for which the BSPs of the MAKS are preserved under certain compositional operators [6,20]. These conditions may provide a starting point for identifying compositionality conditions for our UTP formulation of confidentiality properties.

A further topic for investigation is the compositionality of confidentiality-preserving refinement relations. This topic has not been addressed in the MAKS, but has been investigated elsewhere [21].

Limitations. Like the BSPs of the MAKS, our formulation of confidentiality properties is qualitative w.r.t. information flow. This means that a confidentiality property is violated if even a single bit of information relating to confidential data is disclosed to a low-level user. Small leaks of data from high-level users to low-level users are often acceptable (and sometimes unavoidable) in real-world systems, provided that a low-level user cannot deduce any significant details about confidential data from such a leak. In these circumstances, it may be difficult to work with qualitative confidentiality properties. This difficulty can be overcome by defining confidentiality properties in terms of how much information can flow between users. Recent research has modelled quantitative information flow within the framework of Shannon-style information theory [22].

Another limitation of our treatment of confidentiality properties — which is shared by the MAKS — is that we do not address the probability distribution of the high-level user's activities. This shortcoming could lead to serious security breaches, because if a low-level user has knowledge of this distribution, then it may be able to deduce confidential data with near certainty but without violating the confidentiality property. Some research has investigated *probabilistic* confidentiality properties which account for the likelihood of alternative high-level activities [23,24]. While these properties are attractive in theory, their application in practice is not without difficulty: the probability distribution of the high-level user's interactions with a system may be unknown and, even with this knowledge, it may be intractable to determine whether a non-trivial system model satisfies a probabilistic confidentiality property [25].

A further practical issue with existing frameworks for modelling confidentiality properties (including our own) is that, while they are suitable for reasoning about information flow at the abstract level of system specifications, they do not account for the (potentially confidential) information that a low-level user may deduce by monitoring physical and temporal characteristics of its interface at the implementation level, such as the time interval between requests and responses. These channels may potentially be exploited to obtain confidential information about a system's behaviour, so it is desirable to model these channels formally and to extend the analysis of information flow to them. We regard this as a challenging task that is beyond the scope of this paper.

7 Conclusions

The original contributions of this work are two-fold. First, we have laid the foundations for reasoning about information flow in the UTP and provided a UTP encoding of "possibilistic" confidentiality properties. Second, we have identified a spectrum of confidentiality-preserving refinement relations based on the confidentiality ordering and co-operating refinement.

Our UTP formulation of confidentiality properties in the predicative style is concise and generic in the UTP theory under consideration, yet also provides expressive power equivalent to the MAKS framework for specifying confidentiality properties. Moreover, our approach can be deployed across the various families of specification languages and programming paradigms that have a UTP semantics, rather than just those based on trace semantics.

A drawback of our formulation of confidentiality properties in the UTP is that verifying UTP specifications against confidentiality properties can be cumbersome, due to the need to translate from system-level to interface-level predicates. Indeed, errors can be easily introduced into these calculations if they are carried out manually, and especially when the mapping from system-level to interface-level observations is not straightforward. This difficulty could be alleviated by identifying a collection of laws that can be used to simplify these calculations.

In future work, we intend to integrate our formulation of confidentiality properties with the UTP semantics of *Circus* [26] — a specification language which combines Z and CSP to model the state and behavioural aspects of concurrent systems — in order to realise a unified framework for the specification and development of secure software. Indeed, we envisage that a customer's specification of confidentiality properties can play an integral role in a formal stepwise development process — from constructing an abstract system design that is verified to satisfy the confidentiality specification, through a series of confidentiality-preserving refinement steps — to yield a final implementation that is guaranteed to satisfy the customer's security requirements.

Acknowledgements

Michael Banks is supported by a UK Engineering and Physical Sciences Research Council DTA studentship. Thanks to Ana Cavalcanti for suggestions on improving the structure of this paper; to the anonymous referees for identifying omissions in an earlier draft; and to Chris Poskitt for proofreading.

References

1. Denning, D.E.: Cryptography and Data Security. Addison-Wesley Longman Publishing Company, Inc., Boston (1982)
2. Lampson, B.W.: A note on the confinement problem. Communications of the ACM 16(10), 613–615 (1973)
3. Goguen, J.A., Meseguer, J.: Security policies and security models. In: Proceedings of the 1982 IEEE Symposium on Security and Privacy, pp. 11–20. IEEE Computer Society, Los Alamitos (April 1982)
4. Hoare, C.A.R., He, J.: Unifying Theories of Programming. Prentice Hall International Series in Computer Science. Prentice Hall Inc., Englewood Cliffs (1998)
5. Mantel, H.: Possibilistic definitions of security — an assembly kit. In: 13th IEEE Computer Security Foundations Workshop (CSFW 2000), pp. 185–199 (2000)
6. Mantel, H.: A Uniform Framework for the Formal Specification and Verification of Information Flow Security. PhD thesis, Universität Saarbrücken (July 2003)

7. Banks, M.J., Jacob, J.L.: On Modelling User Observations in the UTP. In: Qin, S. (ed.) UTP 2010. LNCS, vol. 6445, pp. 101–119. Springer, Heidelberg (2010)
8. Jacob, J.L.: On the derivation of secure components. In: Proceedings of the 1989 IEEE Symposium on Security and Privacy, pp. 242–247. IEEE Computer Society, Los Alamitos (1989)
9. McLean, J.: A general theory of composition for trace sets closed under selective interleaving functions. In: Proceedings of the 1994 IEEE Symposium on Security and Privacy, pp. 79–93 (1994)
10. Jacob, J.L.: Security specifications. In: Proceedings of the 1988 IEEE Symposium on Security and Privacy, pp. 14–23 (1988)
11. Jacob, J.L.: Refinement of shared systems. In: McDermid, J.A. (ed.) The Theory and Practice of Refinement: Approaches to the Development of Large-Scale Software Systems, pp. 27–36. Butterworths, London (1989)
12. Focardi, R., Gorrieri, R.: A taxonomy of security properties for process algebras. Journal of Computer Security 3(1), 5–34 (1995)
13. Seehusen, F., Stølen, K.: Maintaining information flow security under refinement and transformation. In: Dimitrakos, T., Martinelli, F., Ryan, P.Y.A., Schneider, S. (eds.) FAST 2006. LNCS, vol. 4691, pp. 143–157. Springer, Heidelberg (2007)
14. Seehusen, F., Stølen, K.: Information flow security, abstraction and composition. IET Information Security 3(1), 9–33 (2009)
15. Roscoe, A.W.: CSP and determinism in security modelling. In: Proceedings of the 1995 IEEE Symposium on Security and Privacy, pp. 114–127. IEEE Computer Society, Los Alamitos (1995)
16. Morgan, C.: The shadow knows: Refinement and security in sequential programs. Science of Computer Programming 74(8), 629–653 (2009)
17. Morgan, C.: How to brew-up a refinement ordering. Electronic Notes in Theoretical Computer Science 259, 123–141 (2009)
18. Morgan, C.: Programming from Specifications, 2nd edn. Prentice Hall International Series in Computer Science. Prentice Hall Inc., Hertfordshire (1994)
19. Alur, R., Černý, P., Zdancewic, S.: Preserving secrecy under refinement. In: Bugliesi, M., Preneel, B., Sassone, V., Wegener, I. (eds.) ICALP 2006. LNCS, vol. 4052, pp. 107–118. Springer, Heidelberg (2006)
20. Mantel, H.: On the composition of secure systems. In: Proceedings of the 2002 IEEE Symposium on Security and Privacy, pp. 88–101 (2002)
21. Santen, T., Heisel, M., Pfitzmann, A.: Confidentiality-preserving refinement is compositional – sometimes. In: Gollmann, D., Karjoth, G., Waidner, M. (eds.) ESORICS 2002. LNCS, vol. 2502, pp. 194–211. Springer, Heidelberg (2002)
22. Smith, G.: On the foundations of quantitative information flow. In: Alfaro, L. (ed.) FOSSACS 2009. LNCS, vol. 5504, pp. 288–302. Springer, Heidelberg (2009)
23. Santen, T.: A formal framework for confidentiality-preserving refinement. In: Gollmann, D., Meier, J., Sabelfeld, A. (eds.) ESORICS 2006. LNCS, vol. 4189, pp. 225–242. Springer, Heidelberg (2006)
24. Santen, T.: Preservation of probabilistic information flow under refinement. Information and Computation 206(2-4), 213–249 (2008)
25. Ryan, P.: Mathematical models of computer security. In: Focardi, R., Gorrieri, R. (eds.) FOSAD 2000. LNCS, vol. 2171, pp. 1–62. Springer, Heidelberg (2001)
26. Oliveira, M., Cavalcanti, A., Woodcock, J.: A UTP semantics for Circus. Formal Aspects of Computing 21(1), 3–32 (2009)

A   Proofs

Lemma 1

Proof. A proof of this lemma is provided elsewhere [7].

Lemma 2

Proof

$$S \preceq_\pi T \wedge \mathbf{C}(\pi, S)$$
$$\Leftrightarrow \qquad \langle \text{ definition of } \preceq \text{ and } \mathbf{C} \rangle$$
$$S \lesssim_\pi T \wedge S \trianglelefteq_\pi T \wedge \left[\begin{array}{l} \mathbf{P}\,(L \wedge H, S) \wedge R \\ \Rightarrow \left(\exists\, \widetilde{u_H}, \widetilde{u'_H} \bullet \mathbf{P}\left(L \wedge \tilde{H}, S \right) \wedge Q \right) \end{array} \right]$$
$$\Rightarrow \qquad \langle \text{ definition of } \lesssim \text{ and transitivity of implication } \rangle$$
$$S \trianglelefteq_\pi T \wedge \left[\mathbf{P}\,(L \wedge H, T) \wedge R \Rightarrow \left(\exists\, \widetilde{u_H}, \widetilde{u'_H} \bullet \mathbf{P}\left(L \wedge \tilde{H}, S \right) \wedge Q \right) \right]$$
$$\Leftrightarrow \qquad \langle \text{ definition of } \trianglelefteq \text{ and predicate calculus } \rangle$$
$$\left[\begin{array}{l} \mathbf{P}\,(L \wedge H, T) \wedge R \Rightarrow \left(\exists\, \widetilde{u_H}, \widetilde{u'_H} \bullet \mathbf{P}\left(L \wedge \tilde{H}, S \right) \wedge Q \right) \\ \wedge \left(\mathbf{P}\,(L \wedge H, T) \wedge R \wedge \mathbf{P}\left(L \wedge \tilde{H}, S \right) \wedge Q \right) \Rightarrow \mathbf{P}\left(L \wedge \tilde{H}, T \right) \end{array} \right]$$
$$\Rightarrow \qquad \langle \text{ predicate calculus } \rangle$$
$$\left[\mathbf{P}\,(L \wedge H, T) \wedge R \Rightarrow \left(\exists\, \widetilde{u_H}, \widetilde{u'_H} \bullet \mathbf{P}\left(L \wedge \tilde{H}, T \right) \wedge Q \right) \right]$$
$$\Leftrightarrow \qquad \langle \text{ definition of } \mathbf{C} \rangle$$
$$\mathbf{C}(\pi, T) \qquad\qquad\qquad\qquad\qquad\qquad\qquad\qquad\qquad\qquad\qquad \square$$

Lemma 3

Proof. First, the proof that $\lesssim_\pi$ is monotonic w.r.t. $\sqsubseteq$ follows from Lemma 1. Second, we show that $\trianglelefteq_\pi$ is anti-monotonic w.r.t. $\sqsubseteq$.

$$S \sqsubseteq T$$
$$\Rightarrow \qquad \langle \text{ by Lemma 1 } \rangle$$
$$\mathbf{P}\left(L \wedge \tilde{H}, S \right) \sqsubseteq \mathbf{P}\left(L \wedge \tilde{H}, T \right)$$
$$\Rightarrow \qquad \langle \text{ predicate calculus } \rangle$$
$$\mathbf{P}\left(L \wedge \tilde{H}, S \right) \sqsubseteq \left(\mathbf{P}\left(L \wedge \tilde{H}, T \right) \wedge R \wedge Q \wedge \mathbf{P}\,(L \wedge H, S) \right)$$
$$\Leftrightarrow \qquad \langle \text{ definition of } \trianglelefteq_\pi \rangle$$
$$T \trianglelefteq_\pi S$$

These two results imply that the relation formed by combining $\lesssim_\pi$ and $\trianglelefteq_\pi$ — namely, $\preceq_\pi$ — is neither monotonic nor anti-monotonic w.r.t. $\sqsubseteq$. $\qquad\qquad \square$

Saoithín: A Theorem Prover for UTP

Andrew Butterfield[*]

School of Computer Science & Statistics
Trinity College Dublin
Rep. of Ireland
Lero: the Irish Software Engineering Research Centre
`Andrew.Butterfield@sccs.tcd.ie`

Abstract. SAOITHÍN is a theorem prover developed to support the Unifying Theories of Programming (UTP) framework. Its primary design goal was to support the higher-order logic, alphabets, equational reasoning and "programs as predicates" style that is prevalent in much of the UTP literature, from the seminal work by Hoare & He [HH98] onwards. This paper describes the key features of the theorem prover, with an emphasis on the underlying foundations, and how these affect the design and implementation choices. These key features include: a formalisation of a UTP Theory; support for common proof strategies; sophisticated goal/law matching ; and user-defined language constructs. A simple theory of designs with some proof extracts is used to illustrate the above features. The theorem prover has been used with undergraduate students and we discuss some of those experiences. The paper then concludes with a discussion of current limitations and planned improvements to the tool.

1 Introduction

SAOITHÍN[1] is an experimental proof assistant for the logic used in UTP, supporting a notion of UTP theory, an intuitive prover interface that supports the equational reasoning style that is prevalent in [HH98] and much other UTP-related literature, with facilities for the user to define the syntax and semantics of their own language constructs. The tool consists of a core equational prover we have developed in concert with a closely-coupled GUI interface. At present its focus is on supporting foundational work in developing UTP, rather than the application of the theory to a "real-world" design problem.

1.1 Motivation

We are doing foundational work in the UTP [HH98], which requires formal reasoning with not only predicates, but also predicate transformers: $\mathbf{R3}(P) \cong II \lhd wait \rhd P$ and predicates over predicates: $P = \mathbf{R3}(P)$. We also need to

---

[*] This paper emanated from work part funded by Science Foundation Ireland, Projects 07/RFP/CMSF186, 08/RFP/CMS1277, 03/CE2/I303-1.

[1] Pronounced "See-heen".

use recursion at the predicate level: $P \widehat{=} \mu\, Q \bullet F(Q)$, as well as partially-defined expressions: $s \leqslant s \frown (tr' - tr) \equiv tr \leqslant tr'$. The logic being used is therefore semi-classical (two-valued logic, but expressions may be undefined) and of least 2nd-order. In addition, tool support for foundational work in UTP requires the ability to easily describe new language constructs, which can themselves be treated just like predicates, in keeping with the "programs are predicates" philosophy [Hoa85] of UTP.

1.2 Structure

We next discuss related work (§2) in order to better justify our decision to "grow our own" theorem proving assistant. We then proceed to look at the logic (§3), type-system (§4), user defined language support (§5), proof procedures (§6), and law matching (§7, with emphasis on the underlying foundations. We then discuss useability and experience (§8) and finally finish with future work and conclusions (§9).

2   Related Work

There are a lot of theorem provers in existence, of which the most prominent feature in [Wie06]. Of these, the most obvious candidates for consideration for UTP prover support are Isabelle/HOL[NPW02], PVS[Sha96], and Coq [BC04]. They are powerful, well-supported, with decades of development experience and large active user communities. They all support higher-order logic of some form, with a command-line interface, typically based around tactics of some form. All three require functions to be total, but support some kind of mechanism for handling partial functions (e.g. dependent types in PVS). Their reasoning frameworks are based on some form of sequent calculus, and do not support equational reasoning in a native fashion.

There has been work done on improving the user interfaces of the above theorem provers. An interesting example was "proof by pointing" [BKT94] for CoQ which allowed the user to select a subterm, whereupon it would generate and apply a tactic based on the subterm's top-level operator. Whilst proof-by-pointing is not supported in more recent versions of CoQ, it has been incorporated into "Proof General" [Asp00], a general purpose user interface for theorem provers, built on top of Emacs. It supports Isabelle and Coq, among others, and is basically a proof-script management system. In essence it supports the command-line tactics of the provers, allowing the user to edit proof scripts at will, whilst maintaining prover consistency behind the scenes.

Within the UTP community, there has been considerable work using Proof-Power-Z to build models of UTP theories in Z in order to mechanise proofs. Early work looked at deep embedding into Z of an imperative language whose semantics were given using UTP [NW06]. Work extending this to a mechanisation of UTP itself was also undertaken, driven by a desire to mechanically verify the semantics of Circus [OCW09]. Recent work has looked at re-working the mechanisation of

UTP in order to better support the hierarchical nature of UTP theory building [ZC09], where alphabetised predicates are restricted to relations, then designs, and so on. Some support for Z-like theories from UTP (such as Circus) can be found as extensions implemented in the Community Z Tools project [MU05].

Whilst all of good pedigree, CoQ, Isabelle/HOL, ProofPower-Z and PVS all have in common that they work best when used in the manner for which they were designed—in none of these cases does this manner match the way we wish to work in UTP, as described in the introduction. Ironically, the key inspiration for the design of SAOITHÍN came not from the above provers, but instead from the one provided as part of the RAISE Development Method [GHH$^+$95]. That theorem prover had mechanisms for selecting sub-expressions and identifying applicable laws for that sub-expression, a feature very close to that required for the proof style that SAOITHÍN supports.

3   The Logic

A subset of the syntax of the predicate logic of SAOITHÍN is shown below:

$$P, Q \in Pred ::= \text{TRUE} \mid \text{FALSE} \mid \neg\, P \mid P \wedge P \mid P \vee P \mid P \Rightarrow P \mid P \equiv P$$
$$\mid\ A \mid \forall\, \overrightarrow{v} \bullet P \mid \exists\, \overrightarrow{v} \bullet P \mid M \mid P[\overrightarrow{e}/\overrightarrow{v}]$$
$$e, f \in Expr ::= v \mid M \mid \text{expressions using } +, \times, \leqslant, \cup, \frown \ldots, v \in Var$$

In addition to the usual propositions and quantifiers, we also have atomic predicates (A, boolean-valued expressions), meta-variables denoting arbitrary predicates or expressions (M), and an explicit substitution notation $P[\overrightarrow{e}/\overrightarrow{v}]$. The predicate meta-variables allow us to write conjectures and laws true for arbitrary predicates, while explicit substitution is required as many definitions in UTP use it in such an explicit manner. The axiomatisation being used is one for equational logic [Tou01], extended to support 2nd-order features, with the inference rules (Liebniz, etc.) effectively being implemented by the law matcher (§7).

Predicates in SAOITHÍN can participate in a number of roles, of which the most basic are *laws* and *conjectures*. Law are either asserted to be true (*axioms*), or are conjectures that have been proven, and are now *theorems*. A theorem is then a conjecture coupled with a proof. Some of the axioms/inference rules of predicate calculus have side-conditions, but given explicit meta-variables and substitutions, we find we can no longer treat side-conditions as statically checkable at law-application time, necessitating an explicit representation:

$$V \in VSet ::= \mathcal{P}\,Var$$
$$sc \in Side ::= True \mid M = V \mid M \subseteq V \mid M \,\not\!\!\cap\, V \mid \text{c}.M \mid \bigwedge\{sc_1, \ldots, sc_n\}$$

We read c.M as asserting that M is a condition (no dashed free variables), and $M \,\not\!\!\cap\, V$ means the free variables of M are disjoint from V. The use of side-condition expressions is discussed further in §7.3.

The basic unit of work in SAOITHÍN is in fact a predicate coupled with a side-condition and from here on we use the terms conjecture and law to refer to such pairs. So we can view a SAOITHÍN theory, as a named collection of named conjectures, theorems and laws:[2]

```
┌─ Theory ──────────────────────────────────────────────────
│   name : Name
│   laws : Name ↦ Pred × Side
│   cnjs : Name ↦ Pred × Side
│   thms : Name ↦ Pred × Side × Proof
└────────────────────────────────────────────────────────────
```

Once a conjecture has been proven it is moved from conjectures to theorems with the same name.

At present, SAOITHÍN is very much an experimental tool, intended in the first instance to support foundational work in the UTP. As a consequence of this, the axioms and inference rules have not, in the main, been hard-coded, but instead the user is free to add their own axioms. This clearly is very dangerous, but does support experimentation. For example, two axiomatisations of predicate calculus have been developed based on [MS89] and [GS94], and initial experimentation suggests that the axiomatisation in the latter leads to easier proofs, due to less choice being available at each step. Versions of SAOITHÍN that disallow user addition of axioms have been implemented for use in teaching, and we envisage future versions of the tool being able to work in different "user-experience" modes.

The interface to the logic presented to the user is, in the main, based on an ASCII-based concrete syntax, that imitates the mathematical syntax as far as is practicable. This ASCII syntax is used for both input and output. For example, the predicates

$$[(\exists\, c \bullet D \wedge L) \Rightarrow S] \qquad P[\text{TRUE}/ok]$$

are written ASCII-style as:

```
[[ ( exists c @ D /\ L ) => S ]]        P[ TRUE // ok ]
```

Similarly, side condition $\bigwedge\{Q \subseteq \{a, b\}, e \oslash \{b, c\}\}$ is written as

```
coverP Q a,b ; notinE e b,c
```

An almost complete theory (less theorems) can be input and output as a ASCII text file, whose extension is .uttxt (UTP Text). The file is structured as a series of sections, each flagged by a header keyword. The first collection of sections, between SYNTAXFROM and ENDSYNTAX keywords provide information to support the parser. The remaining sections provide semantics information. The first line of such text files is the theory name, optionally followed by a version number. So a simple theory defining some laws and conjectures about conjunction and disjunction could be written as:

---

[2] We use Z schema notation here for convenience—we are not presenting a formal Z model of UTP theories.

```
ConjDisj 0
SYNTAXFROM
 Logic
ENDSYNTAX
LAWS
  "/\-comm"  | P /\ Q == Q /\ P .
  "\/-def"   | P \/ Q == ~(~P /\ ~Q)
CONJECTURES
  "\/-comm"  | P \/ Q == Q \/ P
END
```

4 Types

We have a fairly simple notion of types with booleans and integers making up basic types, a basic type *Env* that denotes a program environment (*Name* $\nrightarrow$ *Value*), type variables, and then the capacity to build up set/sequence/map/free types on top of these:

$$
\begin{aligned}
T \in \textit{Type} ::= &\ \mathbb{B} \mid \mathbb{Z} \mid \textit{Env} & \text{Base Types} \\
\mid &\ \tau \mid ? & \text{Type variables} \\
\mid &\ \mathcal{P}\,T \mid T^* \mid T^+ \mid T \times \cdots \times T & \text{Composite types} \\
\mid &\ T \to T \mid T \nrightarrow T \mid T \twoheadrightarrow T & \text{Function types} \\
\mid &\ nm \bullet V\,`|'\ldots`|'\ V & \text{Free Types} \\
V \in \textit{Variant} ::= &\ nm\,\langle\!\langle T \times \cdots \times T\rangle\!\rangle & \text{Free Type Variant} \\
nm \in &\ \textit{Name} & \text{Names}
\end{aligned}
$$

The type-system supports Hindley-Milner style polymorphism, and, for simplicity, treats powerset, sequence and function types as distinct[3]. At present the main role played by types in the prover is to limit the search for applicable laws to those that match the types of expression involved. To this end a type-inferencing algorithm is used to associate types with all expressions. It uses user-supplied information about the types of named functions to deduce the relevant types for entire expressions. This information is stored in a table matching function names to their types, which of course has to be an additional component of a theory:

$$
\begin{array}{|l}
\hline
\ \textit{Theory} \underline{\hspace{10cm}} \\
\ \ldots \\
\ \textit{types} : \textit{Name} \nrightarrow \textit{Type} \\
\hline
\end{array}
$$

Types have an ASCII syntax as well, as exemplified by this example:

$$
\mathbb{Z} \times \mathcal{P}(\tau^*) \to \mathbb{B} \qquad \text{Z x P t* -> B}
$$

We can introduce types into a UTP textfile using a TYPES section, so for example, from a theory of arithmetic, we might have:

---

[3] We could add axioms to a theory relating type-assertion predicates if we wished to link these types.

```
TYPES
 * : (Z x Z) -> Z .
 + : (Z x Z) -> Z .
 neg : Z -> Z
```

5   Adding Language

The main purpose of UTP is to allow the construction, comparison and connection of theories about a variety of modelling, specification and programming languages. This requires us to be able to specify two key aspects:

1. The types of observations of such systems that we wish to discuss, captured by the notion of *observation variables*;
2. A description of the language under study: both its syntax and semantics.

5.1   Alphabets

A key feature of UTP is its use of *alphabetised* predicates, where the alphabet is a collection of typed observation variables. At present, the support in SAOITHÍN is limited to theories with fixed alphabets, such as the standard reactive systems theories, or theories where all program variables are encapsulated in a single *state* : *Name* ↦ *Value* observation. A proposal to broaden this to cover varying alphabets is under consideration for a future revision of the prover. At present, we simply record the (fixed) set of observation variables and their types in a table:

Theory
. . .
obs : *Name* ↦ *Type*

The variables listed in the domain of *objs* are "known" to the theorem prover and this influences the operation of the matcher. This information is also fed into the type-inferencing system, complementing the *types* information. We can specify this in the text file, as in the following example for a theory of designs:

```
OBSVAR
 ok : B .
 ok' : B
```

5.2   User-Defined Language Constructs

In order to be able to describe a theory about the language, we need to be able to describe the language, so we provide facilities to allow the specification (to SAOITHÍN) of the syntax of language constructs.

First, we note that the expression language is easily extendible as the parser automatically converts token streams of the form *nm e* into the application of (function) *nm* to expression argument *e*. However their effective use often requires the user to give them a type, entered in the *types* table. New infix operators however are not automatically parsed, and need to be declared in advance, using a simple form associating an operator name with its precedence and associativity. This infix information is stored in a table in the theory:

```
┌─ Theory ─────────────────────────────────────────────
│ . . .
│ precs : Name ↦ Precedence
└──────────────────────────────────────────────────────
```

A *predecence* is a pair of a number and an associativity (None/Left/Right), with higher numbers denoting tighter binding strengths[4]. In a theory of designs, we want to introduce ⊢ as an infix operator so we can declare it in a PRECEDENCES section:

PRECEDENCES
|- 55 None

A user-defined language construct is an interleaving of existing forms (variables, expressions, types, predicates) with new tokens, including also some list forms with specified delimiters and separators. So a theory needs to contain a table listing syntax specifications:

```
┌─ Theory ─────────────────────────────────────────────
│ . . .
│ lang : Name ↦ SynSpec
└──────────────────────────────────────────────────────
```

There is a simple ASCII syntax for defining new language constructs, basically an interleaving of keywords V (variable), T (type), E (expression) and P (predicate), keysymbols * (list) and # (counted-list) with arbitrary syntactical elements. The keysymbols follow a keyword and are themselves followed by a token denoting a separator. So E*, denotes a comma-separated list of expressions, whereas V#, is a comma-separated list of variables, whose length must match that of any other list present also defined using #. A theory of designs and imperative programming might declare its syntax as follows:

LANGUAGE
```
"|-"    |  " P |- P " .
":="    |  " V := E " .
"::="   |  " V#, ::= E#, " .
";"     |  " P ; P " .
"**"    |  " E ** P "
```

(Here ::= is intended to be simultaneous assignment). All language constructs so specified are considered as new instances of predicates, and so can themselves appear and be parsed as language elements, so allowing easy nesting of such constructs. Any specifications that define an infix operator can also have a precedence declaration.

---

[4] Currently ∧: 80, ∨: 60, ⇒: 30, ≡: 20.

There are no extra facilities provided to describe the semantics of user-constructs, as such laws are simply provided by the user as appropriate axioms in the theory. For our design theory we might give the semantics of ⊢ as follows:

```
LAWS
  "DEF |-" |  P |- Q  ==  ok /\ P => ok' /\ Q
```

Note these axioms can be written using the full predicate calculus language shown here, and hence cannot be considered as some form of conservative extension of pre-existing axioms. In addition, for any law regarding a user-construct to be useable, there must be a non-empty collection of laws satisfying the following conditions:

1. Each law has a name prefixed with "DEF⎵*uname*", where *uname* is the name in *lang* of the user-construct.
2. Each law has the form *LHS* ≡ *RHS* where *LHS* is an instance of the *uname* construct.
3. Any instance of the language construct must match at least one of these laws.
4. The *RHS*s must not mention the construct explicitly, nor should it be possible to construct a cycle via mutual recursion with other user-constructs.

The reason for this set of restrictions is because these laws will be used to automatically expand language definitions "under the hood" in order to evaluate free variables and side-conditions (§7.2). They do not preclude our introducing laws with language recursion, provided their names do not start with "DEF⎵*uname*".

Having introduced our language constructs we then will want to give their semantic definitions as axioms, posit some conjectures, and hopefully prove them to be laws of the language. However, the parser needs to know about language syntax before the rest of the theory text file can be parsed, as we are introducing new lexical elements. So every UTP text file has to have a syntax preamble, immediately after the first line gving the theory name. The preamble has the following format:

```
SYNTAXFROM
```
list of zero or more theory names, separated by spaces
optional **LANGUAGE** and **PRECEDENCES** sections in any order
```
ENDSYNTAX
```
The theories listed are those with syntax sections defining language constructs used in this theory in addition to the ones it introduces itself.

6 Proofs

Given a conjecture in a theory, any attempt to prove it will take place in a general proof context, adopting one of a number of available strategies, and making use of a variety of builtin proof procedures. In general, we do not work with a single theory, but rather a stack of them: the bottommost are the most fundamental and general whilst theories higher up the stack tend to be more specific and higher-level. The key idea is that a proof of a conjecture can depend on its own theory, as well as material from theories below it in the stack. The stack concept is provided to assist in the encapsulation of theories, and for this reason circular dependencies are not allowed.

When initially started, SAOITHÍN has a proof stack with a single entry, the _ROOT theory, defining the precedences of the propositional infix connectives. The user can then load up the desired theories, and the current state of the stack is then displayed in the application's main ("top") window:

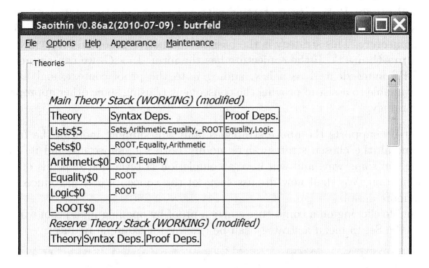

This stack state is saved into a file upon exiting the application, and restored automatically upon re-entry. Double-clicking on a theory name opens up a tabbed window to allow theory components to be inspected:

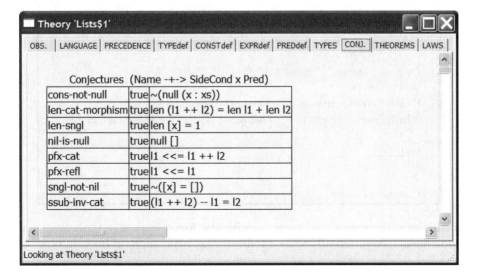

There are a number of strategies we can employ to prove a goal conjecture G, based on its top-level structure:

Reduce/Deduce. We can simply attempt to take G and use proof procedures to transform it to TRUE (or equivalently, an existing law).

LHS-to-RHS. If goal G has the form $L \equiv R$, we can try to transform the LHS L until it is equivalent to R (we could also try **RHS-to-LHS**).

Reduce-Both. Again, for the form $L \equiv R$, a way to proceed might be to try and transform both sides into something equivalent.

Law-Reduce. Rather than starting with the conjecture, we start with an instantiation of an existing law, and transform that until equivalent to our conjecture. This strategy is the basis for inductive proofs in SAOITHÍN.

Assume-then-... If the conjecture has the form $A \Rightarrow C$, we can assume the LHS antecedent A as a law, adding it to the proof context, and have it available to assist in proving the consequent C using some other appropriate strategy.

SAOITHÍN supports the above strategies, and will support more in the future. In general, the chosen strategy may modify both the conjecture and its proof context in some way, and will have a completion criteria that depends on that modification. We shall now discuss some of the concepts just introduced in a little more detail.

Double clicking on a conjecture starts a proof by opening up a proof window. From the Setup menu a strategy can be chosen, for example Reduce:

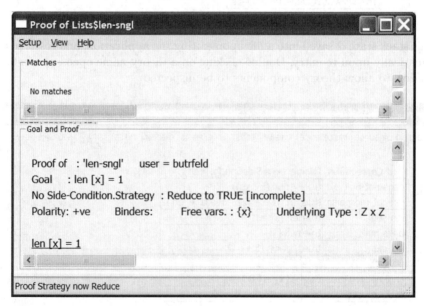

In this case the entire goal appears, with the focus, currently the whole goal, underlined. Given that all atomic predicates are expressions of boolean type, we find more useful typing information to be the notion of *underlying type*: the types of the sub-expressions just below the top-level of the atomic predicate. As the goal is an atomic predicate comparing two integers, we see that its underlying type is $\mathbb{Z} \times \mathbb{Z}$. If attention moves down into sub-expressions, then the full type of that component is displayed, as the notion of underlying type only applies to atomic predicates at the top-level.

6.1   Transformations

We mentioned taking a goal and transforming it in some way. As SAOITHÍN favours the use of equational reasoning, such transformations generally involve replacing the goal, or a sub-part of it, by a logically equivalent expression. So a proof becomes a chain of equivalences linking the initial goal to one that is equivalent to the required final predicate, the specifics of which are of course strategy-dependent.

The primary mechanism for effecting such transformations is a process of selecting a sub-part of the current goal (the "focus") and then applying the desired rule. The rules available for application are dependent on the focus, but always include the option to match it against the laws in all the currently accessible theories. The details of this matching is discussed later (§7), and for now we give a brief survey of other builtin transformers that can be used:

Tidying. Basically a collection of builtin operations to flatten and sort predicates whose top-levels are disjunctions and conjunctions.

Simplify. Effectively constant-folding, doing fairly obvious propositional simplifications.

Normal Forms. Converting predicates to either disjunctive or conjunctive normal form

Application. Reducing applications of abstractions to arguments (β-reduction) or applying explicit substitutions to the underlying predicate.

Quantifiers. Specifying explicit α-substitution, or existential witnesses. If using the Law-Reduce strategy, then we can also strip out top-level universal quantifiers, provided the focus is the whole goal.

Splitting. Given long conjunction/disjunctions, it is often useful to be able to re-structure them into specific groups in order to allow certain laws to become applicable.

Most of these can be invoked by a single key shortcut (see Help menu in Proof Window)

A proof is complete when goal transformation makes it "equivalent" to an endpoint predicate as determined by the strategy in use. The notion of equivalence we use is that of a slight generalisation of α-equivalence, that flattens nested quantifiers of the same type, so that the following are considered equivalent:

$$(\forall x \bullet \forall y \bullet P) \qquad (\forall x, y \bullet P) \qquad (\forall y, x \bullet P) \qquad (\forall y \bullet \forall x \bullet P)$$

6.2   Shorthands

A useful facility in SAOITHÍN is the ability to define meta-variables as shorthands for longer, more complex predicates. Examples of this in UTP include the definition of J in the reactive theory [HH98, Chp.8, p208]:

$$J \mathrel{\hat{=}} (ok \Rightarrow ok') \wedge wait' = wait \wedge tr' = tr \wedge ref' = ref$$

These definitions can be made as part of a theory, or can be introduced on the fly during a proof to replace a long predicate by a shorthand. During a proof it is then possible to replace such a meta-variable by its definition, or even to recursively expand all such shorthands in a predicate—even if the shorthands are themselves mutually recursive. To support this facility, we must add tables to a theory to record these shorthands, which can be introduced for type and predicate meta-variables, as well as regular variables:

```
Theory
  ...
  typedef : Name ⇸ Type
  exprdef : Name ⇸ Expr
  preddef : Name ⇸ Pred
```

All of the names in these tables are "known", which affects how they participate in law matching. These tables also have another use to ensure the soundness of certain strategies, as detailed below.

6.3   Assumptions

The "Assume-" strategies are an implementation of the Deduction Theorem:

$$\Phi \vdash A \Rightarrow C \quad \text{iff} \quad \Phi, A \vdash C$$

where the antecedent is elevated (temporarily) to a law for the purposes of this proof alone. However we need to be careful here [GS94, p72], to ensure that all meta-variables in the "assumption-now-law" can only match against themselves—in essence any such variables in A above must be temporarily restricted to only stand for themselves. We create a temporary theory on the top of the theory-stack, and add in as new laws, the antecedent A, suitably decomposed (e.g.):

$$\Phi \vdash (A_1 \wedge A_2 \wedge A_3) \Rightarrow ((A_4 \wedge A_5 \wedge A_6) \Rightarrow C)$$

$$\downarrow$$

$$\Phi, A_1, A_2, A_3, A_4, A_5, A_6 \vdash C$$

We then use the meta-variable tables just introduced in §6.2, adding in entries of the form $M \mathrel{\hat{=}} M$ for every "unknown" meta-variable in A, and finally renaming all the M in these tables, A_i and C to be fresh, so as to avoid clashes with other laws. This effectively prevents the law matching from binding these meta-variables to anything else during the proof. Once the proof is complete, the temporary theory is removed.

6.4 Induction

The current support for induction is via the Law-Reduce strategy, using the appropriate induction axiom, instantiated appropriately with the conjecture. This is then simplified until the the goal is itself reached. For example, we may have the following inductive axiom for natural numbers:

$$M[0/x] \wedge (\forall y \bullet M[y/x] \Rightarrow M[y+1/x]) \Rightarrow \forall x \bullet M$$

(Note that the assumption here is that x, if free in M is a natural number). Given addition defined recursively on its left argument, we may wish to prove that $n+0 = n$, for all natural n. If we invoke the Induction strategy in SAOITHÍN, and upon selecting the above induction axiom, and identifying n as our induction variable, a goal is generated by substituting our conjecture for M, and n for x, to obtain:

$$(n+0 = n)[0/n] \wedge (\forall y \bullet (n+0 = n)[y/n] \Rightarrow (n+0 = n)[y+1/n]) \Rightarrow \forall n \bullet (n+0 = n)$$

Switching to an Assume strategy here doesn't help as we want to manipulate the antecedents. Successive transformations, applying substitutions and using the definition of $+$, plus other axioms associated with the natural numbers, allow us to reduce the antecedents to true, leaving

$$\forall n \bullet (n + 0 = n)$$

Because we are reducing from an instance of an axiom, this is a theorem, so we can strip off the top-level universal quantification to get our original conjecture:

$$n + 0 = n$$

At present SAOITHÍN requires us to handle induction proofs as one lump as just illustrated, but future strategy/case-handling enhancements will make it possible to do a more "traditional" proof, where the base and inductive cases are effectively proven separately.

6.5 Caveat Emptor

Before moving on to look at the law matching facilities we need to point out an important aspect of the transformations discussed in this section: they have built-in to them certain assumptions regarding such notions as α-equivalence, the associativity, commutativity and idempotence of conjunction and disjunction, and implication trading, to name but a few. It is therefore important that any axioms introduced in theories do not conflict with these internal assumptions regarding the logic[5].

---

[5] This is in fact an argument for having a built-in logic theory that is compatible with the above assumptions.

7 Matching

The basic idea behind law application in SAOITHÍN is that the goal focus is matched against one or many laws. Those matches that succeed return a binding and a replacement template, and the user can then select which successful match to apply. The focus is replaced by the template, instantiated using the bindings. The matching we perform is basic structural matching of one test predicate against another treated as a pattern, with success returning a binding that matches pattern variables to test sub-predicates. We are not performing unification, either in isolation, or w.r.t. to some equational theory [BL98]. This is in contrast to Isabelle, for example, which uses higher-order unification [Pau88]. However, we do not simply match F against all of L —if L has certain forms, we can match against part of the law, offering another part as a replacement:

L is $P \equiv Q$: If the law is an equivalence we look for matches against the LHS and RHS separately, offering the other side as a replacement.

L is $A \Rightarrow C$: Given an implication law, a partial match against either the antecedent or consequent is still useful. Using equational reasoning, a match against A can offer $A \wedge C$ as a replacement, whilst a match against C can be replaced by $C \vee A$.

So the upshot is that we can get a number of different types of matches against laws with a certain structure. We now proceed to discuss the process of matching.

7.1 Basic Matching

The first phase of matching is a basic structural comparison of a test predicate Q (the goal focus) against a pattern predicate P (part of a law), which either fails, or succeeds and returns an incomplete binding, mapping pattern meta-variables to corresponding fragments of the test predicate. A key feature to note is that pattern variables and meta-variables match anything of the appropriate class (expr/type/predicate), provided they are not "known". Remember, a name is "known" if it appears in any of the following theory tables: *obs*, *typedef*, *exprdef* or *preddef*. A known name can only match against either itself or its definition as found in those tables.

None of the above gives any clue as to why basic matching returns an incomplete binding. The reason for this lie in three areas: our use of explicit substitutions, the fact that ordering is not important in substitutions or quantifier lists, and our desire to support a lot of flexibility in matching quantifiers. The motivation for the latter stems from the fact that SAOITHÍN is designed to support foundational work in the UTP, and so we want to be able to derive very general laws. For example, we want to have general laws like:

$$(\forall x, x_1, \ldots, x_n \bullet P) \equiv (\forall x_1, \ldots, x_n \bullet P), \quad x \notin P$$

where we can somehow specify that $n \geq 0$ and avoid listing the x_i. Also, given the above law and the axiom

$$(\exists x_1, \ldots, x_n \bullet P) \equiv \neg (\forall x_1, \ldots, x_n \bullet \neg P)$$

we would like to be able to prove

$$(\exists\, x, x_1, \ldots, x_n \bullet P) \equiv (\exists\, x_1, \ldots, x_n \bullet P), \quad x \notin P$$

To this end, the syntax of quantifiers in the logic of SAOITHÍN is in fact more complex than suggested so far. Instead we view a quantifier as being followed by two comma-separated lists of variables, with a semicolon separating the two lists:

$$\forall\, x_1, \ldots, x_m \,;\, xs_1, \ldots, xs_n \bullet P \qquad m \text{ s-qvars, } n \text{ m-qvars}$$
$$\forall\, x_1, \ldots, x_m \bullet P \qquad m \text{ s-qvars, } 0 \text{ m-qvars}$$
$$\forall\, ;\, xs_1, \ldots, xs_n \bullet P \qquad 0 \text{ s-qvars, } n \text{ m-qvars}$$

Either list may be empty. The first list is of so-called "single" quantifier variables (*s-qvars*), each of which corresponds to a conventional quantifier variable, and, when occurring in a pattern predicate, are required to match distinct s-qvars from the test predicate. The second list is of "multiple" quantifier variables (*m-qvars*), which are intended to represent many quantifier variables. A m-qvar in a pattern can match any mixture of s-qvars and m-qvars, including none. Matching is now complicated by the fact that the ordering of s-qvars, m-qvars is irrelevant, so in principle we have to try every possible permutation. Basic matching will succeed for simple cases, basically those with only one pattern qvar, but otherwise will return a deferred match in the form of a test-qvars/pattern-qvars pair, in addition to any bindings from the quantifier bodies. The basic matching is then followed by two phases, one that tries to resolve the deferred matches, and then a step to check the side-conditions. Both of these phases need to know about the free variables of the goal.

7.2   Free Variables

Many laws have side-conditions attached, all of which are conditions regarding the free-variables. However, the presence of explicit meta-variables and substitution complicates the calculation of the free variables of a predicate. To see this, we first present some clauses of the definition of free variables of a predicate:

$$\mathsf{fv}\, e = \text{all variables free in } e$$
$$\mathsf{fv}(P_1 \wedge P_2) = (\mathsf{fv}\, P_1) \cup (\mathsf{fv}\, P_2)$$
$$\mathsf{fv}(\forall\, \overrightarrow{v} \bullet e) = (\mathsf{fv}\, e) \setminus \overrightarrow{v}$$
$$\mathsf{fv}\, M = \mathsf{fv}.M$$
$$\mathsf{fv}\, P[e_1, \ldots, e_n / v_1, \ldots, v_n] = (\mathsf{fv}\, P) \setminus \{v_1, \ldots, v_n\}$$
$$\cup \bigcup \{i : 1 \ldots n \mid v_i \in \mathsf{fv}\, P \bullet \mathsf{fv}\, e_i\}$$

We see that for meta-variables we need to return the fact that computation of their free variables needs to be held until they are instantiated at some later point in time. With substitution, we see that the resulting set is contingent upon the freeness or otherwise in P of the substitution target variables $(v_1, \ldots, v_n)$. The upshot of all this is that we need to represent the free-variables of predicates using a free-variable set-expression, rather than just a simple variable enumeration. The required syntax of such expressions is as follows:

$$
\begin{array}{llll}
s \in SetExpr & ::= & \{v_1, \ldots, v_n\} & \text{Enumeration, } n \geq 0 \\
& | & \text{fv.}M & \text{Meta free-variables} \\
& | & s_2 \setminus \{v_1, \ldots, v_n\} & \text{Set Difference, } n \geq 0 \\
& | & \bigcup(s_1, \ldots, s_n) & \text{Union, } n \geq 0 \\
& | & m \Rrightarrow s & \text{Conditional Set} \\
m \in Member & ::= & a \in s & \text{Element Membership} \\
& | & \bigwedge(m_1, \ldots, m_n) & \text{Conjunction, } n \geq 2
\end{array}
$$

Most are self explanatory, except conditional set membership $m \Rrightarrow s$, which denotes set s if m is true, otherwise is empty.

A further complication arises with the user-defined language constructs. The free variables of these can only be established by expanding out their definitions. If we were simply to report "cannot tell" for the free variables of such constructs, then we would be unable to match any law involving a user-construct that had a side-condition, and would be forced to expand them out as an explicit proof step in any case. As one of the aims of UTP is to support laws at the language level, without always having to expand out the underlying predicate form, this is not a viable solution.

Accordingly, the algorithm for computing free variables expands language definitions on-the-fly, to get to a predicate form to establish its free-variables. This is why every language construct has to have defining laws with the name and form described in §5. This on-the-fly activity is invisible to the user, occurring behind the scenes. This explains why the language definition laws cannot be mutually recursive, otherwise this procedure could not be guaranteed to terminate.

7.3   Match Completion

Once a basic match is done, we want to try to complete it by using context information to figure out a suitable qvar matching. The context information we use includes the bindings already obtained, some which may pre-determine how qvars should match, as well as any information regarding the free variables of the focus, as well as side-conditions for both the goal and the relevant law. This process is quite complex and we omit any further details, apart form noting that in complicated cases it may fail to find a valid matching even if one exists. However there is a work-around by using other proof steps to re-organise quantifiers until matching does work. For a similar reason, the checking of α-equivalence used to terminate a proof is also incomplete and may fail to detect such an equivalence — the same work-around can be used here as well.

Finally, we check that the law side-condition, if any, when translated in terms of the goal using the bindings, is actually a consequence of the goal side-condition, if any: $sc_{law} \wedge sc_{goal} \equiv sc_{goal}$. This is achieved by code that automatically evaluates/simplifies a side-condition using free-variable set-expressions and then establishes that the above equivalence holds. This is facilitated by the existence of a normal-form for side-conditions.

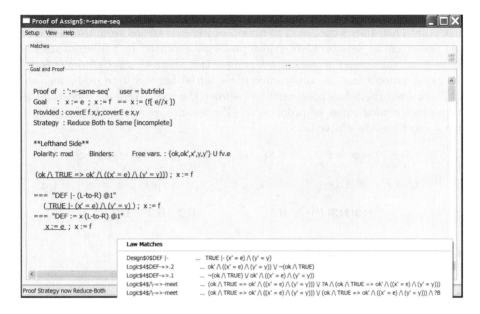

Fig. 1. SAOITHÍN Proof Example

8 Usage

Here we show a proof (that $x := e;\ x := f\ =\ x := f[e/x]$), using the reduce both sides strategy (Fig.1). A number of steps have already been performed, expanding the definitions of $:=$ and $\vdash$, with the steps shown in reverse order (first proof step last). The user has right-clicked, bringing up a possible list of replacements. Law matching can return a large number of successful matches, and these need to be presented to the user in a manner that makes it easy for them to select the law they wish to apply. There are basically two ways for a user to request law matching: one displays all the matches in a special window for the user to peruse, whilst the other displays up to 20 of them in a popup menu for immediate selection. In both cases we need some way to rank matches so the most useful appear first. In essence, we need some form of heuristics that can take a law match and compute a ranking number. There has been a limited amount of experimentation in this area, and it is a difficult area to get right. While at present the heuristics are hard-coded, we expect to improve matters to give the users more control in this area in future. The performance of the law matching is excellent at present, with a virtually instant return of results, while the GUI performance can be a little slow when inspecting large theory tables, so this is an obvious area for improvement.

Earlier versions of SAOITHÍN have been tested on 3rd-year Computer Science students at TCD who have taken an elective module on Formal Methods, which presents the subject through the UTP framework. Initially they were shown the use of the prover using a logic module with initial laws drawn from the axiomatization of equational logic in [GS94], material that they studied in their first year. Then they were asked to prove conjectures arising from useful library theories, such as Sets or Lists. Most problems reported by the students had to do with installation or user-interface behaviour issues—most students found the proof aspects easy to apply once these initial hurdles were overcome, and feedback from them has been used to improve the tool. We have used the tool to produce a wide range of proofs of UTP relevance, of which the following is just a short representative list:

$$(\sigma \frown \tau) - \sigma = \tau \qquad S_1 \cap (S_2 \cup S_3) = (S_1 \cap S_2) \cup (S_1 \cap S_3)$$

$$P \vdash Q \equiv P \vdash P \wedge Q \qquad x := e;\ y := f \equiv y := f[e/x];\ x := e, \quad y \notin e$$

$$\mathbf{R3}(\mathbf{R3}(P)) \equiv \mathbf{R3} \qquad \mathbf{R2} \circ \mathbf{R2} = \mathbf{R2}$$

9   Conclusions and Future Work

We have given motivation for, and presented, SAOITHÍN, a theorem-proving assistant for UTP. The current state of the tool is still experimental, with considerable scope for enhancement and improvement, but is already a useful tool for experienced[6] developers of UTP foundations.

Apart from the obvious need for comprehensive library of useful theorems from general logic, arithmetic, set, list and map theory, there are still a few foundational issues that need to be resolved. The current limitation to fixed alphabets is too restrictive, but we have a plan, using special meta-variables known to the pattern matcher, to be able to describe generic laws that cross a number of theories: the gold standard here would be a definition of sequential composition

$$P;\ Q \mathrel{\widehat{=}} \exists OBS_m \bullet P[OBS_m/OBS'] \wedge Q[OBS_m/OBS], \quad OBS_m \text{ fresh}$$

that works in any theory whose observations are homogenous (meta variables OBS_m, OBS' and OBS would need special pattern matching and binding treatment). The treatment of undefinedness in a way that limits its impact on general proving is still under exploration, and we are exploring various ideas in this area [Art96]. Given the existing work on UTP and Circus using Proofpower-Z, we also hope to explore the ability to take the GUI front-end of SAOITHÍN, and couple it to ProofPower-Z as a backend, given some appropriate transformation of how proofs and theorems are presented.

9.1   Acknowledgments and Availability

We would like to thank Colm Bhandal, Karen Forde, Simon Dardis, Jim Woodcock and the Formal Methods classes of 2009 and 2010 for their work on, and

---

[6] Not too trusting!

feedback about, SAOITHÍN. SAOITHÍN is written in Haskell [JHA$^+$99], managed using the distributed source-code manager Mercurial [O'S09], and is released open-source under GPL v2, at `http://www.scss.tcd.ie/Andrew.Butterfield/Saoithin/`. The version available at the time of writing is $0.86\alpha10$.

References

[Art96]   Arthan, R.D.: Undefinedness in Z: Issues for specification and proof. In: Farmer, W., Kerber, M., Kohlhase, M. (eds.) Proc. Mechanization of Partial Functions Workshop, Affiliated to CADE-13, New Brunswick, pp. 3–12 (1996)

[Asp00]   Aspinall, D.: Proof general: A generic tool for proof development. In: Graf, S., Schwartzbach, M.I. (eds.) TACAS 2000. LNCS, vol. 1785, pp. 38–42. Springer, Heidelberg (2000)

[BC04]   Bertot, Y., Castéran, P.: Interactive theorem proving and program development: Coq'Art: the calculus of inductive constructions. Texts in theoretical computer science. Springer, Heidelberg (2004)

[BKT94]   Bertot, Y., Kahn, G., Théry, L.: Proof by pointing. In: Hagiya, M., Mitchell, J.C. (eds.) TACS 1994. LNCS, vol. 789, pp. 141–160. Springer, Heidelberg (1994)

[BL98]   Baader, F., Leucker, M.: Comparison of two semantic approaches to unification. In: Proceedings of the 12th International Workshop on Unification, number SI-98/8 in Research Report, Universita di Roma, La Sapienza (June 1998)

[GHH$^+$95] George, C., Haxthausen, A.E., Hughes, S., Milne, R., Prehn, S., Pedersen, J.S.: The RAISE Development Method. The BCS Practitioners Series. Prentice Hall Int., Englewood Cliffs (1995)

[GS94]   Gries, D., Schneider, F.B.: A Logical Approach to Discrete Math. Texts and Monographs in Computer Science. Springer, New York (1994)

[HH98]   Hoare, C.A.R., He, J.: Unifying Theories of Programming. Prentice-Hall, Englewood Cliffs (1998)

[Hoa85]   Hoare, C.A.R.: Programs are predicates. In: Proc. of a Discussion Meeting of the Royal Society of London on Mathematical Logic and Programming Languages, pp. 141–155. Prentice-Hall, Inc., Upper Saddle River (1985)

[JHA$^+$99] Peyton Jones, S., Hughes, J., Augustsson, L., Barton, D., Boutel, B., Burton, W., Fasel, J., Hammond, K., Hinze, R., Hudak, P., Johnsson, T., Jones, M., Launchbury, J., Meijer, E., Peterson, J., Reid, A., Runciman, C., Wadler, P.: Report on the programming language haskell 98 (February 1999), `http://haskell.org/onlinereport/`

[MS89]   Morgan, C., Sanders, J.W.: Laws of the Logical Calculi. Oxford University Computing Laboratory, Programming Research Group (1989)

[MU05]   Malik, P., Utting, M.: CZT: A framework for Z tools. In: Treharne, H., King, S., Henson, M.C., Schneider, S.A. (eds.) ZB 2005. LNCS, vol. 3455, pp. 65–84. Springer, Heidelberg (2005)

[NPW02]   Nipkow, T., Paulson, L.C., Wenzel, M.: Isabelle/HOL - A Proof Assistant for Higher-Order Logic. LNCS, vol. 2283. Springer, Heidelberg (2002)

[NW06]   Nuka, G., Woodcock, J.: Mechanising a unifying theory. In: Dunne, S., Stoddart, B. (eds.) UTP 2006. LNCS, vol. 4010, pp. 217–235. Springer, Heidelberg (2006)

156   A. Butterfield

[OCW09]   Oliveira, M., Cavalcanti, A., Woodcock, J.: A UTP semantics for circus.
           Formal Asp. Comput. 21(1-2), 3–32 (2009)
[O'S09]   O'Sullivan, B.: Mercurial: The Definitive Guide. O'Reilly Media, Se-
           bastopol (June 2009)
[Pau88]   Paulson, L.C.: The foundation of a generic theorem prover. Technical Re-
           port TR-130, Computer Laboratory, University of Cambridge (March 1988)
[Sha96]   Shankar, N.: PVS: Combining specification, proof checking, and model
           checking. In: Srivas, M.K., Camilleri, A.J. (eds.) FMCAD 1996. LNCS,
           vol. 1166, pp. 257–264. Springer, Heidelberg (1996)
[Tou01]   Tourlakis, G.: On the soundness and completeness of equational predicate
           logics. J. Log. Comput. 11(4), 623–653 (2001)
[Wie06]   Wiedijk, F. (ed.): The Seventeen Provers of the World, Foreword by Dana
           S. Scott. LNCS (LNAI), vol. 3600. Springer, Heidelberg (2006)
[ZC09]   Zeyda, F., Cavalcanti, A.: Mechanical reasoning about families of UTP
           theories. Electr. Notes Theor. Comput. Sci. 240, 239–257 (2009)

A Formal Approach to Analyzing Interference Problems in Aspect-Oriented Designs⋆

Xin Chen, Nan Ye, and Wenxu Ding

State Key Laboratory for Novel Software Technology, Nanjing University
Department of Computer Science and Technology, Nanjing University
Nanjing, Jiangsu, P.R. China 210093
chenxin@nju.edu.cn,
{yenan,dingwx1987}@seg.nju.edu.cn

Abstract. Interference problems in aspect-oriented designs refer to the undesired interference between aspects and base programs that can lead to the emergence of unexpected behaviors, which do harm to the correctness of the entire system. We present a rigorous approach to analyzing the interference problems in aspect-oriented designs. Formal representations of classes and aspects are defined in terms of *designs* in UTP, while the weaving techniques in AOP are interpreted as the compositions of corresponding formal models. Conflicts between an aspect and base programs as well as between two aspects can be detected by calculating the weakest preconditions. Furthermore, the calculation also provides informative guidelines on how to solve the conflicts it found. Early detecting and removing conflicts in aspect-oriented design models can improve their qualities and save plenty of costs.

1 Introduction

Separation of concerns has been proved as an effective strategy to handle the ever growing complexity of software. It suggests identifying and separating artifacts of a software system relevant to every specific target, requirement or purpose from irrelevant ones, and manipulating them one by one.

Applying this strategy, Aspect-oriented programming (AOP) [10] enables engineers to design and implement a software's core functionalities and crosscutting concerns, as a base system and separate modules, namely aspects, respectively. Before execution, AOP's weaving mechanism can integrate those aspects into the base system on predefined points, called join points. This new paradigm helps to create a more coherent system since it avoids codes of concerns to be scattered everywhere in a system and tangled together with unrelated codes.

Despite of the improvement in reusability and maintainability, AOP brings great difficulty in reasoning the behaviors of software obtained by weaving aspects into base program since base programs and aspects may interfere with each other in an undesired

---

⋆ This work is supported by the National Natural Science Foundation of China (No.90818022, No.60721002), the National Grand Fundamental Research 973 Program of China (No.2009CB320702), and by the National S&T Major Project (2009z01036-001-001-3).

S. Qin (Ed.): UTP 2010, LNCS 6445, pp. 157–171, 2010.

manner. After weaving, unexpected results can emerge. This is the so-called *interference problem* in AOP. To gain a high flexibility in the interactions between aspects and base programs, AOP allows aspects to be woven into the base programs in many positions, including private methods of classes. As a result, aspects may modify any variable's value and change the control flows in base programs arbitrarily. Since on most occasions, base programs and aspects are designed and implemented by different developers, interference, even conflicts between base programs and aspects are prone to occur in large software with usages of AOP.

AOP also aims for the reuse of aspects, as the same concern might be considered in many different systems. It is often the case that more than one aspect is integrated into one system. Unfortunately, when multiple aspects are woven into the same base codes, they may interfere with each other too, as developers of aspects can not anticipate what aspects will be woven together and in which order they are woven.

These two interference problems do harm to the correctness and reliability of software systems using AOP. The weaved software system could be incorrect even both base codes and every aspects individually are correct. Furthermore, when woven with more than one aspects, the weaved software system may be correct in one weaving order and incorrect in another. To ensure the quality of aspect-oriented software systems, the methods to analyze interference problems, to detect and resolve semantics conflicts, need to be carefully studied.

In this paper, we present a formal approach to analyzing interference problems in aspect-oriented designs, detecting and resolving conflicts problems by formal induction techniques. The formal models of base codes and aspects are defined in terms of *designs* in UTP [5]. And, the weaving mechanism is treated as the composition of the formal models. Based on these formal representations, rules for reasoning interferences between a basic system and its aspects, as well as interferences among all its aspects are studied which rely on calculations of weakest preconditions. In addition, when a conflict is detected, the calculating process on weakest preconditions can give guidelines on how to fix it. The approach introduced in this paper can be easily integrated with AOP's development processes, as functional specifications of classes and aspects can be added as annotations to design models and can be analyzed separately. The ability to locate and resolve semantics conflicts in AOP design models in the early develop phase helps to assure the quality of AOP software with less costs.

We begin in Sect. 2, where basic concepts of aspect-oriented programming are introduced. Sect. 3 gives our formal foundations, theories of *design*, which are used in Sect. 4 to formalize classes, aspects and the weaving mechanism in AOP. Sect. 5 studies the methods for detecting conflicts between base programs and an aspect, and between two aspects respectively. We compare our approach with related works in Sect. 6 and conclude our paper in Sect. 7. We use the tele communication simulation system as a case study to illustrate the approach.

2   Aspect-Oriented Programming

Basic concepts of Aspect-oriented programming are illustrated in this section. An example, a tele communication simulation system [12] is given to help the understanding of these concepts. Later in the paper, it is shown that, with the help of our interference analysis method, interference problems in this example will be found and solved.

AOP is built on top of the object-oriented programming. Base programs in AOP are made of *classes* while crosscut concerns in AOP are constructed as *aspects*. An aspect's definition declares that to fulfill a specific concern, in which positions of the base program, according to what rules, what actions need to be injected. In terms of AOP, they are defined as *join points*, *point cuts* and *advices* respectively. Two widely used join points, before the execution of methods and after the execution of methods are considered in the paper. An *advice* is a piece of object-oriented codes, very similar to a method's definition. Three types of advices are treated in this paper. The advice *before* requires to be executed before a join point and after it is executed, the control flow returns to codes next to the join point, while the advice *after* needs to be executed after a join point. Codes in an *around* advice can take the place of the codes in the join point it encounters. Usually, *around* advices are used when some original logics in base programs need to be overridden. The definition of a point cut gives a rule to determine whether or not an advice can be integrated into the base program on a specific join point. Rules defined in point cuts are matched with join points by syntactical comparisons.

To illustrate the use of aspect-oriented programming, we introduce an example, the tele communication simulation system and show how to apply an aspect-oriented design scheme. It is a simple simulation of a telephone system where users can make phone calls. Its base system consists of devices and connections, in which a valid phone call is represented as a connection between two devices. There are two features in consideration to extend the base system's functionality: the *call interruption* and the *call divert*. The feature *call interruption* interrupts the connection on the callee's side when an incoming call is required to reach him and his line is busy. The service *call divert* can forward an incoming call to a busy callee to another device whose number exists in the forwarding list. Here, both features need to intervene at the beginning of a connection and check the status of destination in the incoming call.

In an aspect-oriented design of the system, both features are encapsulated as individual aspects. In the base program, the method *complete* in the class *connection* is responsible for setting up a connection between two devices, the caller and the callee. These two aspects share the same join point, before the execution of the method complete. And, both aspects use the same type of advice, *before*, to handle a busy line according to their own requirements. The point cuts defined in both aspects declare that these two advices should be applied to the method *complete* of the class *connection*.

At first glance, it seems that these two aspects are interference-free with each other since the corresponding concerns they implement are irrelevant. However, in fact, weaving the aspect *call divert* into the base phone service will violate an important invariant assumed by the base program, which means the aspect *call divert* and the base program are not interference-free. Furthermore, adding these aspects into the base phone service according to the order, *call divert, call interruption*, will cause a conflict problem too, since the latter aspects will disable the former's effect. Using this example, we will show how our specification and induction approach can detect potential conflicts arisen from weaving aspects into base programs and give guidelines to remove them.

3   Formal Foundations

Before giving formal specifications to base programs and aspects, we introduce our notation for writing specifications. The most fundamental notion in our framework is a *design* [5]. A design D over an input alphabet $in\alpha$ and an output alphabet $out\alpha$ is a predicate of the form: $p(in\alpha) \vdash R(in\alpha, out\alpha)$ and its meaning is defined by

$$(p \vdash R) \stackrel{def}{=} (ok \wedge p) \Rightarrow (ok' \wedge R).$$

which asserts that if the execution of design D starts successfully, i.e. *ok* is *true*, from a state in which the precondition p holds, it will terminate successfully, i.e. *ok'* is *true*, in a state satisfying the postcondition R. Notice that in a design, an input variable is an unprimed identifier and an output variable is a primed one.

With the use of the auxiliary boolean variables *ok* and *ok'*, designs are closed under the conventional programming operators, such as assignment "$x := e$", sequential composition ";" and conditional choice "$D_1 \lhd b \rhd D_2$" (**if** b **then** D_1 **else** D_2). We also define the special designs $\perp$ as the "weakest design" *true* and $\top$ as "strongest design" *false*. An *assertion* (or *guard*) g is a predicate over the input alphabet and can also be defined as a design, denoted by $g_\top$

$$g_\top \stackrel{def}{=} skip \lhd g \rhd false$$

where *skip* is the design $true \vdash \wedge_{x \in in\alpha} x' = x$ that does not change any variable. Thus, a guarded design $g_\top; D$ behaves like D when g holds, and deadlocks otherwise.

We also define parallel composition, nondeterministic choice and sequential composition as below:

$$
\begin{aligned}
(p_1 \vdash R_1) \parallel (p_2 \vdash R_2) &\equiv (p_1 \wedge p_2 \vdash R_1 \wedge R_2) \\
(p_1 \vdash R_1) \sqcap (p_2 \vdash R_2) &\equiv (p_1 \vee p_2) \vdash ((p_1 \wedge R_1) \vee (p_2 \wedge R_2)) \\
(p_1 \vdash R_1); (p_2 \vdash R_2) &\equiv (p_1 \wedge \neg(R_1; \neg p_2)) \vdash (R_1; R_2)
\end{aligned}
$$

Refinement between designs is defined as logical implication, and data refinement is handled by introducing a refinement mapping between the state spaces of the two designs. All the above operations on designs are monotonic with regard to the refinement relation. Calculus on design refinement can be found in [5].

The *weakest precondition* (**wp**) calculation has been widely used in programs analysis. The link from the design calculus to the theory of predicate transformers is given by the following definition

$$\mathbf{wp}(p \vdash R, q) \stackrel{def}{=} p \wedge \neg(R; \neg q)$$

4   Modeling Base Classes and Aspects

Rather than dealing with aspect-oriented programming languages, this paper focuses on the models used in designing aspect-oriented software. The aspect-oriented programming is built on the basis of object-oriented technologies. Base programs in aspect-oriented software are organized in classes. Class models are the most important artifacts used to present designs of aspect-oriented software. Thus, we begin with the definition of functionality specifications of classes.

Definition 1. *A* **class** *is a collection of fields definitions and methods definitions,* $C = \langle FDef, MDef \rangle$, *where*

- *FDef is a set of field definitions, denoted by C.FDef. Each member of this set has the form* $x : T$ *where* x *and* T *represent the name and type of the field respectively.*
- *MDef is a set of method definitions, denoted by C.MDef. A method* m(**in** *inx*; **out** *outy*) *defines the name* m, *the list of input parameters inx and the list of output parameters outy. Each input or output parameter declaration is of the form* $u : U$ *giving the name* u *and the type* U *of the parameter* m.

For simplicity, we use $\overline{x}$ and $\overline{y}$ to represent the list of input parameters and the list of output parameters respectively.

Example 4.1. For the example, the tele communication simulation system illustrated in section 2, the class *Connection* in its base system can be represented as follows:

$$FDef = \{status : string, origin : Device, dest : Device\}$$
$$MDef = \{locate(onum : string, dnum : string), complete(), drop()\}$$

When class models are used to describe the structure of an application, implementation details of each method will be hidden. Instead, descriptive specifications of methods' functions are given. Thus, when modeling a class's function, we will not break into the body of each method and describe its operation from scratch, but specify its function in terms of states of its fields before and after its execution.

The functional specification of a class is defined as a class's behavior.

Definition 2. *A class* C's **behavior** *is a quadruple Behv*$(C, Init, MSpec, Inv)$, *where*

- *C is a class,*
- *Init is a predicate that defines the initial values of the fields declared in C.FDef,*
- *MSpec assigns each method* $m(\overline{x}; \overline{y})$ *belonging to* $C.MDef$ *a static functionality specification as a pair* $p(x, I.FDef) \vdash R(x, I.FDef, y', I.FDef')$ *of preconditions and postconditions, where non-primed and primed variables represent the values of the variables in the pre and post state of the execution of the method, respectively.*
- *Inv is a class invariant which is assumed to be hold before and after each method's execution.*

The class invariant plays a vital role in designing a class's behavior. It describes important properties of a class needed to be preserved during its execution by enforcing constraints on methods' operation. In practice, business rules and constraints of applications are often translated as invariants of its constituted classes.

Example 4.2. For the class *Connection* given in example 4.1, in short, its methods operate according to the following specifications: Given two phone numbers, the method *locate* can find the corresponding devices. The method *complete* is responsible for connecting two different devices required by an incoming call. The method *drop* can drop the current connection. An important property must be ensured in this class is that a device can not connect to itself. A complete specification of the class *Connection* represented as its behavior are given as follows:

$Init \qquad \stackrel{def}{=} true \vdash status = disconnected \wedge origin = null \wedge dest = null$

$MSpec(locate) \quad \stackrel{def}{=} onum \neq dnum \vdash$
$\qquad\qquad\qquad \exists de1, de2 : Device \bullet de1.num = onum \wedge de2.num = dnum \Longrightarrow$
$\qquad\qquad\qquad origin' = de1 \wedge dest' = de2$

$MSpec(complete) \stackrel{def}{=} status = disconnected \wedge origin \neq null \wedge$
$\qquad\qquad\qquad dest \neq null \wedge origin \neq dest \vdash$
$\qquad\qquad\qquad status' = connected \wedge$
$\qquad\qquad\qquad origin.d\_status' = busy \wedge origin.current' = this \wedge$
$\qquad\qquad\qquad dest.d\_status' = busy \wedge dest.current' = this$

$MSpec(drop) \qquad \stackrel{def}{=} status = connected \vdash$
$\qquad\qquad\qquad status' = disconnected \wedge$
$\qquad\qquad\qquad origin.d\_status' = idle \wedge origin.current' = null \wedge$
$\qquad\qquad\qquad dest.d\_status' = idle \wedge dest.current' = null \wedge$
$\qquad\qquad\qquad origin' = null \wedge desti' = null$

$Inv \qquad\qquad \stackrel{def}{=} status = connected \Longrightarrow origin.num \neq dest.num$

In aspect-oriented models, concerns are constructed in aspects. To achieve a high flexibility in extending a base system's function, most aspect-oriented programming languages permit to add new field variables into classes of a base system. This mechanism is called inter-type declaration in aspects. Besides, aspects include pointcut declarations which provide logical definitions for selecting the join points where a piece of advice is applied. Aspects also have advice definitions where operations on join points are defined. Inter-type declarations, pointcuts and advices compose an aspect definition.

Definition 3. *An* **aspect** *consists of sets of inter-type declarations, pointcuts and advices.* $A = \langle ITDec, PCut, Advs \rangle, where$

- *ITDec is a set of inter-type declaration. Like fields declarations in classes, each inter-type declaration has the form $x : T$, denoting a name x belonging to the type T.*
- *PCut is a set of pointcut definitions. A definition of pointcut pc is of the form pointcut pcname $C.m(\overline{x}, \overline{y})$, where $C.m(\overline{x}, \overline{y})$ is the method m of the class C in base programs. The declaration $C.m(\overline{x}, \overline{y})$ specifies a join point, before the call to the method m of the class C where the advices defined in the set Advs should be applied.*
- *Advs is a set of advices' definitions. An advice is defined in the form $before()|$ $after()|around()$. The advices before and after require to be invoked before or after the join point respectively. And the around advice will replace the codes residing at the join point.*

AOP provides mechanisms that enable an advice to get the execution context of a join point. When defining an advice's specification, descriptions of contexts at the join points must be included. To give a rigorous description to an aspect's function, the behavior of an aspect is introduced.

Definition 4. *An aspect's* **behavior** *is a triple Behv(A, Init, ASpec), where*

- *A is an aspect,*
- *Init is a predicate that defines the initial values of the inter-type declarations declared in A.ITDec.*
- *ASPec assigns each advice adv() $\in$ Advs a functionality specification as a pair:*

$$p(A.ITDec \cup context(C.m)) \vdash R(A.ITDec \cup context(C.m), A.ITDec' \cup context'(C.m)),$$

where context(C.m) $\overset{def}{=}$ C.FDef $\cup$ m.$\overline{x}$ and context'(C.m) $\overset{def}{=}$ C.FDef $\cup$ C.FDef'
$\cup$ m.$\overline{x}$ $\cup$ m.$\overline{y'}$ are the context of a join point C.m before and after adv's execution.
They are the values of fields in the class C and input, output parameters of the method m.

Example 4.3. For the two aspects call interruption and call divert shown in section 2, the specifications of their advices, before, are given as follows:

$$
\begin{aligned}
ASpec(D.before) \overset{def}{=}\ & true \vdash \exists(f,t) \in forwardList, de : Device\bullet \\
& c.dest' = de \wedge c.dest.num = f \wedge de.num = t \\
& \lhd c.dest.d\_status = busy \wedge \exists(f,t) \in forwardList, \\
& de : Device \bullet c.dest.num = f \wedge de.num = t\rhd \\
& c.dest' = c.dest
\end{aligned}
$$

$$
\begin{aligned}
ASpec(I.before) \overset{def}{=}\ & true \vdash (c.dest.d\_status' = idle\wedge \\
& c.dest.current.status' = interrupted\wedge \\
& interruptedC' = interruptedC \cup \{c.dest.current\}) \\
& \lhd c.dest.d\_status = busy \rhd skip
\end{aligned}
$$

For convenience, in the rest of papers, D and I are used to denote the aspect $Call\ Divert$ and $Call\ Interruption$ respectively.

When building an AOP application, an AOP compiler is responsible for weaving classes with aspects. During the weaving operation, the types of classes, the signatures of classes' methods and the required signatures declared in pointcuts' definitions are compared based on their syntactical forms. To record the results of the matching process, a set, $Match(C, A)$ is introduced. A member $(m, ad) \in Match(C, A)$ means that the method m defined in the class C satisfies the signature requirements assumed by the advice ad. Thus, the advice ad should be woven with the method $C.m$ by the compiler. The semantics explanation of a weaving process is defined as the composition of a class's behavior and an aspect's behavior.

Definition 5. *Let C be a class, A be an aspect, such that some pointcuts matches methods m in class C. The woven class obtained by weaving A into C , denoted as $C \oplus A$ is defined as:*

$$(C \oplus A).FDef \overset{def}{=} C.FDef \cup A.ITDec$$
$$(C \oplus A).MDef \overset{def}{=} C.MDef$$

$$(C \oplus A).Init \overset{def}{=} C.Init \wedge A.Init$$

$$(C \oplus A).MSpec \overset{def}{=} \Phi$$

$$(C \oplus A).Inv \overset{def}{=} C.Inv$$

where the function Φ assigns each method $m \in C.MDef$ with a design:

$$\Phi(m) \overset{def}{=} \begin{cases} MSpec(m), & \text{if } \forall ad \in A.Advs \bullet (m, ad) \notin Match(C, A) \\ ASpec(ad)[*/c.*]; MSpec(m) & \text{if } \exists ad \in A.Advs \bullet (m, ad) \in Match(C, A) \\ & \wedge isBefore(ad) \\ MSpec(m); ASpec(ad)[*/c.*] & \text{if } \exists ad \in A.Advs \bullet (m, ad) \in Match(C, A) \\ & \wedge isAfter(ad) \\ ASpec(ad)[*/c.*] & \text{if } \exists ad \in A.Advs \bullet (m, ad) \in Match(C, A) \\ & \wedge isAround(ad) \end{cases}$$

Here, the functions $isBefore(ad), isAfter(ad)$ and $isAround(ad)$ return true correspondingly when the advice ad is a before advice, an after advice or an around advice. The set $Match(C, A)$ consists of pairs of advices and their matched join points. That is, a member (m, ad) means an advice ad 's pointcut definition in the aspect A matches the method m of class C.

Example 4.4. For the example, the tele communication simulation system, the system obtained through weaving the aspect call divert into the class connect, denoted as $C \oplus D$, is represented as follows:

$$(C \oplus D).FDef \overset{def}{=} \{status : string, origin : Device, dest : Device\}$$

$$(C \oplus D).MDef \overset{def}{=} \{locate(onum : string, dnum : string), complete(), drop()\}$$

$$(C \oplus D).Init \overset{def}{=} true \vdash status' = disconnected \wedge origin' = null \wedge dest' = null$$

$$MSpec(locate) \overset{def}{=} C.MSpec(locate)$$

$$MSpec(drop) \overset{def}{=} C.MSpec(drop)$$

$MSpec(complete) \overset{def}{=} status = disconnected \wedge origin \neq null \wedge$
$\qquad (de \neq origin) \lhd dest.d\_status = busy \wedge$
$\qquad \exists (f, t) \in forwardList, de : Device\bullet$
$\qquad dest.num = f \wedge de.num = t \rhd (dest \neq null \wedge origin \neq dest)$
$\qquad \vdash$
$\qquad status' = connected \wedge$
$\qquad origin.d\_status' = busy \wedge origin.current' = this \wedge$
$\qquad (dest' = de \wedge de.d\_status' = busy \wedge de.current' = this$
$\qquad \lhd dest.d\_status = busy \wedge \exists (f, t) \in forwardList, de : Device\bullet$
$\qquad dest.num = f \wedge de.num = t \rhd$

$\qquad\qquad dest' = dest \wedge dest.d\_status' = busy \wedge dest.current' = this$

$$(C \oplus D).Inv \overset{def}{=} status = connected \implies origin \neq dest$$

5   Interference Checking

5.1   Interference Analysis between Base Programs and Aspects

Consider the weaving between an aspect and a base program first. For any weaving, depending on the type of advices, it has to be checked either the base program satisfies the conditions required by the aspect or vice versa. Otherwise, the weaving may lead the execution of the woven method to an unpredictable state. In detail, since the advices, *before* and *around*, will execute before the base program, they require that base program must establish the preconditions of them. That is, for the base program m and its corresponding advice ad for weaving, the condition $(C.inv \wedge \mathbf{pre}(C.MSpec(m))) \implies \mathbf{pre}(A.ASpec(ad))$ holds. At the runtime, the advice $after$ follows the method m. Thus, it requires that when the method m terminates, the precondition of $after$ is established. That is, the condition $\mathbf{pre}(MSpec(m)) \implies \mathbf{wp}((C.MSpec(m), \mathbf{pre}(after))$ holds.

At the same time, the aspect's impact on base programs has to be studied as well. A tight view of the interference-free definition suggests that there is no change in the behaviors of base programs when an aspect is applied. However, in practice, this constraint is too strong. As shown in the example, the tele communication system, the applying of the aspects, Forwarding and interrupting, extends the functions of basic programs largely. In fact, one of the main usages of aspect-oriented designs is to extend the ability of base programs without breaking into their modules. To leave the space for future functional extension, a more flexible view of interference-free definition is preferred. In object-oriented designs, business rules and design constraints are expressed as invariants of classes which impose constraints on behaviors of their methods. Even after the aspects are applied, those constraints should not be violated neither. Thus, rather than considering the behavior of each method before and after weaving, our interference-free definition requires that the invariant of the class should be kept after woven with some aspects. Formally speaking, it requires that once the woven method $(C \oplus A).m$ is invoked on the condition that the precondition of the method $C.m$ is established, the invariant of the class must be held on its termination. By putting all the two conditions into considerations, the definition of interference-free between a class and an aspect is given as follows:

Definition 6. *Let C be a class, A be an aspect, such that some pointcuts in aspect A find their matched join points in class C. The woven class $C \oplus A$ is interference-free if the following conditions hold:*

1. *The preconditions of matched class C's methods and aspect A's advices are satisfied:*

    – *for all $(m, ad) \in \mathbf{Match}(C, A)$, if ad is a before advice or an around advice in the aspect A:*
    $$(C.Inv \wedge \mathbf{pre}(C.MSpec(m))) \implies \mathbf{pre}(A.ASpec(ad))$$
    – *for all $(m, ad) \in \mathbf{Match}(C, A)$, if ad is an after advice in the aspect A:*
    $$(C.Inv \wedge \mathbf{pre}(C.MSpec(m)) \implies \mathbf{wp}((C.MSpec(m), \mathbf{pre}(A.ASpec(ad)))$$
2. *The woven methods hold the invariant of the base program*

    $$(C.Inv \wedge \mathbf{pre}(C.MSpec(m))) \implies \mathbf{wp}((C \oplus A).MSpec(m), (C \oplus A).Inv)$$

Example 5.1. Consider the weaving of the class *connection* and the aspect *Call Divert*. Whether or not they are interference-free can be checked as follows:

For the condition 1, since there is only one matched join point, *connection.complete*(), we need to check that $(connection.Inv \land \mathbf{pre}(connection.MSpec(complete))) \implies$ $\mathbf{pre}(D.ASpec(before))$. It can be easily proved from the fact $\mathbf{pre}(D.ASpec(before)) = true$.

To check the condition 2, we need to calculate $\mathbf{wp}((connection \oplus D).MSpec(complete)$, $(connection \oplus D).Inv)$ and $\mathbf{pre}(connection.MSpec(complete))$.

$\mathbf{wp}((connection \oplus D).MSpec(complete), (connection \oplus D).Inv)$
$= status = disconnected \land origin \neq null \land$
$\quad (de \neq origin) \lhd dest.d\_status = busy \land \exists (f, t) \in forwardList, de : Device \bullet$
$\quad dest.num = f \land de.num = t \rhd (dest \neq null \land origin \neq dest)$
$\mathbf{pre}(C.MSpec(m))$
$= status = disconnected \land origin \neq null \land dest \neq null \land origin \neq dest$

Here, the condition 2 does not hold.

Thus, we conclude that the class *connection* and the aspect *Call Divert* are not interference-free.

Once a semantics conflict between a base system and an aspect is found, the unsatisfied conditions provide direct guidelines on how to refine the design models to remove it. As shown in example 5.1, the condition 2 fails to be satisfied due to the fact that the aspect *Call Divert* may forward a phone call to the caller himself. It prompts the designers to enforce a special check into the aspect *Call Divert*'s design model which ensures the caller is not the destination of the call divert.

5.2   Interference Analysis between Two Aspects

This section studies how to analyze the interference problems between two aspects with respect to a class C. Consider a case: given a class C, two aspects A_1, A_2 are woven into C according to the order: A_1, A_2. First, it is easy to see that to guarantee matched advices in both aspects will not lead the entire system to divergence, their preconditions must be satisfied. In detail, when applying the aspect A_1 into the class C, the preconditions of all matched advices in A_1 must be satisfied which is formally represented as for all the matched before advices or around advices, the condition $(C.inv \land \mathbf{pre}(C.MSpec(m))) \implies \mathbf{pre}(A_1.ASpec(ad))$ holds while for all the after advices, the condition $(C.inv \land \mathbf{pre}(C.MSpec(m)) \implies \mathbf{wp}((C.MSpec(m), \mathbf{pre}(A_1.ASpec(ad))$ holds. Similarly, the system $C \oplus A_1$ must assure the pre conditions of all matched advices in the aspect A_2 to be satisfied. This requirement can be written in formulas using the same pattern.

Notice that if the aspect A_2 doesn't affect the aspect A_1, then the post condition set up by the aspect A_1 will be held after the aspect A_2 is applied. This observation gives an intuitive explanation of the interference-free property between two aspects. In a formal representation, it requires the condition $\mathbf{pre}((C \oplus A_1).MSpec(m)) \Longrightarrow \mathbf{wp}((C \oplus A_1 \oplus A_2).MSpec(m), \mathbf{post}(A_1.ASpec(ad)))$ to be true.

By combining all these conditions together, the definition of interference-free between two aspects with respect to a class is given as follows:

Definition 7. *Let C be a class, A_1, A_2 be two aspects, such that the aspects are woven into the class C in the order A_1, A_2. The aspect A_1 does not interfere with the aspect A_2 with respect to the class C, if the following three conditions hold:*

1. *for all $(m, ad) \in \mathbf{Match}(C, A_1)$, the preconditions of matched class C's methods and aspect A_1's advices are satisfied:*

   - *if ad is a before or an around advice*
     $$(C.Inv \wedge \mathbf{pre}(C.MSpec(m))) \Longrightarrow \mathbf{pre}(A_1.ASpec(ad))$$
   - *if ad is an after advice*
     $$(C.Inv \wedge \mathbf{pre}\ (C.MSpec(m))) \Longrightarrow$$
     $$\mathbf{wp}((C.MSpec(m), \mathbf{pre}(A_1.ASpec(ad)))$$

2. *for all $(m, ad) \in \mathbf{Match}(C \oplus A_1, A_2)$,*
   - *if ad is a before or around advice*
     $$(C.Inv \wedge \mathbf{pre}(C.MSpec(m))) \Longrightarrow \mathbf{pre}(A_2.ASpec(ad))$$
   - *if ad is an after advice*
     $$(C.Inv \wedge \mathbf{pre}\ (C.MSpec(m))) \Longrightarrow$$
     $$\mathbf{wp}((C \oplus A_1).MSpec(m), \mathbf{pre}(A_2.ASpec(ad)))$$

3. *for all $(m, ad) \in \mathbf{Match}(C, A_1)$*

   $$\mathbf{pre}((C \oplus A_1).MSpec(m)) \Longrightarrow$$
   $$\mathbf{wp}((C \oplus A_1 \oplus A_2).MSpec(m), \mathbf{post}(A_1.ASpec(ad)))$$

As shown in the definition, when weaving more than one aspect into a class, the order of weaving is not a trivial issue. Since the results of one aspect woven earlier may be changed by another aspect woven later, the final systems generated by weaving the same set of aspects with different orders may have distinct functionalities with each other. This semantics dependency on weaving orders can be observed in many aspect-oriented languages. Thus, when reasoning the interference problems between two aspects, the orders of weaving should not be overlooked.

Example 5.2. Examine whether or not the aspects *Call Divert* and *Call Interruption* are interference-free with respect to the class *Connection* under the weaving order: first *Call Divert*, then *Call Interruption*.

Referring to the proof in example 5.1, the condition 1 is true.

Then, let us check the condition 2. There is only one matched join point, *conncetion. complete()*, for the advice *before*, we need to check that

$$C.Inv \wedge \mathbf{pre}(C.MSpec(complete)) \Longrightarrow \mathbf{pre}(I.ASpec(before)))$$

Due to the fact $\mathbf{pre}(I.ASpec(before)) = true$, the above condition is true. That is, the condition 2 is satisfied.

To check the condition 3, we need to calculate $\mathbf{pre}((C \oplus D).MSpec(m))$ and $\mathbf{wp}((C \oplus D \oplus I).MSpec(complete), \mathbf{post}(D.ASpec(opComplete)))$.

$$\mathbf{pre}((C \oplus D).MSpec(m))$$
$= status = disconnected \wedge origin \neq null \wedge$
$(de \neq origin) \lhd dest.d\_status = busy \wedge \exists (f,t) \in forwardList, de : Device \bullet$
$dest.num = f \wedge de.num = t \rhd (dest \neq null \wedge origin \neq dest)$
$\mathbf{wp}((C \oplus D \oplus I).MSpec(complete), \mathbf{post}(D.ASpec(opComplete)))$
$= \mathbf{pre}(C \oplus D \oplus I).MSpec(complete) \wedge$
$\neg(status' = connected \wedge origin.d\_status' = busy \wedge origin.current' = this \wedge$
$dest' = dest \wedge dest.d\_status' = busy \wedge dest.current' = this \wedge$
$(dest.current.status' = interrupted) \lhd c.dest.d\_status = busy \rhd skip;$
$\neg(dest' = de \lhd dest.d\_status = busy \wedge \exists (f,t) \in forwardList, de : Device \bullet$
$dest.num = f \wedge de.num = t \rhd dest' = dest))$

Here, the condition 3 does not hold.

As a result, we conclude that with respect to the class *connection*, under the weaving order *Call Divert, Call Interruption*, these two aspects are not interference-free with each other.

Note that, calculations of the weakest preconditions give informative feedbacks on how to get rid of the conflict. As shown in the above example, the calculation process in judging the condition 3 tells us the aspect *Call Interruption* will disable the aspect *Call Divert*'s function permanently by setting all busy callees' status to idle.

6   Related Work

As the interference problem is one of the most challenging issues in AOP, a lot of work has been done in interference detection and resolution.

Authors in [13] use labeled transitions systems to model base programs, aspects as well as the weaving mechanism. For verification, those state-based models of classes are converted into finite state processes, and the model checker LTSA can verify whether or not the woven model satisfies the desired properties. Be specified with particular properties, this method can be used to check the interference between base programs and aspects. Model checking techniques are applied to verify interference between aspects in [7]. It aims at the reuse of aspects called superimpositions. With the help of model checkers, it is assured that when aspects in a superimposition are woven into a basic program that satisfies the superimposition's assumptions, the woven program will satisfy the desired results and conform to the original specification of the basic program. A prototype tool implementing this idea is presented in [2]. It uses the Bandera tool to generate inputs of SPIN or SMV from a Java program. When performing verification, the above works deal with the program after woven with many aspects as a whole. Due to the well-known state explosion problem, these works are difficult to be applied in analyzing aspect-oriented programs in large.

To settle the scalability problem, new verification techniques are introduced. Authors in [11] present an incremental verification approach. It verifies the invariants of the base programs as soon as an aspect is integrated into the base programs. In this way, the verification needs not to be executed over the entire system. It is effective in checking the interference between big base programs and many aspects. In [3], authors suggest an assume-guarantee specification to support modular verification of aspects. In the approach, an aspect is constructed as a single state machine consisting of the linear temporal logic (LTL) description of the assumptions, a description of the join points, and the state machine of the advice. As the assumptions provide enough abstractions to underlying systems, the aspects' guaranteed properties can be checked by model checkers independently. Before an aspect's weaving, only a check on the base state machine with respect to its assumption is needed. The limitation of this work is that it can not handle conflict problems between aspects.

In [1], authors propose a method to detect interference among aspects sharing the same join points. They give a run-time semantics of an AOP language as a graph-transformation production rule system. By simulating the execution of advices, an execution state space is generated which is used to analyze and verify properties of the system at the join points. They also develop means to avoid the simulation of the entire system. The simulation approach requires many resources in computation and memory space. Although it can be applied to aspects without considering the base programs, it may not be suitable to be applied to big base programs with many aspects.

Authors in [12] use the formal specification language Alloy to detect the interference problems in aspect-UML models. Aspect-oriented designs represented as aspect-UML models are translated into Alloy structures, and then a model checker, Alloy analyzer, can be used to verify aspect interactions of an aspect-UML model. Similar to our works, pairs of precondition and postcondition act as the fundaments to describe functions of methods as well as advices in aspects. When detecting a conflict, the Alloy analyzer can give a counterexample explaining under which conditions the conflict happens. Besides the scalability problems coming with a model checker, we believe our calculations of the weakest preconditions can give more direct and complete guides on how to fix conflicts in design models than a counterexample does.

Authors in [8] present a Rely-guarantee approach to reasoning aspect-oriented programs. They treat base programs and aspects as individual processes and introduce a quadruple$(pre, rely, guar, post)$ as the specification of a process, where the pair $(rely, guar)$ gives the specification of processes permitted to be injected in. They insist that the problems of reasoning about AOP programs are very similar to those encountered in reasoning about concurrent programs. Thus, by using their method, theories developed for concurrent programs, such as [14], could be used in reasoning AOP programs. Since in the paper, only a simple example is used to show the idea, its ability to interference detection needs more evidence.

Authors in [6] study the interference problems in aspects' library. They set up an incremental proof strategy that assures the checking for each pairs of aspects are sufficient to detect interference or establish interference freedom for weaving aspects in a library in any order. Our works share similar ideas in defining interference problems among aspects. However, the underlying formal foundations are different. Their work is based on interaction models and interference problems are analyzed by model checkers, while our work is built on a denotational semantics and theorem proving.

Our work is different from the above methods for analyzing interference problems in AOP. In our approach, the formal models of methods and advices in terms of designs are specified with respect to the functionalities of classes and aspects, and deduction based methods are applied to detect and solve semantics conflicts in AOP models, as opposed to the use of behavior models or model checking based techniques. This approach is easily to be integrated with AOP's development processes since functional specifications of methods and advices can be introduced as annotations of AOP design models and be analyzed separately. It supports to analyze interference problems between two aspects as well as between an aspect and base programs in terms of a unified formal model and gives direct feedback on how to solve the conflicts it found.

7   Conclusion

We have presented a rigorous approach to analyzing the interference problems in aspect-oriented designs. Formal representations of classes and aspects are defined on the basis of *designs* in UTP, while the weaving techniques in AOP are interpreted as the compositions of corresponding formal models. Methods for reasoning interference problems between an aspect and base programs as well as between two aspects are given which depend on the calculations of weakest preconditions.

This approach can be easily introduced into the development process of AOP. Functional specifications of methods and advices can be regarded as annotations of AOP models which help developers to record their decisions on functionality designs. In the analysis process, these specifications are separated from AOP models and used independently. Using our approach, the interference analysis process becomes very informative. Once an interference problem is found, it can tell us what is the cause of the interference, and in which weaving order it happens. This information greatly facilitates the developers to refine their design models. Early detecting and removing conflicts in aspect-oriented design models can improve their qualities and save plenty of costs.

Our future work mainly concerns with a formal language for aspect-oriented programs. Based on the formal language for object-oriented language, rCOS [4], we are going to develop a formal language for aspect-oriented programs which includes formal representations for elements in typical aspect-oriented languages, such as AspectJ [9]. The refinement calculus will be studied so that aspect-oriented design models can be related to aspect-oriented programs, which helps developers to maintain the interference-free property derived from design models in codes.

References

1. Aksit, M., Rensink, A., Staijen, T.: A graph-transformation-based simulation approach for analysing aspect interference on shared join points. In: Proceedings of the 8th International Conference on Aspect-Oriented Software Development, AOSD 2009, pp. 39–50. ACM, New York (2009)
2. Corbett, J.C., Dwyer, M.B., Hatcliff, J., Robby: Bandera: a source-level interface for model checking java programs. In: Proceedings of the 22nd International Conference on Software Engineering, ICSE 2000, pp. 762–765. ACM, New York (2000)

3. Goldman, M., Katz, S.: Maven: Modular aspect verification. In: Grumberg, O., Huth, M. (eds.) TACAS 2007. LNCS, vol. 4424, pp. 308–322. Springer, Heidelberg (2007)
4. He, J., Li, X., Liu, Z.: rcos: A refinement calculus of object systems. Theor. Comput. Sci. 365(1-2), 109–142 (2006)
5. Hoare, C.A.R., He, J.: Unifying Theories of Programming. Prentice-Hall, Englewood Cliffs (1998)
6. Katz, E., Katz, S.: Incremental analysis of interference among aspects. In: Proceedings of the 7th workshop on Foundations of Aspect-Oriented Languages, FOAL 2008, pp. 29–38. ACM, New York (2008)
7. Katz, S., Sihman, M.: Aspect validation using model checking. In: Dershowitz, N. (ed.) Verification: Theory and Practice. LNCS, vol. 2772, pp. 373–394. Springer, Heidelberg (2003)
8. Khatchadourian, R., Soundarajan, N.: Rely-guarantee approach to reasoning about aspect-oriented programs. In: Proceedings of the 5th Workshop on Software Engineering Properties of Languages and Aspect Technologies, SPLAT 2007, p. 5. ACM Press, New York (2007)
9. Kiczales, G., Hilsdale, E., Hugunin, J., Kersten, M., Palm, J., Griswold, W.G.: An overview of aspectj. In: Knudsen, J.L. (ed.) ECOOP 2001. LNCS, vol. 2072, pp. 327–353. Springer, Heidelberg (2001)
10. Kiczales, G., Lamping, J., Mendhekar, A., Maeda, C., Lopes, C.V., Loingtier, J.-M., Irwin, J.: Aspect-oriented programming. In: Aksit, M., Matsuoka, S. (eds.) ECOOP 1997. LNCS, vol. 1241, pp. 220–242. Springer, Heidelberg (1997)
11. Krishnamurthi, S., Fisler, K., Greenberg, M.: Verifying aspect advice modularly. In: Proceedings of the 12th ACM SIGSOFT International Symposium on Foundations of Software Engineering, pp. 137–146. ACM, New York (2004)
12. Mostefaoui, F., Vachon, J.: Design-level detection of interactions in aspect-uml models using alloy. Journal of Object Technology 6(7), 137–165 (2007)
13. Xu, D., Alsmadi, I., Xu, W.: Model checking aspect-oriented design specification. In: Proc. of the 31st Annual International Computer Software and Applications Conference, COMPSAC 2007, pp. 491–500. IEEE Computer Society, Los Alamitos (2007)
14. Xu, Q., de Roever, W.P., He, J.: The rely-guarantee method for verifying shared variable concurrent programs. Formal Asp. Comput. 9(2), 149–174 (1997)

Programmable Verifiers in Imperative Programming

Yifeng Chen

HCST Key Lab at School of EECS
Peking University
Beijing 100871, China

Abstract. This paper studies the relation between execution and verification. A simple imperative language called VerExec with execution and verification commands is introduced. A machine only executes execution commands of a program, while the compiler only performs the verification commands. Common commands in other languages can be defined as a combination of execution and verification commands. Design of verifiers then becomes program design using verification commands. It is shown that type checking, abstract interpretation, modeling checking and Hoare Logic are all special verification programs, so are many of their combinations[1].

1 Introduction

A program contains two kinds of information. One kind is used for code generation and machine execution and another for compiler verification. In this paper, verification specifically refers to static verification. The information for verification typically includes various redundant type information such as the class structure and inter-class accessibility control. A compiler performs safety checking and optimisation according to such information, but once that is done, the information is removed and will not appear in the generated code. An example is the access modifiers 'private' and 'protected' in C++. They instruct the compiler to perform extra accessibility checking but do not affect the generated code.

In the past, verification is regarded as additional preprocessing done by the compiler (or verifier). No matter what verification methods are used, a verifier itself is still a program. It is therefore natural to draw an analogy between verifier design and program design.

Two-level languages [16,17] have been widely explored in functional programming mainly for a unifying treatment of code generation. The focus of this paper is to allow a source programmer to control both execution and verification directly so that different verification methods can be applied to different parts of a program.

---

[1] This work is partially supported by National 973 Project 45210130-0442.

S. Qin (Ed.): UTP 2010, LNCS 6445, pp. 172–187, 2010.
© Springer-Verlag Berlin Heidelberg 2010

In type theory, effort is made to design expressive as well as decidable type systems. Guaranteeing decidability is similar to ensuring the termination of a verification program. In abstract interpretation [2], the widening operator forces termination of fixpoint iteration. That is similar to forcing termination of loop in a verifier. Model checking [1] iterates verification for all execution paths. In Hoare logic, the proof obligation of a loop is to maintain loop invariant and decrease loop variant for the loop body. It is noticeable that the ways that various verification methods work are similar to the ways how we use basic program commands like assignments, if-then-else conditionals and while loops in programming.

In this paper, we introduce a language called VerExec, which extends standard imperative languages like Dijkstra's Guarded-Command Language [7] with four verification commands: compile-time error, type assignment, compile-time conditional and compile-time loop. So a program in the language will contain two sets of commands for execution and verification respectively. The machine executes execution commands but ignores those for verification, while the compiler only performs verification commands but ignores those for execution. Upon a successful compilation, verification is only performed once; while the execution commands can be executed for arbitrarily many times after verification. It is normally desirable to conduct as much safety checking and optimisation as possible during compilation.

A more theoretical motivation of this paper is to apply unifying theory of programming [13] to handling traditionally syntactic aspects of programming languages including type checking and symbolic execution. In the past, they are regarded as being "freely available" outside denotational or algebraic semantics. Regarding verifiers as programs means that we can apply denotation-semantic and algebra-semantic methods to these aspects as well.

If a programmer chooses only to use execution commands, the programs are essentially untyped (just like in languages LISP, Self [19] and Smalltalk [9]), all well-definedness checking is conducted in execution. By adding verification commands, a programmer controls the amount of verification to perform. Commands of strongly typed languages such as C and Eiffel [14] can be defined as combination of execution and verification commands. If a programmer chooses only to use such combined commands, the program is essentially strongly typed with a *default scheme* of verification.

Of course, extra flexibility in a programming language sometimes encourages programmers to write unsafe codes. Allowing unrelated codes for execution and verification will permit a compiler to check things unrelated to the dynamic behaviour. Thus appropriate software engineering practice is need to benefit from the extra flexibility as well as restricting undesirable designs (refer to Section 4 for more discussions).

A verifier itself is an imperative program (in this paper). Such a program can change the state of some type variables. Note that a compile-time state is the state of the compiler not the runtime state of the machine. The newly added verification commands mirror what the corresponding execution commands do but change only those type variables. Type assignments can directly update the verifier's state and are useful for verification like abstract interpretation. Verifying conditionals allow a verifier to make decisions according to the current states. They are similar to the use of conditional compilation in existing verifiers (e.g. C). For example, the compile-time conditional (if' q then skip else error$'$) checks the type variables for a property q and generates a compile-time error error$'$ if the property is violated; otherwise, it does nothing. Verifying loops allow a verifier to conduct more in-depth verification such as fixpoint iteration in abstract interpretation and symbolic execution. Note that an execution loop does not necessarily require iterated verification. Most languages simply type-check the boolean condition and the body, although abstract interpretation does use compile-time loop for fixpoint approximation.

The grand challenge of verifying compiler [11] has motivated a lot of research effort. The proposal to combine verification into compilers demands integration of various methods of verification. The current trend in automated verification is to combine different verification methods: combing abstract interpretation and symbolic execution, combining abstract interpretation and type theory [3], combining type theory and model checking [6], and combining Hoare Logic and type theory [15]. This paper studies the relation between execution and verification, and the semantical integration of different verification methods.

The semantics of the new language is a combination of execution semantics and verification semantics. On the contrary to conventional views, verification semantics is not a simple abstraction of execution semantics. They are orthogonal but their relation can be established in a specific verification scheme.

A decision is made in our semantic modelling to distinguish runtime errors and compile-time errors. Runtime errors are represented as the most chaotic command, while compile-time errors become the most infeasible command that generates no final state from every initial state. There has been a long-standing discussion over the use of magic. For example, it can be used in program development as a mechanism to unwind a computation to amend an earlier design mistake. The subtlety is also reflected in the handling of type errors in Z where type error was originally regarded as abort by mistake [10,18].

The rationale behind this decision is related to a view on programming. Programming can be regarded as a game played between the developers and users. In some sense, a compile-time error is 'good', as it causes no damage to the users and it provides a chance to modify the program to pass verification later; in comparison, runtime errors are bad. There are two kinds of nondeterminism. Nondeterminism in development is desirable: if there are two possible designs to choose, and one design passes the verification while another reports compile-time error, then it is reasonable simply to take the passed design. This is why compile-time error is regarded as magic, requiring backtracking at the presence of nondeterminism in compilation. Nondeterminism in execution, for example, occurs in parallel and distributed computing where communication latency is nondeterministic. That makes program behaviour less predictable and is hence undesirable to end users. Runtime error of one component should become error of the whole system and be chaotic.

2   Constants, Variables, Functions, Expressions, Operators and Types

As various entities are handled in the same framework, symbols and notations must be carefully chosen and organised in a logic. The design of the logic is illustrative for typical use of verification methods and can be either extended to be more expressive or simplified to have better decidability and lower decision complexity.

For simplicity, we consider only natural numbers and the boolean values as constants. Let $x, y, z, x_1 \cdots$ denote program variables. A primitive type is simply viewed as a set of constants. A program state is a mapping from variables to constants. Each constant is also regarded as a singleton (primitive) type containing the constant. The empty type is denoted as $\varnothing$. Other primitive types include intervals $[m, n]$ for $m \leqslant n$ and $[n, \infty)$ and boolean type Bool. Note that true and false are two singleton boolean types. Functions (computable) include usual arithmetic operations as well as boolean operations. Note that a function may not be defined for some particular arguments. For example $(1 + \text{true})$ is obviously undefined. An expression is either a constant, a program variable, a membership condition, or a function applied to several expressions. Expressions are used in assignment statements. Boolean expressions, in particular, are used in if-then-else statements and while loops.

A type is a set of states. Constants are regarded as types for singleton sets. For simplicity, we assume that types are closed under union $\cup$, intersection $\cap$, complement $\overline{(\cdot)}$ and some other operators $\nabla, \partial, \cdots$ for widening of abstract interpretation [5], partial extraction (see Section 3.6) etc. In a more general setting, union and intersection are replaceable with lub and glb of a complete lattice. A boolean expression can be regarded as a *relational type* containing states in which the expression is true. For example the type $x < y$ allows any state in which x is less than y; while the type $1 < \text{true}$ is empty as the expression is undefined. A type update $t \dagger u$ evaluates the abstraction of a type after state change. For example, if $t = (x \in [1, 7] \wedge y \in [6, 9])$, then

$$t \dagger \{ x \mapsto (x + y)[t],\ y \mapsto x[t] \} \;=\; x \in [7, 16] \wedge y \in [1, 7].$$

Note that the result type depends on the abstraction of the operation $+$ and is not necessarily the most accurate in the type system. For example, in a type system closed under set union, we may still regard multiplication of types $[1, 2]$ and

$[3, 4]$ as $[3, 8]$ instead of $[3, 4] \cup [6, 6] \cup [8, 8]$ (i.e. all possible results 3, 4, 6 and 8) under a certain abstraction. The semantics of union (or intersection) type is simply set union (or intersection). It is a matter of tradeoff between representation precision and complexity. The notations are organised in the following syntax:

$$\mathbf{C} ::= n \mid \texttt{true} \mid \texttt{false}$$
$$\mathbf{V} ::= x \mid y \mid z \mid x_1 \mid \cdots$$
$$\mathbf{S} ::= \mathbf{C} \mid \varnothing \mid [m, n] \mid [n, \infty) \mid \texttt{Bool}$$
$$\mathbf{F} ::= + \mid - \mid * \mid \div \mid \texttt{succ} \mid \texttt{less} \mid \texttt{eq} \mid \texttt{and} \mid \texttt{or} \mid \texttt{not} \mid \cdots$$
$$\mathbf{E} ::= \mathbf{C} \mid \mathbf{V} \mid \mathbf{E} \in \mathbf{S} \mid \mathbf{F}(\mathbf{E}, \cdots, \mathbf{E})$$

$$\mathbf{O} ::= \cup \mid \cap \mid \overline{(\cdot)} \mid \triangledown \mid \partial \mid \cdots$$
$$\mathbf{U} ::= \mathbf{S} \mid \mathbf{E}$$
$$\mathbf{W} ::= \{\mathbf{V} \mapsto \mathbf{U}, \cdots, \mathbf{V} \mapsto \mathbf{U}\}$$
$$\mathbf{T} ::= \mathbf{E} \mid \mathbf{T} \dagger \mathbf{W} \mid \mathbf{O}(\mathbf{T}, \cdots, \mathbf{T}).$$

Note that a syntactical element may have different semantics under different views. For example, a constant can be a singleton type or a constant function on program variables. Several semantic mappings are needed for capturing the semantics. In the syntax, $\mathbf{T}$ denotes the domain of type assertions (which themselves are types), $\mathbf{U}$ denotes type expressions.

Definition 1.
$$\begin{aligned}
\sigma_\mathbf{S}(c) &\ \hat{=}\ \{c\} \\
\sigma_\mathbf{S}(\varnothing) &\ \hat{=}\ \{\} \\
\sigma_\mathbf{S}([m, n]) &\ \hat{=}\ \{k \mid m \leqslant k \leqslant n\} \\
\sigma_\mathbf{S}([m, \infty)) &\ \hat{=}\ \{k \mid m \leqslant k\} \\
\sigma_\mathbf{S}(\texttt{Bool}) &\ \hat{=}\ \{\texttt{true}, \texttt{false}\}
\end{aligned}$$

We let $|t|$ denote the cardinality of $\sigma_\mathbf{S}(t)$.

Definition 2.
$$\begin{aligned}
\sigma_\mathbf{E}(c, a) &\ \hat{=}\ c \\
\sigma_\mathbf{E}(x, a) &\ \hat{=}\ a(x) \\
\sigma_\mathbf{E}(e \in S, a) &\ \hat{=}\ \texttt{true} \quad (\sigma_\mathbf{E}(e, a) \in \sigma_\mathbf{S}(S)) \\
\sigma_\mathbf{E}(e \in S, a) &\ \hat{=}\ \texttt{false} \quad (otherwise) \\
\sigma_\mathbf{E}(f(e_1, \cdots, e_n), a) &\ \hat{=}\ f(\sigma_\mathbf{E}(e_1, a), \cdots, \sigma_\mathbf{E}(e_n, a))
\end{aligned}$$

Definition 3. $\quad \sigma_\mathbf{W}(w, t) \ \hat{=}\ \lceil w \rceil(t)$

Definition 4.
$$\begin{aligned}
\sigma_\mathbf{T}(e) &\ \hat{=}\ \{a \mid \sigma_\mathbf{E}(e, a) = \texttt{true}\} \\
\sigma_\mathbf{T}(t \dagger w) &\ \hat{=}\ \sigma_\mathbf{W}(w, \sigma_\mathbf{T}(t)) \\
\sigma_\mathbf{T}(\cup(t_1, t_2)) &\ \hat{=}\ \sigma_\mathbf{T}(t_1) \cup \sigma_\mathbf{T}(t_2) \\
\sigma_\mathbf{T}(\cap(t_1, t_2)) &\ \hat{=}\ \sigma_\mathbf{T}(t_1) \cap \sigma_\mathbf{T}(t_2) \\
\sigma_\mathbf{T}(\bar{t}) &\ \hat{=}\ (\mathbf{V} \to \mathbf{C}) \setminus \sigma_\mathbf{T}(t) \\
\cdots &\ \hat{=}\ \cdots
\end{aligned}$$

The mapping $\sigma_\mathbf{S}$ maps primitive types to sets of constants; $\sigma_\mathbf{E}$ maps each expression to a function from states to constants where a is a state (mapping from variables to constants; $\sigma_{\mathbf{W}}$ maps state update to a function from states to states; and $\sigma_{\mathbf{T}}$ maps a type to a set of states where the (computable) operator $\lceil \cdot \rceil$ represents some abstraction that converts a state function to a type function, which is monotonic in the sense that larger input types lead to larger result type.

Let $a \models t$ denote satisfaction $a \in \sigma_{\mathbf{T}}(t)$. A type t is *valid*, written $\models t$, if for any assignment a, we have $a \models t$. The subtyping relation $t_1 \subseteq t_2$ between two types is defined as $\models \overline{t_1} \cup t_2$. There exists algorithm that determines whether a state satisfies a type. The proof of the following theorem takes advantage of the assumption that functions and type operators are computable.

Proposition 1. *Satisfaction* $a \models t$ *is decidable.*

Unfortunately the general validity of types is not decidable. For example, the validity of type $\mathtt{not}(x^5 + x^4 - 100 = 0)$ essentially requires finding integer solutions of the equation. In this particular system (with interval and boolean types), the fragment of types without relational types is decidable.

For dynamic verification (such as Java's array-index-scope checking), satisfaction decidability is sufficient; compilers, however, must handle types as data (or values), and require validity decidability when, for example, checking whether a type is a subtype of another type.

A remedy is to identify a decidable fragment of the logic $\mathbf{T}_0$ and an abstraction mapping $(\cdot)^+ : \mathbf{T} \to \mathbf{T}_0$ as an upper limit such that $\sigma_{\mathbf{T}}(t) \subseteq \sigma_{\mathbf{T}}(\alpha t)$ $t \in \mathbf{T}$ for any $t \in \mathbf{T}$. For example, the relational type $x^2 + y^2 \leqslant 15$ can be abstracted as $x + y \leqslant 10$ relationally. A lot of research [8] has been done for such abstraction. A lower limit can be defined as $t^- \triangleq \overline{\overline{t}^+}$. The upper and lower limits provide estimation for potentially undecidable types. This paper focuses on unification of verification methods and will simply assume the existence of such a computable abstract mapping.

3 An Imperative Language of Execution and Verification

3.1 Execution Semantics

Let $X, Y, Z, X_1, \cdots$ denote type variables, $P, Q, R, P_1, \cdots$ denote programs, $E, E_1, \cdots$ denote type expressions, and $p, q, r, \cdots$ denote type properties (i.e. conditions on type variables). For example, $X \subseteq Y$ denotes that type X is a subtype of Y.

The language that we consider is an extension of Dijkstra's Guarded-Command Language [7]. Command skip does not change the state. Sequential composition has a standard meaning. Command error represents runtime error. Assignment (assign x as e) modifies the program variable x with the value of expression e. Note that an expression may be undefined in a state, generating a runtime error. We adopt the syntax of [12] in which nondeterministic choice, if-then-else conditional and while loop are separate commands. The conditions in conditional and loops are boolean expressions (see Section 2).

Four new commands are added to the standard imperative language. Command error' represents compile-time error (e.g. type error and verification error). Type assignment assign' X as E modifies the type variable X with the type evaluated from the type expression E. Verifying conditional $(\text{if}'$ r then P else $Q)$ tests whether the type property r is satisfied in the current state of the verifier and chooses to perform verification for the program P or Q accordingly. Verifying loop $(\text{while}'$ r do $P)$ repeats verification P if the property r is satisfied.

The execution semantics of the language follows the weakest-precondition semantics [7]. A condition is a set of states. Thus $[P](t)$ is the largest set of states from which the program terminates into a state in t. The execution semantics of the familiar commands are defined as follows:

$$
\begin{aligned}
[\text{skip}](t') &\; \widehat{=} \; t' \\
[P;Q](t') &\; \widehat{=} \; [P]([Q](t')) \\
[P \sqcap Q](t') &\; \widehat{=} \; [P](t') \cap [Q](t') \\
[\text{error}](t') &\; \widehat{=} \; \varnothing \\
[\text{assign } x \text{ as } e](t') &\; \widehat{=} \; \{a \mid a \dagger \{x \mapsto \sigma_{\mathbf{E}}(e,a)\} \in t'\} \\
[\text{if } t \text{ then } P \text{ else } Q](t') &\; \widehat{=} \; (t \cap [P](t')) \cup (\bar{t} \cap [Q](t')) \\
[\text{while } t \text{ do } P](t') &\; \widehat{=} \; (t \cap [P]([\text{while } t \text{ do } P](t'))) \cup (\bar{t} \cap t') \\
[\text{error}'](t') &\; \widehat{=} \; [\text{skip}](t') \\
[\text{assign}' \; X \text{ as } E](t') &\; \widehat{=} \; [\text{skip}](t') \\
[\text{if}' \; r \text{ then } P \text{ else } Q](t') &\; \widehat{=} \; [P;Q](t') \\
[\text{while}' \; r \text{ do } P](t') &\; \widehat{=} \; [P](t').
\end{aligned}
$$

where the semantics of while loop is the least fixpoint (i.e. the smallest set). Note that we also use multiple assignments ($\text{assign } x_1, \cdots, x_n$ as $e_1, \cdots, e_n$ for simultaneous assignment with standard meaning. If an expression e is undefined in some initial state a (e.g. with divided-by-zero error), then the assignment command ($\text{assign } x$ as e) generates a runtime error and the state a does not satisfy the weakest precondition of every postcondition.

The newly added commands error', if', assign' and while', however, have little interesting execution semantics as they require the verification of their branches. For example, the command error' generates a compile-time error without any runtime behaviour. The machine will basically ignore verification commands, which behave like skips in execution.

3.2   Verification Semantics

Verification semantics $\langle P \rangle$ is also defined in the style of the weakest-precondition semantics. However, a program now is a predicate transformer mapping one type (post)condition to the weakest type (pre)condition where a *type condition* is a condition on type variables $X, Y, \cdots$

$$\langle\, \mathtt{skip}\,\rangle(p) \; \triangleq \; p$$
$$\langle\, P;Q\,\rangle(p) \; \triangleq \; \langle\, P\,\rangle(\langle\, Q\,\rangle(p))$$
$$\langle\, P \sqcap Q\,\rangle(p) \; \triangleq \; \langle\, P\,\rangle(p) \wedge \langle\, Q\,\rangle(p)$$
$$\langle\, \mathtt{error}\,\rangle(p) \; \triangleq \; \langle\, \mathtt{skip}\,\rangle(p)$$
$$\langle\, \mathtt{assign}\ x\ \mathtt{as}\ e\,\rangle(p) \; \triangleq \; \langle\, \mathtt{skip}\,\rangle(p)$$
$$\langle\, \mathtt{if}\ r\ \mathtt{then}\ P\ \mathtt{else}\ Q\,\rangle(p) \; \triangleq \; \langle\, P;Q\,\rangle(p)$$
$$\langle\, \mathtt{while}\ r\ \mathtt{do}\ P\,\rangle(p) \; \triangleq \; \langle\, P\,\rangle(p)$$
$$\langle\, \mathtt{error}'\,\rangle(p) \; \triangleq \; true$$
$$\langle\, \mathtt{assign}'\ X\ \mathtt{as}\ E\,\rangle(p) \; \triangleq \; p[E/X]$$
$$\langle\, \mathtt{if}'\ q\ \mathtt{then}\ P\ \mathtt{else}\ Q\,\rangle(p) \; \triangleq \; (q \wedge \langle\, P\,\rangle(p)) \vee (\neg q \wedge \langle\, Q\,\rangle(q))$$
$$\langle\, \mathtt{while}'\ q\ \mathtt{do}\ P\,\rangle(p) \; \triangleq \; (q \wedge \langle\, P\,\rangle(\langle\, \mathtt{while}\ q\ \mathtt{do}\ P\,\rangle(p))) \vee (\neg q \wedge p)$$

The verification semantics mirrors execution semantics. The runtime commands have little interesting function in verification. For example, runtime error and assignment do not require any verification. That means assignment (assign x as $1 + \mathtt{true}$) itself generates runtime error in stead of a type error. So by using only the runtime commands, a programmer is essentially writing an untyped program in which all the checking is left to execution.

This, however, does not mean that the language allows no verification. The newly added commands can be run by the verifier to perform various verification. Compilation error $\mathtt{error}'$, having no runtime function, is the most infeasible computation in verification, also known as *magic* in program specification and refinement. That means if one of the designs of a nondeterministic choice has no compile-time error, the whole program can still be verified. Verification with nondeterminism requires some mechanism of backtracking. Type assignment modifies the type variable with a type expression. Verifying conditional tests a type property in the current verifier's state and performs different verifications. Verifying loop ($\mathtt{while}'\ r\ \mathtt{do}\ P$) repeatedly performs verification P if the type property r is satisfied.

The commands of compiled imperative languages are normally a combination of the runtime commands and compile-time commands. For example, assignment in most languages is type-checked so that if the expression is *never* well-defined (e.g. $(1 + \mathtt{true})$), then a compile-time error is generated. However, type assignment, compile-time conditional and compile-time loop have no direct links to their runtime counterparts. In most languages, assignment does not change any type information during compilation; both branches of a conditional must be verified (not executed) regardless the condition; and in most languages, a loop is only type-checked for its condition and body, and no loop is needed for verification (not the case in abstract interpretation though). On the other hand, a program without runtime loop may be verified with a compile-time loop to enumerate all possible execution paths.

3.3   Relating Execution and Verification

Although the language allows execution and verification to be unrelated in a program, such programs are normally undesirable, as they do not serve the purpose of verifying runtime behaviours of programs in compilation. That means good programming practice and techniques are required to ensure an appropriate correlation between execution and verification.

Definition 5 (Permanent Dynamic Errors). *A program's verification detects permanent dynamic errors, if for any sub-program P (syntactic program fragment) that never terminates successfully $[P](\overline{\varnothing}) = \varnothing$, the program results in a compilation error: $\langle P \rangle(false) = true$.*

Note that this definition does not exclude false alarms, nor does it guarantee to eliminate all dynamic errors (including nontermination). A program satisfying the above property may contain fragments that sometimes terminate successfully but sometimes generate dynamic errors. A typical counterexample is divided-by-zero exception, which is not eliminated. The total-correctness semantics does not distinguish nontermination and undefinedness. Exclusion of only undefinedness requires more discriminating semantic models.

Definition 6 (Dynamic Errors). *A program P's verification detects dynamic errors with type variable X as the abstract state, if for any type t such that $t \not\subseteq [P](\overline{\varnothing})$, we have $(X \supseteq t) \Rightarrow \langle P \rangle(false)$.*

Again this property permits false alarms and does not distinguish nontermination and other dynamic errors. We assume X to be the type variable that records the estimated (type) information about the current state. The definition implies compositionality:

Proposition 2. *If A program P's verification detects dynamic errors with type variable X, t is a type such that $t \not\subseteq [P](\overline{\varnothing})$, and $t = t_1 \cup t_2$, then either $(X \supseteq t_1) \Rightarrow \langle P \rangle(false)$ or $(X \supseteq t_2) \Rightarrow \langle P \rangle(false)$.*

This proposition, a basic property of the wp semantics, reveals that the checking of dynamic errors is compositional in the sense that to determine statically whether a large set of program states may lead to ultimate dynamic errors, we may decompose the set into two smaller sets and perform the checking separately. Any dynamic error will be detected in the checking of either of them.

Definition 7 (Precision of Verification). *Let P and Q be two programs whose verification detects dynamic errors with the type variable X as the abstract state, and they share the same execution semantics $[P] = [Q]$. The verification of P is more precise than that of Q, if $\langle P \rangle(false) \Rightarrow \langle Q \rangle(false)$.*

A verifier is more precise if it has less initial type settings that lead to a compile-time error. A less precise verifier can still be a safe verifier but tends to generate more false alarms.

Indeed, flexibility is a necessary evil when more expressiveness is required for applying different verification methods to different parts of a program. On the other hand, caution is needed as the execution and verification semantics must be appropriately correlated. In practice, this can be achieved by system programmers who establish sets of pre-defined commands that incorporate both execution and verification commands. End programmers only need to choose from these sets in programming. A good verifier must be safe, generate less false alarms and be efficient. The above properties provide some guidance on how pre-defined combined commands should be designed.

3.4   Simple Type Checking

Type checking is useful in reducing runtime errors. If variables x and y are declared to be integer and boolean value respectively (of a relational type $t \mathrel{\hat{=}} x \in [0, \infty) \wedge y \in \texttt{Bool}$), then the assignment ($\texttt{assign } x \text{ as } (x + y)$) contains an expression that is always undefined. Fortunately, it is possible to determine $t \dagger \{x \mapsto (x + y)[t]\} = \varnothing$ in the type system. That means "*always undefinedness*" is detectable as a compile-time error:

$$\texttt{Tvar } x \text{ as } s \ \mathrel{\hat{=}} \ \texttt{if}' \ (X \subseteq (x \in s))$$
$$\texttt{then } (\texttt{assign}' \ X \text{ as } X \dagger \{x \mapsto s\}) \texttt{ else error}'$$
$$\texttt{Tassign } x \text{ as } e \ \mathrel{\hat{=}} \ \texttt{if}' \ (\varnothing \neq X \dagger \{x \mapsto e[X]\} \subseteq X)$$
$$\texttt{then } (\texttt{assign } x \text{ as } e) \texttt{ else error}'.$$

The type variable X is introduced to record the declared type for *all program variables*. The command $\texttt{Tvar}$ declares or re-declares a type. For example $\texttt{Tvar } x \text{ as } [0, 10]$ sets the type of program variable x as an interval. Re-declaration is only allowed to a supertype. $\texttt{Tassign}$ is to replace the command $\texttt{assign}$ by adding type checking against the declared type. If the result type is not a subtype of the declared type or the expression is always undefined in all possible states (empty type), then a compile-time error is generated. Note that the conditions in conditional and while loop are types and always well-defined. In this simple type system, "occasional" dynamic errors such as divided-by-zero are tolerated by the verifier and left to execution unless the divisor has a declared type $[0, 0]$.

Let $\textbf{TC}$ be the language of programs containing only skip, nondeterministic choice, sequential composition, type declaration, type-checked assignment, conditional and while loop. Type checking detects undefinedness but does not detect nontermination:

Theorem 1. *Any finite program (without loops) of* $\textbf{TC}$ *detects permanent dynamic errors.*

3.5   Abstract Interpretation

Abstract interpretation is a technique that simulates the execution of a program statically on "abstract states" (corresponding to states of type variables in this paper). It is not surprising that the verification aspect of a program has a similar structure to the runtime program structure. An abstract state is actually a type (e.g. interval). Such types are abstraction of concrete values and will be handled by the verifier. Most main-stream languages such as C and Java do not handle these subtypes, because their type systems are designed to enable programmers to provide information for code generation, which is not precise enough for verification purposes.

In a type checker, the declared types of program variables are not modified by assignment statements. Abstract interpretation also scans a program, but it records the abstract state of the program at each point as a static estimation of runtime state at that point. The abstract state is always a subtype of the declared type, but it can be modified by an assignment, approximating the way how a runtime state is modified.

We use a new type variable Y to represent the abstract state of the verifier. Again commands with abstract interpretation are a combination of execution and verification commands:

$$
\begin{aligned}
\text{Avar } X \text{ as } t \;&\hat{=}\; \text{Tvar } x \text{ as } t\,;\ \text{assign}'\ Y \text{ as } X \\[4pt]
\text{Aassign } x \text{ as } e \;&\hat{=}\; \text{assign}'\ Y \text{ as } Y \dagger \{x \mapsto e[Y]\}\,; \\
&\quad\ \text{if}'\ (\varnothing \neq Y \subseteq X) \text{ then } (\text{assign } x \text{ as } e)\ \text{else error}' \\[4pt]
\text{Aif } t \text{ then } P \text{ else } Q \;&\hat{=}\; \text{if } t \text{ then } (\text{assign}'\ Z_1, Y \text{ as } Y, (Y \cap t)\,;\ P) \\
&\qquad\qquad\quad \text{else } (\text{assign}'\ Z_2, Y \text{ as } Y, (Z_1 \cap \bar{t})\,;\ Q)\,; \\
&\quad\ \text{assign}'\ Y \text{ as } (Z_2 \cup Y) \\[4pt]
\text{Awhile } t \text{ do } P \text{ on } \nabla \;&\hat{=}\; \text{while } t \text{ do } (\\
&\quad\ \text{assign}'\ Z \text{ as } \varnothing\,; \\
&\quad\ \text{while}'\ Z \neq (Z \nabla Y) \text{ do} \\
&\qquad (\text{assign}'\ Z, Y \text{ as } Z \nabla Y, (Z \nabla Y) \cap t\,;\ P))\,; \\
&\quad\ \text{assign}'\ Y \text{ as } (Z \cap \bar{t})
\end{aligned}
$$

where Z, Z_1, Z_2 are fresh temporary type variables for each conditional and loop. On every type declaration, the abstract state is set to the declared type. Assignment changes the abstract state, which must be a subtype of the declared type to avoid compile-time error. Just before verifying P, the conditional Aif first records the current abstract state Y from which the verification of Q should start. The abstract state Y is then narrowed after checking the condition t. Before verifying Q, the abstract state Y is narrowed by $\bar{t}$, and the result type of P is recorded in Z_2 whose union with the the result type of Q will become the result type of the conditional.

The new loop command is verified by fixpoint iteration based on some widening operator ∇. Widening is a technique proposed by Cousot [4]. It is designed to replace type union $\cup$ (or $\sqcup$ of a complete lattice if type union is not closed in the type system). The widening operator has less accuracy but can help accelerate fixpoint iteration. It satisfies the property that for any t_1 and t_2, $t_1 \nabla t_2$ is a supertype of both types, and for every sequence $\varnothing, t_1, t_2, \cdots$, there exists n such that $\nabla_0^n, t_i = \nabla_0^{n+1} t_i$. The "fresh" variable Z is introduced to record the widened union of all abstract states at the entry of the loop. The loop will iterate until Z reaches a fixpoint (which must exist by definition of ∇). The result type of the loop is the fixpoint of Z intersecting with $\bar{t}$.

Let **AL** be the language of programs containing only skip, nondeterministic choice, sequential composition and commands abstract interpretation.

Theorem 2. *Any program of* **AL** *detects dynamic errors with type variable* Y.

According to Proposition 2, the static analysis is compositional. For example, consider an expression $2*x+(3-x)$. In interval analysis, if x has a range of $[0,1]$, the verifier will try to estimate $[0,2]+[2,3]$, which gives $[2,5]$ instead of $[3,4]$ as expected for an equal expression $(x+3)$. Precision can be improved by breaking $[0,1]$ as $[0,0] \cup [1,1]$. Then the expression yields $[3,3]$ for $[0,0]$ and $[4,4]$ for $[1,1]$, and their merge is $[3,4]$. This suggests that precision can be improved by partitioning an abstract state into small abstract states and apply multiple scans in verification.

The structure of the loop with widening motivates us to improve its precision by further narrowing the abstract state before verifying the body. According to Theorem 2 and Proposition 2, in every iteration, we only need to verify the loop body P for the additional part of the current abstract state not contained by the accumulated abstract state. That leads to the following improved type assignment before the body:

$$\texttt{Awhilst } t \texttt{ do } P \texttt{ on } \triangledown \;\hat{=}\; \texttt{while } t \texttt{ do }($$
$$\texttt{assign}' \; Z \texttt{ as } \varnothing;$$
$$\texttt{while}' \; Z \neq (Z \triangledown Y) \texttt{ do}$$
$$(\texttt{assign}' \; Z, Y \texttt{ as } Z \triangledown Y, (Z \triangledown Y) \cap \overline{Z} \cap t \;;\; P));$$
$$\texttt{assign}' \; Y \texttt{ as } (Z \cap \bar{t}).$$

Proposition 3. *Let* P *be a program of* **AL** *and* Q *be the program obtained by replacing every* **Awhile** *command with an* **Awhilst** *command. Then the verification of* Q *is more precise than that of* P.

3.6   Iterative Symbolic Execution

The basic method of abstract interpretation is to start from an abstract state (i.e. the current type for program variables) and simulate the execution of a program's update of the abstract state, possibly generating false alarms. Symbolic execution essentially simulates a program from (a finite number of) all initial states, requires scanning a program multiple times, and does not generate false alarms.

From the last subsection, we noticed that the abstract state of abstract interpretation can be partitioned for multiple runs of the analyser to obtain better precision. This motivates us to combine the two methods for an analysis without false alarm but can benefit from appropriate abstraction. The following command first scans a program P from the initial abstract state; if the entire resulting abstract state violates the target property t then a compile-time error is generated; if it entirely meets t, then the abstract state becomes the remaining type to be iterated; otherwise the result type partly meets and partly violates the target and then must be sliced by ∂ to obtain a smaller subtype from which the precision of the analysis can be increased:

```
execute P for t by ∂ ≙
    assign' Z as Y ;
    while' Z ≠ ∅ do (
        P ;
        if' Y ⊆ t then assign' Y, Z as Z∩Ȳ, Z∩Ȳ
        else if' Y ⊆ t̄ then error'
        else if' |Y| = 1 then error'
        else assign' Y as ∂Y )
    assign' Y as t.
```

The underlying algorithm is a general adaptive combination of symbolic execution and abstract interpretation. It tries to validates the target properties in as few scans as possible. When the result of analysis is ambiguous, it automatically partitions the abstract state and increases precision. In the rare worst-case scenario, it scans the program no more than twice as many times as the basic symbolic execution, if ∂ tends to partition every (finite) abstract state evenly. The following theorem reveals the improvement of precision:

Theorem 3. *Let P be an* **AL** *program. Then* $[P] = [$execute P for t by $\partial]$ *and* $\langle P \rangle (Y \subseteq t) \Rightarrow \langle$execute P for t by $\partial\rangle(true)$.

Let us consider a simple program:

$$P \;\hat{=}\; \texttt{Aassign } x \texttt{ as } (x * x - x)$$

Then we have $\langle P \rangle (Y = (x \in [80, 390])) = (x \in [10, 20])$ (as

$$[10, 20] * [10, 20] - [10, 20] \;=\; [100, 400] - [10, 20] \;=\; [80, 390]).$$

This analysis by scanning the code once is rather coarse: the accurate result should be $[90, 380]$ instead for the initial range. The precision is improvable with the symbolic-execution command (execute P for t by ∂) where we set the target range $t = (x \in [85, 385])$ and a factoriser $\partial([a, b]) \;\hat{=}\; [a, (a+b)/2]$. The symbolic executer cannot validate the target range in the first scan with the original range $[10, 20]$, but by partitioning it into $[10, 15]$ and $[16, 20]$ with ∂, both subintervals can then validate the target range in two scans.

3.7   Hoare Logic

In Hoare Logic each assertion characterises the property at the point of the assertion in a program. Alternatively, an assertion can be viewed as a relational type for all program variables, i.e. a type containing a logical formula. It is similar to the abstract state in abstract interpretation.

The key rule in Hoare Logic is the rule for loops. We regard a loop invariant as a relational type that is maintained by the loop body. Loop variant is an integer-valued expression whose value is strictly decreased by the body. The following command (Hwhile t do P inv t' dec e) requires the programmer to identify the loop invariant t' and variant e and automates other proof obligation:

Hwhile t do P inv t' dec e $\;\widehat{=}\;$
        if' $(Y \subseteq t')$ then skip else error';
        while t do (
            assign' Y as $(t' \cap t \cap z = e)$;
            P;
            if' $(Y \subseteq (t' \cap 0 \leqslant e < z))$ then skip else error');
        assign' Y as $t' \cap \bar{t}$.

3.8 Combining Widening Loop and Hoare Logic

A loop body is only scanned once in Hoare Logic. The disadvantage is that the loop invariant must be provided by the programmer. On the other hand, widening fixpoint iteration in abstract interpretation scans the body multiple times and can calculate a loop invariant using the given widening operator. Thus it is possible to combine the two approaches by employing abstract fixpoint iteration to discover the loop invariant and using decreasing variant of Hoare Logic to check termination:

AHwhile t do P on $\triangledown$ dec e $\;\widehat{=}\;$
        while t do (
            assign' Z as $\varnothing$;
            while' $Z \neq (Z \triangledown Y)$ do (
                assign' Z, Y as $Z \triangledown Y,\ (Z \triangledown Y) \cap t \cap (z = e)$;
                P;
                if' $(Y \subseteq (Z \cap 0 \leqslant e < z))$ then skip else error')
            );
            assign' Y as $Z \cap \bar{t}$)

where Z is a fresh temporary type variable, and z is a fresh program variable not used in P.

4 Conclusions

The main contribution of this paper is conceptual. The advantage of VerExec is that various verification methods can now be naturally integrated and allow programmers to apply different verification methods to different parts of a program. This flexibility is not supported by existing languages.

Caution is required for such extra flexibility. Execution and verification commands of a source program should be appropriately correlated. Such correlation is captured by several desirable properties. A possible application scheme is to expect system programmers to design sets of commands with pre-defined execution and verification functions in a library (of different verification methods).

Such commands will possess the desirable properties, and the end programmers may simply choose one for each piece of code to be verified.

An interesting question is whether programmers should be required to write verification code. Both choices are supported by the language. On one hand, if a programmer writes programs using the language directly, then the distinction between execution and verification commands is explicit responsibility of the programmer; on the other hand, new commands combining execution and verification can be defined in the language, and if a programmer uses only such commands, verification becomes a pre-defined default process of the compiler.

The design of the logic for types, expressions and so on in Section 2 is illustrative. Various other designs are possible to extend it with more expressive logical operators such as quantifiers (e.g. for assertions) or simplify it to sub-logical fragments with better decidability and lower decision complexity.

As any existing verifier is a program, and any verification program can be extracted from some source program in the extended imperative language, the technique of this paper is general enough to derive all existing verification methods and algorithms. A possible future extension is to add input and output commands so that the verification process becomes interactive. Missing information about verification can then be added via a Human-Computer Interface.

It is proposed that *"the verifying compiler does not itself have to be verified, though it would be desirable to do so, at least partially"* [11]. A reasonable scheme is to use a verifier to check programs automatically but apply manual reasoning calculi to the correctness proof of the verifier itself.

Acknowledgement

The author is very grateful to Tony Hoare, Zhiming Liu and Jeff Sanders for their comments on early drafts of this paper.

References

1. Clarke, E., Emerson, E.A., Sistla, A.P.: Automatic verification of finite-state concurrent systems using temporal logic specifications. ACM Transactions on Programming Languages and Systems 8(2), 244–263 (1986)
2. Cousot, P.: Abstract interpretation. ACM Computing Surveys 28(2), 324–328 (1996)
3. Cousot, P.: Types as abstract interpretations. In: Proceedings of POPL, pp. 316–331. ACM, New York (1997)
4. Cousot, P., Cousot, R.: Abstract interpretation: A unified lattice model for static analysis of programs by construction or approximation of fixedpoints. In: Proceedings of 4th POPL, pp. 238–252. ACM, New York (1977)
5. Cousot, P., Cousot, R.: Comparing the Galois connection and widening/narrowing approaches to abstract interpretation. In: Bruynooghe, M., Wirsing, M. (eds.) PLILP 1992. LNCS, vol. 631, pp. 269–295. Springer, Heidelberg (1992)
6. Debbabi, M., Benzakour, A., Ktari, B.: A synergy between model-checking and type inference for the verification of value-passing higher-order processes. In: Haeberer, A.M. (ed.) AMAST 1998. LNCS, vol. 1548, pp. 214–230. Springer, Heidelberg (1998)

7. Dijkstra, E.W.: A discipline of programming. Prentice-Hall, Englewood Cliffs (1976)
8. Bagnara, R., et al.: Precise widening operators for convex polyhedra. Science of Computer Programming 58(1-2), 28–56 (2005)
9. Goldberg, A., Robson, D.: Smalltalk-80: The Language and Its Implementation. Addison-Wesley, Reading (1983)
10. Henson, M.C., Reeves, S.: Revising Z: Part I - logic and semantics. Formal Asp. Comput. 11(4), 359–380 (1999)
11. Hoare, C.A.R.: The verifying compiler: A grand challenge for computing research. Journal of the ACM 50(1), 63–69 (2003)
12. Hoare, C.A.R., et al.: Laws of programming. Communications of the ACM 30(8), 672–686 (1987)
13. Hoare, C.A.R., He, J.: Unifying Theories of Programming. Prentice Hall, Englewood Cliffs (1998)
14. Meyer, B.: Object-Oriented Software Construction, 2nd edn. Prentice-Hall, Englewood Cliffs (1997)
15. Nanevski, A., Morrisett, G., Birkedal, L.: Polymorphism and separation in Hoare type theory. SIGPLAN Not. 41(9), 62–73 (2006)
16. Nielson, F., Nielson, H.R.: Two-level semantics and code generation. Theoretical Computer Science 56(1), 59–133 (1988)
17. Nielson, F., Nielson, H.R.: Two-level functional languages. Cambridge University Press, Cambridge (1992)
18. Spivey, J.M.: The Z Notation: A Reference Manual, 2nd edn. Prentice Hall International Series in Computer Science (1992)
19. Ungar, D., Smith, R.B.: Self: The power of simplicity. SIGPLAN Notice 22(12), 227–242 (1987)

Unifying Theories in Isabelle/HOL[*]

Abderrahmane Feliachi, Marie-Claude Gaudel, and Burkhart Wolff

Univ Paris-Sud, Laboratoire LRI, UMR8623, Orsay, F-91405, France
and
CNRS, Orsay, F-91405, France
{Abderrahmane.Feliachi,Marie-Claude.Gaudel,Burkhart.Wolff}@lri.fr

Abstract. In this paper, we present various extensions of Isabelle/HOL by theories that are essential for several formal methods. First, we explain how we have developed an Isabelle/HOL theory for a part of the Unifying Theories of Programming (UTP). It contains the theories of alphabetized relations and designs. Then we explain how we have encoded first the theory of reactive processes and then the UTP theory for CSP. Our work takes advantage of the rich existing logical core of HOL.

Our extension contains the proofs for most of the lemmas and theorems presented in the UTP book. Our goal is to propose a framework that will allow us to deal with formal methods that are semantically based, partly or totally, on UTP, for instance CSP and *Circus*. The theories presented here will allow us to make proofs about such specifications and to apply verified transformations on them, with the objective of assisting refinement and test generation.

Keywords: UTP, Theorem Proving, Isabelle/HOL, CSP, *Circus*.

1 Introduction

The fundamental problem of the *combination* of programming paradigms has raised significant interest recently; a framework to combine different languages describing various facets and artifacts of software development in a seamless, logically consistent way is vital for its solution. Hoare & He gave one of the most significant approaches towards unification [10]. A relational theory between an initial and subsequent states or observations of computer devices is used to give meaning to specifications, designs, and programs. States are expressed as predicates over observational variables. They are constrained by invariants, called healthiness conditions, that characterize theories for imperative, communicating, or reactive processes and their designs.

The UTP framework has proved to be powerful enough for developing a theory of CSP processes, and more recently for giving semantics to languages like *Circus* [13] that combines CSP and Z features and enables states, concurrency and communications to be easily expressed in the same specification.

The motivation of this paper is to provide effective deductive support of UTP theories, in particular those related to *Circus*. Effective deduction is needed for

---

[*] This work was partially supported by the Digiteo Foundation.

S. Qin (Ed.): UTP 2010, LNCS 6445, pp. 188–206, 2010.
© Springer-Verlag Berlin Heidelberg 2010

practically useful transformations on *Circus* specifications, and for our objective of refinement support and automated test generation. Therefore, it is of major importance to find a semantic representation that has a small "representational distance" to the logic used in the implementing proof-environment: since *Circus* comprises typed sets, only frameworks for higher-order logics (HOL, Z, ...) are coming into consideration.

Textbook UTP presentations reveal a particular syntactic flavor of certain language aspects, a feature inherited from the Z tradition. The UTP framework is centered around the concept of *alphabetized* predicates, relations, etc, which were written $(\alpha P, P)$ where αP is intended to produce the *alphabet* of the predicate P implicitly associated to a superset of the free variables in it. In prior works based on *ProofPower*[2], providing a formal semantics theory for UTP in HOL [12], [14], [15], the authors observed the difficulty that "the name of a variable is used to refer both to the name itself and to its value". For instance, in the relation

$$(\{x, x'\}, x > 0 \wedge (x' = x + 1 \vee x' = x - 1)), \tag{1}$$

the left-most x, x' indicates the names x resp. x', while the right-most x, x' stand for their value. Since Oliveira et al. [12] aimed at the proof of refinement laws, the authors saw no alternative to proving meta-theorems using a so-called *deep embedding*; thus, an explicit data type for abstract syntax and an explicit semantic interpretation function was defined that relates syntax and semantic domain. However, such a representation has a number of drawbacks, both conceptually as well as practically wrt. the goal of efficient deduction:

1. there are necessarily ad-hoc limitations of the cardinality of the semantic domain *VAL* (e.g. sets are limited to be *finite* in order to keep the recursive definition of the domain well-founded),
2. the alphabet uses an untyped presentation — there is no inherent link from names and their type, which must be established by additional explicit concepts adding a new layer of complexity, and
3. the reasoning over the explicit alphabet results in a large number of nasty side-conditions ("provisos") hampering deduction drastically. For example, the rule for the sequential composition $\_;_{C}\_$ in *Circus* reads as follows:

$$\forall\, a, b, c : CA \mid \alpha a = \alpha b \wedge \alpha b = \alpha c \wedge\ a;_C (b;_C c) = (a;_C b);_C c \tag{2}$$

where CA abbreviates $CIRCUS\_ACTION$.

In contrast to this "deep embedding" approach we opt for a "shallow embedding". The characterizing feature for the latter is the following: if we represent an object-language expression E of type T into the meta-language by some expression E' of type T', then the mapping is injective for both E and T (provided that E was well-typed with T). In contrast, conventional representations are a surjective map from object-expressions to, say, a data type AST (abstract syntax tree) and therefore not shallow. Due to injective map on types, the types are implicit in a shallow representation, and thus reference to them in provisos in rules is unnecessary. It means that type-inference is used to perform a part of the deduction task beforehand, once and for all, as part of a parsing process prior to deduction.

At this point, we will already recklessly reveal the only essential idea of this paper to the knowledgeable reader: we will represent equation (1) by the λ-abstraction:

$$\lambda \sigma \bullet \sigma.x > 0 \wedge (\sigma.x' = \sigma.x + 1 \vee \sigma.x' = \sigma.x - 1) \tag{3}$$

having the record type $\langle x \rightsquigarrow \mathbb{Z}, x' \rightsquigarrow \mathbb{Z}, ... \rangle \Rightarrow$ bool, which is, in other words, a set of records in HOL. The reader familiar with SML-like record-pattern-match notation may also recognize expression (3) as equivalent to:

$$\lambda \{x, x', ...\} \bullet x > 0 \wedge (x' = x + 1 \vee x' = x - 1)$$

Note that in record notation, the order of the names is insignificant (in contrast to, say, a representation by tuples). Further note that we use *extensible* records — the dots represent the possibility of their extensions, allowing to build up the UTP in an incremental way similar to Brucker and Wolff's approach [6].

Represented in the form of expression (3), the rule (2) above is practically an immediate consequence of rules of a HOL-library. The function αP becomes a meta-function (implemented in the meta language of the target HOL system, typically SML), and the notation $(\alpha P, P)$ is a particular pretty-print of P for sets of records.

Note that in a shallow embedding, the injective representation function must not be a one-to-one translation of operator symbols; rather, it can introduce coercions in E' on the basis of object-language types. For example, it can be necessary to coerce isomorphically a $\langle x \rightsquigarrow \mathbb{Z}, x' \rightsquigarrow \mathbb{Z}, ... \rangle$ set-predicate to a $(\langle x \rightsquigarrow \mathbb{Z}, ... \rangle \times \langle x \rightsquigarrow \mathbb{Z}, ... \rangle)$ set-relation in order to support the semantics of the UTP dash-notation x' in terms of relational composition. Similar compiler techniques are necessary to add or remove fields in extensible records, for example when entering and leaving the scope of a local variable declaration.

Another price we are ready to pay is that there may be *rules* in Textbook UTP, which must be implemented by a *rule scheme* in our representation. That is, there will be specific tactic support that implements a rule scheme, e. g., by inserting appropriate coercions in a more general rule and applying the result in a specific context. This technique has been used for the Z schema calculus by Brucker et al. [3].

As concrete implementation platform, we chose Isabelle/HOL [11] which is a well established tool for formal proof development. As member of the LCF-style prover family, it offers support for user-programmed extensions in a logically safe way. This choice is motivated by our wish to exploit, in a future step, the semantic *Circus* theory developed here with HOL-TestGen [4,5], a powerful test-case generation system that has been built on top of the specification and theorem proving environment Isabelle/HOL.

The paper is organized as follows: Section 2 recalls briefly some useful aspects of various background concepts: UTP, Isabelle/HOL, some advanced aspects of

HOL; Section 3 presents how we have expressed in HOL the part of UTP that is relevant for the *Circus* semantics; Section 4 introduces the *Circus* language and the theory we have developed in HOL from its denotational semantics; Section 5 gives a small example of a *Circus* specification defined in Isabelle/HOL; and the last section summarizes our current contributions and sketches our future work.

2   Background

2.1   Isabelle and Higher-Order Logic

Higher-order logic (HOL) [9,1] is a classical logic based on a simple type system. It provides the usual logical connectives like $\_ \wedge \_$, $\_ \rightarrow \_$, $\neg \_$ as well as the object-logical quantifiers $\forall x \bullet P\,x$ and $\exists x \bullet P\,x$; in contrast to first-order logic, quantifiers may range over arbitrary types, including total functions $f : : \alpha \Rightarrow \beta$. HOL is centered around extensional equality $\_ = \_ : : \alpha \Rightarrow \alpha \Rightarrow$ bool. HOL is more expressive than first-order logic, since, e. g., induction schemes can be expressed inside the logic. Being based on some polymorphically typed λ-calculus, HOL can be viewed as a combination of a programming language like SML or Haskell and a specification language providing powerful logical quantifiers ranging over elementary and function types.

Isabelle/HOL is a logical embedding of HOL into the generic proof assistant Isabelle. The (original) simple-type system underlying HOL has been extended by Hindley/Milner style polymorphism with type-classes similar to Haskell. While Isabelle/HOL is usually seen as "proof assistant", systems like HOL-TestGen[4,5] also use it as symbolic computation environment. Implementations on top of Isabelle/HOL can re-use existing powerful deduction mechanisms such as higher-order resolution, tableaux-based reasoners, rewriting procedures, Presburger Arithmetic, and via various integration mechanisms, also external provers such as Vampire and the SMT-solver Z3. Isabelle/HOL offers support for a particular methodology to extend given theories in a logically safe way: A theory-extension is *conservative* if the extended theory is consistent provided that the original theory was consistent. Conservative extensions can be *constant definitions, type definitions, datatype definitions, primitive recursive definitions* and *well-founded recursive definitions*.

For example, typed sets were built in the Isabelle libraries conservatively on top of the kernel of HOL as functions to bool; consequently, the constant definitions for membership is as follows:[1]

types α set $= \alpha \Rightarrow$ bool
definition Collect :: $(\alpha \Rightarrow$ bool$) \Rightarrow$ α set $---$ set comprehension
where   " Collect S $\equiv$ S"
definition member :: $\alpha \Rightarrow$ bool $---$ membership test
where   "member s S $\equiv$ S s"

---

[1] To increase readability, we use a slightly simplified presentation.

Isabelle's powerful syntax engine is instructed to accept the notation $\{x \bullet P\}$ for Collect $(\lambda x.\ P)$ and the notation $s \in S$ for member s S. As can be inferred from the example, constant definitions are axioms that introduce a fresh constant symbol by some closed, non-recursive expressions; this type of axiom is logically safe since it works like an abbreviation. The syntactic side-conditions of this axiom are mechanically checked, of course. It is straight-forward to express the usual operations on sets like $\_\cup\_, \_\cap\_ :\ :\ \alpha\,\mathrm{set} \Rightarrow \alpha\,\mathrm{set} \Rightarrow \alpha\,\mathrm{set}$ as conservative extensions, too, while the rules of typed set-theory were derived by proofs from these definitions.

2.2   Advanced Concepts of the HOL-Language

Similarly, a logical compiler is invoked for the following statements introducing the types option and list:

datatype α option   = None | Some α
datatype α list = Nil | Cons a l

Here, [] or $a\#l$ are an alternative syntax for Nil or Cons $a\ l$; moreover, $[a, b, c]$ is defined as alternative syntax for $a\#b\#c\#[]$. These (recursive) statements were internally represented in by internal type- and constant definitions. Besides the *constructors* None, Some, there are match-operations like:

case x of None $\Rightarrow F$ | Some $a \Rightarrow G\ a$.

Finally, there is a compiler for primitive and well-founded recursive function definitions.

Isabelle/HOL also provides a rich collection of library theories like sets, pairs, relations, partial functions lists, multi-sets, orderings, and various arithmetic theories which only contain rules derived from conservative definitions. Setups for the automated proof procedures like simp, auto, and the arithmetic types such as int have been done.

Isabelle/HOL's support for *extensible records* is of particular importance for this work. Record types are denoted, for example, by:

record $\mathsf{T} = \mathsf{a} :: \mathsf{T}_1$
         $\mathsf{b} :: \mathsf{T}_2$

which implicitly introduces the record constructor $(\!|\mathsf{a} := \mathsf{e1}, \mathsf{b} := \mathsf{e2}|\!)$ and the update of record r in field a, written as $\mathsf{r}(\!|\mathsf{a} := \mathsf{x}|\!)$. Extensible records are represented internally by cartesian products with an implicit free component δ, i.e. in this case by a triple of the type $\mathsf{T}_1 \times \mathsf{T}_2 \times \delta$. Thus, the record T can be extended later on using the syntax:

record $\mathsf{ET} = \mathsf{T} +$
         $\mathsf{c} :: \mathsf{T}_3$

The key point is that theorems can be established, once and for all, on T types, even if future parts of the record are not yet known, and reused in the later definition and proofs over ET-values. Thus, we can model the effect of defining the alphabet of UTP processes incrementally while maintaining a fully typed shallow embedding with full flexibility on the types T_1, T_2 and T_3. In other words, extensible records give us the means to implement the dots in the representation type of the alphabetized predicate (3):

$$\langle x \rightsquigarrow \mathbb{Z}, x' \rightsquigarrow \mathbb{Z}, ...\rangle set$$

shown in the introduction.

3 Representing UTP in HOL

3.1 Core UTP

In this section, we present the most general features of UTP: the concept of alphabetized predicates, and sub-concepts such as alphabetized relations. As already unveiled in the introduction, we semantically represent alphabetized predicates by sets of extensible records, and the latter by sets of pairs of extensible records; for the latter, there is already the theory Relation.thy in the Isabelle library that provides a collection of derived rules for sequential relational composition _ o _ or operators for least and greatest fixpoints (lfp, gfp).

In order to support a maximum of common UTP look-and-feel, we implement on the SML level implementing Isabelle a function that computes for a term denoting an alphabetized predicate (a cterm in Isabelle terminology) the alphabet of a theorem, be it in the format of an alphabetized predicate or an alphabetized relation. This function is suitably integrated into the command language ISAR of Isabelle such that we can define and query on the ISAR shell:

define_pred sample "($\{x :: int, x' :: int, ...\}$, $x = x' + 1$) "
alpha   sample
inalpha   sample
outalpha   sample

The first statement will be expanded internally into definitional constructions of an alphabetized predicate; the latter three statements make Isabelle execute the common alphabet projection functions α sample, the input alphabet **in**α sample and the output alphabet outα sample (which are $\{x, x', ...\}, \{x, ...\}$ and $\{x', ...\}$, respectively). In more detail, the alphabetized predicate mechanism expands internally the **define_pred**-command as follows:

record   sample_type = $x :: int$, $x' :: int$
definition sample "sample $\equiv \{A :: sample\_type. A.x = A.x' + 1\}$"

where the latter introduces per default a *constant* sample with the right type and a *theorem* sample_def containing the constant definition for sample. Note that leaving out the dots "..." in the **define_pred**-declaration leads to non-extensible records (the internal δ type-variable representing future extensions is instantiated with the trivial unit-type); the query-functions will reflect this in the output accordingly.

Alphabetized Predicates. We introduce the abbreviation α alphabet as a syntactic marker to highlight types that we use for alphabetized elements; on this basis, alphabetized predicates as sets of records are defined as follows:

types α alphabet $= "\alpha"$
types α predicate $= "\alpha$ alphabet $\Rightarrow$ bool"

The standard logical connectives on predicates are simply introduced as abbreviations:

abbreviation   true :: "α predicate"
where "true $= \lambda$A. True"

abbreviation   false :: "α predicate"
where "false $= \lambda$A. False"

abbreviation   not :: "α predicate $\Rightarrow \alpha$ predicate" ("$\neg$ _")
where "$\neg$ P $= \lambda$A. $\neg$ (P A)"

abbreviation   conj :: "[α predicate, α predicate] $\Rightarrow \alpha$ predicate" (infix "$\wedge$")
where "P $\wedge$ Q $= \lambda$A. (P A) $\wedge$ (Q A)"

abbreviation   disj :: "[α predicate, α predicate] $\Rightarrow \alpha$ predicate" ("_ $\vee$ _")
where "P $\vee$ Q $= \lambda$A. (P A) $\vee$ (Q A)"

abbreviation impl :: "[α predicate, α predicate] $\Rightarrow \alpha$ predicate" ("_ $\longrightarrow$ _")
where "P $\longrightarrow$ Q $= \lambda$A. (P A) $\longrightarrow$ (Q A)"

Note that our typing requires that all arguments range over the *same* alphabet. This is a significant restriction compared to textbook UTP, where all alphabets were merged (by the union of the underlying sets), pretty much in the style of Z. Thus, there are implicit coercions between sub-expressions in UTP alphabetized predicates that have to be made explicit in suitable coercion functions. For example, if we have the additional alphabetized predicate:

define_pred sample2 "({y :: int, ...}, y $= 5$) "

an expression like sample $\longrightarrow$ sample2 is simply ill-typed since they are both built over different alphabets. In order to make this work, it is necessary to insert suitable coercion functions (whose definition will be shown below):

$$(Inj_{\alpha sample \mapsto \alpha sample \cup \alpha sample2} \; sample) \longrightarrow (Inj_{\alpha sample2 \mapsto \alpha sample \cup \alpha sample2} \; sample2)$$

The insertion of such coercion functions can be done automatically (based on an SML- computation of the alphabet of each sub-expression) and in an optimized form (only in cases where the alphabets are not just inclusion, only at the "leaves", i.e. around constants denoting alphabetized predicates). The details of such an automated coercion inference are out of the scope of this paper; the technique, however, has already been applied elsewhere [3].

It remains to define universal and existential quantifications in terms of HOL quantifications.

abbreviation ex ::"$'\beta \Rightarrow ['\beta \Rightarrow '\alpha$ predicate] $\Rightarrow '\alpha$ predicate" ("$\exists$ _ _")
where "$\exists$ x P $\equiv \lambda$A. $\exists$ x. (P x) A"

abbreviation all ::"$'\beta \Rightarrow ['\beta \Rightarrow '\alpha$ predicate] $\Rightarrow '\alpha$ predicate" ("$\forall$ _ _")
where "$\forall$ x P $\equiv \lambda$A. $\forall$ x. (P x) A"

Alphabetized Relations. the alphabetized relations type is defined as a HOL relation over $in\alpha P$ and $out\alpha P$. Some programming constructs are then defined over relations, for example the *conditional expression*. The condition expression is represented as a predicate over $in\alpha P$, the symbols are kept as defined in the UTP book.

types α relation $=$ "$(\alpha$ alphabet $\times \alpha$ alphabet) set"
types α condition $=$ "$\alpha \Rightarrow$ bool"

abbreviation cond::"[α relation , α condition , α relation] $\Rightarrow \alpha$ relation" ("_ $\lhd$ _ $\rhd$_")
where "(P $\lhd$ b $\rhd$ Q) $= \lambda$(A, A'). (b A $\wedge$ P (A, A')) $\vee$
$\qquad\qquad\qquad\qquad\qquad (\neg$ (b A) $\wedge$ Q (A, A'))"

The second definition concerns the *sequential composition*; we use a predefined HOL relation operator, which is the relation composition. This operator corresponds exactly to the definition of sequential composition of alphabetized relations.

abbreviation comp::"α relation $\Rightarrow \alpha$ relation $\Rightarrow \alpha$ relation" ("_ ;; _")
where "(P ;; Q) $=$ P o Q"

Since the alphabet is defined as an extensible record, an update function is generated automatically for every field. For example, let **a** be a field in some record, then there is the function r(|a := x|), or represented internally _update_ name a x. We use this internal representation to define by a syntactic paraphrasing the update relation family defined as {(A,A'). A'= (|a := E A|)}.

The syntactic transformation of the assignment to the update function is instrumented as follows:

syntax
"_Assign"   :: "[idt , $\alpha \Rightarrow \beta$] $\Rightarrow \alpha$ relation "   ("_ :== _")
translations
"x :== E" $=>$ "{(A,A'). A' = _update_ name x (E A)}"

A last construct is the *Skip* relation, which keeps all the variable values as they were. We use an equality over $in\alpha P$ and $out\alpha P$ to represent this. By using the record type for the alphabet, this equality is considered as values equality.

abbreviation skip_r ::"α relation" ("Π_r")
where "Π_r $= \lambda$(A, A'). (A' = A)"

The notion of *refinement* is equivalent to the universal implication of predicates, it is defined using the universal closure used in the UTP.

abbreviation closure :: " α predicate $\Rightarrow$ bool" ("[_]")
where "[P] = $\forall$ A. P A"

abbreviation refinement :: " [αpredicate, α predicate] $\Rightarrow$ bool" ("_$\sqsubseteq$_")
where "P $\sqsubseteq$ Q = [Q $\longrightarrow$ P]"

Coercions. As mentioned earlier, it is crucial for our approach to generate coercions in order to make our overall approach work. While it is impossible to *define* coercion function once and for all for an arbitrary αP inside HOL, it is however possible for any concrete alphabet, say $\{x :: int, x' :: int, ...\}$, a coercion, and compute this concrete alphabet for each UTP theory context outside the logic in suitable parsing functions.

More concretely, we have:

1. $Inj_{A \mapsto B}\ P$ which embeds pointwise. Elements of the P-set with alphabet αP are mapped to elements with identical field content if field $a \in \alpha P$, and with arbitrary values if $a \in A$. For example we consider the case $Inj_{\alpha sample \mapsto \alpha sample \cup \alpha sample2}$ which is just: $Inj_{\{x,x',...\} \mapsto \{x,x',y...\}}$. Then we define it by:

    λ P. $\{\sigma$. P $(\!|$x:=x σ, x' := x' σ, ... $|\!)\}$

2. $Proj_A\ P$ projects pointwise. Elements of the P-set with alphabet αP are mapped to elements with identical field content if field $a \in \alpha P$; the fields were ommited otherwise.

3. $Inj_{A \mapsto (B \times C)}\ P$ is a version of $Inj_{A \mapsto B}\ P$ that splits into pairs (useful for the transition between predicates and relations). Example: $Inj_{\alpha sample \mapsto \alpha insample \times \alpha outsample}$ or concretely:

    λ P. $\{(\sigma, \sigma')$. P $(\!|$x:=x σ, x' := x σ', ... $|\!)\}$

4. $Proj_{A \times B \mapsto A \cup B}\ P$ is the inverse of the latter.
5. etc.

3.2   Designs Theory

The *Designs* theory is centered around a new concept which is captured by the extra name ok. Thus, we consider alphabets that contain at least this variable. This fits well to our representation of alphabets in extensible records: any theorem that we prove once and for all in the *Designs* theory will hold in future theories, too.

The name ok. For short, the definition proceeds straightforwardly:

define_pred alpha_d " ({ok :: bool, ...}, true) "

However, it is worthwhile to look at the internal definitions generated here:

record alpha_d   = ok::bool
types 'α alphabet_d = "'α alpha_d_scheme alphabet"
types 'α relation_d = "'α alphabet_d relation "

In this construction, we use the internal type synonym alpha_d_scheme which Isabelle introduces internally for the cartesian product format where δ captures the possible type extension.

Since the definition of alphabets and relations uses a polymorphic type, we declare a new alphabet and relation type by instantiating this type to an extensible alpha_d. All the expressions defined for the first, more general type, will be directly applicable to this new specific type.

Designs. Designs are a subclass of relations than can be expressed in the form:

$$(\text{ok} \wedge P) \rightarrow (\text{ok'} \wedge Q)$$

which means that if a program starts with its precondition P satisfied, it will finish and satisfy its post condition Q. The definition of designs uses the previous definitions of relations and expressions.

definition design :: " [α relation_d , α relation_d] ⇒ α relation_d " ("(_ ⊢ _)")
where " (P ⊢ Q) ≡λ(A, A'). (ok A ∧ P (A, A')) ⟶ (ok A' ∧ Q (A ,A'))"

As seen above, ok is an automatically generated function over the record type alpha_d, it returns the value of field ok

Once given the definition of designs, new definitions for *skip* are stated as follows:

abbreviation skip_d :: "α relation_d " (" Π_d")
where " Π_d ≡(true ⊢ Π_r)"

Our definitions make it possible to lead some proofs using Isabelle/HOL, as for the *true−; left zero* lemma. More details about proofs are given in Sect. 3.5.

3.3   Reactive Processes

As for designs, reactive processes require more observational variables to be defined. They are used for modeling the interaction of a process with its environment. Proceeding like we did with ok, we extend the alphabet with the variables wait, tr and ref. The corresponding extended alphabet and the definition of reactive processes are given in our *Reactive Process* theory. This kind of alphabet is called a *reactive alphabet*.

The names wait, tr and ref. The variable wait expresses whether a process has terminated or is waiting for an interaction with its environment. The variable tr records the trace of events (interactions) the process has already performed. The ref variable is an event set, that encodes the events (interactions) that the process may refuse to perform at this state.

198   A. Feliachi, M.-C. Gaudel, and B. Wolff

The new alphabet is an extension of the alphabet of designs, using the same construct: extensible records. The traces are defined as polymorphic events lists, and the refusals as polymorphic events sets.

datatype α event $=$ ev α
types α trace $=$ "(α event) list "
types α refusals $=$ "(α event) set"

define_pred alpha_rp
          "(alpha_d $\cup$ {wait :: bool, tr :: α trace, ref :: α refusals ,...}, true)"

and we add the handy type abbreviation:

types $(\alpha,\ \delta)$ relation_rp $=$ "$(\alpha,\ \delta)$ alpha_rp_scheme relation "

Again, the δ is used to make the record-extensions explicit.

Reactive Processes. Reactive processes are characterised by three healthiness conditions. The first healthiness condition **R1** states that a reactive process cannot change the history of performed event.

$$\mathbf{R1}\ P = P \wedge (tr \le tr')$$

This healthiness condition is encoded as a relation, it uses a function $\le$ on traces, which is defined in our theory.

abbreviation R1::"$(\alpha,\ \delta)$ relation_rp "
where "R1 (P) $\equiv \lambda$ (A, A'). P (A, A') $\wedge$ (tr A $\le$tr A')"

To express the second healthiness condition **R2**, we use the formulation proposed by Cavalcanti and Woodcock [7].

$$\mathbf{R2}\ (P(tr, tr')) = P(<>, tr - tr')$$

It states that a process description should not rely on what took place before its activation, and should restrict only the new events to be recorded since the last observation. These are the events in $tr - tr'$.

abbreviation R2::"$(\alpha,\ \delta)$ relation_rp "
where "R2 (P) $\equiv \lambda$ (A, A'). P (A(|tr:=[]|),A'(|tr:= (tr A ' − tr A) |))"

The last healthiness condition for reactive processes, **R3**, states that a process should not start if invoked in a waiting state.

$$\mathbf{R3}\ (P) = \Pi \triangleleft wait \triangleright P$$

A definition is given to Π (Skip process), and the healthiness condition is expressed as a conditional expression over predicates.

abbreviation R3::"$(\alpha,\ \delta)$ relation_rp "
where "R3 (P) $\equiv (\Pi\_rp \triangleleft (wait\ o\ fst) \triangleright P)$"

We can now define a reactive process as a relation over a reactive alphabet that satisfies these three healthiness conditions. This condition can be expressed as a functional composition of the three conditions.

definition R::"(α, δ) relation_rp "
where "R $\equiv$ R3 o R2 o R1"

3.4   CSP Processes

As for reactive processes, a theory *CSP Process* corresponds to the CSP processes healthiness conditions. In UTP, a reactive process is a CSP process if it satisfies two additional healthiness conditions **CSP1** and **CSP2**.

definition CSP1::"(α, δ) relation_rp "
where "CSP1 (P) $\equiv \lambda$ (A, A'). (P (A, A')) $\vee$ ($\neg$ ok A $\wedge$ tr A $\leq$ tr A')"

definition J_csp ::"(α, δ) relation_rp "
where "J_csp $\equiv \lambda$ (A, A'). ok A $\longrightarrow$ ok A' $\wedge$ tr A = tr A' $\wedge$ wait A = wait A'
$\wedge$ ref A = ref A' $\wedge$ more A = more A' "

definition CSP2::"(α, δ) relation_rp "
where "CSP2 (P) $\equiv$ P ;; J_csp"

CSP basic processes and operators can be encoded using their definitions as reactive designs. Isabelle can be used to prove that these reactive designs are CSP healthy. This could be an extension of our theory, which contains only the definitions of the two CSP healthiness conditions above. There are three other CSP healthiness conditions that we don't mention here. However, they will be considered in the *Circus* theory since they are required for *Circus* processes.

3.5   Proofs

As mentioned above, the theories contains also proofs for some theorems and lemmas. In the relations theory, 100 lemmas are proved using 250 lines of proof, and in the designs theory 26 lemmas are proved using 120 lines of proof. Since our definitions are close to the library definitions of Isabelle/HOL, we can exploit the power of the standard Isabelle proof procedures. For example, we consider the proof of the *true$-$; left zero* lemma. There are almost the same proof steps as those used in the textbook proof.

lemma t_comp_lz: "(true;;(P $\vdash$ Q)) = true"
  apply (auto simp: expand_fun_eq design_def rel_comp_def_raw mem_def)
  apply (*rule_tac* x="b(|ok:=False|)" **in** exI)
  by (simp add: mem_def)

In the previous proof we first apply some simplifications using the operators definitions (eg. *design_def*), then we fix the ok value to false and finally some simplifications will finish the proof.

4   *Circus*

4.1   A Brief Introduction into the *Circus* Language

Circus is a formal specification and development approach providing a combination of process algebra and model-based abstract data types, with an integrated notion of refinement. As a language, it combines CSP, Z and refinement.

channel $out : \mathbb{N}$

process $Fib \; \hat{=} \;$ **begin**
  state $FibState \;==\; [\, x, y : \mathbb{N} \,]$
  $InitFibState \;==\; [\, FibState' \mid x' = y' = 1 \,]$
  $InitFib \; \hat{=} \; out\,!1 \to out\,!1 \to InitFibState$
  $OutFibState \;==\; [\, \Delta FibState;\; next! : \mathbb{N} \mid next! = y' = x + y \wedge x' = y \,]$
  $OutFib \; \hat{=} \; \mu\, X \bullet (\, \mathbf{var}\; next : \mathbb{N} \bullet OutFibState\,;\, out\,!next \to X\,)$
  $\bullet \; InitFib\,;\; OutFib$
end

Fig. 1. The Fibonacci suite in *Circus*

Syntactically, a *Circus* specification is a sequence of paragraphs, just like in Z or Isabelle/ISAR, with the possibility to declare schemas, channels and processes. In the example of Fig. 1, there is first a paragraph where a channel is declared, namely $out : \mathbb{N}$. Then comes the definition of the Fib process as a sequence of (1) a state definition, which is just a couple of natural numbers, (2) an initialization operation $InitFibState$ on the state defined by a Z schema, (3) a *Circus* action named $InitFib$ defined as a CSP-like process with the specificity that the $InitFibState$ operation appears as an event, (4) a normal operation on the state $OutFibState$, defined by a Z schema and (5) a recursive action $OutFib$ defined by CSP-like constructs where $OutFibState$ operation appears as an event. Finally, the main action of the Fib process is given by just the sequential composition of the two actions above.

This example just shows the description of a process with an encapsulated state, where the behavior combines CSP-like external interactions and Z-like internal state operations. The small example gives only a flavor of *Circus*, which comprises a combined semantics for features like parallelism, internal choices, encapsulated complex data types, imperative statements, and refinements.

4.2   The *Circus* Theory

The denotational semantics of *Circus* was defined by Oliveira et al. [13], based on UTP. *Circus* actions are defined as CSP healthy reactive processes. The Circus_Actions theory contains the definition of the type Action, which restricts the relations to the subset of CSP healthy relations.

typedef(Action)

    (α,δ) action $=$ " $\{$p::(α,δ) relation_rp . is_CSP_process p$\}$"

proof $-$

    have "true $\in \{$p::(α,δ) relation_rp . is_CSP_process p$\}$"

        by(auto simp add: Collect_def mem_def Healthy_def)

    thus ? thesis **by** auto

qed

We assume here the predicate is_CSP_process capturing the known healthiness conditions of CSP (not shown here). Isabelle methodology imposes that type definitions should be non-empty. In the action type definition, the first part declares the actions as subset of CSP healthy relations, and the second part is the proof that this subset is not empty.

Every *Circus* operator is defined as an alphabetized predicate. the first definitions concern the basic processes Stop, Skip and Chaos. Some other examples of operators are also shown in the sequel of the paper.

Basic Processes. Stop is defined as a reactive design, with a precondition true and a postcondition stating that the system deadlocks and the traces are not evolving.

definition

    Stop :: " (α,δ) action"

where

    "Stop $\equiv$ Abs_Action (R (true $\vdash \lambda$ (A, A'). tr A' $=$ tr A $\wedge$ wait A'))"

Skip is defined as a reactive design, with a precondition *true* and a postcondition stating that the system terminates and all the variables of the state are not changed.

definition

    Skip :: " (α,δ) action"

where

    "Skip $\equiv$ Abs_Action (R (true $\vdash \lambda$ (A, A'). tr A' $=$ tr A $\wedge \neg$ wait A'

                                  $\wedge$ more A $=$ more A'))"

The Chaos process is defined as a reactive design with false as precondition and true as postcondition.

Communications. The prefixed actions definition is based on the definition of a special predicate do_C. In the *Circus* denotational semantics, different forms of prefixing were defined, we define in our theory one general form, and the other notations can be defined using this form.

abbreviation

    do_C :: " [α event, α event set] $\Rightarrow (\alpha,\delta)$ relation_rp ''

where

  "do_C x S $\equiv$ (λ (A, A'). (tr A $=$ tr A') $\wedge$ (S $\cap$ (ref A') $= \{\}$))

              $\triangleleft$ wait $\triangleright$

              (λ (A, A'). $\exists$ e. e $\in$ S $\wedge$ (tr A') $=$ (tr A)@[e] $\wedge$ x $=$ e)"

The definition of do_C is different from Oliveira et al.'s definition [13], because we want our definition to be more general. The prefixing action can then be defined, using the same denotational semantics definition.

definition

       Prefix :: "[α event set, α event ⇒ (α,δ) action] ⇒ (α,δ) action"
where
  "Prefix S P ≡Abs_Action((∃ e. R (true ⊢ (λ (A,A'). ((do_C e S)(A,A')
                             ∧ more A' = more A)))) ;; P e)"

Different types of communication are considered below. The channels are defined as functions over communicated values. We distinguish three types of communications:

- Inputs: the set of communications contains all possible values.
- Outputs: the set of communications contains only one value.
- Synchronizations: the set is empty, there is just a channel name.

Below, we define these three communications forms

definition

  read   :: "[α ⇒ β event, α set, α ⇒ (β, δ) action] ⇒ (β, δ) action"
"read c S P ≡ Prefix (c ' S) (P o (inv c))"
  write   :: "[α ⇒ β event, α, (β, δ) action] ⇒ (β, δ) action"
"write c a P ≡ Prefix {c a} (λ x. P)"
  write0   :: "[β event, (β, δ) action] ⇒ (β, δ) action"
"write0 a P ≡ Prefix {a} (λ x. P)"

and configure the Isabelle syntax-engine such that it parses the usual communication primitives:

syntax

"_read"   :: "[id, pttrn, (α,δ) action] ⇒ (α, δ) action" ("_‘?‘_→_")
"_readS" :: "[id, pttrn, β⇒bool, (α,δ)action] ⇒ (α,δ)action" ("_‘?‘_‘:‘_→_")
" _write" :: "[id, β,(α,δ)action] ⇒   (α,δ) action"   ("_‘!‘_ → _")
" _writeS" :: "[α,(α,δ)action] ⇒ (α,δ)action"   ("_ → _")
translations
"c ‘?‘ p → P"   ≡"CONST read c CONST UNIV (λp. P)"
"c ‘?‘ p ‘:‘ b → P" ≡"CONST read c {p. b} (λp. P)"
"c ‘!‘ p → P"   ≡"CONST write c p P"
"a → P"   ≡"CONST write0 a P"

Guarded Actions. A guarded action is defined with a condition and an action, we define a special function Spec that fixes the values of wait and ok' for a given predicate.

abbreviation
   Spec
where
  "Spec b b' P ≡λ (A,A'). P (A(|wait := b'|), A'(|ok := b|))"

definition

   Guard :: " [(α,δ) relation_rp ,(α,δ)action] $\Rightarrow$ (α,δ)action" (" _ & _")

where

  "g & P $\equiv$ Abs_Action(R ((g $\rightarrow$ $\neg$ Spec False False P) $\vdash$

                      ((g$\wedge$Spec True False P) $\vee$

                      ($\neg$ g $\wedge$ λ (A,A').(tr A'=trA$\wedge$ waitA'))))))"

Sequencing. Actions may be composed sequentially using the squential composition operator. The definition is based on the UTP relation composition.

definition

   Seq :: " [(α,δ)action ,(α,δ)action] $\Rightarrow$ (α,δ)action"   (" _ ' ; ' _")

where

  "P ' ; ' Q $\equiv$ Abs_Action (Rep_Action P ;; Rep_Action Q)"

    The complete *Circus* theory contains the definition of all actions operators, constructs, healthiness conditions and the proofs of some theorems over them.

Circus **Processes.** Finally, the *Circus* process definition contains the alphabet declaration, schema expressions and actions. The alphabet is defined by extending the alpha_rp record with the process variables. The normalized schema expressions are defined separately as *relations* over the defined alphabet. The actions are defined as *Circus actions* over the alphabet.

    The next section gives an example of how a *Circus* process is written using the previous theories.

5   Example: Using Isabelle/*Circus*

To illustrate the *use* of the *Circus* theory we come back to our example in Fig. 1 of a process that calculates and outputs the Fibonacci suite. The process uses only one channel *out* that communicates natural numbers. The process state is defined by two natural variables x and y. The process contains two schema expressions *InitFibState* and *OutFibState*, and two actions *InitFib* and *OutFib*. *InitFibState* initializes the state variables to the value 1. *InitFib* action outputs twice the value 1 over the channel *out*, then calls *InitFibState*. *OutFibState* performs the Fibonacci suite step, and returns a value *next*. The *OutFib* action recursively calls *OutFibState* and outputs the value of *next*. The main action of the process performs initialization with *InitFib*, then generates the fibonacci suite with *OutFib*.

    In the following, we will encode this example in our *Circus* theory. Note that we deliberately refrain from a front-end here that hides the Isabelle/*Circus* internals from the user (such a front-end consisting of the existing CZT-parser and type-checker for Circus will be integrated in the future); the purpose of this section is to have a glance at our *Circus* semantics "at work".

5.1   Channels and Alphabet

We first define the channels, types and alphabets. The state definition corresponds to the extension part of the defined alphabet.

datatype channel = out nat

record fib_state = "channel alpha_rp" +
                             x   :: nat
                             y   :: nat

types my_alpha = " fib_state alphabet"
types my_pred = " my_alpha relation"

types my_action = "(channel, (|x :: nat, y :: nat|)) action"

5.2   Schema Expressions and Actions

Normalized schema expressions are defined as reactive processes. The predicate value corresponds to the schema formula, and the input/output variables are passed as parameters (eg. **next**). The actions are defined as *Circus actions*.

definition
        InitFibState :: "my_pred"
where
      " InitFibState $\equiv$ R (λ(A, A'). (x A' = 1 $\wedge$y A' = 1))"

definition
        InitFib :: "my_action"
where
      " InitFib $\equiv$ (out '!' 1 $\rightarrow$ (out '!' 1 $\rightarrow$ Abs_Action InitFibState))"

definition
        OutFibState:: "nat $\Rightarrow$ my_pred"
where
     "OutFibState **next** $\equiv$ R (λ(A, A'). x A' = y A
                                        $\wedge$ y A' = x A + y A $\wedge$**next** = x A + y A)"

definition
   OutFib :: "my_action"
where
    "OutFib $\equiv$$\mu$ X. Abs_Action (λ A. $\exists$ **next**.
                  ((OutFibState **next**) ;; (Rep_Action (out '!' **next** $\rightarrow$ X))) A)"

5.3   Main Action

The main action is also defined as a *Circus Action*, by a sequential composition of the defined actions InitFib and OutFib.

definition
   Fib :: "my_action"
where
   "Fib ≡ InitFib ';' OutFib"

6   Conclusions and Future Work

This paper introduces the Isabelle/*Circus* proof environment. It is conceived as a shallow embedding into Isabelle/HOL and aims for effective deductive support of those UTP theories related to *Circus* and to *Circus* itself. This is work in progress: while the foundation of the UTP is done and most textbook proofs have been formalized, there is at present still very little automated proof support with respect to our ultimate goal, the development of efficient deductive support for verification and test generation for *Circus*.

Our choice of Isabelle as a foundation is justified by the fact that this proof environment comes with a rich set of deduction machinery, and the powerful binding mechanism and type inference system of HOL that we can re-use. However, our main motivation is that we plan to use the HOL-TestGen system [4,5], that is developed on the top of Isabelle/HOL, for developing well-founded test generation strategies from *Circus* specifications, on similar formal bases as those presented by Cavalcanti and Gaudel [8] for CSP.

When developing these theories, it turned out that using HOL extensible records for representing alphabetized predicates is extremely convenient and allows an incremental encoding that remains very close to the original UTP definitions.

Moreover, a significant advantage is that we do not encode the alphabet in our key formalization of the "alphabetized predicate": after a pre-processing, we do everything in the semantic representation with the *type* (as in HOL-Z). This means

- that P is not of type boolean ("predicate"), but of form $\alpha => bool$, which is equivalent to $\alpha\ set$.
- for α, we uses the fact that the fields of the extensible records correspond to the elements of the alphabet,
- the function $\alpha\ P$ becomes a meta-function in ML.

The price to pay are a number of coercions that we have currently to add by hand (and that might be generated by a future front-end using the CZT-Parser, in the way the "Encoder" works in HOL-Z).

From prior experiments, for instance the HOL-Z system mentioned above, we expect this approach to lead to the deductive efficiency required to support proofs about *Circus* specifications, to apply verified transformations on them, with the objective of assisting refinement and test generation.

References

1. Andrews, P.B.: Introduction to Mathematical Logic and Type Theory: To Truth through Proof, 2nd edn. (2002)
2. Arthan, R.: The ProofPower homepage (2009),
   http://www.lemma-one.com/ProofPower/index/
3. Brucker, A.D., Rittinger, F., Wolff, B.: Hol-z 2.0: A proof environment for z-specifications. Journal of Universal Computer Science 9(2), 152–172 (2003)
4. Brucker, A.D., Wolff, B.: Symbolic test case generation for primitive recursive functions. In: Grabowski, J., Nielsen, B. (eds.) FATES 2004. LNCS, vol. 3395, pp. 16–32. Springer, Heidelberg (2004)
5. Brucker, A.D., Wolff, B.: Test-sequence generation with hol-testgen with an application to firewall testing. In: Gurevich, Y., Meyer, B. (eds.) TAP 2007. LNCS, vol. 4454, pp. 149–168. Springer, Heidelberg (2007)
6. Brucker, A.D., Wolff, B.: An extensible encoding of object-oriented data models in hol with an application to imp++. Journal of Automated Reasoning (JAR) 41(3-4), 219–249 (2008); Autexier, S., Mantel, H., Merz, S., Nipkow, T. (eds)
7. Cavalcanti, A.L.C., Woodcock, J.C.P.: A Tutorial Introduction to CSP in Unifying Theories of Programming. In: Cavalcanti, A., Sampaio, A., Woodcock, J. (eds.) PSSE 2004. LNCS, vol. 3167, pp. 220–268. Springer, Heidelberg (2006)
8. Cavalcanti, A., Gaudel, M.C.: A note on traces refinement and the *conf* relation in the Unifying Theories of Programming. In: Butterfield, A. (ed.) UTP 2008. LNCS, vol. 5713, pp. 42–61. Springer, Heidelberg (2008)
9. Church, A.: A formulation of the simple theory of types, vol. 5(2), pp. 56–68 (June 1940)
10. Hoare, C.A.R., Jifeng, H.: Unifying Theories of Programming. Prentice Hall International Series in Computer Science (1998)
11. Nipkow, T., Paulson, L.C., Wenzel, M.: Isabelle/hol!—A Proof Assistant for Higher-Order Logic. LNCS, vol. 2283. Springer, Heidelberg (2002)
12. Oliveira, M.V.M., Cavalcanti, A.L.C., Woodcock, J.C.P.: Unifying theories in ProofPower-Z. In: Dunne, S., Stoddart, B. (eds.) UTP 2006. LNCS, vol. 4010, pp. 123–140. Springer, Heidelberg (2006)
13. Oliveira, M., Cavalcanti, A., Woodcock, J.: A denotational semantics for Circus. Electron. Notes Theor. Comput. Sci. 187, 107–123 (2007)
14. Zeyda, F., Cavalcanti, A.: Encoding Circus programs in ProofPowerZ. In: Butterfield, A. (ed.) UTP 2008. LNCS, vol. 5713, pp. 218–237. Springer, Heidelberg (2009), http://www.cs.york.ac.uk/circus/publications/docs/zc09b.pdf
15. Zeyda, F., Cavalcanti, A.: Mechanical reasoning about families of UTP theories. Science of Computer Programming (2010) (in Press) (Corrected Proof, Available online March 17, 2010)

Unifying Recursion in
Partial, Total and General Correctness

Walter Guttmann

Department of Computer Science, University of Sheffield, UK
walter.guttmann@uni-ulm.de

Abstract. We give an algebraic semantics of non-deterministic, sequential programs which is valid for partial, total and general correctness. It covers full recursion based on a unified approximation order. We provide explicit solutions in terms of the refinement order. As an application, we systematically derive a semantics of while-programs common to the three correctness approaches.

UTP's designs and prescriptions represent programs as pairs of termination and state transition information in total and general correctness, respectively. We show that our unified semantics induces a pair-based representation which is common to the correctness approaches. Operations on the pairs, including finite and infinite iteration, can be derived systematically. We also provide the effect of full recursion on the unified, pair-based representation.

1 Introduction

In previous works [17,18] we have identified common axioms which underlie the approaches of partial, total and general correctness [24], and we have given a unified semantics of while-programs which is valid in all three correctness approaches. Results stated in terms of this semantics and proved by applying the common axioms hold in partial, total and general correctness. For example, this includes complex program transformations, such as those used to prove the normal form theorem for while-programs.

In this paper, we extend the unified semantics to cover full recursion. Fixpoints are taken with respect to a common approximation order, which is expressed in terms of the common refinement order and based on the Egli-Milner order typically used in general correctness. By adding axioms specific to partial, total and general correctness, respectively, we obtain the appropriate semantics of recursion in each particular approach. This covers in particular the sequential, non-deterministic fragment of UTP.

The unified recursion can be used to systematically derive a semantics of programming constructs which is common to all three correctness approaches. As an example, we calculate the unified semantics of while-programs. This improves the previous method of deriving or defining the semantics independently for partial, total and general correctness.

Theories of total and general correctness often represent a program as a pair whose components describe termination information and possible state

S. Qin (Ed.): UTP 2010, LNCS 6445, pp. 207–225, 2010.

transitions, respectively [5,3,30,28,19]. In UTP they emerge as designs for total correctness [22] and prescriptions for general correctness [14].

We show that our unified semantics induces such a pair-based representation, and systematically derive the operations and programming constructs on the pairs. Since it relies only on the common axioms, the same representation is valid for all correctness approaches. Informally speaking, this achieves a unification of UTP's designs and prescriptions.

We generalise previous investigations about the solution of recursions on the pair-based representations, which are specified by a pair of functions. This exemplifies that besides dealing with specific kinds of recursion, such as those necessary for while-programs, the unified recursion is also useful for general results.

Our approach is algebraic: laws of programs are taken as the axioms of algebraic structures with programs as elements. Thus our results hold in any model that satisfies the underlying axioms. In fact, this is essential for our unification as partial, total and general correctness have quite different models. Since the axioms are typically first-order conditional equations, another benefit is the support by automated theorem provers and counterexample generators.

Section 2 provides the axioms and some of their consequences. Most axioms are well investigated in the literature; the few of Section 2.3, including a new one, are specific to our aim of unification.

In Section 3 we contribute the unified approximation order, based on which we unify the semantics of recursion. Our main consequences are explicit representations of the unified fixpoint and explicit conditions for its existence. The application to while-loops is last.

The topic of Section 4 is to contribute a unified, pair-based representation of programs. Two more axioms are required and provided at the beginning. Based on them we map our algebraic structure to a structure of pairs. Operations on the pairs are derived via this isomorphism. We combine these results with the unified fixpoint representation of Section 3 to solve recursions on pairs.

To summarise, the contributions of this paper are to unify approximation, the semantics of recursion, representations of fixpoints, and pair-based representations of programs for partial, total and general correctness.

2   Axioms for Partial, Total and General Correctness

Partial-correctness approaches such as Hoare logic [21], weakest liberal preconditions [12] and Kleene algebra with tests [26] treat programs by ignoring their non-terminating executions. In total correctness, which includes weakest preconditions [12], UTP [22], demonic refinement algebra [31] and demonic algebra [6], terminating executions are ignored in the presence of any non-terminating ones starting from the same states. General correctness [2,5,24,3,30,14,28,17] models terminating and non-terminating executions independently.

Although these approaches give programs different semantics, they support a number of common laws about programs. For example, these laws are sufficient to prove complex program transformations, which then hold in all three correctness approaches [18]. In this section we discuss some of the common axioms, which are subsequently used in this paper. We also mention laws characteristic for particular correctness approaches.

2.1 Basic Axioms

Throughout this paper we assume that programs are elements of an algebraic structure $(S, +, 0, \curlywedge, \top, \cdot, 1)$ such that $(S, +, 0, \curlywedge, \top)$ is a bounded distributive lattice and $(S, +, 0, \cdot, 1)$ is a semiring without the right zero law. We thus have the following axioms:

$$x + 0 = x \qquad\qquad x \curlywedge \top = x$$
$$x + y = y + x \qquad\qquad x \curlywedge y = y \curlywedge x$$
$$x + (y + z) = (x + y) + z \qquad x \curlywedge (y \curlywedge z) = (x \curlywedge y) \curlywedge z$$
$$x \curlywedge (x + y) = x \qquad x \curlywedge (y + z) = (x \curlywedge y) + (x \curlywedge z)$$

$$1 \cdot x = x \qquad\qquad x \cdot (y + z) = (x \cdot y) + (x \cdot z)$$
$$x \cdot 1 = x \qquad\qquad (x + y) \cdot z = (x \cdot z) + (y \cdot z)$$
$$x \cdot (y \cdot z) = (x \cdot y) \cdot z \qquad 0 \cdot x = 0$$

They characterise a lattice-ordered monoid [4] in which the lattice is bounded and distributive and the left zero law $0 \cdot x = 0$ holds. In contrast to our previous works [17,18] we now include the $\curlywedge$ operation, which we use to represent fixpoints in Section 3.2 and programs as pairs in Section 4.2. The operation $\cdot$ has highest precedence; it is frequently omitted by writing xy instead of $x \cdot y$.

By $x \leq y \Leftrightarrow_{\mathrm{def}} x + y = y \Leftrightarrow x \curlywedge y = x$ we obtain the partial order $\leq$ on S with join $+$, meet $\curlywedge$, least element 0 and greatest element $\top$. The operations $+$, $\curlywedge$ and $\cdot$ are $\leq$-isotone. Further consequences of the above axioms are

$$x + x = x \qquad x + (x \curlywedge y) = x$$
$$x \curlywedge x = x \qquad x + (y \curlywedge z) = (x + y) \curlywedge (x + z)$$

In relational models such as UTP, the operation $+$ is interpreted as set union (non-deterministic choice), $\curlywedge$ as set intersection, and $\cdot$ as relational (sequential) composition. The relation $\leq$ is the subset or refinement order, where $x \leq y$ expresses that x refines y. In partial correctness, the constants 0, $\top$ and 1 are the empty, universal and identity relation, respectively. In terms of UTP designs, 0 is $(true \vdash false)$, $\top$ is $(false \vdash true)$, and 1 is $(true \vdash \vec{v}' = \vec{v})$; prescriptions have similar instances. Without further notice, we assume that designs and prescriptions satisfy the healthiness condition H3; these are called 'normal' by [14].

2.2 Domain

The domain $d(x)$ of the program x represents the initial states from which a transition under x is possible. Its complement, the anti-domain $a(x)$, is used in a compact axiomatisation given in [11,10], which we adopt:

$$d(x) = a(a(x))$$
$$a(x)x = 0$$
$$a(xd(y)) = a(xy)$$
$$d(x) + a(x) = 1$$

In our bounded setting the characterisation $d(x) \leq d(y) \Leftrightarrow x \leq d(y)\top$ given by [1] follows. The domain operation is idempotent and $\leq$-isotone, whence the domain elements $d(S)$ are the fixpoints of d. They form a Boolean algebra $(d(S), +, 0, \cdot, 1, a)$ [11,10], in which the operations $\cdot$ and $\curlywedge$ coincide. Further consequences are

$$
\begin{array}{lll}
d(0) = 0 & d(xd(y)) = d(xy) & x \leq d(x)\top \\
d(\top) = 1 & d(d(x)y) = d(x)d(y) & x\top \leq d(x)\top \\
d(x)x = x & d(x + y) = d(x) + d(y) & xd(y)\top \leq d(xy)\top
\end{array}
$$

In UTP and other relational models of total correctness, the domain operation can be defined explicitly by $d(x) = x\top \curlywedge 1$, but this is not valid in general correctness. The domain of a design is reduced to that of its components by $d(P \vdash Q) = (true \vdash a(P) \vee d(Q))$, and similarly for prescriptions.

Domain elements can be used as tests to model conditions: for example, the sequential composition px of $p \in d(S)$ with the program $x \in S$ restricts the transitions of x to those starting in a state that satisfies p.

2.3   Loop

Notably missing from our axioms for S is the right zero law $x \cdot 0 = 0$, or equivalently, $\top \cdot 0 = 0$. This law is characteristic of partial correctness, but it does not hold in total and general correctness. In fact, $\top \cdot 0 = \top$ in total correctness, which in UTP is a consequence of the healthiness condition H1 for designs [22, Theorem 3.2.2]. In general correctness, the element $\top \cdot 0$ is neither 0 nor $\top$: in terms of prescriptions we obtain $(false \Vdash true) \cdot (true \Vdash false) = (false \Vdash false)$.

The element $\top \cdot 0$ occurs in several contexts, such as infinite computations and temporal logic [13,29,27]. Its role in the present work is that in all three correctness approaches $\top \cdot 0$ represents the endless loop or never terminating program; we denote it by $\mathsf{L} =_{\mathrm{def}} \top \cdot 0$.

We assume the following, independent axioms about L:

$$
\begin{array}{ll}
(\mathsf{L1}) & d(x)\mathsf{L} = x\mathsf{L} \\
(\mathsf{L2}) & d(\mathsf{L})x \leq xd(\mathsf{L})
\end{array}
$$

Axiom (L1) and the more restrictive $d(\mathsf{L}) = 1$ are used in our algebraic treatment of general correctness [17,18]; the current (L2) is new.

Axiom (L1) generalises a law typical for relational models of total correctness such as UTP, namely $d(x)\top = x\top$. The latter follows from the explicit $d(x) = x\top \curlywedge 1$ by $d(x)\top = (x\top \curlywedge 1)\top \leq x\top\top = x\top \leq d(x)\top$, but it is not valid in general correctness.

Axiom (L2) holds in partial correctness, where $\mathsf{L} = 0$ and hence $d(\mathsf{L}) = 0$; in total correctness, where $\mathsf{L} = \top$ and hence $d(\mathsf{L}) = 1$; and in general correctness where also $d(\mathsf{L}) = 1$. For prescriptions, the latter is obtained by

$$
\begin{aligned}
d(\mathsf{L}) &= d(false \Vdash false) = (true \Vdash a(false) \vee d(false)) \\
&= (true \Vdash (\neg false \wedge \vec{v}' = \vec{v}) \vee false) = (true \Vdash \vec{v}' = \vec{v}) = 1 \ .
\end{aligned}
$$

The endless loop L is a particular case of an element being formed by sequential composition with 0. Intuitively, this operation cuts out all terminating executions, thus $x0$ retains only the non-terminating executions of x [27,23]. In presence of (L2), the axiom (L1) can be replaced by its instance (L3) for such non-terminating elements:

$$\text{(L3)} \quad d(x0)\mathsf{L} = x0$$
$$\text{(L3')} \quad x \leq y \Leftrightarrow x \leq y + \mathsf{L} \wedge x \leq y + d(y0)\top$$

Along with a few other facts, including the equivalence of (L3) and (L3'), this is shown in the following lemma.

Lemma 1.

1. $\text{(L1)} \wedge \text{(L2)} \Leftrightarrow \text{(L3)} \wedge \text{(L2)}$.
2. $\text{(L1)} \Rightarrow x\top \curlywedge \mathsf{L} = x\mathsf{L}$.
3. $\text{(L1)} \Rightarrow (x0 \curlywedge y0)0 = x0 \curlywedge y0$.
4. $\text{(L2)} \Rightarrow xa(\mathsf{L})\top \leq x0 + a(\mathsf{L})\top$.
5. $\text{(L3)} \Leftrightarrow \text{(L3')}$.

Proof.

1. The forward implication is clear since (L3) is an instance of (L1). The backward implication follows by

$$d(x)\mathsf{L} = d(x)d(\mathsf{L})\mathsf{L} = d(\mathsf{L})d(x)\mathsf{L} = d(d(\mathsf{L})x)\mathsf{L} \leq d(xd(\mathsf{L}))\mathsf{L} = d(x\mathsf{L})\mathsf{L}$$
$$= d(x\top0)\mathsf{L} = x\top0 = x\mathsf{L} \leq d(x)\top\mathsf{L} = d(x)\mathsf{L} \ .$$

2. Since $\cdot$ is $\leq$-isotone we have $x\mathsf{L} \leq x\top$ and $x\mathsf{L} \leq \top\mathsf{L} = \mathsf{L}$. Hence $x\mathsf{L} \leq x\top \curlywedge \mathsf{L} = d(x\top \curlywedge \mathsf{L})(x\top \curlywedge \mathsf{L}) \leq d(x\top)\mathsf{L} = x\top\mathsf{L} = x\mathsf{L}$.

3. We use (L1) in

$$x0 \curlywedge y0 = d(x0 \curlywedge y0)(x0 \curlywedge y0) \leq d(x0 \curlywedge y0)\mathsf{L} = (x0 \curlywedge y0)\mathsf{L}$$
$$= (x0 \curlywedge y0)\top0 \leq (x0\top \curlywedge y0\top)0 = (x0 \curlywedge y0)0 \leq x0 \curlywedge y0 \ .$$

4. The claim is proved by separating the cases $d(\mathsf{L})$ and $a(\mathsf{L})$:

$$xa(\mathsf{L})\top = 1xa(\mathsf{L})\top = (d(\mathsf{L}) + a(\mathsf{L}))xa(\mathsf{L})\top = d(\mathsf{L})xa(\mathsf{L})\top + a(\mathsf{L})xa(\mathsf{L})\top$$
$$\leq xd(\mathsf{L})a(\mathsf{L})\top + a(\mathsf{L})\top = x0 + a(\mathsf{L})\top \ .$$

5. Assume (L3). The forward implication of (L3') is clear since $+$ is the join operator. For the backward implication let $x \leq y + \mathsf{L}$ and $x \leq y + d(y0)\top$. We then obtain $x \leq y$ by separating the cases $d(y0)$ and $a(y0)$:

$$x = d(y0)x + a(y0)x \leq d(y0)(y + \mathsf{L}) + a(y0)(y + d(y0)\top)$$
$$= d(y0)y + d(y0)\mathsf{L} + a(y0)y + a(y0)d(y0)\top \leq y + y0 + 0 = y \ .$$

Assume (L3'). We then obtain $d(x0)\mathsf{L} \leq x0$ since $d(x0)\mathsf{L} \leq \mathsf{L} \leq x0 + \mathsf{L}$ and $d(x0)\mathsf{L} \leq d(x0)\top \leq x0 + d(x0 \cdot 0)\top$, thus (L3) by $x0 = d(x0)x0 \leq d(x0)\mathsf{L}$. $\square$

2.4 Specific Laws

The axioms discussed so far are common to partial, total and general correctness. Table 1 presents a sample of laws which hold in some correctness approaches only. These, and further ones, can be imposed as axioms or derived from other axioms when reasoning in a particular sub-theory. We do not consider them further as our goal is a theory unifying the three correctness approaches.

Table 1. Laws of particular correctness approaches

	partial	total	general
$\mathsf{L} = 1$	−	−	−
$\mathsf{L} = 0$	+	−	−
$\mathsf{L} = \top$	−	+	−
$d(\mathsf{L}) \le \mathsf{L}$	+	+	−
$\mathsf{L} \curlywedge 1 = a(\mathsf{L})$	−	−	+
$\mathsf{L} \curlywedge 1 = 0$	+	−	+
$d(\mathsf{L}) = 1$	−	+	+
$d(\mathsf{L})\top \le \top d(\mathsf{L})$	+	+	+

3 Unified Semantics

In this section, we describe the unified semantics of partial, total and general correctness. Sequential composition and non-deterministic choice are modelled by the operations $+$ and $\cdot$, respectively. Hence $\le$ is the common refinement order. Also traditional is the conditional statement given by if p then x else $y =_{\text{def}}$ $px + a(p)y$ for domain elements p. A unified semantics of finite and infinite iteration has been presented in [18]. It arises in Section 3.3 as a special case of the unified semantics of recursion, which we first discuss.

3.1 Approximation

In contrast to the refinement order, the approximation order is used to fix the meaning of recursively defined programs. Both orders coincide in the case of partial and total correctness, but not in general correctness, where approximation is given by the Egli-Milner order [30]. For general correctness, we have expressed the Egli-Milner order algebraically in terms of the refinement order [17,18]. Based on that, we use the following generalisation to cover partial, total and general correctness:

$$x \sqsubseteq y \Leftrightarrow_{\text{def}} x \le y + \mathsf{L} \wedge d(\mathsf{L})y \le x + d(x0)\top .$$

Let us instantiate the approximation relation $\sqsubseteq$ for each correctness approach to see why it is appropriate:

- In partial correctness we have $\mathsf{L} = 0$, hence $x \sqsubseteq y \Leftrightarrow x \le y$. Refinement and approximation coincide.

- In total correctness we have $\mathsf{L} = \top$, hence $x \sqsubseteq y \Leftrightarrow y \leq x + d(x0)\top = x + x0 = x$ assuming the law $d(x)\top = x\top$ valid in UTP and other relational models. Thus approximation is the converse of refinement, which enables us to take the same (least) fixpoints as in the other approaches.
- In general correctness we exemplify $\sqsubseteq$ for prescriptions. A calculation similar to the one in [17] yields

$$(P_1 \Vdash Q_1) \sqsubseteq (P_2 \Vdash Q_2) \Leftrightarrow P_1 \leq P_2 \wedge Q_1 \leq Q_2 \wedge P_1 \curlywedge Q_2 \leq Q_1 .$$

This is the Egli-Milner order given by [15].

Although we know that in these three instances the relation $\sqsubseteq$ is a partial order, we still have to show this in general. This is done by the following theorem, which also shows that the basic operators are $\sqsubseteq$-isotone. Our previous result for the Egli-Milner order in [18] is similar, but due to subtle differences between the orders we provide a new proof.

Theorem 2. *The relation $\sqsubseteq$ is a preorder with least element L. It is a partial order if and only if (L3) holds. The operations $+$ and $\cdot z$ are $\sqsubseteq$-isotone. The operation $z\cdot$ is $\sqsubseteq$-isotone if (L2) holds.*

Proof. Reflexivity is clear since $x \leq x + \mathsf{L}$ and $d(\mathsf{L})x \leq x$. The least element is L since $\mathsf{L} \leq y + \mathsf{L}$ and $d(\mathsf{L})y \leq d(\mathsf{L})\top \leq \mathsf{L} + d(\mathsf{L}0)\top$. For transitivity let $x \sqsubseteq y$ and $y \sqsubseteq z$. Thus $x \leq y + \mathsf{L}$ and $y \leq z + \mathsf{L}$, whence $x \leq y + \mathsf{L} \leq z + \mathsf{L}$. Moreover $d(\mathsf{L})y \leq x + d(x0)\top$ and $d(\mathsf{L})z \leq y + d(y0)\top$, whence

$$
\begin{aligned}
d(\mathsf{L})z &= d(\mathsf{L})d(\mathsf{L})z \leq d(\mathsf{L})(y + d(y0)\top) = d(\mathsf{L})y + d(\mathsf{L})d(y0)\top \\
&= d(\mathsf{L})y + d(d(\mathsf{L})y0)\top \leq x + d(x0)\top + d((x + d(x0)\top)0)\top \\
&= x + d(x0)\top + d(x0 + d(x0)\mathsf{L})\top = x + d(x0)\top + d(x0)d(\mathsf{L})\top \\
&= x + d(x0)\top .
\end{aligned}
$$

Hence $x \sqsubseteq z$. By Lemma 1.5 we can use (L3') to show that $\sqsubseteq$ is antisymmetric. Let $x \sqsubseteq y$ and $y \sqsubseteq x$, then $x \leq y + \mathsf{L}$ and $d(\mathsf{L})x \leq y + d(y0)\top$. Thus

$$x = d(\mathsf{L})x + a(\mathsf{L})x \leq d(\mathsf{L})x + a(\mathsf{L})y + a(\mathsf{L})\mathsf{L} \leq y + d(y0)\top .$$

We therefore have $x \leq y$ by (L3'), and a symmetric argument shows $y \leq x$. On the other hand, we obtain (L3) by assuming that $\sqsubseteq$ is antisymmetric since $d(x0)\mathsf{L} \sqsubseteq x0$ and $x0 \sqsubseteq d(x0)\mathsf{L}$ follow from

$$
\begin{aligned}
&d(x0)\mathsf{L} \leq \mathsf{L} = x0 + \mathsf{L} , &&d(\mathsf{L})x0 \leq x0 \leq d(x0)\mathsf{L} \leq d(x0)\mathsf{L} + d(d(x0)\mathsf{L}0)\top , \\
&x0 \leq \mathsf{L} = d(x0)\mathsf{L} + \mathsf{L} , &&d(\mathsf{L})d(x0)\mathsf{L} \leq d(x0)\top \leq x0 + d(x0 \cdot 0)\top .
\end{aligned}
$$

For the isotony claims assume $x \sqsubseteq y$, hence $x \leq y + \mathsf{L}$ and $d(\mathsf{L})y \leq x + d(x0)\top$. Then $x + z \sqsubseteq y + z$ follows from $x + z \leq y + z + \mathsf{L}$ and $d(\mathsf{L})(y + z) \leq d(\mathsf{L})y + z \leq x + z + d(x0)\top \leq x + z + d((x + z)0)\top$. Moreover $xz \sqsubseteq yz$ follows from $xz \leq (y + \mathsf{L})z = yz + \mathsf{L}$ and $d(\mathsf{L})yz \leq (x + d(x0)\top)z = xz + d(x0)\top z \leq xz + d(xz0)\top$. Finally $zx \sqsubseteq zy$ follows from $zx \leq z(y + \mathsf{L}) \leq zy + \mathsf{L}$ and $d(\mathsf{L})zy \leq zd(\mathsf{L})y \leq z(x + d(x0)\top) = zx + zd(x0)\top \leq zx + d(zx0)\top$ using (L2). $\qquad\square$

By developing the unified semantics algebraically in a first-order theory, we considerably profit from tools such as automated theorem provers and counterexample generators. For example, the converse of the last claim in Theorem 2 does not hold as witnessed by a 12-element counterexample generated by Mace4, even if (L1) is assumed additionally.

3.2 Recursion

With the approximation order in place, we can define the unified semantics of recursion. Let $f : S \to S$ be the characteristic function of the recursion. The unified semantics of the recursion is the $\sqsubseteq$-least fixpoint of f, denoted by κf provided it exists. We furthermore use the $\leq$-least prefixpoint and the $\leq$-greatest postfixpoint of f, which are denoted by μf and νf, respectively, provided they exist. To be precise, we require that these elements satisfy the following laws:

$$
\begin{aligned}
f(\kappa f) &= \kappa f & f(x) = x &\Rightarrow \kappa f \sqsubseteq x \\
f(\mu f) &= \mu f & f(x) \leq x &\Rightarrow \mu f \leq x \\
f(\nu f) &= \nu f & x \leq f(x) &\Rightarrow x \leq \nu f
\end{aligned}
$$

It follows that μf and νf are the $\leq$-least and $\leq$-greatest fixpoints of f, respectively. By the discussion about the unified approximation order in Section 3.1 we immediately obtain that κf is appropriate in all three correctness approaches. In particular, $\kappa f = \mu f$ in partial correctness, and $\kappa f = \nu f$ in total correctness.

The main result of this section gives explicit representations of κf and conditions for its existence. We denote by $x \sqcap y$ the greatest lower bound of x and y with respect to $\sqsubseteq$, provided it exists.

Theorem 3. *Let $f : S \to S$ be $\leq$- and $\sqsubseteq$-isotone, and assume that μf and νf exist. Then the following are equivalent:*

1. κf exists.
2. $\kappa f = \mu f \sqcap \nu f$.
3. $\kappa f = (\nu f \curlywedge L) + \mu f$.
4. $d(L)\nu f \leq (\nu f \curlywedge L) + \mu f + d(\nu f 0)\top$.
5. $(\nu f \curlywedge L) + \mu f \sqsubseteq \nu f$.
6. $\mu f \sqcap \nu f = (\nu f \curlywedge L) + \mu f$.
7. $\mu f \sqcap \nu f \leq \nu f$.

Proof. Abbreviate $\ell =_{\text{def}} (\nu f \curlywedge L) + \mu f$ and $m =_{\text{def}} \mu f \sqcap \nu f$. Since $\nu f 0 \leq \nu f$ and $\nu f 0 \leq L$ we have $\nu f 0 \leq \nu f \curlywedge L \leq \ell \leq \nu f + \mu f = \nu f$, whence $\nu f 0 = \ell 0$. We first show that statements (4)–(7) are equivalent:

(4) $\Rightarrow$ (5): Because $\ell \leq \nu f \leq \nu f + L$ and $d(L)\nu f \leq \ell + d(\nu f 0)\top = \ell + d(\ell 0)\top$ we obtain $\ell \sqsubseteq \nu f$.

(5) $\Rightarrow$ (6): We have $\ell \leq \mu f + L$ and $d(L)\mu f \leq d(L)\nu f \leq \ell + d(\ell 0)\top$, thus $\ell \sqsubseteq \mu f$. Let $x \sqsubseteq \mu f$ and $x \sqsubseteq \nu f$, then $x \leq \mu f + L \leq \ell + L$ and $d(L)\ell \leq d(L)\nu f \leq x + d(x0)\top$, whence $x \sqsubseteq \ell$.

(6) $\Rightarrow$ (7): This is immediate since $\ell \leq \nu f$.

$(7) \Rightarrow (4)$: From $m \sqsubseteq \mu f$ we obtain $m \leq \mu f + \mathsf{L}$, whence $m \leq \nu f \curlywedge (\mu f + \mathsf{L}) = (\nu f \curlywedge \mu f) + (\nu f \curlywedge \mathsf{L}) = \ell$ by distributivity and the meet property of $\curlywedge$. Thus $m \sqsubseteq \nu f$ implies $d(\mathsf{L})\nu f \leq m + d(m0)\top \leq \ell + d(\ell 0)\top = \ell + d(\nu f 0)\top$.

We next add statements (1)–(3) to this cycle:

$(1) \Rightarrow (2)$: Clearly $\kappa f \sqsubseteq \mu f$ and $\kappa f \sqsubseteq \nu f$. Let $x \sqsubseteq \mu f$ and $x \sqsubseteq \nu f$, then $x \leq \mu f + \mathsf{L} \leq \kappa f + \mathsf{L}$ and $d(\mathsf{L})\kappa f \leq d(\mathsf{L})\nu f \leq x + d(x0)\top$, whence $x \sqsubseteq \kappa f$.

$(2) \Rightarrow (7)$: This is immediate since $\kappa f \leq \nu f$.

$(7) \Rightarrow (3)$: This step uses isotony of f. From $m \sqsubseteq \mu f$ we get $f(m) \sqsubseteq f(\mu f) = \mu f$ and $m \leq \mu f + \mathsf{L} = f(\mu f) + \mathsf{L} \leq f(m) + \mathsf{L}$ since $\mu f \leq m$ by (6). From $m \sqsubseteq \nu f$ we get $f(m) \sqsubseteq f(\nu f) = \nu f$ and $d(\mathsf{L})f(m) \leq d(\mathsf{L})f(\nu f) = d(\mathsf{L})\nu f \leq m + d(m0)\top$ by (7). Hence $m \sqsubseteq f(m) \sqsubseteq m$, thus $f(\ell) = \ell$ by (6) and Theorem 2. Let $f(x) = x$, then $\mu f \leq x \leq \nu f$, whence $\ell \leq \mu f + \mathsf{L} \leq x + \mathsf{L}$ and $d(\mathsf{L})x \leq d(\mathsf{L})\nu f \leq \ell + d(\nu f 0)\top = \ell + d(\ell 0)\top$ by (4). Thus $\ell \sqsubseteq x$.

$(3) \Rightarrow (1)$: This is clear. □

Statements (3) and (4) of this theorem describe the $\sqsubseteq$-least fixpoint κf and its existence in terms of the refinement order $\leq$. In all representations, the $\leq$-least and $\leq$-greatest fixpoints are separated; this is in contrast to the partitioned fixpoint of [7] which nests one fixpoint operator inside another.

In partial and general correctness the additional representation $\kappa f = \nu f 0 + \mu f$ holds [17,18]. The counterexample $f(x) = x \curlywedge 1$ with $\mu f = 0$ and $\nu f = 1$ shows that in total correctness this representation cannot be added as an equivalent condition to Theorem 3. Yet we obtain the following, sufficient conditions that describe when $\kappa f = \nu f 0 + \mu f$ in partial, total and general correctness.

Corollary 4. *Let $f : S \to S$ be $\leq$- and $\sqsubseteq$-isotone, and assume that μf and νf exist. Then the following are equivalent:*

1. $\kappa f = \nu f 0 + \mu f$.
2. $d(\mathsf{L})\nu f \leq \mu f + d(\nu f 0)\top$.
3. $\nu f 0 + \mu f \sqsubseteq \nu f$.
4. $\mu f \sqcap \nu f = \nu f 0 + \mu f$.

They imply the statements of Theorem 3.

Proof. Abbreviate $\ell =_{\text{def}} (\nu f \curlywedge \mathsf{L}) + \mu f$ and $n =_{\text{def}} \nu f 0 + \mu f$. Since $\nu f 0 \leq \nu f$ and $\nu f 0 \leq \mathsf{L}$ we have $n \leq \ell$. Assuming (2) we obtain $n = \ell$ since Lemma 1.2 gives

$$\nu f \curlywedge \mathsf{L} = \nu f \curlywedge \mathsf{L} \curlywedge \mathsf{L} = d(\nu f \curlywedge \mathsf{L})(\nu f \curlywedge \mathsf{L}) \curlywedge \mathsf{L} \leq d(\mathsf{L})\nu f \curlywedge \mathsf{L}$$
$$\leq (\mu f + d(\nu f 0)\top) \curlywedge \mathsf{L} \leq \mu f + (d(\nu f 0)\top \curlywedge \mathsf{L}) = \mu f + d(\nu f 0)\mathsf{L} = n \ .$$

But (2) also implies Theorem 3.4 and therefore (1), (3) and (4) by setting $\ell = n$ in statements (3), (5) and (6) of Theorem 3. Conversely, $(3) \Rightarrow (2)$ by

$$d(\mathsf{L})\nu f \leq n + d(n0)\top = \nu f 0 + \mu f + d(\nu f 0)\top = \mu f + d(\nu f 0)\top \ ,$$

and $(1) \Rightarrow (3)$ since $\kappa f \sqsubseteq \nu f$ and $(4) \Rightarrow (3)$ since $\mu f \sqcap \nu f \sqsubseteq \nu f$. □

3.3   Iteration

In partial, total and general correctness, the semantics of the loop while p do y is obtained as the appropriate solution of the equation $x = pyx + a(p)$, using a domain element p. As discussed above it is given by the fixpoint operator κ. To represent the solution of this particular recursion we use the Kleene star and omega operations given by the following axioms [25,8,27]:

$$1 + y^*y \le y^* \qquad\qquad z + xy \le x \Rightarrow zy^* \le x$$
$$1 + yy^* \le y^* \qquad\qquad z + yx \le x \Rightarrow y^*z \le x$$
$$yy^\omega = y^\omega \qquad\qquad x \le yx + z \Rightarrow x \le y^\omega + y^*z$$

It follows that $y^*z = \mu(\lambda x.yx + z)$ and $y^\omega + y^*z = \nu(\lambda x.yx + z)$. We also have the decomposition laws $(x + y)^* = x^*(yx^*)^*$ and $(x + y)^\omega = (x^*y)^\omega + (x^*y)^*x^\omega$. Moreover $y^\omega = y^\omega\top$ and $y^*0 \le y^\omega 0$. The operations * and $^\omega$ are $\le$-isotone.

The unified semantics of the while-loop is obtained by the following result.

Corollary 5. *Let* $y \in S$ *and* $p, q \in d(S)$ *and* $f(x) =_{\text{def}} pyx + q$. *Then* $\kappa f = (py)^\omega 0 + (py)^*q$.

Proof. We have $\mu f = (py)^*q$ and $\nu f = (py)^\omega + (py)^*q$. The function f is $\le$-isotone and by Theorem 2 also $\sqsubseteq$-isotone. Thus κf exists since Corollary 4.2 holds by

$$\nu f 0 = ((py)^\omega + (py)^*q)0 = (py)^\omega 0 + (py)^*0 = (py)^\omega 0 = (py)^\omega L \ ,$$
$$d(L)(py)^\omega \le (py)^\omega d(L) \le d((py)^\omega d(L))\top = d((py)^\omega L)\top = d(\nu f 0)\top \ ,$$
$$d(L)\nu f = d(L)((py)^\omega + \mu f) \le d(L)(py)^\omega + \mu f \le d(\nu f 0)\top + \mu f \ ,$$

using (L2). Hence Corollary 4.1 gives $\kappa f = \nu f 0 + \mu f = (py)^\omega 0 + (py)^*q$.   □

We have thus replaced the incidental observation of [18], that $(py)^\omega 0 + (py)^*a(p)$ is an adequate semantics of while p do y for partial, total and general correctness, by a systematic derivation.

This section is concluded by showing that both finite and infinite iteration are $\sqsubseteq$-isotone, which generalises our previous result for finite iteration in general correctness [18]. Hence by Theorem 2 also while p do y is $\sqsubseteq$-isotone in y.

Theorem 6. *Let* $x, y \in S$ *such that* $x \sqsubseteq y$. *Then* $x^* \sqsubseteq y^*$ *and* $x^\omega \sqsubseteq y^\omega$.

Proof. From $x \sqsubseteq y$ we obtain $x \le y + L$ and $d(L)y \le x + d(x0)\top$. For $x^* \sqsubseteq y^*$ we have $x^* \le (y + L)^* = y^*(Ly^*)^* = y^*L^* = y^* + y^*LL^* = y^* + L$, whence it suffices to show $d(L)y^* = d(L)(d(L)y)^* \le z =_{\text{def}} x^* + d(x^*0)\top$. The first step imports the test $d(L)$ into the iteration by [18, Lemma 9] using (L2). The second step follows by instantiating a star axiom with $d(L) + zd(L)y \le 1 + z(x + d(x0)\top) \le z$ using $x^*d(x0)\top \le d(x^*x0)\top \le d(x^*0)\top$. For $x^\omega \sqsubseteq y^\omega$ we have

$$x^\omega \le (y + L)^\omega = (y^*L)^\omega + (y^*L)^*y^\omega = y^*L(y^*L)^\omega + y^\omega + y^*L(y^*L)^*y^\omega = y^\omega + L$$

since $y^*Lw = y^*L = L$ for any $w \in S$, and

$$d(L)y^\omega = (d(L)y)^\omega \le (x + d(x0)\top)^\omega = (x^*d(x0)\top)^\omega + (x^*d(x0)\top)^*x^\omega$$
$$= x^*d(x0)\top(x^*d(x0)\top)^\omega + x^\omega + x^*d(x0)\top(x^*d(x0)\top)^*x^\omega$$
$$\le x^\omega + x^*d(x0)\top \le x^\omega + d(x^*0)\top \le x^\omega + d(x^\omega 0)\top$$

again by importing $d(L)$, this time into the infinite iteration.   □

4 Representation by Pairs

In this section, we give a unified representation of programs as pairs of termination and state transition information. Describing programs this way is standard in total correctness, exemplified by UTP's designs, and in general correctness, exemplified by the prescriptions of [14]. Hoare and He argue that the pair-based representation is helpful for practical application [22, page 81].

Algebraic accounts of designs and prescriptions are given in [28,19,17,20]. In the following we describe a representation which is suitable for total and general correctness at the same time. Partial correctness is included as an extreme case, too.

4.1 Havoc

In Section 2.3 we have already discussed the operation $\cdot 0$ which cuts out the terminating executions of a program, giving rise to the loop element L. This operation can be used to obtain one component of the pair-based representation: that which describes the (non-)termination information. For the other component we need an operation that gives us the terminating executions, cutting out the non-terminating ones. We proceed in two steps.

First, we axiomatise the greatest element which contains only terminating executions. In general correctness, it corresponds to the command havoc of [30], whence we denote the element by H. In UTP's total-correctness approach, it corresponds to the design $(true \vdash true)$. We use the following axioms (not to be confused with the healthiness conditions H1–H4 of UTP):

$$\begin{array}{ll} \text{(H1)} & \mathsf{H}0 = 0 \\ \text{(H2)} & x \le x0 + \mathsf{H} \end{array}$$

Axiom (H2) and the more restrictive $x \le y + \mathsf{L} \wedge x \le y + \mathsf{H} \Rightarrow x \le y$ are used in our algebraic treatment of general correctness [17]. The latter implies (H1), but is not suitable for total correctness.

A few facts about H are shown in the following lemma. By instantiating its first claim with $y = 0$, we obtain that H is indeed the greatest terminating element. As such, it is axiomatised in [31] in a total-correctness setting, but as a counterexample generated by Mace4 shows, those axioms do not imply (H2) which we need for our representation as pairs in Section 4.2.

Lemma 7. *Assume* (H1) *and* (H2).

1. $x0 \le y \Leftrightarrow x \le y + \mathsf{H}$.
2. $1 \le \mathsf{H} = \mathsf{H}^2 = \mathsf{H}^*$.
3. $\mathsf{L} + \mathsf{H} = \top$.

Proof.

1. $(x + \mathsf{H})0 = x0 + \mathsf{H}0 = x0 + 0 \le x$ by (H1). With (H2) and $\le$-isotony of $\cdot$ and $+$ the claimed Galois connection follows by [9, Lemma 7.26]. Furthermore, the Galois connection conversely implies (H1) and (H2).

2. $1 \leq H$ by part 1 since $1 \cdot 0 = 0$. Hence $H = 1H \leq H^2$, while $H^2 \leq H$ by part 1 since $H^2 0 = H0 = 0$. Hence $1 + H^2 \leq H$, which implies $H^* \leq H$. Finally, $H = 1H \leq H^*H \leq H^*$.
3. $\top \leq L + H$ by part 1 since $\top 0 = L$.   □

Second, we cut out the non-terminating executions by forming the meet with H. Intuitively, $x \curlywedge H$ retains only the terminating executions of x since H contains all terminating executions and no non-terminating ones. It should be noted that although $L + H = \top$, we do not have $L \curlywedge H = 0$, so H is not a complement of L in S; hence they are not partitioning elements [7]. In particular, $L \curlywedge H = H \neq 0$ in total correctness, where $L = \top$. In partial correctness $H = \top$ because $L = 0$. There and in general correctness $L \curlywedge H = 0$ holds.

4.2   Pair Programming

We represent the program $x \in S$ by the pair $(x0, x \curlywedge H)$. The first component $x0$ describes those states from where non-terminating executions are possible. The second component $x \curlywedge H$ describes the possible state transitions for terminating executions.

UTP's designs remind us that the representation as pairs is not necessarily unique. For example, the two designs $(false \vdash false)$ and $(false \vdash true)$ are equal. This is in contrast to prescriptions, which uniquely represent programs in general correctness. A unique representation for designs can be obtained by choosing a canonical representative, for example, by requiring $\neg P \Rightarrow Q$ for each design $(P \vdash Q)$. We follow this strategy to obtain a unique common representation.

Formally, we take representatives from the set $S' =_{\text{def}} \{(x0, x \curlywedge H) \mid x \in S\}$. The representation and abstraction functions are given by

$$\rho : S \to S' \qquad\qquad \pi : S' \to S$$
$$\rho(x) =_{\text{def}} (x0, x \curlywedge H) \qquad\qquad \pi((x, y)) =_{\text{def}} x + y$$

We write $\pi(x, y)$ instead of $\pi((x, y))$ and similarly for other functions on pairs. The following lemma shows that ρ and π are in fact bijections.

Lemma 8.

1. $x = x0 + (x \curlywedge H)$, hence $\pi \circ \rho = \text{id}_S$ and $\rho \circ \pi = \text{id}_{S'}$.
2. $S' = \{(x0, y \curlywedge H) \mid x, y \in S \land x0 \curlywedge H \leq y\}$.

Proof.

1. $x = x \curlywedge (x0 + H) = (x \curlywedge x0) + (x \curlywedge H) = x0 + (x \curlywedge H)$ by (H2). This shows $\pi \circ \rho = \text{id}_S$ or ρ is injective. But ρ is surjective by definition.
2. The inclusion ($\subseteq$) is immediate from $x0 \curlywedge H \leq x0 \leq x$. For the inclusion ($\supseteq$) let $x, y \in S$ with $x0 \curlywedge H \leq y$ and consider $z =_{\text{def}} x0 + (y \curlywedge H)$. Then

$$z0 = (x0 + (y \curlywedge H))0 = (x0)0 + (y \curlywedge H)0 = x0 + 0 = x0 ,$$
$$z \curlywedge H = (x0 + (y \curlywedge H)) \curlywedge H = (x0 \curlywedge H) + (y \curlywedge H) = y \curlywedge H ,$$

by using (H1) in the first calculation. Hence $(x0, y \curlywedge H) = \rho(z) \in S'$.   □

Part 2 of the preceding lemma shows the necessary restriction to obtain the dependence between the two components of a pair, and hence the unique representation. In partial and general correctness $x0 \curlywedge \mathsf{H} = 0$, whence the restriction is vacuous; it is only needed for total correctness.

Part 1 gives a decomposition of programs into their terminating and non-terminating executions. Similar decompositions of elements are admitted by separated IL-semirings [27] and quemirings [16]. We cannot use these structures since their axioms include $x0 \curlywedge \mathsf{H} = 0$, which is not valid in the unified setting.

In the extreme case of partial correctness, we have $\rho(x) = (x0, x \curlywedge \mathsf{H}) = (0, x)$, hence S' is just a copy of S with 0 attached in the first component of each pair. Nevertheless this correctly represents that there are no non-terminating executions in this approach.

4.3   Induced Operations on Pairs

Operations on the pairs S' can now be derived from operations on S by using the bijections ρ and π as an isomorphism. From the unary operation $f : S \to S$ we derive the operation $f' : S' \to S'$ defined by $f' =_{\mathrm{def}} \rho \circ f \circ \pi$, and similarly for binary operations; for the constant $c \in S$ we obtain $c' =_{\mathrm{def}} \rho(c) \in S'$. We denote an operation and its derived counterpart by the same symbol, relying on the context for disambiguation. The following theorem gives the derived operations.

Theorem 9. *Let* $(t, x) \in S'$ *and* $(u, y) \in S'$. *Then,*

$$
\begin{aligned}
(t, x) + (u, y) &= (t + u, x + y) & 0' &= (0, 0) \\
(t, x) \cdot (u, y) &= (t + xu, (t + xu + xy) \curlywedge \mathsf{H}) & 1' &= (0, 1) \\
(t, x) \curlywedge (u, y) &= (t \curlywedge u, x \curlywedge y) & \top' &= (\mathsf{L}, \mathsf{H}) \\
d(t, x) &= (0, d(t + x)) & \mathsf{L}' &= (\mathsf{L}, \mathsf{L} \curlywedge \mathsf{H}) \\
(t, x)^* &= (x^* t, (x^* t + x^*) \curlywedge \mathsf{H}) & \mathsf{H}' &= (0, \mathsf{H}) \\
(t, x)^\omega &= (x^\omega 0 + x^* t, (x^\omega + x^* t) \curlywedge \mathsf{H})
\end{aligned}
$$

Proof. Observe that $t0 = t$ and $x \curlywedge \mathsf{H} = x$ and $t \curlywedge \mathsf{H} \le x$ by Lemma 8.2 and $x0 = (x \curlywedge \mathsf{H})0 \le \mathsf{H}0 = 0$ by (H1). Similar properties hold for u and y. Hence

$$
\begin{aligned}
(t, x) + (u, y) &= \rho(\pi(t, x) + \pi(u, y)) = \rho(t + x + u + y) \\
&= ((t + x + u + y)0, (t + x + u + y) \curlywedge \mathsf{H}) \\
&= (t0 + x0 + u0 + y0, (t \curlywedge \mathsf{H}) + (x \curlywedge \mathsf{H}) + (u \curlywedge \mathsf{H}) + (y \curlywedge \mathsf{H})) \\
&= (t + u, x + y) \,.
\end{aligned}
$$

Moreover $xy0 = x0 = 0$ and $tz = t0z = t0 = t$ for any $z \in S$, whence

$$
\begin{aligned}
(t, x) \cdot (u, y) &= \rho(\pi(t, x) \cdot \pi(u, y)) = \rho((t + x)(u + y)) = \rho(t(u + y) + x(u + y)) \\
&= \rho(t + xu + xy) = (t0 + xu0 + xy0, (t + xu + xy) \curlywedge \mathsf{H}) \\
&= (t + xu, (t + xu + xy) \curlywedge \mathsf{H}) \,.
\end{aligned}
$$

This equals $(t + xu, ((t + xu) \curlywedge \mathsf{H}) + xy)$ since $xy \le \mathsf{HH} = \mathsf{H}$ by Lemma 7.2. A simplification to $(t + xu, (t \curlywedge \mathsf{H}) + xy)$ would require the additional axiom $(w \curlywedge \mathsf{H})z \curlywedge \mathsf{H} = (w \curlywedge \mathsf{H})(z \curlywedge \mathsf{H})$ that is valid in partial, total and general correctness.

Next, $t \curlywedge y = t \curlywedge y \curlywedge \mathsf{H} \leq x \curlywedge y$ and symmetrically $u \curlywedge x \leq x \curlywedge y$, whence

$$
\begin{aligned}
(t, x) \curlywedge (u, y) &= \rho(\pi(t, x) \curlywedge \pi(u, y)) = \rho((t + x) \curlywedge (u + y)) \\
&= \rho((t \curlywedge u) + (t \curlywedge y) + (x \curlywedge u) + (x \curlywedge y)) = \rho((t \curlywedge u) + (x \curlywedge y)) \\
&= ((t \curlywedge u)0 + (x \curlywedge y)0, (t \curlywedge u \curlywedge \mathsf{H}) + (x \curlywedge y \curlywedge \mathsf{H})) \\
&= ((t \curlywedge u)0, x \curlywedge y \curlywedge \mathsf{H}) = (t \curlywedge u, x \curlywedge y) \,,
\end{aligned}
$$

using Lemma 1.3 in the last step. Since $d(z) \leq 1 \leq \mathsf{H}$ by Lemma 7.2, we obtain the domain operation as

$$
d(t, x) = \rho(d(\pi(t, x))) = \rho(d(t + x)) = (d(t + x)0, d(t + x) \curlywedge \mathsf{H}) = (0, d(t + x)) \,.
$$

For the Kleene star we use $x^*0 \leq \mathsf{H}^*0 = \mathsf{H}0 = 0$ by Lemma 7.2 to calculate

$$
\begin{aligned}
(t, x)^* &= \rho((\pi(t, x))^*) = \rho((t + x)^*) = \rho(x^*(tx^*)^*) = \rho(x^*t^*) = \rho(x^* + x^*tt^*) \\
&= \rho(x^* + x^*t) = (x^*0 + x^*t0, (x^* + x^*t) \curlywedge \mathsf{H}) = (x^*t, (x^*t + x^*) \curlywedge \mathsf{H}) \,.
\end{aligned}
$$

This equals $(x^*t, (x^*t \curlywedge \mathsf{H}) + x^*)$ since $x^* \leq \mathsf{H}$. With the additional axiom above this could be further simplified to (x^*t, x^*). For the omega operation we calculate

$$
\begin{aligned}
(t, x)^\omega &= \rho((\pi(t, x))^\omega) = \rho((t + x)^\omega) = \rho((x^*t)^\omega + (x^*t)^*x^\omega) \\
&= \rho(x^*t(x^*t)^\omega + x^\omega + x^*t(x^*t)^*x^\omega) = \rho(x^*t + x^\omega) \\
&= (x^\omega 0 + x^*t, (x^\omega + x^*t) \curlywedge \mathsf{H}) \,.
\end{aligned}
$$

The derived constants are obtained by

$$
\begin{aligned}
0' &= \rho(0) = (0 \cdot 0, 0 \curlywedge \mathsf{H}) = (0, 0) \\
1' &= \rho(1) = (1 \cdot 0, 1 \curlywedge \mathsf{H}) = (0, 1) \\
\top' &= \rho(\top) = (\top 0, \top \curlywedge \mathsf{H}) = (\mathsf{L}, \mathsf{H}) \\
\mathsf{L}' &= \rho(\mathsf{L}) = (\mathsf{L}0, \mathsf{L} \curlywedge \mathsf{H}) = (\mathsf{L}, \mathsf{L} \curlywedge \mathsf{H}) \\
\mathsf{H}' &= \rho(\mathsf{H}) = (\mathsf{H}0, \mathsf{H} \curlywedge \mathsf{H}) = (0, \mathsf{H})
\end{aligned}
$$

using Lemma 7.2 and (H1). $\qquad\qquad\qquad\qquad\qquad\qquad\qquad\qquad\qquad\qquad\quad\square$

Let us remark that the domain elements of S' are $d(S') = \{(0, p) \mid p \in d(S)\}$ with complements taken in the second component of each pair.

From the choice operation, we immediately obtain the refinement order on pairs $(t, x) \leq (u, y) \Leftrightarrow t \leq u \wedge x \leq y$, which is the same as the induced order $\pi(t, x) \leq \pi(u, y)$. Another calculation shows that the approximation order on pairs induced by $(t, x) \sqsubseteq (u, y) \Leftrightarrow_{\text{def}} \pi(t, x) \sqsubseteq \pi(u, y)$ can be explicitly expressed, too, by $x \leq y + \mathsf{L} \wedge u \leq t \wedge d(\mathsf{L})y \leq x + d(t)\top$.

Note that both ρ and π preserve both $\leq$ and $\sqsubseteq$ by definition. Hence a function $f' : S' \to S'$ is $\leq$- or $\sqsubseteq$-isotone if and only if $f = \pi \circ f' \circ \rho$ is so. In particular, we obtain

$$
\varphi f' = \varphi(\rho \circ \pi \circ f') = \rho(\varphi(\pi \circ f' \circ \rho)) = \rho(\varphi f)
$$

for any fixpoint operator $\varphi \in \{\kappa, \mu, \nu\}$ by rolling [9, Rule 8.29]. For $\varphi = \kappa$ this requires that f' is $\sqsubseteq$-isotone, and otherwise that f' is $\leq$-isotone.

We thus obtain one method to calculate fixpoints of functions on S'. Another way, which works directly on the pairs, is discussed next.

4.4   Recursion

A function h on the pair-based representation may be specified by two functions f, g applied separately to the pairs as in

$$h(t, x) =_{\text{def}} (f(t, x), g(t, x)) .$$

For total correctness, this is investigated in UTP, where [22, Theorem 3.1.6] shows how to obtain the $\leq$-greatest fixpoint of h by a 'mutually recursive formula'. In an algebraic context, this is generalised to $\leq$-least fixpoints in [20] and to general correctness in [17].

In the following we show how to obtain the $\sqsubseteq$-least, $\leq$-least and $\leq$-greatest fixpoints of h for our unified representation, and hence for partial, total, and general correctness at the same time.

Consider the function $h : S' \to S'$ as defined above. Hence the types of f and g are $f : S' \to S_0$ and $g : S' \to S_{\text{H}}$ where $S_0 =_{\text{def}} \{x0 \mid x \in S\}$ and $S_{\text{H}} =_{\text{def}} \{x \curlywedge \text{H} \mid x \in S\}$. As subsets of S, both S_0 and S_{H} are partially ordered by $\leq$. By Lemma 8.2 we also have $f(t, x) \curlywedge \text{H} \leq g(t, x)$ for each $(t, x) \in S'$.

We assume that h is $\leq$-isotone, whence both f and g preserve $\leq$ in both arguments as shown by

$$t \leq u \wedge x \leq y \Leftrightarrow (t, x) \leq (u, y)$$
$$\Rightarrow (f(t, x), g(t, x)) = h(t, x) \leq h(u, y) = (f(u, y), g(u, y))$$
$$\Leftrightarrow f(t, x) \leq f(u, y) \wedge g(t, x) \leq g(u, y) .$$

Motivated by [22] we define for $\varphi \in \{\mu, \nu\}$ the auxiliary functions

$$
\begin{array}{ll}
P_\varphi : S_{\text{H}} \to S_0 & P_\varphi(x) =_{\text{def}} \varphi(\lambda t.f(t, (t \curlywedge \text{H}) + x)) \\
R_\varphi : S_{\text{H}} \to S_{\text{H}} & R_\varphi(x) =_{\text{def}} (P_\varphi(x) \curlywedge \text{H}) + g(P_\varphi(x), (P_\varphi(x) \curlywedge \text{H}) + x) \\
Q_\varphi : S_{\text{H}} & Q_\varphi =_{\text{def}} \varphi R_\varphi
\end{array}
$$

We assume that the fixpoints taken in P_φ and Q_φ exist. Being composed from $\leq$-preserving operations, including the fixpoint operators by [9, Rule 8.28], both P_φ and R_φ preserve $\leq$.

Theorem 10. $\mu h = (P_\mu(Q_\mu), Q_\mu)$ and $\nu h = (P_\nu(Q_\nu), Q_\nu)$.

Proof. Let $\varphi \in \{\mu, \nu\}$. We first show that $(P_\varphi(Q_\varphi), Q_\varphi)$ is a fixpoint of h:

$$P_\varphi(Q_\varphi) \curlywedge \text{H} \leq R_\varphi(Q_\varphi) = Q_\varphi ,$$
$$P_\varphi(Q_\varphi) = f(P_\varphi(Q_\varphi), (P_\varphi(Q_\varphi) \curlywedge \text{H}) + Q_\varphi) = f(P_\varphi(Q_\varphi), Q_\varphi) ,$$
$$R_\varphi(Q_\varphi) = (P_\varphi(Q_\varphi) \curlywedge \text{H}) + g(P_\varphi(Q_\varphi), (P_\varphi(Q_\varphi) \curlywedge \text{H}) + Q_\varphi)$$
$$= (P_\varphi(Q_\varphi) \curlywedge \text{H}) + g(P_\varphi(Q_\varphi), Q_\varphi) ,$$
$$h(P_\varphi(Q_\varphi), Q_\varphi) = (f(P_\varphi(Q_\varphi), Q_\varphi), g(P_\varphi(Q_\varphi), Q_\varphi))$$
$$= (f(P_\varphi(Q_\varphi), Q_\varphi), (f(P_\varphi(Q_\varphi), Q_\varphi) \curlywedge \text{H}) + g(P_\varphi(Q_\varphi), Q_\varphi))$$
$$= (P_\varphi(Q_\varphi), (P_\varphi(Q_\varphi) \curlywedge \text{H}) + g(P_\varphi(Q_\varphi), Q_\varphi))$$
$$= (P_\varphi(Q_\varphi), R_\varphi(Q_\varphi)) = (P_\varphi(Q_\varphi), Q_\varphi) .$$

Now let $(f(t,x), g(t,x)) = h(t,x) \leq (t,x)$, whence $t \curlywedge \mathsf{H} \leq x$ by Lemma 8.2 and $f(t, (t \curlywedge \mathsf{H}) + x) = f(t,x) \leq t$ and $g(t,x) \leq x$. Then

$$
\begin{aligned}
P_\mu(x) &\leq t \,, \\
P_\mu(x) \curlywedge \mathsf{H} &\leq t \curlywedge \mathsf{H} \leq x \,, \\
g(P_\mu(x), (P_\mu(x) \curlywedge \mathsf{H}) + x) = g(P_\mu(x), x) &\leq g(t,x) \leq x \,, \\
R_\mu(x) &\leq x \,, \\
Q_\mu &\leq x \,, \\
P_\mu(Q_\mu) \leq P_\mu(x) &\leq t \,.
\end{aligned}
$$

Hence $(P_\mu(Q_\mu), Q_\mu) \leq (t,x)$, and thus $\mu h = (P_\mu(Q_\mu), Q_\mu)$.

The proof for νh is a bit different. Let $(t,x) \leq h(t,x) = (f(t,x), g(t,x))$, whence $t \curlywedge \mathsf{H} \leq x$ by Lemma 8.2 and $t \leq f(t,x) = f(t, (t \curlywedge \mathsf{H}) + x)$ and $x \leq g(t,x)$. Then

$$
\begin{aligned}
t &\leq P_\nu(x) \,, \\
x &\leq g(t,x) \leq g(P_\nu(x), (P_\nu(x) \curlywedge \mathsf{H}) + x) \leq R_\nu(x) \,, \\
x &\leq Q_\nu \,, \\
t &\leq P_\nu(x) \leq P_\nu(Q_\nu) \,.
\end{aligned}
$$

Hence $(t,x) \leq (P_\nu(Q_\nu), Q_\nu)$, and thus $\nu h = (P_\nu(Q_\nu), Q_\nu)$.   □

We thus obtain the $\leq$-least and $\leq$-greatest fixpoints on pairs. But now we can apply the unified fixpoint representation of Section 3.2 to obtain the $\sqsubseteq$-least fixpoint as well. To this end, assume additionally that h is $\sqsubseteq$-isotone, and observe that $P_\mu \leq P_\nu$ and $R_\mu \leq R_\nu$ and $Q_\mu \leq Q_\nu$.

Corollary 11. *The following are equivalent:*

1. *κh exists.*
2. *$\kappa h = (P_\nu(Q_\nu), (Q_\nu \curlywedge \mathsf{L}) + Q_\mu)$.*
3. *$d(\mathsf{L})Q_\nu \leq (Q_\nu \curlywedge \mathsf{L}) + Q_\mu + d(P_\nu(Q_\nu))\mathsf{T}$.*

Proof. Let $P =_{\text{def}} P_\nu(Q_\nu)$ and $Q =_{\text{def}} (Q_\nu \curlywedge \mathsf{L}) + Q_\mu$. By Theorems 9 and 10,

$$
\begin{aligned}
(\nu h \curlywedge \mathsf{L}') + \mu h &= ((P, Q_\nu) \curlywedge (\mathsf{L}, \mathsf{L} \curlywedge \mathsf{H})) + \mu h = (P \curlywedge \mathsf{L}, Q_\nu \curlywedge \mathsf{L} \curlywedge \mathsf{H}) + \mu h \\
&= (P, Q_\nu \curlywedge \mathsf{L}) + (P_\mu(Q_\mu), Q_\mu) = (P + P_\mu(Q_\mu), Q) = (P, Q)
\end{aligned}
$$

using $P_\mu(Q_\mu) \leq P \leq \mathsf{L}$ and $Q_\nu \leq \mathsf{H}$, and

$$
d(\mathsf{L}')\nu h = d(\mathsf{L}, \mathsf{L} \curlywedge \mathsf{H})\nu h = (0, d(\mathsf{L}))(P, Q_\nu) = (d(\mathsf{L})P, d(\mathsf{L})(P + Q_\nu) \curlywedge \mathsf{H}) \,,
$$

and

$$
\begin{aligned}
d(\nu h 0')\mathsf{T}' &= d((P, Q_\nu)(0,0))\mathsf{T}' = d(P + Q_\nu 0, (P + Q_\nu 0) \curlywedge \mathsf{H})\mathsf{T}' \\
&= d(P, P \curlywedge \mathsf{H})\mathsf{T}' = (0, d(P))(\mathsf{L}, \mathsf{H}) = (d(P)\mathsf{L}, d(P)(\mathsf{L} + \mathsf{H}) \curlywedge \mathsf{H}) \\
&= (P, d(P)\mathsf{T} \curlywedge \mathsf{H})
\end{aligned}
$$

using (H1), (L3) and Lemma 7.3.

Hence we obtain

$$d(\mathsf{L}')\nu h \le (\nu h \curlywedge \mathsf{L}') + \mu h + d(\nu h 0')\top'$$
$$\Leftrightarrow (d(\mathsf{L})P, d(\mathsf{L})(P + Q_\nu) \curlywedge \mathsf{H}) \le (P, Q + (d(P)\top \curlywedge \mathsf{H}))$$
$$\Leftrightarrow d(\mathsf{L})(P + Q_\nu) \curlywedge \mathsf{H} \le Q + (d(P)\top \curlywedge \mathsf{H})$$
$$\Leftrightarrow d(\mathsf{L})Q_\nu \curlywedge \mathsf{H} \le Q + (d(P)\top \curlywedge \mathsf{H})$$
$$\Leftrightarrow d(\mathsf{L})Q_\nu \curlywedge \mathsf{H} \le Q + d(P)\top$$
$$\Leftrightarrow d(\mathsf{L})Q_\nu \le Q + d(P)\top$$

using $d(\mathsf{L}) \le 1$ and $P \le d(P)\top$. The claim follows by the isomorphism of Section 4.3 and Theorem 3. □

5 Conclusion

This paper shows how to extend the unification of partial, total and general correctness all the way to full recursion. We obtain a common semantics of programs and common laws to reason about programs. It is possible to derive a unified semantics of recursively specified operations.

All of this applies as well to programs specified on pairs of termination information and state transitions. For this pair-based representation the lessons learned from UTP's designs were very helpful. We also observe that reasoning in an axiomatic style fits well into UTP.

Future work will unify pre-post specifications and refinement laws, based on their algebraic treatments in total and general correctness [31,17,15], and program transformations between different kinds of recursions, based on their development in total correctness [20].

Acknowledgement. I thank Georg Struth for helpful discussions and the anonymous referees for valuable remarks.

This work was supported by a fellowship within the Postdoc-Programme of the German Academic Exchange Service (DAAD).

References

1. Aarts, C.J.: Galois connections presented calculationally. Master's thesis, Department of Mathematics and Computing Science, Eindhoven University of Technology (1992)
2. de Bakker, J.W.: Semantics and termination of nondeterministic recursive programs. In: Michaelson, S., Milner, R. (eds.) Automata, Languages and Programming: Third International Colloquium, pp. 435–477. Edinburgh University Press, Edinburgh (1976)
3. Berghammer, R., Zierer, H.: Relational algebraic semantics of deterministic and nondeterministic programs. Theoretical Computer Science 43, 123–147 (1986)
4. Birkhoff, G.: Lattice Theory, 3rd edn. Colloquium Publications, vol. XXV. American Mathematical Society, Providence (1967)

5. Broy, M., Gnatz, R., Wirsing, M.: Semantics of nondeterministic and noncontinuous constructs. In: Bauer, F.L., Broy, M. (eds.) Program Construction. LNCS, vol. 69, pp. 553–592. Springer, Heidelberg (1979)
6. De Carufel, J.-L., Desharnais, J.: Demonic algebra with domain. In: Schmidt, R. (ed.) RelMiCS/AKA 2006. LNCS, vol. 4136, pp. 120–134. Springer, Heidelberg (2006)
7. Chen, Y.: A fixpoint theory for non-monotonic parallelism. Theoretical Computer Science 308(1–3), 367–392 (2003)
8. Cohen, E.: Separation and reduction. In: Backhouse, R., Oliveira, J.N. (eds.) MPC 2000. LNCS, vol. 1837, pp. 45–59. Springer, Heidelberg (2000)
9. Davey, B.A., Priestley, H.A.: Introduction to Lattices and Order, 2nd edn. Cambridge University Press, Cambridge (2002)
10. Desharnais, J., Struth, G.: Domain axioms for a family of near-semirings. In: Meseguer, J., Roşu, G. (eds.) AMAST 2008. LNCS, vol. 5140, pp. 330–345. Springer, Heidelberg (2008)
11. Desharnais, J., Struth, G.: Modal semirings revisited. In: Audebaud, P., Paulin-Mohring, C. (eds.) MPC 2008. LNCS, vol. 5133, pp. 360–387. Springer, Heidelberg (2008)
12. Dijkstra, E.W.: A Discipline of Programming. Prentice Hall, Englewood Cliffs (1976)
13. Dijkstra, R.M.: Computation calculus bridging a formalization gap. Science of Computer Programming 37(1–3), 3–36 (2000)
14. Dunne, S.: Recasting Hoare and He's Unifying Theory of Programs in the context of general correctness. In: Butterfield, A., Strong, G., Pahl, C. (eds.) 5th Irish Workshop on Formal Methods, Electronic Workshops in Computing. The British Computer Society (July 2001)
15. Dunne, S.E., Hayes, I.J., Galloway, A.J.: Reasoning about loops in total and general correctness. In: Butterfield, A. (ed.) UTP 2008. LNCS, vol. 5713, pp. 62–81. Springer, Heidelberg (2010)
16. Elgot, C.C.: Matricial theories. Journal of Algebra 42(2), 391–421 (1976)
17. Guttmann, W.: General correctness algebra. In: Berghammer, R., Jaoua, A.M., Möller, B. (eds.) RelMiCS/AKA 2009. LNCS, vol. 5827, pp. 150–165. Springer, Heidelberg (2009)
18. Guttmann, W.: Partial, total and general correctness. In: Bolduc, C., Desharnais, J., Ktari, B. (eds.) MPC 2010. LNCS, vol. 6120, pp. 157–177. Springer, Heidelberg (2010)
19. Guttmann, W., Möller, B.: Modal design algebra. In: Dunne, S., Stoddart, W. (eds.) UTP 2006. LNCS, vol. 4010, pp. 236–256. Springer, Heidelberg (2006)
20. Guttmann, W., Möller, B.: Normal design algebra. Journal of Logic and Algebraic Programming 79(2), 144–173 (2010)
21. Hoare, C.A.R.: An axiomatic basis for computer programming. Communications of the ACM 12(10), 576–580/583 (1969)
22. Hoare, C.A.R., He, J.: Unifying theories of programming. Prentice Hall Europe (1998)
23. Höfner, P., Möller, B.: An algebra of hybrid systems. Journal of Logic and Algebraic Programming 78(2), 74–97 (2009)
24. Jacobs, D., Gries, D.: General correctness: A unification of partial and total correctness. Acta Informatica 22(1), 67–83 (1985)
25. Kozen, D.: A completeness theorem for Kleene algebras and the algebra of regular events. Information and Computation 110(2), 366–390 (1994)

26. Kozen, D.: On Hoare logic and Kleene algebra with tests. ACM Transactions on Computational Logic 1(1), 60–76 (2000)
27. Möller, B.: Kleene getting lazy. Science of Computer Programming 65(2), 195–214 (2007)
28. Möller, B., Struth, G.: WP is WLP. In: MacCaull, W., Winter, M., Düntsch, I. (eds.) RelMiCS 2005. LNCS, vol. 3929, pp. 200–211. Springer, Heidelberg (2006)
29. Moszkowski, B.C.: A complete axiomatization of Interval Temporal Logic with infinite time. In: Proceedings of the 15th Annual IEEE Symposium on Logic in Computer Science, pp. 241–252. IEEE, Los Alamitos (2000)
30. Nelson, G.: A generalization of Dijkstra's calculus. ACM Transactions on Programming Languages and Systems 11(4), 517–561 (1989)
31. von Wright, J.: Towards a refinement algebra. Science of Computer Programming 51(1–2), 23–45 (2004)

Halting Still Standing – Programs versus Specifications

Cornelis Huizing, Ruurd Kuiper, and Tom Verhoeff

Technische Universiteit Eindhoven, Department of Mathematics and Computer
Science, Den Dolech 2, 5600 MB Eindhoven, The Netherlands
{c.huizing,r.kuiper,t.verhoeff}@tue.nl

Abstract. In UTP'06 [4], Hehner claims that the traditional proof of
the incomputability of the Halting Function is rather a proof of the
inconsistency of its specification. We identify where his argument fails.

Hehner claims that assuming a well-defined Halting Function for specifications leads to a contradiction by a very similar argument as assuming
a computable Halting Function for programs does. In the case of programs, this argument leads to concluding that the Halting Function is not
computable, porting the proof to the case of specifications, it is claimed
to allow concluding that the Halting Function is ill-defined. He reasons
that if the Halting Function for specifications is ill-defined, then the concept of the Halting Function in general is inconsistent, including the one
for programs. We do not challenge this generalization, but rather point
out a flaw in his argument for the specification case. We formalize his
argument in UTP-style. This enables us to show that there is a subtle
tacit assumption being made about the recursive definition that is used
to arrive at the contradiction, namely that the defining equation has a
solution. We also explain why this does not affect the proof for the program case. Furthermore, we analyze whether recursion in the language
Hehner uses is essential for his argument and our refutation. Porting the
arguments to a language without recursion shows that the issue of the
existence of the contradicting specification remains. We conclude that
this line of argument does not challenge the healthiness of the concept
of the Halting Function, including its extension to specifications.

1 Introduction

Hehner has conducted a long standing, in fact ongoing, stimulating investigation
into the relationship between the foundations of programming and of mathematics. We have followed the development of his thoughts on this from the unpub-
lished [1], the published [2–4], through to recent (2010), momentarily unavailable,
contributions on his web site, e.g., [5]. The investigations are wide-ranging, from
general, almost philosophical issues like the validity of Cantor's onto function
approach as a comparison of set sizes, to more UTP-specific issues like whether
specified termination should include a time bound and what is acceptable as a
bound.

S. Qin (Ed.): UTP 2010, LNCS 6445, pp. 226–233, 2010.

In this paper we address a concrete, published claim made in this context, as described in section "The Problem with Halting" in his contribution "Retrospective and Prospective for Unifying Theories of Programming" for UTP'06, [4].

Informally, the answer to the Halting Problem states that there cannot exist a computable Halting Function that decides for every program whether or not it will terminate. Hehner argues that the traditional interpretation of the proof is mistaken and rather proves the inconsistency of the specification of the Halting Function. He gives his argument in the intuitive setting of a simple programming and specification language with recursion.

The argument is quite concrete and touches on many of the aspects of Hehner's general investigations: the proof of the Halting Theorem that he challenges is a fundamental one and the framework in which he carries out the argument has various aspects that are of relevance to UTP. We analyze and refute the argument. Furthermore, we go beyond just refuting the argument, in that we clarify that the setting of a simple programming language with recursion plays a significant role.

In section 2 we briefly introduce some UTP-style formalization to present the arguments. In section 3 we summarize Hehner's argument. Section 4 contains our refutation. In section 5 we step back to take a fresh look at the whole issue to see what happens if recursion is avoided. Conclusions are provided in section 6.

2 Preliminaries

We, very concisely, sketch what essentially we use from UTP. In particular, we use the notions of specification, implementation and satisfaction as common in UTP, provided, for example, in Hehner's [3] and in Hoare and He Jifeng's [6].

A state is a value assignment to a set of state variables – the domains of the values of the variables are given. A computation has an initial and a final state.

Syntactically, a specification is a first order predicate containing as free variables just unprimed state variables for the initial values and primed state variables for the final ones, i.e., relating these. There are two extra Boolean variables ok and ok', denoting start and termination of a program, respectively. Furthermore, there are recursive equations (containing variables that range over the predicates). The semantics of specifications is based on first order logic, together with a fixed-point as the solution of equations. The semantics of a specification thus is a relation between initial and final states.

The syntax of programs is that of sequential programs, with recursion, as in the specification case, through equations. The semantics is, again as in the specification case, a relation between initial and final states. A program gives for any initial state one final state, obtained by a computation performed by the program.

Although syntactically different, specifications and programs are both defining a relation between initial and final states. A program is, in that sense, a special case of a specification: it has special features like being deterministic and being implementable (in the UTP sense: for each initial state providing a final one).

A program P satisfies a specification S if $P \Rightarrow S$.

With respect to $\Leftarrow$, specifications (including programs) form a complete lattice, with top element $false$ and bottom element $true$. Note that in this ordering $ok \Rightarrow true$ and $ok' \Rightarrow true$, but not vice versa for either case.

There are various subtleties about the existence, uniqueness or selection of fixed points for the equations in the formalism. For our argumentation it is only relevant to observe that the following theorem holds (again, see [3, 6] for details).

Theorem 1

1. *If the operator corresponding to the recursive equation is monotonic and the lattice is complete, then fixed- point solutions, in particular the weakest and strongest, exist (Tarski).*
2. *Under appropriate restrictions, as presented in [6], this can be strengthened to the existence of a particular unique fixed point.*

For a programming language as described above, monotonicity and the further restrictions hold, thereby providing every syntactically correct program with a semantics. Note that this does not hold for specifications, e.g., $X = \neg X$ does not have a solution: not even $true$ or $false$.

3   Hehner's Argument

We summarize Hehner's exposition of the Halting Theorem (the theorem that the Halting Problem is not algorithmically solvable) and the proof, and his arguments against that proof.

Hehner uses a sequential, deterministic, imperative programming language that is universal and has the following properties. Programs are represented as text. No input commands are present; initialization is incorporated in the program. A program may return a value. A program may have parameters. Program text may contain identifiers. For each such identifier X there is a corresponding program text `text` in a dictionary, the dictionary entry then being $X = $ `"text"`. This entry defines the program that the identifier represents. An identifier can both be used for a procedure call and for inspection of the text.

In a standard manner, this can be turned into a precise notion of syntactically correct program. It is also standard to show that the language satisfies the requirements as stated in Theorem 1, i.e., that every syntactically correct program has a semantics in the UTP-style. We assume that all this has been done.

The proof of the Halting Theorem then is that one assumes that the Halting Function H is computable: H returns **true** for texts that represent a program that terminates and **false** for texts that represent a program that does not terminate.

Then $P = $ " $(\textbf{true} * \Pi) \triangleleft H(P) \triangleright \Pi$ " defines a program. This leads to a contradiction: if P represents a program that terminates, then $H(P)$ must return **true**, hence P represents an infinite loop, i.e., a program that does not terminate, and vice versa. The conclusion is that the assumption of computability is wrong.

We remind the reader that in $P =$ " $(\mathbf{true} * \Pi) \lhd H(P) \rhd \Pi$ " the application of H to P must mean that the text that P identifies is analyzed. This might involve, for example, that this text is looked up in the library, likewise for further identifiers that may occur in the text, and so on. It cannot mean that the P is recursively replaced by the text in the library, as this would cause an infinite regress. There will always remain occurrences of P and some kind of library is needed to know what these identifiers mean. Again, all this can be formalized in the UTP-style.

Next, Hehner considers the case where texts represent specifications that incorporate requirements about (non)termination. Since specifications need not be implementable, he drops the requirement that H is computable. H is now defined as the function that delivers **true** for a specification that requires termination (ok') and **false** for a specification that does not $(\neg ok')$.

He then defines

$$S = \text{`` } \neg ok' \lhd H(S) \rhd ok' \text{ ''} \tag{1}$$

Again, a contradiction is derived and Hehner concludes that function H is not properly defined: '...we cannot consistently say the sentence "H tells us, for all specification texts S, whether S specifies terminating behavior." ' ([4], p. 12).

From the similarity of the statements and the reasoning between the case of programs and specifications, Hehner concludes that H will have similar definitional problems in the case of programs as well. We do not further consider whether or not the similarity warrants suspicion of the definition of H in the program case, but directly refute the conclusion that in the specification case H would not be well-defined.

4   Refutation

Our objection to the conclusion in section 3 is that there is a tacit assumption, underlying the proof, that should be withdrawn instead of doubting the well-definedness of H. This is the assumption that a semantic object S exists. Hehner defines S as specification text, but the contradiction is derived from semantic properties of S. In observation 1 we show this.

Observation 1. *Specification S is defined as text, but the contradiction is derived from a semantic object (a specification relation). In particular, 'If S specifies terminating behavior...', which is a semantic property of S. Furthermore, '...then H(S) is* **false***, and so S specifies terminating behavior.' ([4], p. 12). The conclusion relies on the semantics of the right-hand side of (1), where the conditional is replaced by the then-part, because H(S) is* **true***. Finally, the contradiction is concluded because the result of this replacement, $\neg ok'$, is compared to the left-hand side of formula (1) and both sides are not equal, semantically, since H(S) is* **true** *(by assumption) and H("$\neg ok'$") is* **false** *(by definition of H).*

From this analysis of the argument we see that equation (1) is used semantically (without quotes) to define the semantics of S.

Observation 2. *The semantic object S is defined by the equation*

$$S = \neg ok' \triangleleft H(S) \triangleright ok' \qquad (2)$$

Now the question arises whether this semantic object S (a relation between initial and final states) exists. So the question is whether (2) has a solution, or in other words, whether the function $F(S) = \neg ok' \triangleleft H(S) \triangleright ok'$ has a fixed point. In the setting of UTP, existence of a fixed point is guaranteed when the corresponding function is monotonic. The function F is not monotonic, however. Take for instance the elements **true** and ok'. Then $F(\textbf{true}) = ok'$ and $F(ok') = \neg ok'$, which are incomparable, whereas $\textbf{true} \Leftarrow ok'$.

The fact that F is not monotonic alone does not imply that there is no specification S with the desired properties. It does, however, justify that its existence should be an explicit assumption and since a contradiction is derived based on this assumption, the assumption should be withdrawn. The contradiction does not give reason to doubt whether H is properly specified.

Why is this not a problem in the program case? We have a definition that looks very similar. Although we didn't use directly that P is a fixed point to derive the contradiction, the semantics of P can indeed be considered as a fixed point. The answer is that the restricted syntax of programs guarantees that all functions defining fixed points (called *constructors* in [3]) are monotonic. For specifications, this is not the case. This language is much more liberal. We see this in particular in the case of the Halting Function. To define the program P, we need the assumption that H is computable and infer that some, probably very complex, UTP program exists that examines program texts (without executing them!). The resulting semantic function is monotonic by construction. To define the text of the specification S, however, we only need that the specification of $H(S)$ can be expressed, which is, for example, $S \Rightarrow ok'$. This is a much simpler expression, but it doesn't guarantee monotonicity.

> When we try to prove that the operator in the program case is monotonic using the meaning of H (not the syntax, which we don't have), we will see that it isn't. This is not disturbing, however, because the assumption of computability is not valid and no UTP-program can be constructed to implement it. In fact, the proof that the operator is not monotonic is tantamount to deriving the contradiction.

Remark. There are formal settings where equations like (2) do have a fixed point, e.g., the cpo of partial functions. A solution would then be the function $\bot$ that is everywhere undefined and in this setting it is required that $H(\bot) = \bot$ (or undefined) and $\neg ok' \triangleleft \bot \triangleright ok' = \bot$. This will give us a semantic object S, but there is no contradiction anymore, since the righthand side of (2) will not always yield $\neg ok'$ or ok', but can also result in $\bot$.

5   Approach without Recursive Definitions

Although the formulation with recursive definitions is concise, it caused troubles. The usual formulation of the proof of the Halting Theorem (cf. [7]) does not use recursive definitions. Therefore, it is interesting to see what happens when we do not use them. The necessary self-reference is achieved by diagonalizing with a second argument. We give a short presentation of this proof, staying close to Hehner's notation.

Proof of Halting Theorem without recursion.
Let $\mathbf{T}$ be the set of texts and $\mathbf{B}$ the boolean domain. We extend the notion of programs and specifications with a text parameter, usually considered as input. $P(I)$ stands for executing program P with input I, $S(I)$ specifies behavior of a program with input I. Then define function $H : \mathbf{T} \times \mathbf{T} \to \mathbf{B}$ with $H(P, I) = \mathbf{true}$ if and only if execution of program with text P on input I will terminate.

Now assume, aiming for a contradiction, that H is computable. Then define program $P(I)$ by $(\mathbf{true} * \mathit{\Pi}) \lhd H(I, I) \rhd \mathit{\Pi}$, where I is the input of P. Since H is computable, it can be written as a program in our programming language and hence this is the definition of a legal program, and it has a program text. What is now the termination behavior of program $P(P)$, i.e., P with the text of P itself as input? If this execution terminates, then $H(P, P)$ is $\mathbf{true}$ and execution of P will take the left branch, resulting in an infinite loop. If the execution does not terminate, then $H(P, P)$ is $\mathbf{false}$ and execution will take the right branch and terminate.

Both cases will lead to a contradiction and we will have to withdraw our assumption that H is computable. Note that this assumption is essential for the derivation of the contradiction, since it implies that execution of $H(P, P)$ will always terminate, also in the case that $H(P, P)$ is $\mathbf{false}$, since it is a proper implementation of a computable function.

The next step is to generalize this theorem to specifications. So $\mathbf{T}$ will include specification texts and we define $H(S, I)$ as $\mathbf{true}$ if and only if specification S requires termination on input I.

We try to give the proof for this situation. Define specification $S(I)$ by $\neg ok' \lhd H(I, I) \rhd ok'$, where I is the input. What does S specify about termination on input S (the text of S)? If S requires termination on S, then $H(S, S)$ is $\mathbf{true}$ and S is $\neg ok'$, hence does not require termination. If S does not require termination, then $H(S, S)$ is $\mathbf{false}$ and S is ok', hence does require termination. Again we have a contradiction.

The question is, however, whether $S(S)$, used to derive the contradiction, exists. One approach to guarantee existence is to assume that H is expressible in the specification language. Then $S(S)$ is defined as well and we find a contradiction. So we have to withdraw the assumption and conclude that H is *not* expressible in the specification language. This does not, however, give reason to doubt the well-definedness of H.

Another approach is to drop the assumption that H is expressible in the specification language.

This has as a consequence that we cannot define S by giving text. Instead we define S, with the same intended semantics, by

$$S(I) = \begin{cases} \neg ok' & \text{if } H(I, I) = \mathbf{true} \\ ok' & \text{otherwise} \end{cases} \tag{3}$$

Since H is not given by text, neither can be S and since we want to apply S to S, the parameter I can not be text either. Consequently, we have to define S as a function from $\mathcal{S}$ to $\mathcal{S}$, where $\mathcal{S}$ is the set of all specifications.

First assume that S is defined on the domain $\mathcal{S}$ of all specification. If (3) is a valid definition of a specification for every $I \in \mathcal{S}$, we can define more specifications like this and get a contradiction. Note that H is a function from the set $\mathcal{S}$ of specifications to the boolean domain $\mathbf{B}$. Now let a set $R \subseteq \mathcal{S}$ be given. Define $H_R : \mathcal{S} \rightarrow \mathbf{B}$ by $H_R(I) = \mathbf{true}$ if and only if $I \in R$. Then $S_R(I) = \neg ok' \triangleleft H_R(I) \triangleright ok'$ defines a specification for every set R. Now for every two sets R_0 and R_1 that are different, S_{R_0} and S_{R_1} are different, because there must be an $s \in R_0$ and $s \notin R_1$ (or the other way around), so $S_{R_0}(s) = \neg ok'$ and $S_{R_1}(s) = ok$. Consequently, the set of specifications S_R, which is a subset of $\mathcal{S}$, has the same cardinality as the set of subsets of $\mathcal{S}$. This is not possible, since the powerset always has greater a cardinality than its base set. Note that this contradiction does not depend on the Halting Function. So the assumption that the domain of S is $\mathcal{S}$ has to be withdrawn and we have to define S as a function from $\mathcal{S}' \rightarrow \mathcal{S}$ for some subset $\mathcal{S}'$ of $\mathcal{S}$.

Now the question is: is $S \in \mathcal{S}'$? First assume it is. Then $S(S)$ is a legitimate specification and we have the contradiction shown above. So we have to withdraw this assumption and conclude that $S \notin \mathcal{S}'$, which implies that the problematic specification can not be constructed.

> **Remark.** In the program case, we have a similar situation. A program can be considered as a function from programs to programs. The cardinality problem does not occur here, however, since the domain is restricted to program texts, which is possible because of the assumption that H is computable and hence expressible as program text. Similarly, for the case of specifications that are expressible.

Again, we see that the counter example from the program case cannot be ported to the specification case. Whether we assume a syntax for specifications or we do not, the counter example cannot be defined.

6   Conclusions

Self-reference is at the root of the contradictions in the Halting Theorem proof. The approach by Hehner, using recursive definitions, makes this explicit. It is interesting to see that the approach with only programs without input as parameters for the Halting Function is easy and intuitive but requires great care in handling the recursive definitions that result from this approach. In particular, we show that in the specification case the counterexample that Hehner proposes is not well-defined.

This subtle difference between the program and specification case carries over to the two-parameter approach without recursion, where programs have input and both program text and input are input for the halting function: here the self-reference is indirect and, again, the counterexample for the specification case cannot be constructed.

UTP provides the framework to carry out these investigations with its intuitive yet formal style. Especially, the equal footing of programs and specifications is important in analyzing the Halting Theorem. However, our investigations show that the subtle difference that programs have to be computable whereas specifications need not be gives rise to different conclusions from the contradictions that are derived in the two domains, even though their construction is very similar.

Acknowledgment

We thank the reviewers and Rick Hehner for their stimulating and helpful comments.

References

1. Hehner, E.C.R.: Formalist Heresy: Mathematics is Based on Programming (1986)
2. Hehner, E.C.R.: Beautifying Goedel. In: Feijen, V.G., Gries, M. (eds.) Beauty is our Business, New York. Springer-Verlag silver series, pp. 163–172 (1990)
3. Hehner, E.C.R.: A Practical Theory of Programming. Springer, Heidelberg (1993); also version 2004 on website Hehner
4. Hehner, E.C.R.: Retrospective and Prospective for Unifying Theories of Programming. In: Dunne, S., Stoddart, B. (eds.) UTP 2006. LNCS, vol. 4010, pp. 1–17. Springer, Heidelberg (2006) ISBN 978-3-540-34750-7
5. Hehner, E.C.R.: Problems with the Halting Problem, pp. 0–8, May 19 (2010), http://www.cs.toronto.edu/~hehner/PHP.pdf
6. Hoare, C.A.R., He, J.: Unifying Theories of Programming. Prentice-Hall, Englewood Cliffs (1998)
7. Turing, A.: On computable numbers, with an application to the Entscheidungs problem. In: Proceedings of the London Mathematical Society. Series, vol. 2(42), pp. 230–265 (1936)

Promoting Models

Qin Li, Yongxin Zhao, Xiaofeng Wu, and Si Liu

Software Engineering Institute,
East China Normal University,
Shanghai, China
{qli,yxzhao,xfwu,sliu}@sei.ecnu.edu.cn

Abstract. There can be multitudinous models specifying aspects of the same system. Each model has a bias towards one aspect. These models often override in specific aspects though they have different expressions. A specification written in one model can be refined by introducing additional information from other models. The paper proposes a concept of promoting models which is a methodology to obtain refinements with support from cooperating models. It refines a primary model by integrating the information from a secondary model. The promotion principle is not merely an academic point, but also a reliable and robust engineering technique which can be used to develop software and hardware systems. It can also check the consistency between two specifications from different models. A case of modeling a simple online shopping system with the cooperation of the guarded design model and CSP model illustrates the practicability of the promotion principle.

1 Introduction

There are many modeling techniques can be used to model our diversified views of software systems. The Model Driven Architecture (MDA) [1] [15] is a promising direction which is capable to generate implementation codes from abstract models. The analysis on the model level is more convenient than on the implementation level.

The Unified Modeling Language (UML) [7] [6] is a popular modeling technique supporting the model-driven development. It provides many standard models to specify corresponding aspects of the whole system. It makes a design criterion to divide a system into many design aspects such that each aspect is precisely specified by one model. In UML standards, designing an object-oriented system mainly needs to consider three aspects corresponding to the following three models: class model, state model and interaction model. The class model shows the static structure of classes and objects in the system. The state model specifies the dynamic behavior of each object in its life cycle. The interaction model describes the interactions between objects. UML uses diagram syntax which is intuitive and easy to understand. It is helpful to establish a consistent view among the system designers and programmers. Therefore, UML receives increasingly concerning by software engineers and is widely used in software engineering though its formal semantics is still obscure.

S. Qin (Ed.): UTP 2010, LNCS 6445, pp. 234–252, 2010.

Formal methods also provide many formal models such as CSP, Z and B to specify the behavior of the software system according to different aspects. CSP is a typical event-based model which aims to specify the communication sequences of processes [13] [21]. It regulates whether an action can be performed after a certain sequence. Z notation is a mature state-based formalism which specifies the behavior of every operation in the system with pre-condition, post-condition and invariant [24] [28]. It can be used by designers to specify the abstract structure of the system and the functionality of every operation. B method is a variant of Z which specify the behavior of a program with a state machine [3] [22]. As a formal method, it has been applied by software engineers to analyze some industrial scale projects.

People have abandoned the idea of adopting a universal model to include every information of a system because it increases the complexity of the model to an unacceptable degree. Also, It is an unaffordable process in translating the existing models to this universal one. However, the independency of the existing formal models makes the model-driven methodology difficult to apply.

In most scenes, one model is not sufficient to provide us the whole behavioral view of a system. One kind of modeling techniques often has the capability to deeply reveal one kind of properties of the system but contains little information in other aspects even though it has such expressivity. The key issue is synthesizing the information from different models without violating their own advantages in specifying certain aspects of the system.

This paper proposes a promotion calculus towards drawing information from cooperation models to gain a refinement. Given a model specifying an aspect of a whole system, if there exists another model having information which can be used to concretize the former model, a refined model can be obtained by applying the promoting operation to these two models. It provides a method to enrich a model with other models either in different domains or have different appearances. The promoting operation can also be used to check the consistency of two models since the inconsistency will lead to the promoted model being an unachievable miracle. With support from the promoting operation, the analyzers can make a model more concrete and deterministic by introducing additional constraints from other cooperation models. It obtains an implementation compatible to the constraints acquired by other models, which realizes the model-driven development more feasibly. It can further help the analyzers to determine which model is more compatible to an existing standard specification without concerning the model integration issues. A case of modeling an online shopping system is discussed in this paper. We model the system with two formalisms, guarded design and CSP, and then promote each model with another and obtain more concrete versions of the two models.

The reminder of the paper is organized as follows. Section 2 proposes a general definition to concepts related to the promoting operation. Section 3 demonstrates an application of the promoting approach in the pair of CSP and Guarded Design domains. Section 4 adopts the results of section 3 on an online shopping system case. Section 5 states some researches related to our work. Section 6 finally concludes the paper and mentions some future works.

2 Model Promotion

In the section, we propose a general definition of model promotion which is a methodology to obtain refinements involving two models for the same system. The algebraic
laws are explored to provide precise and adequate comprehension of model promotion.
Furthermore, the concept of compatibility and consistency are defined in terms of the
promoting calculi.

Definition 1 (Translation)

*Given two model domains $\mathcal{D}_1$, $\mathcal{D}_2$ with their own refinement relation $\sqsupseteq_{\mathcal{D}_1}, \sqsupseteq_{\mathcal{D}_2}$, a func-
tion $\psi : \mathcal{D}_2 \to \mathcal{D}_1$ is called a **translation** from $\mathcal{D}_2$ to $\mathcal{D}_1$ if it is order-preserved.*

(Order-Preservation) $\forall B, B' \in \mathcal{D}_2$, $\psi(B) \sqsupseteq_{\mathcal{D}_1} \psi(B')$ if $B \sqsupseteq_{\mathcal{D}_2} B'$.

The translation maps each element in domain $\mathcal{D}_2$ to a unique element in domain $\mathcal{D}_1$. The
requirement for order-preserved property is nature since a more concrete cooperation
model always provides more benefits in the promoting process.

The information quantum depends on the selection of the translation. A model may
lose part of its information during the translation process. Thus constructing reasonable
translations is essential when we extract information from a model. In general, the algebraic structure of the domain and codomain can affect the form of the translation.
Furthermore, we should also take into account the variety and granularity of the model
and the perspective from which we abstract the information. In this paper, we assume
that the codomain should be a complete lattice where we can define two binary operations $\sqcup$ and $\sqcap$ which obtain the least up-bound and the greatest low-bound of their
participants respectively.

Definition 2 (Promoting)

*Assume that $\mathcal{D}_1$ be a complete lattice, ψ is a translation from $\mathcal{D}_2$ to $\mathcal{D}_1$, and let $A \in \mathcal{D}_1$,
$B \in \mathcal{D}_2$.*

$$A \, prt_\psi \, B =_{df} A \sqcup_{\mathcal{D}_1} \psi(B)$$

*where the calculi $\sqcup_{\mathcal{D}_1}$ gets the least up-bound of the two sides in domain $\mathcal{D}_1$. We say
$A \, prt_\psi \, B$ promotes A by $\psi(B)$ or A can be promoted with B through ψ.*

In this case, we call A as **primary model**, B as **secondary model** and the result of
the promoting operation $A \, prt_\psi \, B$ as **promoted model**. The translation ψ interprets the
information of model B in terms of $\psi(B)$ in the domain $\mathcal{D}_1$ while the promoting calculi integrates the information to model A. As a result, the promoted model *'promotes'*
(refines) model A in virtue of model B. Therefore, the promoting calculi supports the
model driven development by developing a system through synthesizing existing models which specify the system from different aspects at the beginning of the project.
Furthermore, it enhance the robustness and reliability of the system since the promoted
model reflects the consistency and correctness among the existing models. Figure 1
illustrates the framework of the model promotion process.

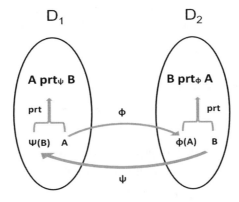

Fig. 1. Framework of Model Promotion

The promoting calculi has the following algebraic laws.

Theorem 1 (Promoting Laws)

Let $A, A' \in \mathcal{D}_1$, $B, B' \in \mathcal{D}_2$, ψ *is a translation from* $\mathcal{D}_2$ *to* $\mathcal{D}_1$.

(1.1) $A\,prt_\psi\,B \sqsupseteq_{\mathcal{D}_1} A$

(1.2) $(A\,prt_\psi\,B)\,prt_\psi\,B = A\,prt_\psi\,B$

(1.3) If $A \sqsupseteq_{\mathcal{D}_1} A'$, *then* $A\,prt_\psi\,B \sqsupseteq_{\mathcal{D}_1} A'\,prt_\psi\,B$

(1.4) If $B \sqsupseteq_{\mathcal{D}_2} B'$, *then* $A\,prt_\psi\,B \sqsupseteq_{\mathcal{D}_1} A\,prt_\psi\,B'$

(1.5) $A \sqsupseteq_{\mathcal{D}_1} \psi(B)$ *iff* $A\,prt_\psi\,B = A$

(1.6) $(A \sqcup_{\mathcal{D}_1} A')\,prt_\psi\,B = (A\,prt_\psi\,B) \sqcup_{\mathcal{D}_1} (A'\,prt_\psi\,B)$

(1.7) $(A \sqcap_{\mathcal{D}_1} A')\,prt_\psi\,B = (A\,prt_\psi\,B) \sqcap_{\mathcal{D}_1} (A'\,prt_\psi\,B)$

The theorem reflects the following facts.

(1.1) The promoted model is the refinement of primary model. The primary model gets concretized according to the information from secondary model.

(1.2) The promoting calculi is idempotent. Promoting a primary model twice with the same secondary model through the same translation cannot gain more benefits.

(1.3) The promoting calculi is monotonic with respect to the domain $\mathcal{D}_1$. Promoting a better primary model can always obtain a better promoted model when it is promoted with the same model through the same translation.

(1.4) The promoting calculi is monotonic with respect to the domain $\mathcal{D}_2$. A better secondary model can provide more information so that it can obtain a better promoted model.

(1.5) The promoting calculi has no effect if the secondary model cannot provide any useful information through the translation.

(1.6) The promoting calculi is $\sqcup$-distributable in the domain $\mathcal{D}_1$. This law implies that the componentwise promotion is feasible.

(1.7) The promoting calculi is $\sqcap$-distributable in the domain $\mathcal{D}_1$. This law implies that the promotion of a primary model can be applied on each of its nondeterministic component.

Proof

(1.1) $A\,\mathrm{prt}_\psi\,B = A \sqcup_{\mathcal{D}_1} \psi(B) \sqsupseteq_{\mathcal{D}_1} A$.

(1.2) $(A\,\mathrm{prt}_\psi\,B)\,\mathrm{prt}_\psi\,B = (A \sqcup_{\mathcal{D}_1} \psi(B)) \sqcup_{\mathcal{D}_1} \psi(B) = A \sqcup_{\mathcal{D}_1} \psi(B) = A\,\mathrm{prt}_\psi\,B$.

(1.3) $A\,\mathrm{prt}_\psi\,B = A \sqcup_{\mathcal{D}_1} \psi(B) \sqsupseteq_{\mathcal{D}_1} A' \sqcup_{\mathcal{D}_1} \psi(B) = A'\,\mathrm{prt}_\psi\,B$

(1.4) Since the translation ψ is order-preserved, we have $\psi(B) \sqsupseteq_{\mathcal{D}_1} \psi(B')$. Therefore $A\,\mathrm{prt}_\psi\,B = A \sqcup_{\mathcal{D}_1} \psi(B) \sqsupseteq_{\mathcal{D}_1} A \sqcup_{\mathcal{D}_1} \psi(B') = A\,\mathrm{prt}_\psi\,B'$.

(1.5) $A \sqsupseteq_{\mathcal{D}_1} \psi(B)$ iff $A \sqcup_{\mathcal{D}_1} \psi(B) = A$ iff $A\,\mathrm{prt}_\psi\,B = A$

(1.6) $(A \sqcup_{\mathcal{D}_1} A')\,\mathrm{prt}_\psi\,B = (A \sqcup_{\mathcal{D}_1} A') \sqcup_{\mathcal{D}_1} \psi(B)$

$$= (A \sqcup_{\mathcal{D}_1} \psi(B)) \sqcup_{\mathcal{D}_1} (A' \sqcup_{\mathcal{D}_1} \psi(B))$$

$$= (A\,\mathrm{prt}_\psi\,B) \sqcup_{\mathcal{D}_1} (A'\,\mathrm{prt}_\psi\,B)$$

(1.7) $(A \sqcap_{\mathcal{D}_1} A')\,\mathrm{prt}_\psi\,B = (A \sqcap_{\mathcal{D}_1} A') \sqcup_{\mathcal{D}_1} \psi(B)$

$$= (A \sqcup_{\mathcal{D}_1} \psi(B)) \sqcap_{\mathcal{D}_1} (A' \sqcup_{\mathcal{D}_1} \psi(B))$$

$$= (A\,\mathrm{prt}_\psi\,B) \sqcap_{\mathcal{D}_1} (A'\,\mathrm{prt}_\psi\,B)$$

Sometimes two models may have opposite constraints for the same physical object in the system. We consider it as a conflict blocking the way of consistent system development. With the support of the model promotion operation, conflicts between co-operation models can be easily exposed. In most modeling domains, the top element is never implementable which we call a miracle. We use it as the mark of the confliction. In other words, if the promotion ends up as a miracle, the promotion fails and there exists conflicts between the primary model and secondary model.

Definition 3 (Compatibility)

Assume $\mathcal{D}_1$ is a complete lattice and let $A \in \mathcal{D}_1$, $B \in \mathcal{D}_2$, ψ is a translation from $\mathcal{D}_2$ to $\mathcal{D}_1$. If $A\,\mathrm{prt}_\psi\,B \not\sqsupseteq_{\mathcal{D}_1} \top_{\mathcal{D}_1}$ where $\top_{\mathcal{D}_1}$ is the top element of $\mathcal{D}_1$, we say model B is **compatible** *to model A with respect to function ψ, denoted as $A \mathrel{\backsim}_\psi B$.*

Promoting one model is not sufficient when developing a software or hardware system using the model promotion technique. The information extracted from model B may compatible with the current primary model A, but inconsistency may still occur when interpreting A's information to B. The consistency properties need to guarantee that both models are compatible with each other. The compatibility relation is asymmetrical while the consistency relation which is symmetrical can be defined by conjuncting the compatibility relation in both directions.

Definition 4 (Consistency)

Assume $\mathcal{D}_1$ and $\mathcal{D}_2$ are complete lattices and let $A \in \mathcal{D}_1$, $B \in \mathcal{D}_2$, ϕ is a translation from $\mathcal{D}_1$ to $\mathcal{D}_2$, ψ is a translation from $\mathcal{D}_2$ to $\mathcal{D}_1$. If $A \mathrel{\backsim}_\psi B$ and $B \mathrel{\backsim}_\phi A$, then we say A

*and B are **consistent** with respect to translations ϕ, ψ, denoted as $A \overset{\phi}{\underset{\psi}{\rightleftarrows}} B$. Otherwise, there exists a conflict between model A and model B with respect to ϕ, ψ.*

The consistency of various models is increasingly concerned in both model analysis and model driven development. The promoting operation provides a formal theory to determine whether two models are consistent with each other. In practice, designers usually concerns the consistency issue involving several aspects of the system only. The model promotion approach can reflect the designers' concerns with the selection of the translations. In this case, a translation maps the secondary model to its projection according to the designers' concerning points.

The model promotion calculi can have more elegant property if the two model domains and the two translations forms a Galois Connection.

The Galois theory tells us certain problems in the concrete domain can be solved equivalently in the abstract domain if there exists a Galois connection between the two domains [4] [10] [14]. The information may lose when we adopt the function to transform the concrete model to an abstract domain. Actually, the information loss could not be fatal. Firstly, the stepwise refinement is an applicable and effective formal method in developing systematic softwares. Analyses and verifications in the abstract model may be easy to operate. The refinement preserves the validated properties and implement to the concrete model step by step. Secondly, the loss information in transforming the program into other model may be out of our concerns and we focus on the remained information.

Definition 5 (Galois Domains)

If the two translations ϕ, ψ consist Galois connection which satisfies that for any $A \in \mathcal{D}_1$ and $B \in \mathcal{D}_2$, $\phi(A) \sqsupseteq_{\mathcal{D}_2} B$ iff $A \sqsupseteq_{\mathcal{D}_1} \psi(B)$, we say the two domains are Galois domains.

We call two models A, B as a Galois pair with respect to the Galois connection ϕ, ψ if $\phi(A) \sqsupseteq_{\mathcal{D}_2} B$ iff $A \sqsupseteq_{\mathcal{D}_1} \psi(B)$. Models in a Galois pair has no promoting effect to each other though their information is not equal.

The special properties of the promoted calculi involving the Galois domains are exhibited below.

Theorem 2 (Promoting Laws in Galois Domains)

Let $A \in \mathcal{D}_1, B \in \mathcal{D}_2$ with two translations ϕ, ψ consisting Galois connection. Let $C_1 = A\,prt_\psi\,B, C_2 = B\,prt_\phi\,A$. Then we have

(2.1) $\phi(C_1) \sqsupseteq_{\mathcal{D}_2} C_2$ iff $C_1 \sqsupseteq_{\mathcal{D}_1} \psi(C_2)$

(2.2) $C_1\,prt_\psi\,C_2 = C_1$ and $C_2\,prt_\phi\,C_1 = C_2$

(2.3) $A\,prt_\psi\,B = A\,prt_\psi\,C_2$

(2.4) $B\,prt_\phi\,A = B\,prt_\phi\,C_1$

The above laws can be explained as

(2.1) The promoted models C_1 and C_2 form a Galois pair with respect to ϕ, ψ.
(2.2) A promoted model cannot be promoted using its partner in a Galois pair.

(2.3) The promotion A prt$_\psi$ C_2 cannot get a better model than A prt$_\psi$ B since the additional information in C_2 compared to B is totally extracted from A itself.

(2.4) The inverse version of (2.3).

Example 1

Consider modeling a temperature control system. Model A from domain $\mathcal{D}_1$ is a design with the alphabet $\alpha_{\mathcal{D}_1} = \{ok, ok', st, st', mod, mod'\}$ where the variable st represents the temperature level in the room and mod stands for the running mode of the control system. We set three temperature levels for the system: low, medium and high. Model B from domain $\mathcal{D}_2$ is a design with the alphabet $\alpha_{\mathcal{D}_2} = \{ok, ok', t, t', mod, mod'\}$ where the variable t is an integer showing the current temperature of the room. Obviously model A is an abstract model while model B is a concrete model. We define two translations

$$\phi(A) =_{df} \mathbf{var}\, t;\ A;\ t := L(st);\ \mathbf{end}\ st$$
$$\psi(B) =_{df} \mathbf{var}\, st;\ B;\ st := R(t);\ \mathbf{end}\ t$$

where

$$R(t) =_{df} \begin{cases} low & t < 14 \\ medium & 14 \le t < 16 \\ high & t \ge 16 \end{cases}$$

$$L(st) =_{df} \begin{cases} \{t \mid t < 14\} & st = low \\ \{t \mid 14 \le t < 16\} & st = medium \\ \{t \mid t \ge 16\} & st = high \end{cases}$$

We can figure out that $\psi(B) \sqsupseteq_{\mathcal{D}_1} A$ iff $B \sqsupseteq_{\mathcal{D}_2} \phi(A)$. Hence ϕ, ψ forms a Galois connection and $\mathcal{D}_1, \mathcal{D}_2$ are Galois domains.
Let

$$A = true \vdash \begin{pmatrix} st = low \wedge mod' = on \wedge st' \in \{low, medium\} \\ \vee\ st = medium \wedge mod' \in \{on, off\} \wedge st' = medium \\ \vee\ st = high \wedge mod' = off \wedge st' \in \{high, medium\} \end{pmatrix}$$

$$B = true \vdash \begin{pmatrix} t < 15 \wedge mod' = on \wedge t' = t + 1 \\ \vee\ t \ge 15 \wedge mod' = off \wedge t' = t - 1 \end{pmatrix}$$

Then we can see from B that if the pre-temperature is near 15 centigrade, the post-temperature of the room is stable around it. This information is not represented in model A. According to the model promotion approach, we can integrate this information into A to concretize it.

$$A\ \text{prt}_\psi\ B = \psi(B) = true \vdash \begin{pmatrix} st = low \wedge mod' = on \wedge st' \in \{low, medium\} \\ \vee\ st = medium \wedge mod' \in \{on, off\} \wedge st' = medium \\ \vee\ st = high \wedge mod' = off \wedge st' \in \{high, medium\} \end{pmatrix}$$

$$\phi(A) = true \vdash \begin{pmatrix} t < 10 \wedge mod' = on \wedge t' < 16 \\ \vee\ 14 \le t < 16 \wedge mod' \in \{on, off\} \wedge 14 \le t' < 16 \\ \vee\ t \ge 16 \wedge mod' = off \wedge t' \ge 14 \end{pmatrix}$$

$$B \operatorname{prt}_\phi A = B = true \vdash \left(\begin{array}{l} t < 15 \wedge mod' = on \wedge t' = t + 1 \\ \vee \ t \geq 15 \wedge mod' = off \wedge t' = t - 1 \end{array} \right)$$

With the fact that $B \sqsupseteq_{\mathcal{D}_2} \phi(\psi(B))$, we can easily obtain that $A \operatorname{prt}_\psi B =_{\mathcal{D}_1} \psi(B \operatorname{prt}_\phi A)$ and $B \operatorname{prt}_\phi A \sqsupseteq_{\mathcal{D}_2} \phi(A \operatorname{prt}_\psi B)$. Furthermore, we can say A and B are consistent with respect to translations ϕ, ψ, denoted as $A \stackrel{\phi}{\rightleftarrows}_\psi B$.

If we modify model B slightly, an incompatibility occurs when we select a proper translation. For instance, let

$$B' = true \vdash \left(\begin{array}{l} t < 15 \wedge mod' = on \wedge t' = t + 2 \\ \vee \ t \geq 15 \wedge mod' = off \wedge t' = t - 2 \end{array} \right)$$

We select the following translation

$$\phi' = AND_{t=15} \circ \phi$$

where $AND_{t=15}(A) =_{df} A \wedge t = 15$

Then we have

$$\phi'(A) = t = 15 \wedge mod' \in \{on, off\} \wedge 14 \leq t' < 16$$

Unfortunately, model B' specifies that $t = 15 \wedge mod' = off \wedge t' = 13$, so the result of the promotion $B' \operatorname{prt}_{\phi'} A = False$. We say A is not compatible to B' with respect to ϕ', denoted as $B' \not\succ_{\phi'} A$.

The promoting calculi has more special properties when the domains have special relations. For example, if the two domains are isomorphic, the promoted models $A \operatorname{prt}_\psi B$ and $B \operatorname{prt}_{\psi^{-1}} A$ should be equivalent and the promoting calculi is distributable with respect to $\sqcap, \sqcup$. Furthermore, the promoting calculi will collapse to $\sqcap$ calculi if the two domains are identical.

3   Promoting Models of CSP and Guarded Design System

As an application case study, we use the model promotion approach to the pair of models: guarded design system and CSP model.

The guarded design model is proposed by He to specify the behavior of web services [12]. It models a program as a predicate $Guard\&(Pre \vdash Post)$ which includes three components: precondition Pre, postcondition $Post$ and guard condition $Guard$. The precondition specified whether the program terminates. The postcondition represents the changes between the initial and final data states. Finally the guard condition reflects when the program can be invoked. If the precondition is violated, the program diverges. If the guard condition is violated, the program stays await. In our case study, we consider a model called guarded design system which can be represented by a tuple $(\alpha, A, [\![ ]\!])$ where α is the alphabet of the system which contains all data variables; A is a set of action names which represent computations and communications; $[\![ ]\!] : A \to GD$ is a function mapping every action to a guarded design specification, eg. $[\![a]\!]$ denotes the guarded design semantics for action $a \in A$. And the refinement relation defined in this domain is as follows.

Definition 6

Let $G_1 = (\alpha, A_1, [\![\,]\!]_1)$, $G_2 = (\alpha, A_2, [\![\,]\!]_2)$ be guarded design systems with the same alphabet. $G_1 \sqsupseteq_{\mathcal{G}} G_2$ iff $A_1 \supseteq A_2$ and $\forall s \in A_2^+ \bullet [\![s]\!]_1 \sqsupseteq_{GD} [\![s]\!]_2$.

where $[\![s]\!] =_{df} [\![a_1]\!]; [\![a_2]\!]; ...; [\![a_n]\!]$ if $s = \langle a_1, a_2, ..., a_n \rangle$.

And we define $G_1 \sqcup_{\mathcal{G}} G_2 =_{df} (\alpha, A_1 \cup A_2, [\![\,]\!]_{12})$ where

$$[\![a]\!]_{12} =_{df} \begin{cases} [\![a]\!]_1 & a \in A_1 \backslash A_2 \\ [\![a]\!]_2 & a \in A_2 \backslash A_1 \\ [\![a]\!]_1 \sqcup_{GD} [\![a]\!]_2 & a \in A_1 \cap A_2 \end{cases}$$

CSP notation is convenient for designers to specify the relations of interactions between objects in a concurrent system [13]. The failure-divergence semantics of CSP specifies which event sequences lead to divergences and which events will be rejected after certain event sequences. Although it seldom involves data state explicitly, its synchronous communication mechanism implies the dependency between the interactions. In this case, we represent a CSP model as a tuple (α, A, Fal, Div) where α contains all data variables, A is a set of action names, Fal and Div are the set of failures and divergences respectively. The refinement relation defined on CSP domain is as follows.

Definition 7

Let $S_1 = (\alpha, A, Fal_1, Div_1)$, $S_2 = (\alpha, A, Fal_2, Div_2)$ be CSP models with the same alphabet and action set. $S_1 \sqsupseteq_S S_2$ iff $Div_1 \subseteq Div_2$ and $Fal_1 \subseteq Fal_2$. And we define $S_1 \sqcup_S S_2 =_{df} (\alpha, A, Fal_1 \cap Fal_2, Div_1 \cap Div_2)$.

Obviously these two formalisms can share information. A designer who makes a guarded design specification for a system can combine the communication sequence constraints from the CSP model. The CSP designer also need the state based decisions made by the guarded design model to reduce the nondeterminism. The cooperation of the two designers can improve their specifications or find some conflicts between the two modeling. The model promotion provides a feasible approach for designers to achieve this purpose.

In order to promote the two models, we need to define two translations between the CSP domain and the guarded design domain. Let G be a guarded design system and S be a CSP model. For simplicity, we assume the two models has the same reference to data variables $G.\alpha = S.\alpha$ and the same reference to actions $G.A = S.A$ so that every action occur in the CSP model has a guarded design specification.

Then we can define a translation ψ from the CSP model to Guarded design system. It maps the CSP model S to a guarded design system

$$\psi(S) = (S.\alpha, S.A, [\![\,]\!]')$$

where $[\![\,]\!]'$ can be obtained as the follows.

For any action $a \in S.A$, we define

$$[\![a]\!]' =_{df} a.GUARD \,\&\, (a.PRE \vdash a.POST)$$

where

$$a.GUARD(x) =_{df} (\forall s \forall v \bullet s \in reftr(a) \Rightarrow \neg(Init; [\![s]\!][true/ok', false/wait']))[x/v']$$

where x is the vector of the data variables in α, $Init$ is a special guarded design which initialize the local data variables,

$$reftr(a) =_{df} \{s \mid a \in X \wedge (s, X) \in Fal \wedge s \notin Div\}$$

$$a.PRE(x) =_{df} (\forall s \forall v \bullet s \cdot \langle a \rangle \in Div \Rightarrow \neg(Init; [\![s]\!][true/ok', false/wait']))[x/v']$$

$$a.POST(x, x') =_{df} \bigvee_{b \in next(a)} b.Guard[x'/x]$$

where $next(a) =_{df} \{b \mid \exists s \bullet s \cdot \langle a, b \rangle \in Tr\}$

$$Tr =_{df} \{s \mid \exists X \bullet (s, X) \in Fal \wedge s \notin Div\}$$

Note that this translation from CSP model to guarded design system needs the reference of the original specification of each action $[\![\,]\!]$ in the guarded design system. It uses the action sequence restricted in the CSP model to reason the guard condition of each action. The divergence set implies the preconditions of the actions after which the process diverges. From the translation we can see an action's final data state should enable at least one of its following actions according to the CSP traces.

We define a translation ϕ which derives the failure-divergence semantics for CSP from the guarded design model.

$$\phi(G) = (G.\alpha, G.A, Fal', Div')$$

where

$$Div' =_{df} \{\langle a_1.(x_1), a_2.(x_2), ..., a_k.(x_k) \rangle \cdot s \mid \exists v, v', wait, wait' \bullet$$
$$(Init; [\![a_1]\!][x_1/x]; [\![a_2]\!][x_2/x]; ...; [\![a_k]\!][x_k/x])[true/ok, false/ok']\}$$

$$Fal' =_{df} \{(s, X) \mid s \in Div \wedge X \subseteq G.A\} \cup$$
$$\{(\langle a_1.(x_1), ..., a_k.(x_k) \rangle, X) \mid \exists v' \bullet$$
$$(Init; [\![a_1]\!][x_1/x]; ...; [\![a_k]\!][x_k/x])[true/ok, false/wait, true/ok', false/wait']$$
$$\wedge \forall a.(x) \in X \bullet \neg a.GUARD[v'/x]\} \cup$$
$$\{(\langle a_1.(x_1), ..., a_k.(x_k) \rangle, X) \mid \exists v' \bullet$$
$$(Init; [\![a_1]\!][x_1/x]; ...; [\![a_k]\!][x_k/x])[true/ok, false/wait, true/ok', true/wait']\}$$

Theorem 3

Translation ϕ and ψ establish a Galois connection between CSP and guarded design system.

It can be proved with the fact $\phi(\psi(S)) \sqsupseteq_S S$ and $G \sqsupseteq_G \psi(\phi(G))$. Therefore each of the two models can be promoted by taking another as the secondary model.

It is only one instance of the model promotion over Galois domains. In UTP method, many pairs of domains have been proved to be Galois domains. Hence, the model promotion approach can be used to these domains to improve specifications in these models.

4   Practical Design Cases

In this section we discuss the scenario of modeling an online shopping system to demonstrate the practical application of the model promotion approach. We select modeling techniques of CSP and guarded design system to model the online shopping system independently so that the conclusion of the last section can be adopted in the promotion process.

Consider a simple online shopping system. It contains three kinds of participants: customers, web broker and warehouse. The web broker lists the products to the customers for the warehouse. A customer can login/logout to the system, add/remove goods to/from cart and place an order for them. A customer has an individual session and only a logged customer can submit a order with a nonempty cart. A good with insufficient quantity cannot be placed to cart. The system provides these functionalities as services responding customers' requests and finally return the order number when a order is successfully accepted. Figure 2 shows the structure of the online shopping system.

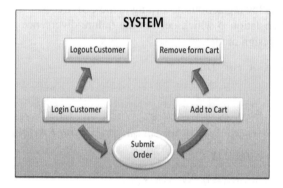

Fig. 2. Structure of a online shopping system

Assume we already have a guarded design model specifying state changes caused by operations and a CSP model restricting the interaction sequences for a valid transaction.

The online shopping system we consider includes four main objects: customers, goods, carts, orders. In detail, a customer has name, password and a IP address to access the network. A good has its identifier, price and the quantity in stock. Cart keeps a list of requested goods and the order records the purchase information involving the customers and their purchased goods. In general, we give some types to the data states of these basic objects. *NAME* is the set of all names used to distinguish the users. *KEY* is a collection of users passwords for login. *GID* and *OID* stand for the identifiers of goods and orders respectively. *IP* is the set of IP addresses of users. The declaration for the data states is shown as follows.

```
System
 CONSTANTS
      register : NAME ⇸ KEY
      price : GID → ℝ⁺
 VARIABLES
      log : IP ⇸ NAME
      stock : GID → [0..100]
      cart : IP ⇸ (GID ⇸ [1..100])
      order : OID ⇸ (GID ⇸ [1..100])
      buyer : OID ⇸ NAME
 INVARIANT
      ran log ⊆ dom register
      dom order = dom buyer
      ran buyer ⊆ dom register
 INITIALIZATION
      log, stock, cart, order, buyer := ∅, ∅, ∅, ∅, ∅
```

The system schema describes the construct of the online shopping system as well as the guarded design system

$$G = (\alpha_G, A_G, [\![\ ]\!])$$

The data variable set $\alpha_G = \{log, stock, cart, order, buyer\}$. The *register* contains information of all registered users of the system. Each user owns a corresponding key for security. The *price* describes the price of good which are identified by *GID*. Each available good has a corresponding price. In the model, we assume that the *register* and *price* is the constant of the system that cannot be changed by any operations.

log is a link between IP address and user name used to record the login users. The login user must be a registered one which is specified by the invariant of the system. The *stock* reflects the number of the good in the warehouse. We assume the maximum quantity of each good is 100. The *cart* is a temporary shopping status of each IP address. When applied to a certain IP address, the *cart* lists the goods which have been chosen with associated quantity. The *order* contains the order identifier *oid* and the corresponding information about purchased goods. The *buyer* gives who submitted the order.

The schema also specifies the initial state of the system. We can written it as the following guarded design.

$$Init =_{df} true \& (true \vdash \overrightarrow{V}' = \overrightarrow{\varnothing} \wedge \neg wait')$$

where the notation $\overrightarrow{\varnothing}$ means a vector of empty-domain functions.

The action set $A_G = \{Login, Logout, AddtoCart, RemovefromCart, SubmitOrder\}$. The guarded design semantics $[\![a]\!]$ for any action $a \in A_G$ is shown as a Z-like schema where a label *GUARD* is introduced to represent the guard condition g, label *PRE* leads the precondition b and *POST* corresponds to the postcondition R.

```
┌─ Login ──────────────────────────────────────────────────
│ Δlog
│ name? : NAME
│ key? : KEY
│ ip? : IP
├───────────────────────────────────────────────────────────
│ GUARD
│     ip? ∉ dom log
│     register(name?) = key?
│ POST
│     log' = log ∪ {ip? ↦ name?}
│
└───────────────────────────────────────────────────────────
```

```
┌─ Logout ─────────────────────────────────────────────────
│ Δlog
│ name? : NAME
├───────────────────────────────────────────────────────────
│ GUARD
│     name? ∈ dom log
│ POST
│     log' = log ▷ {name?}
└───────────────────────────────────────────────────────────
```

Operation *Login* changes the logging state of customers. After the correct input of name and key, the state changes from logout to login by adding the name to the domain of function *log*. In contrast, operation *Logout* removes the customer's name from *log*.

```
┌─ AddtoCart ──────────────────────────────────────────────
│ Δcart
│ ip? : IP
│ gid? : GID
│ n? : [1..100]
├───────────────────────────────────────────────────────────
│ POST
│     IF stock(gid?) ≥ n? THEN
│         cart' = cart ⊕ {ip? ↦ (gid? ↦ n?)}
│     ELSE
│         cart' = cart
└───────────────────────────────────────────────────────────
```

RemovefromCart _____

$\Delta cart$
$ip? : IP$
$gid? : GID$

GUARD
    $ip? \in \operatorname{dom} cart$
    $gid? \in \operatorname{dom} cart(ip?)$
POST
    $IF \operatorname{dom} cart(ip?) = \{gid?\}\ THEN$
        $cart' = cart \rhd \{ip?\}$
    $ElSE$
        $cart'(ip?) = cart(ip?) \rhd \{gid?\}$

Operation *AddtoCart* allows the user to change the quantity of the present good or add new goods with associated quantity. Operation *RemovefromCart* is used to delete the appointed good and corresponding quantity from the cart.

SubmitOrder _____

$\Delta order, \Delta stock, \Delta cart, \Delta buyer$
$ip? : IP$
$oid! : OID$

GUARD
    $ip? \in \operatorname{dom} log$
    $\operatorname{dom} cart(ip?) \neq \emptyset$
POST
    $oid! \notin \operatorname{dom} order$
    $order' = order \uplus \{oid! \mapsto cart(ip?)\}$
    $buyer' = buyer \uplus \{oid! \mapsto log(ip?)\}$
    $cart' = cart \rhd \{ip?\}$
    $\forall gid \in \operatorname{dom} cart(ip?) \bullet stock'(gid) = stock(gid) - cart(ip?)(gid)$
    $\forall gid \notin \operatorname{dom} cart(ip?) \bullet stock'(gid) = stock(gid)$

Operation *SubmitOrder* generates a new order for a login user. When a login user submits his order, the information about his trade will be add to the new generated order and be removed from the cart at the same time. The quantity of good in stock also will be change according to the newest order.

The CSP model specifies the sequence of communications between processes. The online shopping system can be modeled by a CSP model

$$S = (\alpha_S, A_S, Fal, Div)$$

where $\alpha_S = \alpha_G$ and $A_S = \{c.x \mid c \in Channel\}$. *Channel* is a set of channel names.

$Channel = \{Login(ip), Logout(ip), AddtoCart(ip), RemovefromCart(ip),$
        $SubmitOrder(ip) \mid ip \in IP\}$

Each observable communication action in A_S corresponds to an operation in the action set A_G from guarded design system. In this case, the action sets of the two models are slightly different. But there exists an action transformation rule. For example the nonresponse action $AddtoCart(ip?, gid?, n?)$ in the guarded design system corresponds to the receiving communication action $AddtoCart(ip)?(g, n)$ in CSP model where we consider the computation is done when the receiving is complete. The response action $SubmitOrder(ip?, oid!)$ corresponds to a pair of sequential communication actions $SubmitOrder(ip)?$ and $SubmitOrder(ip)!oid$ in the same channel where the computation is considered to be finished at the end of the sending action. The computation of this operation is considered to be executed after the communication.

The CSP formulas are listed as follows. Its failure-divergence semantics is straight forward so it is omitted here.

$$System =_{df} |||_{ip \in IP} (Log(ip) \parallel Cart(ip, C) \parallel Order(ip))$$
$$\backslash \{submit(ip), log\_order(ip), cart\_order(ip)\}$$
$$Cart(ip, \varnothing) =_{df} AddtoCart(ip)?(g, n) \rightarrow (Cart(ip, \{g \mapsto n\}) \sqcap Cart(ip, \varnothing))$$
$$Cart(ip, C) =_{df} submit(ip) \rightarrow cart\_order(ip)!C \rightarrow skip \qquad [C \neq \varnothing]$$
$$\square AddtoCart(ip)?(g, n) \rightarrow (Cart(ip, C \oplus \{g \mapsto n\}) \sqcap Cart(ip, C))$$
$$\square RemovefromCart(ip)?g \rightarrow Cart(ip, C \rhd \{g\})$$

$$Log(ip) =_{df} Login(ip)?(name \mapsto key) : register \rightarrow$$
$$(submit(ip) \rightarrow log\_order(ip)!name \rightarrow skip$$
$$\square Logout(ip)?name \rightarrow Log(ip))$$

$$Order(ip) =_{df} SubmitOrder(ip)? \rightarrow$$
$$submit(ip) \rightarrow log\_order(ip)?name \rightarrow cart\_order(ip)?C \rightarrow$$
$$SubmitOrder(ip)!oid \rightarrow skip$$

The system consists of three parallel components with channels for communications. The components synchronize on the actions which have the same name. A customer can login to the system, add goods to his cart, remove goods from the cart and submit his order. The cart process reflects the goods information selected by the user with IP address ip. The parameter C is a function corresponding to the function $cart(ip)$ defined in guarded design model. It changes the status of the process when the user adds or removes goods. Note that the $Cart$ process is nondeterministic since sometimes the action $AddtoCart$ may have no effect. When the user submits his order, the goods information will be send to process $Order$ through an internal communication $cart\_order$. If there is no good in user's cart, the user cannot submit his order. The login process records the login state of customers. It ensures that a customer cannot login or logout continuously. If the user performs login, his name will be record with his IP address. Then the process is waiting for the user to submit the order or logouts. When the user submits his order, the login process send the name of user to process $Order$ through an internal communication log_order. The $Order$ process generates the order using both the customer's information and his purchase information. Note that the channels $cart\_order$

and *log_order* are concealed in the system so that they do not appear in the semantical level. In other words, communications in these channels are not collected in the action set. There are two restriction shown by the CSP formula: a customer can only submit order after login and a order should contain at least one good.

According to the translation ϕ in section 3, the *AddtoCart* operation has no effect only when the request quantity of the good exceeds its stock. It converts the nondeterministic choice to a deterministic choice. In other words, we can modify the cart process as follows.

$$Cart(ip, \varnothing) =_{df} addtocart(ip)?(g, n) \rightarrow$$
$$(Cart(ip, \{g \mapsto n\} \lhd n \geq stock(g) \rhd Cart(ip, \varnothing))$$
$$Cart(ip, C) =_{df} submit(ip) \rightarrow cart\_order(ip)!C \rightarrow skip \qquad\qquad [C \neq \varnothing]$$
$$\Box addtocart(ip)?(g, n) \rightarrow$$
$$(Cart(ip, C \oplus \{g \mapsto n\}) \lhd n \geq stock(g) \rhd Cart(ip, C))$$
$$\Box removefromcart(ip)?g \rightarrow Cart(ip, C \rhd \{g\})$$

We can see that the guarded design system can promote the CSP model by complementing the information about when the action *AddtoCart* has no effect. Note that the CSP model actually has no contribution to the guarded design system in this case study. It is also an evidence that the two models are consistent since the guard conditions specified in guarded design system are not violated by the CSP restriction to the action sequence. Actually, we can figure out $G^\phi \rightleftarrows_\psi S$, because neither G' nor S' is a top element of their domain.

5 Related Work

Model Driven Architecture pictures a promising blue map for an alternative way of software development. The perspective is software can be produced automatically if we have elegant models which precisely reflect its requirements, are consistent with each other and decidable and implementable for code generation. The Object Management Group (OMG) proposes the concept of model transformation [2] to expose the relations between models. Models can be transformed to other models in order to fit the needs of certain scenarios. The general approach of model transformation defines a set of transformation rules which describe the process of the transformation [9] [18]. The source model and target model are often interpreted in a metamodel. Our model promotion approach uncovers the relations between models with the translations which give interpretations for constraints in other models and apply them to the primary model. It can be somehow considered as a vertical transformation method since it achieves program refinement which transform an abstract model to a concrete model. But the support of a metamodel is not necessary in model promotion.

The combination of formal models such as CSP-OZ [11], Circus [25] and CSP‖B [8] propose a new model which consists of the characters of the component models. They all have their own syntax and develop new semantics to interpret the features caused by the combination. The combination of CSP and Z is introduced since 1989 by Benjamin [5]. A unified theory of CSP and Z is also applied to specify the classical case of steam boiler by Woodcock [26]. The theory leads to a new concurrent language called circus which combines CSP and Z as well as refinement calculus [25]. Its semantics has been deeply studied [27] [20] and a systematic method has been discussed for developing an industrial system using circus [19]. At last, with the industrial application of the B method, developers eager to compose the B machine with the CSP process. The new framework is denoted as CSP||B by Schneider et al. [23]. It has been applied to model and analyze particular software and hardware systems [16] [17]. Our model promotion approach does not combine two models together to form a new model. It simply interpret elements from other models in the primary model in order to complement the specification. The result will keep the form of the primary model so that the analysis and verification techniques can be also applied on the result model. And it is more concrete and consistent with other cooperating models because the promoting is based on the information provided by them.

6   Conclusion and Future Work

This paper proposes a promoting calculi which is a refinement approach combining information from other models to concretize the primary model. This approach avoids the cost of transforming models to a unified domain which is too complicated for analysis and implementation. The promoted model has the following promising properties.

- The promoted model lies in the same domain of primary model. Every analyzing method applied to the primary model can be also used to the promoted model.
- The promoted model satisfies every specification satisfied by the primary model.
- The promoted model is subject to every additional restriction specified by secondary models. The consistency of models can be guaranteed if the promoting process does not end in antinomy.

The above advantages make the model promotion approach become a promising engineering technique. Software designers can use the approach to improve their models by sharing specific information of each model. It helps to reduce the gap between designers and makes the models more convincing and the system consisting of these models more clear. Its modeling power is listed as following.

- This approach can be applied to arbitrary models only requiring they have lattice-semantics.
- This approach is flexible because the designers can combine information according to their own concern without introducing abundant ones.
- This approach does not modify the existing models when combining their information so that it can take advantage of the existing properties and verification techniques for these models directly.
- This approach can complement the primary model with the information from more than one secondary model. Conversional combination methodologies cannot easily realize this kind of improvement.
- This approach can be used to compare two models according to their contributions to the same primary model. A model-level ordering based on this aspect can be easily defined to assistant designing and analyzing models.

- This approach can take advantage of the existing relations between models and use them to promote models. As we know, the UTP method has researched links between many formalisms and concluded that there exists a Galois connection between their domains. Our approach can use these conclusions directly and make these models cooperate with each other to obtain their refinements.

In the next step, we want to further reduce the restriction of applying this approach. The model promotion may not need the lattice restriction to the domains if we are not concern the refinement issues. A model can be improved in many other aspects according to orderings concerned by designers. For example, we expect it can compose two models which is totaly independent with each other but are both interacted with a common environment. In this foundation, we will consider how to generate translations in special modeling domains such as UML diagrams. Then we can concretize an existing UML model and make the model driven methodology applied to it more feasible. Besides, the promoting process can be stepwise with the composition of different translations. The properties generated by the stepwise promotion need to be discussed in detail.

Acknowledgement. This work was supported by the Open Fund of the State Key Laboratory of Software Development Environment under Grant No. SKLSDE-2009KF-2-05, Beijing University of Aeronautics and Astronautics, and by National Basic Research Program of China (No. 2005CB321904), National High Technology Research and Development Program of China (No. 2007AA010302), National Natural Science Foundation of China (No. 90718004), Shanghai Leading Academic Discipline Project (No. B412), and PhD Program Scholarship Fund of ECNU (No. 2010046).

References

1. The Model-Driven Architecture, Guide Version 1.0.1, OMG Document: omg/2003-06-01
2. Object Management Group, MOF 2.0 Query / Views / Transformations RFP, OMG Document: ad/2002-04-10, revised on April 24 (2002)
3. Abrial, J.-R.: The B-book: assigning programs to meanings. Cambridge University Press, New York (1996)
4. Artin, E.: Galois Theory. Dover Publications, New York (1998)
5. Benjamin, M.: A message passing system: An example of combining csp and z. In: Proc. 4th Z Users Workshop, Workshops in Computing, pp. 221–228. Springer, Heidelberg (1989)
6. Blaha, M.R., Rumbaugh, J.R.: Object-Oriented Modeling and Design with UML, 2nd edn. Prentice Hall, Englewood Cliffs (2004)
7. Booch, G., Rumbaugh, J., Jacobson, I.: The Unified Modeling Language User Guide, 2nd edn. Addison Wesley Professional, Reading (2005)
8. Butler, M.J., Leuschel, M.: Combining csp and b for specification and property verification. In: Fitzgerald, J.S., Hayes, I.J., Tarlecki, A. (eds.) FM 2005. LNCS, vol. 3582, pp. 221–236. Springer, Heidelberg (2005)
9. Czarnecki, K., Helsen, S.: Classification of model transformation approaches (2003)
10. Erne, M., Koslowski, J., Melton, A., Strecker, G.E.: A primer on galois connections. In: Proc. 1991 Summer Conference on General Topology and Applications in Honor of Mary Ellen Rudin and Her Work, Annals of the New York Academy of Sciences, vol. 704, pp. 103–125 (1993)

11. Fischer, C.: Csp-oz: a combination of object-z and csp. In: Proc. FMOODS 1997: IFIP TC6 WG6.1 International Workshop on Formal Methods for Open Object-Based Distributed Systems, London, UK, pp. 423–438. Chapman & Hall, Ltd., Sydney (1997)
12. He, J.: Service refinement. Science in China Series F: Information Sciences 51(6), 661–682 (2008)
13. Hoare, C.A.R.: Communicating Sequential Processes. Prentice Hall International Series in Computer Science (1985)
14. Hoare, C.A.R., He, J.: Unifying Theories of Programming. Prentice Hall International Series in Computer Science (1998)
15. Kleppe, A., Warmer, J., Bast, W.: MDA Explained: The Model Driven Architecture: Practice and Promise. Addison Wesley Professional, Reading (2003)
16. McEwan, A.A., Schneider, S.: A verified development of hardware using csp/spl par/b. In: Proc. MEMOCODE 2006: 4th ACM & IEEE International Conference on Formal Methods and Models for Co-Design, p. 81 (2006)
17. McEwan, A.A., Schneider, S.: Modeling and analysis of the amba bus using csp and b. In: Proc. CPA 2007: The 30th Communicating Process Architectures Conference. Concurrent Systems Engineering Series, vol. 65, pp. 379–398. IOS Press, Amsterdam (July 2007)
18. Mens, T., Czarnecki, K., Gorp, P.V.: A taxonomy of model transformation. Electronic Notes Theoritical Computer Science 152, 125–142 (2006)
19. Oliveira, M., Cavalcanti, A., Woodcock, J.: Formal development of industrial-scale systems in circus. Innovations in Systems and Software Engineering 1(2), 125–146 (2005)
20. Oliveira, M., Cavalcanti, A., Woodcock, J.: A denotational semantics for circus. Electronic Notes in Theoretical Computer Science 187, 107–123 (2007); Proceedings of the 11th Refinement Workshop (REFINE 2006)
21. Roscoe, A.W.: The Theory and Practice of Concurrency. Prentice Hall International Series in Computer Science (1997)
22. Schneider, S.: The B-Method: An Introduction. Atlantic, London (2001)
23. Schneider, S., Treharne, H.: Csp theorems for communicating b machines. Formal Aspect of Computing 17(4), 390–422 (2005)
24. Spivey, J.M.: The Z Notation: A reference manual, 2nd edn. International Series in Computer Science. Prentice-Hall, Englewood Cliffs (1992)
25. Woodcock, J., Cavalcanti, A.: A concurrent language for refinement. In: Proc. IWFM 2001: 5th Irish Workshop on Formal Methods. BCS, Moscow (July 2001)
26. Woodcock, J., Cavalcanti, A.: The steam boiler in a unified theory of z and csp. In: Proc. APSEC 2001: 8th Asia-Pacific Software Engineering Conference, pp. 291–298. IEEE Computer Society, Los Alamitos (December 2001)
27. Woodcock, J., Cavalcanti, A.: The semantics of circus. In: Bert, D., Bowen, J.P., Henson, M.C., Robinson, K. (eds.) B 2002 and ZB 2002. LNCS, vol. 2272, pp. 184–203. Springer, Heidelberg (2002)
28. Woodcock, J., Davies, J.: Using Z: Specification, Refinement, and Proof. Prentice-Hall, Englewood Cliffs (1997)

Probabilistic Choice, Reversibility, Loops, and Miracles

Bill Stoddart[1] and Pete Bell[2]

[1] University of Teesside, UK
[2] Consultant

Abstract. We consider an addition of probabilistic choice to Abrial's Generalised Substitution Language (GSL) in a form that accommodates the backtracking interpretation of non-deterministic choice. Our formulation is introduced as an extension of the Prospective Values formalism we have developed to describe the results from a backtracking search. Significant features are that probabilistic choice is governed by feasibility, and non-termination is strict. The former property allows us to use probabilistic choice to generate search heuristics. In this paper we are particularly interested in iteration. By demonstrating sub-conjunctivity and monotonicity properties of expectations we give the basis for a fixed point semantics of iterative constructs, and we consider the practical proof treatment of probabilistic loops. We discuss loop invariants, loops with probabilistic behaviour, and probabilistic termination in the context of a formalism in which a small probability of non-termination can dominate our calculations, proposing a method of limits to avoid this problem. The formal programming constructs described have been implemented in a reversible virtual machine (RVM).

Keywords: prospective values, probabilistic choice, expectations, reversibility, iteration.

1 Introduction

Probabilistic algorithms exist for many applications, with some well known examples being primality testing (Rabin's algorithm), Quicksort with random pivot selection (which has optimum expected performance against a hostile oracle), Buffon's algorithm for the evaluation of π, Quantum algorithms such as Shor's algorithm, and randomised back-off algorithms for resolving symmetric choice [11]. This has motivated researchers to add probabilistic choice to formalisms which underpin formal software development, such as GCL, GSL, and Hoare-He Designs,

Tractable formulations for doing this have not been easy to find. A major difficulty has been in the interaction between non-deterministic and probabilistic forms of choice, and this is seen in all approaches. The semantics of probabilistic programs was first formulated using measure theoretic approaches by Kozen[9]. A more immediately practical approach based on pGCL (the Guarded Command

S. Qin (Ed.): UTP 2010, LNCS 6445, pp. 253–270, 2010.

Language extended with probabilistic choice) has been developed by He, Morgan, McIver, Sanders and others[13,14,3]. A discursive exposition of this approach is available in the monograph of McIver and Morgan[10]. Hurd[6,7] has developed an approach based on a shallow embedding of probabilistic programming concepts in HOL, in which random events are modelled by popping elements from an assumed infinite series of coin flips, and has worked with Morgan and McIver on the mechanisation, in HOL, of probabilistic guarded commands. Meinicke and Hayes [12] have given an extensive account of algebraic properties of probabilistic action systems. The combination of reversibility and probability is addressed by He Jifeng and J Sanders in [8].

In previous work, we have explored the use of non-deterministic choice within search procedures, both in the B Formalism and in terms of Hoare and He's unifying theories [18]. We propose the formalism $S \diamond E$ to represent all the values E might take after executing the program S. We add probabilistic choice to our language and formulate the expectation of expression E following the execution of program S. We exploit reversibility to support backtracking, and in our approach both probabilistic and non-deterministic choice are "governed by feasibility". By this we mean that if a choice subsequently leads to an infeasible continuation, execution will backtrack to the point of choice and try a different alternative.

Abrial's Generalised Substitution Language provides a suitable vehicle for representing computations based on UTP Designs minus Healthiness Condition H4, which expresses the "Law of the Excluded Miracle". In particular GSL includes naked guarded commands, able to express miraculous behaviour. Our particular interest is reversible computation, and in this context an infeasible operation will simply cause execution to engage reverse gear, recommencing forward execution when it encounters an unexplored choice.

Central to our project is the provision of an execution platform for the constructs we investigate, in the form of the "Reversible Virtual Machine".[19] We propose a programming language in which we can use terms of the form $S \diamond E$. This yields the value (or bunch of values) E would take after executing S, but *does not change the system state*. Operationally it represents the execution of S, the recording of the value of E, and the restoration of the previous system state by a stepwise reversal of the computation of S. This method of organising a computation, and in particular stepwise reversibility, has a thermodynamic significance: the requirements for power consumption in a computation arise from the damping required to reconcile previously incompatible system states, a requirement that is not present if computations are organised in a stepwise reversible manner. Our reversible execution platform in a virtual machine implemented on non-reversible technology, and therefore offers none of the advantages of reversibility in terms of power consumption. However, reversibility has other advantages which we can exploit, for example in terms of garbage collection, and in providing a number of new programming structures [19,17].

The theory of probabilistic programming given here is more fully described in our paper "A Unification of Probabilistic Choice within a Design-based Model of Reversible Computation"[15] and in an associated technical report[16]. The original contributions of the current paper are the re-expression of our theory in GSL, the establishment of a semantic foundation for probabilistic iterations in our formalism based on fixed point theory, the practical proof treatment of loops with probabilistic loop bodies, and consideration of probabilistic loop termination within a formalism which has a strict approach to probabilistic termination. Aspects of our approach which are covered in our previous report [15] include: the ability to derive a relational model from a probabilistic program text, the expression of blind non-determinism within the same model as demonic non-determinism, the characterisation of probabilistic refinement as containment of convex closures in distribution space, and the linking of probabilistic and non-probabilistic models via a Galois connection.

The paper is organised as follows. In Section 2 we review our Prospective Values formalism; in Section 3 we introduce probabilistic choice and review our previous work on expectations; In section 4 we consider some algebraic properties of expectations, establishing sub-conjunctivity and monotonicity; in section 5 we establish the basis for a fixed point semantics of iterative constructs; in section 6 we discuss practical proof treatment of loops and probabilistic termination; in section 7 we draw our conclusions and discuss future work.

2   Backtracking and Prospective Values

In [20] we introduce $S \diamond E$, to represent the bunch[4,5] of values that could be taken by expression E after executing the program S. The binding power of $\diamond$ is below that of program connectives ($[\![$, $\Longrightarrow$ etc).

We remind the reader that, in Hehner's Bunch Theory, a bunch is "the contents of a set"; thus $1, 2$ is the bunch of elements which are in the set $\{1, 2\}$, and the comma is now an operator, signifying bunch union. The type of a bunch is the same as that of its elements, and there is no difference between an element and the bunch consisting of just that element. The empty bunch is written as **null**. We write $E : F$ to express bunch containment, for example $1, 2 : 1, 2, 3$. Some simple but important properties are $E : E$, $E, F = F, E$, $E : E, F$ and **null** $: E$.

Operators applied to bunches are lifted. For example if $A = 1, 2$ and $B = 4, 5$, then $A + B = 1 + 4, 1 + 5, 2 + 4, 2 + 5$.

The guarded bunch $g \longrightarrow S$ has the value of S where g holds, and is otherwise *null*.

In our approach we add an improper bunch $\bot$, (more strictly an improper bunch for each type) to represent the value of an expression after a non-terminating computation. For any other bunch E of the same type we have $E : \bot$ and $\neg \bot : E$. The improper bunch has a number of absorptive properties, e.g. $E, \bot = \bot$, $E + \bot = \bot$, $E * \bot = \bot$. Full details of our use of Bunch theory are given in [15][1].

---

[1] Available from `http://tees.openrepository.com`

We use a large equals $=$ with the same meaning but lower precedence than $=$. It is particularly useful because $\diamond$ has a lower precedence than $=$. We use $[P]$ to assert that P is true everywhere.

Returning now to the construct $S \diamond E$, in [20] and [18] we prove that it has the properties:

Name	Rule	Side Cond
Precondition	$P \mid S \diamond E = P \mid S \diamond E$	
Skip	$skip \diamond E = E$	
Assignment	$x := F \diamond E = E[F/x]$	
Guard	$g \Longrightarrow S \diamond E = g \longrightarrow S \diamond E$	
Choice	$S [\![T \diamond E = S \diamond E, T \diamond E$	
Choice from set	$x :\in A \diamond E = \S a \bullet a \in A \longrightarrow E[a/x]$	$a \setminus E$
Seq Comp	$S;\ T \diamond E = S \diamond T \diamond E$	
Local Variable	$var\ z.S.\ end \diamond E = \S z \bullet S \diamond E$	$z \setminus E$

This characterisation of prospective values has two uses. It can serve as a semantic description of our reversible language, within a total correctness framework. It can also serve as a description of values terms of the form $S \diamond E$ take when they occur as executable constructs in our programming language. The RVM executes such terms by following each non-deterministic choice within S and collecting the results. The resulting value ????

3   Probabilistic Choice and Expectations

In [15,16] we add probabilistic choice. In common with pGSL, pGCL and other formalisms we use $S\ _p\oplus\ T$ for the operation that will choose S with probability p and T with probability $1 - p$. Thus the following program represents an experiment in which a coin is tossed two times and the number of heads is recorded in the variable X.

$$Experiment \mathrel{\widehat{=}} X := 0;$$
$$X := X + 1\ _{0.5}\oplus\ skip;$$
$$X := X + 1\ _{0.5}\oplus\ skip$$

The expression X has its value assigned according to a random process; it complies with our intuitive understanding of a "random variable".[2] We reason about expressions that can take random values following some operation in terms of expectations. After each run of $Experiment$, X will be set at random to one of the values 0,1 or 2. If enough runs are performed to iron out random fluctuations, we wool,expect its long term average value to approach 1. It will be set to 0 approximately 25.

---

[2] Though it is not a random variable as formulated in classical probability theory, where a random variables is a real valued function on a sample space, and its random properties are implied from a probability measure over this space.

We write the expected value of a numeric expression or numeric vector E after performing a computation S as $\mathbf{E}(S \diamond E)$. This is a non compositional notation, in the sense that the value of $\mathbf{E}(S \diamond E)$ is *not* evaluated by applying the expectation operator $\mathbf{E}$ to $S \diamond E$. Rather, the expectation is calculated from S and E, and the diamond just serves as a syntactic separator between them. A compositional alternative would be to write this as $S \diamond_{\mathbf{E}} E$, but this is less easy to write in a notebook or email discussion.

We will often be interested in the expectations of "numerotized predicates". For any predicate Q we define $| Q | \hat{=} Q \longrightarrow 1, \neg Q \longrightarrow 0$, so that the value of $| Q |$ will be 1 if Q is true and 0 if Q is false.

Before giving the rules for calculating expectations, we note that the expectations associated with the operation *Experiment* noted above are

$\mathbf{E}(\textit{Experiment} \diamond X) = 1$
$\mathbf{E}(\textit{Experiment} \diamond | X = 0 |= 0.25$
etc

In the following table the effect of probabilistic choice is captured through a weighted addition of expectations. The tricky part is to decide the meaning of a probabilistic choice between a feasible operation (i.e. one that is able to run) and an infeasible one (i.e. one which will place execution in reverse gear if invoked).

Name	Rule	Side Cond
Precondition	$\mathbf{E}(P \mid S \diamond E) = P \mid \mathbf{E}(S \diamond E)$	
Skip	$\mathbf{E}(\textit{skip} \diamond E) = E$	
Assignment	$\mathbf{E}(x := F \diamond E) = E[F/x]$	
Guard	$\mathbf{E}(g \Longrightarrow S \diamond E) = g \longrightarrow \mathbf{E}(S \diamond E)$	
Choice	$\mathbf{E}(S \, [\!] \, T \diamond E) = \mathbf{E}(S \diamond E), \mathbf{E}(T \diamond E)$	
Choice from set	$\mathbf{E}(x :\in A \diamond E) = \S \, a \bullet a \in A \longrightarrow E[a/x]$	$a \setminus E$
Seq Comp	$\mathbf{E}(S; \; T \diamond E) = \mathbf{E}(S \diamond \mathbf{E}(T \diamond E))$	
Local Variable	$\mathbf{E}(\textit{var } z.S.\textit{end} \diamond E) = \S \, z \bullet \mathbf{E}(S \diamond E)$	$z \setminus E$
Prob Choice	$\mathbf{E}(S \, _p\!\oplus \, T) \diamond E = \mathbf{E}(S \diamond E) \, _p\!+ \, \mathbf{E}(T \diamond E)$	$0 < p < 1$
Prob Choice	$\mathbf{E}(S \, _0\!\oplus \, T) \diamond E = \mathbf{E}(T \diamond E)$	
Prob Choice	$\mathbf{E}(S \, _1\!\oplus \, T) \diamond E = \mathbf{E}(S \diamond E)$	

To model probabilistic choice we use the weighted bunch addition $_p\!+$. We define $E_1 \, _p\!+ \, E_2$ where E_1 and E_2 are bunches and p is an element with $0 \leq p \leq 1$ by

$$E_1 \, _p\!+ \, E_2 \hat{=} E_1 = \mathbf{null} \longrightarrow E_2 \, , \, E_2 = \mathbf{null} \longrightarrow E_1 \, , \, p * E_1 + (1 - p) * E_2$$

The body of this key definition consists of the bunch union of three terms. The definition covers nine cases, these being that each of E_1 and E_2 could be a proper non-empty bunch, or **null**, or $\perp$. Where E_1 and E_2 are non-empty the first two terms equate to **null** and thus do not contribute to the result, which is given by the third term. If either E_1 or E_2 is **null**, then, by the absorptive properties of **null**, the third term will be **null** and the result will be given by the first two terms, at most one of which will be non-null. If either E_1 or E_2 is $\bot$, the third term of will be $\bot$ (by the absorptive power of $\bot$), and the whole expression will equate to $\bot$.

As an (unsatisfactory) alternative we might have used the rule: $\mathbf{E}(S \ {}_p\oplus\ T) \diamond E = p * \mathbf{E}(S \diamond E) + (1-p) * \mathbf{E}(T \diamond E)$ which would be correct in the case of feasible S and T, but would have the unwanted effect of making our formalism strict with respect to feasibility, i.e. a possibly infeasible operation would *certainly* be infeasible. That is the case in pGSL, but we must reject it as a possible formulation because its implementation in a programming environment which includes possibly infeasible commands would require all branches to be tested for feasibility. We prefer the view that execution will resolve possible infeasibility by use of a backtracking mechanism, and the rule we adopt makes *magic* ${}_p\oplus$ *skip* = *skip*. Thus *magic* is a zero element with respect to our probabilistic choice, just as it is with respect to non-deterministic choice: probabilistic choice, like demonic choice, is governed by feasibility.

A property of our probabilistic choice is that it is strict with respect to non-termination. We define $trm(S)$ as $\mathbf{E}(S \diamond null) : null$. The idea here is that the only way the expected value of the null bunch after running S can be larger than the null bunch is if we cannot guarantee termination of S. As an example of how this works consider $abort \mathrel{\widehat{=}} false \mid skip$ and let S be the program $abort \ {}_{0.5}\oplus\ skip$ Then we have:

$\mathbf{E}(S \diamond null) = \mathbf{E}(abort \ {}_{0.5}\oplus\ skip \diamond null)$
$= \mathbf{E}(abort \diamond null) \ {}_{0.5}+\ \mathbf{E}(skip \diamond null)$
$= \mathbf{E}(false \mid skip \diamond null) \ {}_{0.5}+\ null$
$= \mathbf{E}(false \mid skip \diamond null) = false \mid null$
$= \bot$

hence

$trm(S) = \bot : null = false$ Using the lenient approach to termination of pGSL or pGCL, the above program would terminate with probability 0.5.

A possible advantage of a strict treatment of non-termination is that use of an operation outside of its pre-condition would be easier to detect during the discharge of proof obligations. The disadvantage is that vanishingly small probabilities of non-termination will dominate our expectations, and require special treatment; we discuss a case later. He and Sanders[8] have engineered a version of pGCL which is strict with respect to non-termination. To do this they introduce angelic choice and view an operation S as an angelic choice over a set of "fibres". The fibre at x_0 behaves like S for $x = x0$ and like abort elsewhere.[8]. We achieve strictness from the properties of the improper bunch.

The effect of non-determinism is that we may have more than one expected value for an expression, with different values corresponding to different combinations of non-deterministic choices. We capture this property, in our rule for $\mathbf{E}(S \ [\!]\ T \diamond E)$, by using bunch union. We could have used a set of expectations at this point, but the advantage of using bunches is that we obtain a smooth transformation from the deterministic (but probabilistic) case to the non-deterministic case. We are able to apply our rule for weighted addition equally well to individual expectations or bunches of expectations. Use of set theory to express our theory would require us to use sets even for the deterministic case, and to define our already complex weighted addition operator to work on sets of expectations rather than on expectations themselves.

If A is a predicate on the state space we write $Prob(S, A)$ for the probability that A is true after executing S, defined as $Prob(S, A) = \mathbf{E}(S \diamond \mid A \mid)$. Where S is nondeterministic the result may be a non-elemental bunch, and we will typically be interested in the minimum probability of obtaining some desired result A.

Whereas $S \diamond E$ terms are part of our programming language, expectations are not, and are used only for semantic analysis of programs. We also note that we have not defined the meaning of $S \diamond E$ terms where S includes probabilistic choice.

4 Algebraic Properties of Our Expectation Calculus

Predicate transformers in B-GSL and UTP designs are conjunctive. i.e. $wp(S, Q_1 \land Q_2) = wp(S, Q_1) \land wp(S, Q_2)$. I.e. S will establish post condition $Q_1 \land Q_2$ exactly when it will establish Q_1 and will also establish Q_2.

The equivalent property in PV semantics is $S \diamond E, F = (S \diamond E), (S \diamond F)$.

This correspondence can be illustrated by the use of the conjunctivity property in establishing that sequential composition distributes through choice, i.e. $S; T \mathbin{[\!]} U = (S; T) \mathbin{[\!]} (S; U)$. In wp semantics we establish the equality of program expressions S and T by showing $wp(S, Q) = wp(T, Q)$ for arbitrary Q, Thus to establish the given distributivity rule we proceed as follows:

$wp(S; T \mathbin{[\!]} U, Q) =$ "wp rule for sequential composition"
$wp(S, wp(T \mathbin{[\!]} U, Q)) =$ "wp rule for choice"
$wp(S, wp(T, Q) \land wp(U, Q)) =$ "wp conjunctivity"
$wp(S, wp(T, Q)) \land wp(S, wp(U, Q)) =$ "wp rule for sequential composition"
$wp(S; T, Q) \land wp(S; U, Q) =$ "wp rule for choice"
$wp((S; T) \mathbin{[\!]} (S; U), Q)$

and hence $S; T \mathbin{[\!]} U = (S; T) \mathbin{[\!]} (S; U)$

Using PV semantics we establish the equality of S and T by showing the equivalence of their prospective value effect, i.e. that for an arbitrary expression E defined on the current state, that $(S \diamond E) = (T \diamond E)$. To establish the given distributivity rule in PV semantics we proceed as follows:

$S; T \mathbin{[\!]} U \diamond Q =$ "pv rule for sequential composition"
$S \diamond (T \mathbin{[\!]} U \diamond Q) =$ "pv rule for choice"
$S \diamond (T \diamond Q, U \diamond Q) =$ "pv conjunctivity"
$(S \diamond T \diamond Q), (S \diamond U \diamond Q) =$ "pv rule for sequential composition"
$(S; T \diamond Q), (S; U \diamond Q) =$ "pv rule for choice"
$(S; T) \mathbin{[\!]} (S; U) \diamond Q$

and again we establish our result. We notice that the appeal to the respective conjunctivity properties is made at the same point in both these proofs.

One important property of conjunctivity is that it implies monotonicity, which is a pre-requisite for establishing a fixed point semantics of loops. We would formulate the conjunctivity property for expectations as:

$$\mathbf{E}(S \diamond (A, B)) \;=\; \mathbf{E}(S \diamond A), \mathbf{E}(S \diamond B)$$

Our expectation calculus, however is not conjunctive, or more exactly is only conjunctive for operations that do not include probabilistic choice. We see we do not in general have conjunctivity from the following counter example.

Let $S \;\widehat{=}\; x := 0 \;_{0.5}+\; x := 1$ then applying the rules for probabilistic choice to $\mathbf{E}(S \diamond x, x + 1)$ we have

$$\mathbf{E}(S \diamond (x, x + 1)) \;=\; 0.5, 1, 1.5$$

but

$$\mathbf{E}(S \diamond x), \mathbf{E}(S \diamond x + 1) = 0.5, 1.5$$

We can however show "sub-conjunctivity". We follow Hehner in defining a bunch refinement $A \sqsubseteq B \;\widehat{=}\; B : A$.

Theorem 1. sub-conjunctivity of expectations

$$\mathbf{E}(S \diamond (A, B)) \;\sqsubseteq\; \mathbf{E}(S \diamond A), \mathbf{E}(S \diamond B)$$

Proof
The proof is by structural induction with base cases for *skip* and assignment and proofs for each program connective, these making appeals to the inductive case. Here we give just the base case for assignment and the inductive proof for probabilistic choice.

For assignment we have:

$\mathbf{E}(x := E \diamond (A, B)) \;=\;$ "expectation rule for assignment"
$(A, B)[E/x] \;=\;$ "distributivity of substitution through bunch union"
$A[E/x], B[E/x] \;=\;$ "expectation rule for assignment"
$\mathbf{E}(x := E \diamond A), \mathbf{E}(x := E \diamond B) \sqsubseteq$ "property of bunch refinement"
$\mathbf{E}(x := E \diamond A), \mathbf{E}(x := E \diamond B)$

For probabilistic choice with $0 < p < 1$ we have:

$\mathbf{E}(S_p \oplus T \diamond (A, B)) \;=\;$ "rule for prob choice"
$\mathbf{E}(S \diamond (A, B)) \;_p+\; \mathbf{E}(T \diamond (A, B)) \sqsubseteq$ "inductive case and property of $_p+$ "
$\mathbf{E}(S \diamond A), \mathbf{E}(S \diamond B) \;_p+\; \mathbf{E}(T \diamond A), \mathbf{E}(T \diamond B)) \;=\;$
"lifted application of $_p+$ "
$\mathbf{E}(S \diamond A) \;_p+\; \mathbf{E}(T \diamond A), \mathbf{E}(S \diamond A) \;_p+\; \mathbf{E}(T \diamond B),$
$\mathbf{E}(S \diamond B) \;_p+\; \mathbf{E}(T \diamond A), \mathbf{E}(S \diamond B) \;_p+\; \mathbf{E}(T \diamond B) \sqsubseteq$
"defn of bunch refinement"
$\mathbf{E}(S \diamond A) \;_p+\; \mathbf{E}(T \diamond A), \mathbf{E}(S \diamond B) \;_p+\; \mathbf{E}(T \diamond B) \;=\;$
"rule for prob choice"
$\mathbf{E}(S_p \oplus T \diamond A), \mathbf{E}(S_p \oplus T \diamond B)$

Other cases follow in an obvious way.   □

We now return to the subject of monotonicity, which fortunately is implied by sub-conjunctivity. Our proof of this will use the following obvious lemma:

Lemma 1. *Bunch refinement lemma*

$$[A \sqsubseteq B] \Rightarrow A = A, B$$

Theorem 2. Monotonicity of expectations

$$A \sqsubseteq B] \Rightarrow \mathbf{E}(S \diamond A) \sqsubseteq \mathbf{E}(S \diamond B)$$

Proof. We must prove $\mathbf{E}(S \diamond A) \sqsubseteq \mathbf{E}(S \diamond B)$ under the assumption $[A \sqsubseteq B]$

$\mathbf{E}(S \diamond A) \quad = \quad$ "assumption, lemma, and referential transparency"
$\mathbf{E}(S \diamond (A, B)) \sqsubseteq$ "sub-conjunctivity of expectations"
$\mathbf{E}(S \diamond A), \mathbf{E}(S \diamond B) \sqsubseteq$ "defn of bunch refinement"
$\mathbf{E}(S \diamond B)$

□

The monotonicity of expectations will be of use in the next section, when it allows us to infer the monotonicity of a function used in a fixed point equation to characterise the transitive opening of an operation, and which we subsequently use to define the meaning of a while loop in terms of expectation calculus.

5   Expectations and Iterative Commands

In this section we are concerned with asking whether it makes any mathematical sense to talk about an expectation of some expression following an iterative command, and how such commands may be defined in terms of the basic table of commands for which expectation rules have been given in Section 3. We construct an argument based on fixed point theory, following the approach Abrial takes in [1] to justify iterative constructs in a predicate transformer context. We first define the "transitive opening" of an operation, and examine its expectation properties. We then use transitive opening as the basis for defining a while loop.

5.1   Expectations and Transitive Opening

We make use of Abrial's definition of the transitive opening $S^\wedge$ of a command S, defined as:

$$S^\wedge \mathrel{\widehat{=}} \mu X.(X;\ S) \, [\!] \, skip$$

In this definition of $S^\wedge$ in terms of a fixed point equation, the associated cpo is the lattice of operations, with top element magic and bottom element abort, and the ordering is reverse refinement. We choose the weakest fixed point to include infinite behaviour. The corresponding strongest fixed point would give us S^*, the transitive closure of S.

We first prove the following

Lemma 2. *The expectation effect of transitive opening*

$$\mathbf{E}(S^\wedge \diamond E) \;=\; \mu\, Y.\mathbf{E}(S \diamond Y), E$$

Proof. From the definition of $S^\wedge$ we have that $S^\wedge$ is the least (least refined) operation that satisfies

$$S^\wedge \;=\; (S;\, S^\wedge) \,[\!]\, skip$$

Taking expectations (and by referential transparency)

$$\mathbf{E}(S^\wedge \diamond E) \;=\; \mathbf{E}((S;\, S^\wedge)\,[\!]\, skip \diamond E) \;=$$
"expectation rule for choice"
$$\mathbf{E}(S;\, S^\wedge \diamond E), \mathbf{E}(skip \diamond E) \;=$$
"expectation rules for sequential composition and skip"
$$\mathbf{E}(S \diamond \mathbf{E}(S^\wedge \diamond E)), E$$

Thus we obtain the following fixed point equation for $\mathbf{E}(S^\wedge \diamond E)$

$$\mathbf{E}(S^\wedge \diamond E) \;=\; \mathbf{E}(S \diamond \mathbf{E}(S^\wedge \diamond E)), E$$

We have thus transformed a fixed point equation on operations to a fixed point equation on expectations. Our cpo is now the lattice of bunches of values that can be taken by expectations , and our order is reverse bunch refinement, with top element *null* and bottom element the improper bunch $\perp$. Once again, to include infinite behaviour we take the least solution, giving

$$\mathbf{E}(S^\wedge \diamond E) \;=\; \mu\, Y.\mathbf{E}(S \diamond Y), E$$

We may assure ourselves that such a fixed point indeed exists by appeal to Tarski's fixed point theorem. This states that an equation of the form $X = f(X)$ will have solutions if the domain of f is a cpo and f is monotonic. in our case the function f is given by $f(Y) = \mathbf{E}(S \diamond Y), Y$ the domain of f is a lattice (and therefore a cpo) and the monotonicity of f is assured by the monotonicity property of expectations, proved in the previous section.   □

5.2   WHILE Loops

We now take Abrial's definition of a while loop and again we will investigate it's effect on expectations, showing that the usual "unwinding" interpretation of a while loop is valid within our expectation semantics.

We define:

$$\text{while } G \text{ do } S \text{ end } \,\widehat{=}\, (G \Longrightarrow S)^\wedge \,;\; \neg\, G \Longrightarrow skip$$

And the following theorem describes the effect of a while loop within the expectation calculus.

Theorem 3

$$\mathbf{E}(\text{ while } G \text{ do } S \text{ end } \diamond E \ = \ \mu\, Y.\, \text{if } G \text{ then } \mathbf{E}(S \diamond Y) \text{ else } E \text{ end}$$

Proof. We consider the expectation effect of a while loop on an arbitrary expression.

$\mathbf{E}(\text{ while } G \text{ do } S \text{ end } \diamond E) \ = \ $ "defn of while loop"
$\mathbf{E}((G \Longrightarrow S)^{\wedge} \,;\, \neg\, G \Longrightarrow skip \diamond E) \ = \ $
"expectation rule for sequential composition"
$\mathbf{E}((G \Longrightarrow S)^{\wedge} \diamond \mathbf{E}(\neg\, G \Longrightarrow skip \diamond E)) \ = \ $
"expectation rules for guard and skip"
$\mathbf{E}((G \Longrightarrow S)^{\wedge} \diamond \neg\, G \longrightarrow E) \ = \ $ "Lemma 2"
$\mu\, Y.\mathbf{E}(G \Longrightarrow S \diamond Y), \neg\, G \longrightarrow E \ = \ $ "expectation rule for guard"
$\mu\, Y.G \longrightarrow \mathbf{E}(S \diamond Y), \neg\, g \longrightarrow E \ = \ $
"rewriting as a conditional expression"
$\mu\, Y.\, \text{if } G \text{ then } \mathbf{E}(S \diamond Y) \text{ else } E \text{ end}$

□

We terminate this section with a note on our choice of the weakest fixed point in our interpretation of loop expectation semantics. This seems intuitively correct, for the same reason that the weakest fixed point is chosen to describe the predicate transformer effect of loop semantics, i.e. to include the infinite case. We now check this intuition for a particular extreme case.

Writing   while G do S end   as W, theorem 3 tells us that $\mathbf{E}(W \diamond E)$ is characterised by the equation

$$\mathbf{E}(W \diamond E) = \text{ if } G \text{ then } \mathbf{E}(S \diamond \mathbf{E}(W \diamond E)) \text{ else } E \text{ end}$$

which is the classical unwinding interpretation of a loop, expressed in terms of expectations. If we set G to true, and thus make a non-terminating loop, and (for simplicity) set S to *skip*, the equation reduces to

$$\mathbf{E}(W \diamond E) = \mathbf{E}(skip \diamond \mathbf{E}(W \diamond E))$$

which by the rule for skip reduces to

$$\mathbf{E}(W \diamond E) = \mathbf{E}(W \diamond E)$$

an equation which conveys no information and thus admits any solution. However, since we are taking the weakest fixed point as our solution we obtain the improper bunch $\perp$ as the expected value of an expression following the termination of this non-terminating loop, and this is what we expect.

6   Practical Proof Treatment of Loops and Termination

The preceding section demonstrates that our expectation calculus gives an interpretation of loops which is able to give a mathematic interpretation to the meaning of the expectation of some expression after executing a loop. As with other formalisms, however, practical proof treatment of loops is not based directly on such a treatment, but rather uses a technique in which loop behaviour is characterised in terms of loop variants and invariants, which capture the programmers intuition about what the loop is intended to achieve and why it is sure to terminate.

Treatment of loops and heuristics for finding probabilistic loop invariants follow the approach described by McIver and Morgan in [10] with the exception that, due to our strict interpretation of non-determinism, possibly non-terminating loops become definitively non-terminating. We consider first an example in which termination is deterministic but the result achieved is probabilistic and illustrate the loop invariant method for this case. We then consider two contrasting loops with different forms of probabilistic termination. The first has an arbitrarily small probability of not terminating, which will nevertheless dominate our expectations unless we calculate them in the form of limits. The second can easily be shown to terminate with probability one, but is better regarded as non-terminating for practical purposes.

For our first example we have a sequence of Bernoulli trails and we are interested in the probability distribution of number of successes obtained, i.e. the classical binomial distribution. We define a program $prog$ to be used in subsequent discussion.

$prog \mathrel{\widehat{=}} r := 0;\ i := n;\ /*\ init\ */$
while $i \neq 0$ do
$\quad r := r + 1 \ {}_p\oplus\ skip;\ i := i - 1 \ /*\ body\ */$
$\quad$ variant i
$\quad$ invariant $c(i, k - r) * p^{k-r} * (1 - p)^{i-k+r} * \mid 0 \leq k - r \wedge k - r \leq i \mid$
end

We want to show that $prog \diamond r$ follows a binomial $b(n, p)$ distribution, i.e. that for any k with $k \in 0..n$ we have $Prob(prog, r = k) = c(n, k) * p^k * (1 - p)^{n-k}$. Here c is the binomial coefficient function defined by $c(n, k) = n!/((n - k)! * k!)$.

The probabilistic loop invariant, found by one of the heuristics proposed in [10], has the form $p* \mid pred \mid$. We consider the computation from some general point at which r successes have been achieved and i trials remain. At that point $pred$ is the necessary condition it is still possible to finish with k successes, and p is the probability that this will occur assuming $pred$. If the loop invariant can be preserved the value of $Prob(prog, r = k)$ is given by $\mathbf{E}(init \diamond I)$ where I is the loop invariant. i.e.

$$\mathbf{E}(r := 0;\ i := n \ \diamond\ c(i, k - r) * p^{k-r} * (1 - p)^{i-k+r} * \mid 0 \leq k - r \wedge k - r \leq i \mid)$$
$$= \ c(n, k) * p^k * (1 - p)^{i-k} * \mid 0 \leq k \wedge k \leq i \mid$$

The loop preservation rule in our style of presentation is:
$\mid g \mid * I \implies \mathbf{E}(body \diamond I)$
where we use $\implies$ for "everywhere less than or equal to" (the equivalent to "everywhere implies" when working with numerotized predicates). We also use $\Longleftarrow$ with an obvious similar meaning.

To show the invariant property we reason from the left hand side:

$\mathbf{E}(body \diamond I) =$

$\mathbf{E}(r := r+1 \,_p\oplus\ skip;\ i := i-1 \diamond c(i, k-r) * p^{k-r} * (1-p)^{i-k+r} * \mid 0 \le k - r \wedge k - r \le i \mid)$

$= $ "seq comp and assignment"

$\mathbf{E}(r := r+1 \,_p\oplus\ skip \diamond c(i-1, k-r) * p^{k-r} * (1-p)^{i-1-k+r} * \mid 0 \le k - r \wedge k - r \le i - 1 \mid)$

$= $ "prob choice and assignment"

$p * c(i-1, k-r-1) * p^{k-r-1} * (1-p)^{i-k+r} \mid 0 \le k - r - 1 \wedge k - r \le i \mid$
$\quad \mathbf{E}(x := E \diamond A), \mathbf{E}(x := E \diamond B) +$
$(1-p) * c(i-1, k-r) * p^{k-r} * (1-p)^{i-1-k+r} * \mid 0 \le k - r \wedge k - r \le i - 1 \mid)$

$= $ "collecting terms"

$c(i-1, k-r-1) * p^{k-r} * (1-p)^{i-k+r} \mid 0 \le k - r - 1 \wedge k - r \le i \mid$
$\quad +$
$c(i-1, k-r) * p^{k-r} * (1-p)^{i-k+r} * \mid 0 \le k - r \wedge k - r \le i - 1 \mid)$

$\Lleftarrow$ "comparing numerotized predicates"

$(c(i-1, k-r-1) + c(i-1, k-r)) * p^{k-r} * (1-p)^{i-k+r} * \mid 0 \le k - r \wedge k - r \le i \mid)$

$= $ "Pascal's Triangle property of binomial coefficients"

$c(i, k-r) * p^{k-r} * (1-p)^{i-k+r} * \mid 0 \le k - r \wedge k - r \le i \mid)$

$\Lleftarrow$ " since $\mid i \ne 0 \mid \le 1$

$\mid i \ne 0 \mid * c(i, k-r) * p^{k-r} * (1-p)^{i-k+r} * \mid 0 \le k - r \wedge k - r \le i \mid)$

$= \mid g \mid *I$ □

In the next two examples we consider loops with probabilistic termination. These illustrate potential problems both with our strict approach to non-termination and with the concept of "termination with probability one". First we consider a loop for which termination is always possible, where the probability of termination in the first iterations may be arbitrarily close to one, and only moves slowly away from this value in each subsequent iteration. Nevertheless we will be able to show that there is a non-zero probability of non-termination of this loop. On termination the loop will leave a variable i set to the number of iterations performed. We will not be able to derive a numeric value for the expected value of i by considering the expected value of i following the loop, because even an arbitrarily small probability of non-termination will dominate our calculations. However, we will be able to obtain the result we require by taking limits. In the second example we will have a very different situation: a loop that can easily be shown to terminate with probability one but for which, in practice, it would be very imprudent to assume that termination would occur in any human time scale.

The first example makes use of the binomial trials described above, which we now assume are packaged in an operation Bin with output r.

$r \leftarrow Pterm1(p) \ \widehat{=}\ 0 < p \wedge p < 1 \mid$
$\quad k := 1;\ i := 0;$
$\quad$ while $k \ne i$ do
$\quad\quad i := i + 1;\ k \leftarrow Bin(i, p)$
$\quad$ end
$\quad r := i;$

At the ith iteration the program performs i Bernoulli trials and terminates if all are successful. The probability of termination on the 1st iteration is p. Termination on the second iteration occurs only if we have non-termination on the first iteration followed by termination on the second. It has probability $(1-p)*p^2$. Probability of termination on the third iteration is $(1-p)*(1-p^2)*p^3$ and so on. It seems we should be able to show, within our formalism, that the expected number of iterations required for termination is:

$$\mathbf{E}(r \leftarrow Pterm1(p) \diamond r) = p + 2*(1-p)*p^2 + 3*(1-p)*(1-p^2)p^3 + ..$$

The reason we cannot do so is that termination is not guaranteed. The probability of non-termination is given by the infinite product whose ith term is the probability that termination does not occur at the ith iteration, i.e. $P(p) = (1-p)*(1-p^2)*(1-p^3)....$ For $p = 1/2$ the value of this product has a known analytic form and its value is given in [2] as approximately 0.288788. As we increase p from $1/2$ and approach 1 we can make the probability of termination on the first iteration as close to 1 as we like. We therefor wonder if there is some value p_0 for p with $p_0 < 1$ but $P(p_0) = 0$. In fact this cannot be the case, and we will always have a finite probability of non-termination for our loop. As a first step in showing why this must be so assume some p_0 exists with $P(p_0) = 1$ and let it also be the smallest such value. Then consider p_0^2. We have $p_0^2 < p_0$, so if we can show $P(p_0^2) = 0$ we will have contradicted our assumption that p_0 is the smallest value with this property and thus have shown that no such smallest value exists. We have:

$P(p_0^2) = (1-p_0^2)*(1-p_0^4)*(1-p_0^6)...$ =   "since $(1-x^2) = (1-x)*(1+x)$"
$(1-p_0)*(1-p_0^2)*(1-p_0^3)...(1+p_0)*(1+p_0^2)*(1+p_0^3)...$ =   "since $P(p_0) = 0$"
$0*(1+p_0)*(1+p_0^2)*(1+p_0^3)...$

This will be zero so long as $(1+p_0)*(1+p_0^2)*(1+p_0^3)...$ has a finite value, and this will be the case so long as $log((1+p_0)(1+p_0^2)(1+p_0^3)...)$ has a finite value. Recalling that $log(1+x) = x - x^2/2 + x^3/3..$ and noting that therefore $0 < x < 1 \Rightarrow log(1+x) < x$ we have

$log((1+p_0)*(1+p_0^2)*(1+p_0^3)..) = log(1+p_0) + log(1+p_0^2) + log(1+p_0^3)... <$
$p_0 + p_0^2 + p_0^3 + ...$ =   "standard geometric progression"
$p_0/(1-p0)$ which has a finite value for $p_0 \in openinterval(0,1)$

Thus we conclude there is no smallest p such that $P(p) > 0$. That is not yet enough to prove that we cannot have $p \in openinterval(0,1) \wedge P(p) = 0$, but since $P(p)$ is continuous and monotonic decreasing, the only remaining possibility is that the region for which $P(p) > 0$ runs up to and includes some $p_1 \in openinterval(0,1)$. Then we would have $P(p_1) > 0$ but $p \in openinterval(p_1, 1) \Rightarrow P(p) = 0$. However, we can also dispose of this possibility: if such a p_1 exists let $p_2 = p_1 + \epsilon$, and we can show in an obvious way that we can choose ϵ such that $p_2^2 < p_1$.

Having concluded that the operation $Pterm1$ will always have some finite probability of non-termination, given by $P(p)$, we return to our expression of the expected value for the number of loop iterations in $Pterm1$ but we now include this term and calculate its effect:

$\mathbf{E}(r \leftarrow (Pterm1(p) \diamond r) = p + 2*(1-p)*p^2 + 3*(1-p)*(1-p^2)p^3 + .. + P(p)*\perp$
$= \text{``since } e * \perp = \perp \text{ for any term } e\text{''}$
$\mathbf{E}(r \leftarrow (Pterm1(p) \diamond r) = p + 2*(1-p)*p^2 + 3*(1-p)*(1-p^2)p^3 + .. + \perp$
$= \text{``since } e + \perp = \perp \text{ for any term } e\text{'' } \perp$

Not surprisingly the absorptive effect of the improper bunch dominates the calculation, however small the term multiplying it might be.

Looking for an alternative approach that would allow us to calculate the termination probability of a loop that may be non-terminating, and to calculate the probability of some the loop terminating and establishing some post condition, we recall that in Theorem 3 we proved that the "unwinding" interpretation of a loop remains valid in the context of expectations. For the loop $L \triangleq$ while G do S end we have by repeated application of the unwinding result that:

$$\mathbf{E}(L \diamond E) \ = \ \mathbf{E}((\text{ if } G \text{ then } S \text{ end })^n; \ L \diamond E))$$

The probability of termination within the first n iterations of L can be calculated as

$$\mathbf{E}((\text{ if } G \text{ then } S \text{ end })^n \diamond \mid \neg G \mid)$$

and the probability of termination and establishing some post condition Q can be calculated as

$$lim_{n \to \infty} \mathbf{E}((\text{ if } G \text{ then } S \text{ end })^n \diamond \mid \neg G \wedge Q \mid)$$

We now consider the second of our two examples. This time we take a loop whose termination is readily provable by the zero one law, but, with suitably chosen parameters, is effectively non-terminating on any practical time scale.
$r \leftarrow Pterm2(p, b) \triangleq 0.5 < p \wedge p < 1 \wedge b > 0 \mid$
$\quad i := 1 \ _p\oplus \ i := 1;$
$\quad$ while $i \neq 0$ do
$\quad\quad i := i + 1 \ _p\oplus \ i := i - 1;$
$\quad\quad$ if $i > b$ then $i := b$ end
$\quad\quad$ if $i < -b$ then $i := -b$ end
$\quad$ end
$\quad r := i;$

The program represents a random walk, biased to move in a upward directions and with barriers at $-b$ and b. To apply the zero-one law to show termination with probability 1 we need to show the loop always has some probability of termination bounded away from zero. Here, such a bound is given by $(1-p)^b$, which is the probability of terminating in b steps when we are at the upper barrier. Every other position gives a better probability of terminating within the next b steps, and obviously all such probabilities are less that the overall probability of termination from any current position.

We have a trivial application of the zero one law for proving the termination of this loop with probability one and the impossibility of proving termination occurs with probability one in the previous case, but we also have the following: given any integer $N > 0$, however large and some $\epsilon \in openinterval(0, 1)$, however small, we can choose p and b such that the probability of the first loop terminating within N iterations is greater than $1 - \epsilon$ (i.e arbitrarily close to 1) and the probability of the second terminating within N iterations is less that ϵ (i.e. arbitrarily close to 0). We conclude from this that we need to supplement a proof of termination with probability 1 with a proof that termination is highly likely to occur in some sensible number of iterations given by the contact of the application. Also we need to be aware that loops which look extremely likely to terminate may not, in fact, terminate with probability one, and may need to have termination imposed after some suitable number of iterations, since the slightest possibility of non-termination of a loop will dominate our calculations.

7   Conclusions and Future Work

In this paper we consider the fixed point semantics and proof treatment of iterative constructs within an expectation calculus designed to describe reversible computations. To arrive at this calculus from UTP Designs, we remove healthiness condition H4, the law of the excluded miracle, and we consider perspective value terms of the form $S \diamond E$ which represent the value expression E would take if S were to be executed. This has a semantic role, but is also a term in our extended language of expressions, which is implemented by executing S, evaluating E, and reversing execution of E to uncompute its effects. Where S is non-deterministic, this is captured by $S \diamond E$ yielding a bunch of possible values and the corresponding execution of $S \diamond E$ executing all possible branches of the corresponding search tree.

A prospective value calculus allows us to make a smooth transition to an expectation calculus, but we must treat probabilistic choice in a manner that suits the execution behaviour of a reversible machine. This requires *magic* to be a unit of probabilistic choice, as it is of demonic choice.

Our previous work on expectation gives a relation model and links our prospective value calculus and our expectation calculus by means of a Galois Connection.

In this paper we consider the expectation effects of iterative constructs. We provide a fixed point theory by interpreting Abrial's definitions for recursive constructs in terms of our expectation calculus. To do this we first had to establish a monotonicity property for our calculus, which we derived by first proving that expectations are sub-conjunctive.

We also consider the practical proof treatment of probabilistic iterations, using the technique of loop variants and invariants, and we show how to look for an appropriate loop invariant. We consider at some length the problem of probabilistic termination, giving an example to show that even a loop that seems intuitively certain to terminate may retain a residual possibility of non-termination. Since our approach to termination is strict, we must be on the look our for such possibilities, as they will swamp any terminating behaviour. In such cases however, a alternative approach to evaluating the probabilities of terminating in some post condition can be taken by calculating the probability of establishing termination and the required post condition after n iterations of the loop, and taking the limit of this value as n tends to infinity. We also argue that termination with probability one is not a strong enough property to provide practical assurance of loop termination, and should be supplemented by calculating how likely termination is after a sensible number of iterations.

We conclude with a short note on plans for future work. In our present approach, non-deterministic choice plays two roles. It can represent provisional choice, subject to revision by backtracking, or implementors choice, which may be removed during the refinement process. For some problems it may be more appropriate to replace non-deterministic choice used as provisional choice by a preferential choice, and make this distinct from implementors choice. We have described a calculus which does this in [17]; this also describes in a more concrete way the execution behaviour of provisional choice strutters implemented on the RVM. At present this calculus of preferences does not incorporate probabilistic choice, and part of our future work will be to perform this additional unification.

References

1. Abrial, J.-R.: The B Book. Cambridge University Press, Cambridge (1996)
2. Finch, S.R.: Mathematical Constants. Cambridge (2003)
3. He, J., Seidel, K., McIver, A.: Probabilistic models for the guarded command language. Science of Computer Programming 28(2-3), 171–192 (1997)
4. Hehner, E.C.R.: Bunch theory: A simple set theory for computer science. Information Processing Letters 12.1, 26–31 (1981)
5. Hehner, E.C.R.: A Practical Theory of Programming. Springer, Heidelberg (1993); Latest version available on-line
6. Hurd, J.: Formal Verification of Probabilistic Algorithms. PhD thesis, Computer Laboratory, University of Cambridge (2001)
7. Hurd, J.: A Formal Approach to Probabilistic Termination. In: Carreño, V.A., Muñoz, C.A., Tahar, S. (eds.) TPHOLs 2002. LNCS, vol. 2410, pp. 230–245. Springer, Heidelberg (2002)
8. He, J., Sanders, J.W.: Unifying probability. In: Dunne, S.E., Stoddart, W. (eds.) UTP 2006. LNCS, vol. 4010, pp. 173–199. Springer, Heidelberg (2006)
9. Kozen, D.: Semantics of Probabilistic Programs. Journal of Computer and System Sciences 22(3), 328–350 (1981)
10. McIver, A., Morgan, C.: Abstraction, Refinement And Proof For Probabilistic Systems. Springer, Heidelberg (2004)
11. McIver, A., Morgan, C., Hoang, T.S.: Probabilistic Termination in B. In: Bert, D., Bowen, J., King, S., Walden, M. (eds.) ZB 2003. LNCS, vol. 2651, pp. 216–239. Springer, Heidelberg (2003)
12. Meinickel, L., Hayes, I.J.: Algebraic reasoning for probabilistic action systems and while-loops. Acta Informatica 45(5) (2008)
13. Morgan, C., McIver, A., Seidel, K., Sanders, J.W.: Tr-4-95, probabilistic predicate transformers. Technical report, Oxford University Programming Research Group (1995)

14. Morgan, C., McIver, A., Seidel, K.: Probabilistic predicate transformers. ACM Transactions on Programming Languages and Systems 18(3), 325–353 (1996)
15. Stoddart, W.J., Zeyda, F.: A Unification of Probabilistic Choice within a Design-based Model of Reversible Computation. Formal Aspect of Computing (2007) (Published on line), doi:10.1007/s00165-007-0048-1
16. Stoddart, W.J., Zeyda, F.: Probabilistic Choice. Technical report, University of Teesside, UK, p. 35 (2008)
17. Stoddart, W.J., Zeyda, F., Dunne, S.E.: Preference and non-deterministic choice. In: Proceedings of ICTAC 2010. LNCS. Springer, Heidelberg (to appear, 2010)
18. Stoddart, W.J., Zeyda, F., Lynas, A.R.: A Design-based model of reversible computation. In: Dunne, S., Stoddart, B. (eds.) UTP 2006. LNCS, vol. 4010, pp. 63–83. Springer, Heidelberg (2006)
19. Stoddart, W.J., Zeyda, F., Lynas, A.R.: A virtual machine for supporting reversible probabilistic guarded command languages. Electronic Notes in Theoretical Computer Science 253 (2010), doi:10.1016/j.entcs.2010.02.005
20. Zeyda, F., Stoddart, W.J., Dunne, S.: A Prospective-value Semantics for the GSL. In: Treharne, H., King, S., Henson, M., Schneider, S. (eds.) ZB 2005. LNCS, vol. 3455, pp. 187–202. Springer, Heidelberg (2005)

Towards a Pomset Semantics for a Shared-Variable Parallel Language

Yongxin Zhao[1], Xu Wang[2], and Huibiao Zhu[1]

[1] Shanghai Key Laboratory of Trustworthy Computing
East China Normal University, Shanghai, China
[2] International Institute for Software Technology
United Nations University, Macau, China
{yxzhao,hbzhu}@sei.ecnu.edu.cn, wx@iist.unu.edu

Abstract. In this paper we present a pomset semantics for a shared-variable parallel language which is an extension of the one studied by Brookes in [5]. The pomset semantics lifts the transition trace semantics to the non-interleaving setting, where parallel events in a pomset transition trace are labeled by *conditionally independent* actions. Most of the important laws from the interleaving setting also hold in the non-interleaving setting. Similarities and differences with other related works are discussed.

1 Introduction

In comparison to the more established *interleaving* models of concurrency, non-interleaving (a.k.a. partial-order or truly concurrent) models of concurrency is less developed in theoretical foundations as well as in practical applications. While the interleaving models are largely unified in using semantic structures like *sequences* and *state transition systems*; there is little consensus on what are the 'canonical structures' underpinning in non-interleaving models, denotationally or operationally. Added to this confusion is the fact that interleaving models are generally simpler and less 'plastic', than its non-interleaving counterparts, in the formulation of definitions and that they are adequate for the most purposes of functional correctness. So it seems there is little justification to study an alternative, more complicated, model of concurrency.

However, the other side of the coin is that, in contrast to interleaving approach which reduces concurrency to nondeterminism and sequential composition, non-interleaving approach models concurrency explicitly and partial orders give a more realistic treatment of parallel executions. This is very important because the price non-interleaving pays in complication will be more than compensated by its gains in efficiency and expressiveness.

- Superfluous interleaving of *independent actions* induces combinatorial explosion in model representation, which can be avoided in non-interleaving models. The more efficient and succinct representation by partial orders greatly ameliorates the state-explosion problem in algorithmic verification.

S. Qin (Ed.): UTP 2010, LNCS 6445, pp. 271–285, 2010.

- With the rise of multicore processors, hardware and software have increasingly shifted its dependency for performance improvements onto better exploitation of parallelism. Modeling parallelism explicitly saves later work of intra-thread and inter-thread commutativity analysis for code parallelisation.
- Interleaving assumes sequential consistency on memory models, which is no longer valid on modern multicore processors. For weak memory models, parallelism is irreducible to other semantic elements; they need be explicitly expressed in order to construct a correct semantics for multicore programming.
- It is widely known in the theoretical community that interleaving framework cannot properly express the important (but under-developed) notion of action/atomicity refinement: action refinement on processes is not preserved by most interleaving equivalences.

In this paper we are going to present a non-interleaving semantics for a shared-variable parallel language. Previously, Brookes has presented a fully abstract interleaving semantics for a similar shared-variable parallel language [6]. Brookes has also developed non-interleaving semantics [8] for communicating processes, where the interprocess communication is accomplished by synchronous or asynchronous message-passing rather than by writing and reading shared variables. His semantics is based on pomsets [3] but no full abstraction results are given. Similarly our work will present a pomset semantics with no full abstraction result. But our pomsets differ from his pomsets [8] in that Brookes' is a lifting of action traces while ours is a lifting of (global) transition traces[1].

There are also other related works on non-interleaving denotational semantics for synchronous communicating processes. A resource-trace based semantics is given to a deterministic subset of CSP-like language by Gastin and Mislove [12]. Resource traces are an extension of Mazurkiewicz traces [13], so a limitation is that *independence* is a static relation over actions: the dynamic independence relations abundant in concurrent programs can only be coarsely approximated.

Using pomsets independence can be expressed as relations over instances of action occurrences (a.k.a. events) so that the same action in different contexts can be related differently to other actions. Actions are denoted very differently in communicating processes, i.e., as primitive symbols, than in shared-variable programs, i.e., as transition functions over states. Given a context the action independence in communicating processes can be derived from the conflict and synchronization relations, whereas in shared-variable threads the action independence is calculated using the semantic criteria of function commutativity. It is what is called *conditional independence* by Peled [14], which forms the basis for later work on dynamic partial order reduction by Flanagan [15], Wang [16], etc.

The rest of this paper is organised as follows. In section 2 we present our shared-variable parallel language which is an extension of Brookes' language by introducing *thread-local* variable which is different from localised shared variable. Section 3 introduces and then formally defines actions for shared-variable programs. Section 4 uses the defined actions and pomsets to lift transition traces

---

[1] In addition to global transition traces, a new variant of transition traces that is defined on footprints is called local transition traces.

to the non-interleaving settings. The resulted pomset transition traces are used to give a denotational semantics to our language. In section 5, we use the pomset semantics to prove some algebraic laws of parallel programs. Section 6 discusses the related works and section 7 concludes the paper.

2   The Language

We slightly extend a standard shared-variable parallel language as in [5]. Our language expands assignment command into three types, i.e., *read*, *write* and *local* operation. The thread-local variable is introduced to distinguish from *localised* shared variable dealt with by Brookes [6].

$$P, Q ::= \ Skip \mid Stop \mid x := E \mid I := E \mid I := x \mid P; Q \mid$$
$$P \parallel Q \mid If \ B \ then \ P \ else \ Q \mid While \ B \ do \ P \mid$$
$$\langle b \to SP \rangle \mid Let \ I := E \ in \ P$$

In the syntax above the metavariables $x, y, z, \cdots$ range over the set SV of shared variables. $I, J, K, \cdots$ range over the set LV of thread-local variables. All the variables are assumed to be of integer type ($\mathbb{Z}$). Commands $Let \ I := E \ in \ P$ is the localisation/scoping construction for the thread-local variables.

Similar distinction is also imposed on *expressions* in our syntax. $LExp$ and $LBExp$ (for the arithmetic expressions ranged over by E, E' and boolean types ranged over B, B' respectively) define the sets of *local expressions*, i.e., only thread-local variables are employed in such expressions. $BExp$ (ranged over by b, b') defines the set of usual boolean expressions on both shared variables and thread-local ones.

The thread-local variable in our language is highly different from localised shared variable [6]. The latter is implemented as a single copy in the store which is shared by multiple threads. For instance, the variable x is a *localised* shared variables in $Let \ x := 0 \ in \ (x := 1 \parallel x := x + 2)$ and the computations of the two assignments on x can interfere with each other. On the other hand, the former, thread-local variable, is implemented as many copies on the stacks of the threads. Each thread owns a private copy in its local stack. When a thread forks, its thread-local variables are generated into multiple copies, one for each offspring thread; whereas when multiple threads join the different copies of the same thread-local variable are merged back into one copy, with its value non-deterministically inherited from one of the ancestors. Thus in the context $Let \ I := 0 \ in \ (I := 1 \parallel I := I + 2)$, the two assignments on thread-local variable I do not interfere.

The set of command Com is ranged over by P, Q. Note that $Stop$ is not essential in our language as it is semantically equivalent to $\langle false \to SP \rangle$. Command $\langle b \to SP \rangle$ is the so-called *conditional atomic action* (CAA), where SP is a loop-free sequential program defined as below:

$$SP, SQ ::= \ Skip \mid Stop \mid x := E \mid I := E \mid I := x \mid SP; SQ$$
$$Let \ I := E \ in \ SP \mid If \ B \ then \ SP \ else \ SQ$$

Now we give more detailed explanation for all commands.

(1) CAA uses b to monitor the state (including shared and local state) and the evaluation of b is done in one atomic step even though b may use a number of shared or thread-local variables. The command $\langle b \rightarrow SP \rangle$ is blocked if b does not hold at the current state. Otherwise, SP is converted to execute in one indivisible step. The restriction of CAAs to sequential loop-free program is not strictly necessary. It can be extended to loop as well as parallel programs if one prefers to treat CAAs more as locks rather than atomic transactions. Furthermore, $\langle True \rightarrow SP \rangle$ can be abbreviated to $\langle SP \rangle$.

(2) Assignment command in our language is allowed to make at most *one access to a shared variable* in its execution. Thus, according to the nature of the accesses there are three types of assignment: local operation $I := E$, write $x := E$, and read $I := x$. Local operation $I := E$ makes no access to shared variables; it only reads and writes thread-local variables and thus does not interfere with other commands in parallel. The write operation $x := E$ writes to shared variable x after reading from the thread-local variables contained in E. It might interfere with other parallel commands which are writing into x. The operation $I := x$ reads from shared variable x and writes into thread-local variable I. It might interfere with other parallel commands that access to x.

(3) Command *Skip*, *Stop*, $P; Q$, $P \| P$, *If B then P else Q* and *While B do P* are idle operation, deadlock, sequential, parallel, conditional and loop respectively. The informal interpretations about these commands are just like in traditional parallel languages. Note that the boolean expressions in conditional and loop are restricted to use thread-local variable only[2].

(4) Command *Let I := E in P* declares a thread-local variable I for the scope P. Assignment initialises I to E.

3   Semantics of Actions

Like a large class of related works on concurrent program semantics, the semantics of our language will also be based on *traces*. A trace describes a trail of interactions on shared state between agents in a concurrent system. Each interaction takes the form of an (atomic) action which represents an uninterrupted *state transitions* made by one agent in the concurrent system. The trace can be modeled as an ordered set of (atomic) actions (either a partial order or a total order). Atomicity guarantees that the intermediate states of an action will not be observable to other agents, or even to other actions of the same agent. Thus only the initial and final states are recorded in the semantics of actions. It is somehow in agreement with classical transformational approach to sequential program semantics.

In this paper there are three types of atomic actions, i.e., the *stutter* action *Skip*, the *write* action $x := E(l)$ and CAA action $\langle b \rightarrow SP \rangle_l$, where the latter two

---

[2] Actually, the restriction is not critical; the conditional *If x > E then P else Q* can be reformulated as *Let I = 0 in (I := x; If I > E then P else Q)*.

actions perform from the thread-local state l. The read, local and idle operations are all regarded as the stutter actions since they don't modify the shared states. It is close to programmers' intuition on realistic language like Java and the fine-grained semantics of Brookes. Giving semantics to the stutter and write action is straightforward, whereas the semantics of CAAs depends on the transformational semantics for SP. Thus we first investigate the transformational semantics for the sequential programs.

Formally the set of thread-local states is $\mathbb{L} = LV \rightarrow \mathbb{Z}$, which is ranged over by l, l'; whereas the set of shared states is $\mathbb{S} = SV \rightarrow \mathbb{Z}$, which is ranged over by s, s'. In transformational semantics the effect of a program's execution is reflected in the change of state (i.e., from initial states to terminating states). A state, (s, l), records the values of all the variables, either thread-local one (l) or shared one (s). A sequential program can be viewed as a set of state pairs, i.e., $[\![SP]\!] = \{(s, l, s', l') \mid s \in \mathbb{S}, l \in \mathbb{L}\}$.

$$[\![Skip]\!] =_{df} \{(s, l, s, l) \mid s \in \mathbb{S}, l \in \mathbb{L}\}$$

$$[\![Stop]\!] =_{df} \emptyset$$

$$[\![x := E]\!] =_{df} \{(s, l, s', l) \mid s' = [s|x = E(l)], s \in \mathbb{S}, l \in \mathbb{L}\}$$

$$[\![I := x]\!] =_{df} \{(s, l, s, l') \mid l' = [l|I = s(x)], s \in \mathbb{S}, l \in \mathbb{L}\}$$

$$[\![I := E]\!] =_{df} \{(s, l, s, l') \mid l' = [l|I = E(l)], s \in \mathbb{S}, l \in \mathbb{L}\}$$

where, $E : L \rightarrow \mathbb{Z}$ is an integer expression over thread-local states, $[s|x = E(l)]$ denotes a shared state that is identical to s except that the value of shared variable x is replaced by the evaluated value of expression E over l. Similar definitions are given for the thread-local states $[l|I = s(x)]$ and $[l|I = E(l)]$.

The command $Skip$ produces a stuttering step (s, l, s, l) on both shared and thread-local states. The command $Stop$ is identified with deadlock and has an empty set of state pairs. The write operation computes the value of local expressions and then updates the shared state while the read operation accesses to the shared variable and updates the thread-local state. The local operation works entirely on local variables.

$$[\![Let\ I := E\ in\ SP]\!] =_{df} \{(s, l, s', [l'|I = l(I)]) | (s, [l|I = E], s', l') \in [\![SP]\!]\}$$

The command $Let\ I := E\ in\ SP$ introduces the new variable with name I (initialized to the evaluated value of E) for the scope SP. In the exit point of the scope, the variable I would reinstate the original value of the entrance point.

$$[\![SP; SQ]\!] =_{df} [\![SP]\!]; [\![SQ]\!]$$

where, $[\![SP]\!]; [\![SQ]\!] =_{df} \{(s, l, s', l') | \exists s_0, l_0 : (s, l, s_0, l_0) \in [\![SP]\!] \wedge$
$$(s_0, l_0, s', l') \in [\![SQ]\!]\}$$

$$[\![If\ B\ then\ SP\ else\ SQ]\!] =_{df} \{(s, l, s', l') \mid (s, l, s', l') \in [\![SP]\!] \wedge$$
$$b(s, l) = true \vee (s, l, s', l') \in [\![SQ]\!] \wedge b(s, l) = false\}$$

The semantics of sequential composition and conditional is the same as in other sequential languages.

Now we can give semantics to actions. Note that the basic actions involved in evaluating B and E are ignored as the action effect shall be observably the same as that of $Skip$. All the actions in this paper are deterministic and therefore an action denotes a set of state pairs (initial and final state) which gives rise to a partial function. Thus the semantics of an action would be a partial function over $\mathbb{S}$, i.e., $\mathcal{A}[\![a_l]\!] : \mathbb{S} \rightharpoonup \mathbb{S}$ for an action a_l, where the subscript l means the action performs under thread-local state l. The semantics of three types of actions is listed below:

$$\mathcal{A}[\![Skip]\!] =_{df} \{(s, s) \mid s \in \mathbb{S}\}$$

$$\mathcal{A}[\![x := E(l)]\!] =_{df} \{(s, s') \mid s' = [s|x = E(l)], s \in \mathbb{S}\}$$

$$\mathcal{A}[\![\langle b \rightarrow SP \rangle_l]\!] =_{df} \{(s, s') \mid \exists l' \in \mathbb{L} \cdot (s, l, s, l') \in [\![SP]\!]\}$$

After we achieves the semantics of action, we apply ourself to the definition of action independence/conflicts. There are many possible definitions of conflict in the literature based on either semantic or syntactic criteria. One of the most general semantic definition is *conditional conflict*, which basically says that at the current state two actions running in parallel are in conflict iff the terminating state will differ if their executions are interleaved differently. Conversely we say two actions are *conditional independent* if the different interleavings give the same terminating state.

Action conflict is inherently related to the phenomenon of data race, i.e., two actions accessing a data variable simultaneously and at least one of them is a write operation. Some people, such as Dijkstra, Hoare, Reynolds and Brookes, tend to believe that accesses to shared variables should occur mutual exclusively, either through the use of locks or through ownership transfer, and data races indicate errors in program and should be completely banned. Brookes' work [6] largely concentrates on giving a race-banning semantics (or race-detecting called by Brookes) to concurrent programs. One of the nice property of race-free programs is that the atomicity will be grainless.

However, race-freedom also rules out some parallel independent actions. For instance, two write operations to x will not be conflict if they are both $x := 1$. Similarly many people also impose interleaving on CAA actions even though they may be semantically independent, e.g. $\langle true \rightarrow (I := x; \ x := I + 1) \rangle$ and $\langle true \rightarrow (I := x; \ x := I + 1) \rangle$. This is not the case in our semantics, where CAAs are treated exactly as basic actions.

Formally we define action independence as below:

Definition 3.1. Action a_l and $a'_{l'}$ are independent on state s iff

1) $\mathcal{A}[\![a_l]\!](s'') = \mathcal{A}[\![a'_{l'}]\!](s')$

2) $L([\![a]\!](s'', l)) = L([\![a]\!](s, l))$ and $L([\![a']\!](s', l')) = L([\![a']\!](s, l'))$.

Where $s' = \mathcal{A}[\![a_l]\!](s)$, $s'' = \mathcal{A}[\![a'_{l'}]\!](s)$, and $L((s, l)) =_{def} l$.

Note that the two actions work on different copies of local states and that the independence is relative to a *shared state* s. Hence the independence is *conditional* on s and it is quite different from unconditional or static independence in semantic models like Mazurkiewicz traces.

Independence is a symmetric relation derivable from an asymmetric relation:

Definition 3.2. Action a_l does not interfere with action $a'_{l'}$ on state s iff

1) $\mathcal{A}[\![a_l]\!](s'') = \mathcal{A}[\![a'_{l'}]\!](s')$

2) $L([\![a']\!](s', l')) = L([\![a']\!](s, l'))$.

Where $s' = \mathcal{A}[\![a_l]\!](s)$, $s'' = \mathcal{A}[\![a'_{l'}]\!](s)$.

Theorem 3.3. Action a and b are independent on state s iff neither interfere with the other on s.

4 Pomset Semantics of Parallel Program

Syntactically the parallel languages are a small upgrade of the sequential languages by the addition of parallel composition. Semantically, however, an overhaul of mathematic tools is required to deal properly with parallel composition.

In Brookes' interleaving semantics a parallel program denotes a set of transition traces. A transition trace is a finite sequence of pairs of states recording a possible interaction of the command with its environment. Formally, a transition trace of command P is defined as $(s_0, s'_0)(s_1, s'_1) \ldots (s_k, s'_k)$ such that it is possible for P to perform a computation from s_0 to s'_k if the execution is interrupted k time, where the ith interruption changes the state from s'_i to s_{i+1} $(0 \le i < k)$ [6]. The transition from the environment is implicit in the transition trace. Thus the system and environment alternate in making transitions.

We will lift interleaving transition traces into pomset transition traces (non-interleaving setting) and the resulted pomset are used to give a denotational semantics to our parallel language. However, some attentions are needed on potential technical complications in lifting:

- In non-interleaving setting, two actions are ordered in a trace either because they are ordered in program order (i.e., sequential composition) or because they are in conflict and have to be interleaving or sequentialized. Thus in a trace any pairs of actions in parallel (i.e., not ordered) must be independent (i.e., not in conflict).
- In pomset semantics the alternation between the system and environment may not exist since independent actions are executed in parallel in non-interleaving setting. Moreover, the transition from the environment should appear in the pomset trace explicitly.
- In the transition trace, an action is enabled only on one state. So a degenerated partial function, i.e., a state pair, suffices for action. In a partial order, due to the existence of parallel actions, an action can be enabled on many states and thus requires the full power of partial functions.

– Due to parallel actions, the large numbers of different execution paths may exist when we induce the transition trace from the pomset trace. All executions should lead to the same terminating state. Otherwise some action conflicts occur in the pomset trace, i.e., some parallel actions don't meet the independent condition.

In the next subsections, we will develop our non-interleaving semantics.

4.1   Labeled Partial Order

In our semantic model we draw a distinction between events and actions. An event is an instance of action occurrence. A finite execution of a program is a partially ordered set of events. Different events in the set can be labeled by the same or different actions.

Formally, a labeled partial order (LPO) is a 4-tuple $m = (V, V_S, \leq, \alpha)$, consisting of

(1) a finite set V of events including *system* events and *environment* ones.
(2) a set of *system* events $V_S \subseteq V$. Obviously, $V \backslash V_S$ is the set of the *environment* events V_E.
(3) a reflexive partial order (PO) $\leq$ over V ($<$ is the corresponding irreflexive partial order). We say e precedes f (or f succeeds e) if $e \leq f$, and we say e and f are incomparable if neither $e \leq f$ nor $f \leq e$.
(4) a labeling function $\alpha : V \to (\mathbb{S} \rightharpoonup \mathbb{S})$ assigning actions to events.

Label-Isomorphism: The LPO $m = (V, V_S, \leq, \alpha)$ and $m' = (V', V_S', \leq', \alpha')$ are label-isomorphic iff there exists a bijection $\Psi : V \leftrightarrow V'$ satisfies the properties below:

(1) $\Psi \lceil_{V_S}$ is a *bijection* from V_S to V_S'.
(2) $\forall e_1, e_2 \in V \cdot ((e_1, e_2) \in \leq \;\Rightarrow\; (\Psi(e_1), \Psi(e_2)) \in \leq')$.
(3) $\forall e \in V \cdot \alpha(e) = \alpha'(\Psi(e))$.

A *pomset* denoted $[V, V_S, \leq, \alpha]$ is the labeled-isomorphism class of the LPO $(V_S, V_E, \leq, \alpha)$. By taking LPOs up to labeled-isomorphism, we concentrate on the actions and internal structure of the LPO other than the events.

Some events in partial order (PO) $V^{\leq}$ may have no strict predecessors, while some may have no strict successors. We denote the set of the formers as $Min(V^{\leq})$ while the set of the latters as $Max(V^{\leq})$.

A *linearization* ll of PO $V^{\leq}$ is a total order over V that is an extension of $\leq$. The set of linearizations of $V^{\leq}$ is denoted $Lin(V^{\leq})$. Each $ll \in Lin(V^{\leq})$ can be alternatively represented as a sequence (over V) and ll_i, for $1 \leq i \leq |V|$, is used to denote the i-th event in the sequence.

A subset Δ of $V^{\leq}$ is a *prefix* of $V^{\leq}$ iff it is downwards-closed w.r.t. $\leq$. The projection of $m = (V, V_S, \leq, \alpha)$ onto a subset Δ of V gives rise to another LPO $m \lceil_{\Delta} = (\Delta \cap V, \Delta \cap V_S, \leq \cap (\Delta \times \Delta), \alpha \triangleright \Delta)$ where $\alpha \triangleright \Delta$ stands for the domain restriction of the function α onto Δ.

4.2 Pomset Transition Traces

The purpose of this subsection is to define the counterpart of transition traces in non-interleaving settings.

In our semantic model LPOs denote *complete* executions of a program. An execution is complete if it starts from *the initialisation state* $0_S \in S$ and ends in (successful) termination. Note that our semantics is geared towards partial correctness. Infinite executions, i.e., non-termination, should be discarded similarly as deadlock executions.

An LPO $m = (V, V_S, \leq, \alpha)$ is *executable*, or is an eLPO, iff for all $ll \in Lin(V^{\leq})$, ll is executable. A linearization ll of m is executable iff there exists a (unique) sequential execution trace[3], $s_0 \xrightarrow{a_1} s_1 \xrightarrow{a_2} s_2 \dots s_{|V|-1} \xrightarrow{a_{|V|}} s_{|V|}$ such that $s_0 = 0_S$, $a_i = \alpha(ll_i)$ and $(s_{i-1}, s_i) \in a_i$ for $1 \leq i \leq |V|$. The state $s_{|V|}$ is called the *terminating state* of ll.

Given any $e \in V$, $^{\bullet}e_{ll}$ is used to denote the *pre-state* of e in ll, i.e., $^{\bullet}e_{ll} = s_{i-1}$ for $e = ll_i$ and $e_{ll}^{\bullet}$ used to denote the *post-state* of e in ll, i.e., $e_{ll}^{\bullet} = s_i$ for $e = ll_i$. If $sl = ll \upharpoonright_{V_S}$, then we say $tt(sl) = (^{\bullet}e_{sl_1}, e_{sl_1}^{\bullet})(^{\bullet}e_{sl_2}, e_{sl_2}^{\bullet})\dots(^{\bullet}e_{sl_n}, e_{sl_n}^{\bullet})$, is the transition trace and $ltt(sl) = (^{\bullet}e_{sl_1}, e_{sl_1}, e_{sl_1}^{\bullet})(^{\bullet}e_{sl_2}, e_{sl_2}, e_{sl_2}^{\bullet})\dots(^{\bullet}e_{sl_n}, e_{sl_n}, e_{sl_n}^{\bullet})$, is the labeled transition trace induced by ll respectively, where $n = |V_S|$.

Thus the set of transition traces induced by an eLPO m is, $TT(m) = \{tt(sl)|sl = ll \upharpoonright_{V_S} \wedge ll \in Lin(V^{\leq})\}$. Similarly the set of labeled transition traces induced by an eLPO m is, $LTT(m) = \{ltt(sl)|sl = ll \upharpoonright_{V_S} \wedge ll \in Lin(V^{\leq})\}$.

Given an eLPO $(V, V_S, \leq, \alpha)$, the *pre-state set* of $e \in V$ is defined to be $^{\bullet}e = \{^{\bullet}e_{ll}|ll \in Lin(V^{\leq})\}$ and the *post-state set* is $e^{\bullet} = \{e_{ll}^{\bullet}|ll \in Lin(V^{\leq})\}$.

Definition 4.1. An eLPO $(V, V_S, \leq, \alpha)$ is *well-connected* iff for all $e \in V$, we have $dom(\alpha(e)) = {}^{\bullet}e$.

Definition 4.2. An eLPO $(V, V_S, \leq, \alpha)$ is *consistent* iff for all prefix $V_0^{\leq}$ of $V^{\leq}$, all the linearisations of $V_0^{\leq}$ terminate in the same state.

Finally, we say an eLPO m is *well-formed* iff m is consistent and well-connected. All the above definition can be lifted onto pomsets.

Pomset transition trace: A pomset $[V, V_S, \leq, \alpha]$ is a pomset transition trace, or simply a pomset trace, iff $(V, V_S, \leq, \alpha)$ is a consistent and well-connected eLPO with $V_S \neq \{\}$.

4.3 Semantics of Parallel Programs

In our semantics program P is identified with a set of extended traces. An extended trace is a pomset trace augmented with a pair of local state, i.e., (l, t, l'). It is a combination of trace and state-transition semantics: t is the pomset trace part on the shared states while (l, l') is the state-transformation part on the thread-local states.

---

[3] Execution traces are called *behaviours* in [1].

Thus the semantics of program P is a set of extended traces: $\mathcal{P}[\![P]\!] = \{(l, [V, V_S, \leq, \alpha], l') \mid ...\}$. The equivalence of two programs is the equality of their extended trace sets. We define a refinement relation on concurrent programs. Program P refines program Q if the extended trace set of P is a subset of Q's, i.e., $Q \sqsubseteq P$ iff $\mathcal{P}[\![P]\!] \subseteq \mathcal{P}[\![Q]\!]$.

Given a trace $(l, [V, V_S, \leq, \alpha], l')$ of program P, it denotes a possible execution of P with the cooperation of a suitable environment E. The set of system events V_S arising from the execution of commands in P depends crucially on that E supplies a suitable $V_E\ (= V - V_S)$ supporting V_S.

Given V_S there are an infinite number of V_Es that provide the same type of support. The semantics of P quantifies over all such environments. V_S is combined with each of the possible V_Es to form a pomset trace. The resultant subset of traces denotes an *abstract trace* (AT) of P, characterising one type of V_S with one type of ordering constraint and assuming one type of support from E. The formal definition of abstract traces is based on *AT-refinement*.

AT-Refinement: Given a pair of pomset traces $t = [em]$ and $t' = [em']$, where $em = (V, V_S, \leq, \alpha)$ and $em' = (V', V_S, \leq', \alpha')$, we say t' is an AT-refinement of t, or $t' \lesssim t$ iff $LTT(em') \subseteq LTT(em)$.

The extended trace set of programs in our semantics satisfies the two properties:

AT-Refinement Closure: The extended trace set of a program P is closed under AT-refinement: $(l, t, l') \in \mathcal{P}[\![P]\!] \wedge t' \lesssim t \implies (l, t', l') \in \mathcal{P}[\![P]\!]$.

S-Stutter Addition (SSA) Closure: The extended trace set of a program P is closed under system stutter addition. That is, given any pomset trace $t = [m]$ with $m = (V, V_S, \leq, \alpha)$ and $\Delta \subset V_S$ such that $\forall e \in \Delta \cdot \alpha(e) \subseteq \mathcal{A}[\![Skip]\!]$, we have $(l, [m \upharpoonright_{V \setminus \Delta}], l') \in \mathcal{P}[\![P]\!] \implies (l, t, l') \in \mathcal{P}[\![P]\!]$.

The AT-refinement closure property can be established by the structural induction on the *Com*. Given an extended trace set T, $T^{\ddagger}$ denotes the SSA closure of T. We say a set of extended pomsets is closed if the set is closed under AT-refinement and SSA. Let $\mathbb{P}$ denote the set of the closed set of the extended pomsets, ordered by inclusion. Obviously $(\mathbb{P}, \subseteq)$ forms a partially ordered space with least element the empty set.

$$\mathcal{P}[\![Skip]\!] =_{df} \{(l, [V, \{e\}, \leq, \alpha], l) \mid \alpha(e) \subseteq \mathcal{A}[\![Skip]\!]\}^{\ddagger}$$

$$\mathcal{P}[\![Stop]\!] =_{df} \emptyset$$

Program *Skip* generates and situates a system event e inside an environment V_E. e is a stutter restricted to a sub-domain, $dom(\alpha(e))$. The sub-domain defines the set of states on which e can be enabled within V_E. Program *Stop* generates only deadlock executions. So its semantics is an empty set of traces.

$$\mathcal{P}[\![x := E]\!] =_{df} \{(l, [V, \{e\}, \leq, \alpha], l) \mid \alpha(e) \subseteq \mathcal{A}[\![x := E(l)]\!]\}^{\ddagger}$$

$$\mathcal{P}[\![I := E]\!] =_{df} \{(l, [V, \{e\}, \leq, \alpha], l') \mid \alpha(e) \subseteq \mathcal{A}[\![Skip]\!] \wedge l' = [l|I = E(l)]\}^{\ddagger}$$

$$\mathcal{P}[\![I := x]\!] =_{df} \{(l, [V, \{e\}, \leq, \alpha], l') \mid \alpha(e) \subseteq \mathcal{A}[\![Skip]\!] \wedge \\ \{s(x)|s \in {}^{\bullet}e\} = \{v\} \wedge l' = [l|I = v]\}^{\ddagger}$$

Program $x := E$ and $I := E$ are assignments to shared and thread-local variables respectively while program $I := x$ reads from a shared variable. The event e generated by $I := x$ is a stutter. Still e may potentially be involved in conflict with other actions that modify x. To remove the potential conflicts, the domain of $\alpha(e)$ is restricted to a set of states across which x holds a consistent value.

$$\mathcal{P}[\![Let\ I := E\ in\ P]\!] =_{df} \{(l, t, l') \mid (l, t, l'') \in \mathcal{P}[\![I := E; P]\!] \wedge \\ l' = [l''|I = l(I)]\}$$

Variable localisation first creates a new copy of the variable, then initialises and feeds it to the fragment of program (i.e. P) which is its scope, and finally (upon the exit from P) reinstates the original copy of the variable.

$$\mathcal{P}[\![If\ B\ then\ P\ else\ Q]\!] =_{df} \{(l, t, l') \mid B(l) \wedge (l, t, l') \in \mathcal{P}[\![P]\!] \vee \\ \neg B(l) \wedge (l, t, l') \in \mathcal{P}[\![Q]\!]\}$$

Program $\langle b \to P \rangle$ is executed in one big indivisible step, giving rise to the system event e. e can transform a global state (l, s) to another one (l', s') iff (l, s) satisfies b and P can be collapsed into a single action transforming (l, s) to (l', s').

$$\mathcal{P}[\![\langle b \to SP \rangle]\!] =_{df} \{(l, [V, \{e\}, \leq, \alpha], l')|\alpha(e) \subseteq \mathcal{A}[\![\langle b \to SP \rangle_l]\!] \wedge \\ l' \in \{l'|\forall(s, s') \in \alpha(e), (s, l, s', l') \in [\![SP]\!]\} \wedge \forall s \in {}^{\bullet}e \cdot b(s, l)\}^{\ddagger}$$

There are two composition operators in our language: sequential and parallel compositions. In our semantics composition is interpreted as conjunction (after throwing out the system/enviroment event distinction in traces): (l, t, l') is a trace of a composition iff it is a trace of each of its components.

$$\mathcal{P}[\![P\|Q]\!] =_{df} \mathcal{P}[\![P]\!]\|\mathcal{P}[\![Q]\!]$$

Where $T_1\|T_2 =_{df} \{(l, [V, V_S, \leq, \alpha], l') \mid (l, [V, V_S^1, \leq, \alpha], l_1) \in T_1 \wedge \\ (l, [V, V_S^2, \leq, \alpha], l_2) \in T_2 \wedge V_S = V_S^1 \uplus V_S^2 \wedge l' \in \{l_1, l_2\}\}.$

$T_1\|T_2$ picks a pair of otherwise identical traces, one each from T_1 and T_2, with disjoint sets of system events, combines the sets of system events (by union), and produces a new trace in $T_1\|T_2$.

$T_1; T_2$ is a more constrained version of $T_1\|T_2$, in which the picked pairs of traces need to satisfy in addition the condition that one set of system events (for the trace from T_1) should be placed behind the other set of system events (for the trace from T_2) in the partial order.

$$\mathcal{P}[\![P; Q]\!] =_{df} \mathcal{P}[\![P]\!]; \mathcal{P}[\![Q]\!]$$

Where $T_1; T_2 =_{df} \{(l, [V, V_S, \leq, \alpha], l') \mid (l, [V, V_S^1, \leq, \alpha], l_0) \in T_1 \wedge$
$(l_0, [V, V_S^2, \leq, \alpha], l') \in T_2 \wedge V_S = V_S^1 \uplus V_S^2 \wedge (V_S^1 \times V_S^2) \subseteq \leq\}.$

It is straightforward to verify that all operators in our language are monotonic and continuous. Thus iteration can be as given a fixed-point semantics.

$$\mathcal{P}[\![While\ B\ do\ P]\!] =_{df} \mu T.(\{(l, t, l') \in \mathcal{P}[\![P]\!] \mid B(l)\}; T \cup$$
$$\{(l, t, l') \in \mathcal{P}[\![Skip]\!] \mid \neg B(l)\})$$

The semantics of $While\ B\ do\ P$ is the least fixed-point ordered by subsethood of trace sets, or the greatest fixpoint ordered by program refinement. An alternative definition of iteration is:

$$\mathcal{P}[\![While\ B\ do\ P]\!] = \bigcup_n \{(l, t, l') \in \mathcal{P}[\![P]\!] | B(l)\}^n; \{(l, t, l') \in \mathcal{P}[\![Skip]\!] \mid \neg B(l)\}$$

Where, $[\![P]\!]^n =_{df} [\![P]\!]; [\![P]\!]^{n-1}$. An operator F is monotonic if $F(P) \sqsupseteq F(Q)$ such that $P \sqsupseteq Q$. And an operator F is continuous if $F(\sqcap_n P_n) = \sqcap_n F(P_n)$ and $F(\sqcup_n P_n) = \sqcup_n F(P_n)$, where $\sqcap_n P_n = \cup_n [\![P_n]\!]$ and $\sqcup_n P_n = \cap_n [\![P_n]\!]$. The Kleene theorem ensures that the two definitions are equivalent.

Now, we instantiate the extended pomset semantics for $Q = \langle P \rangle \| \langle P \rangle$ where $P = (I := x; \ x := I + 1)$. The action semantics $\mathcal{A}[\![\langle P \rangle]\!]$ is $\{(s, s') | s' = [s | x = s(x) + 1]\}$.

The pomset semantics of $\langle P \rangle$ would be $\{(l, [V, \{e\}, \leq, \alpha], l') \mid \alpha(e) \subseteq \{(s, s') | s' = [s | x = s(x) + 1]\} \wedge l' = [l | I = s(x)]\}^{\ddagger}$. We therefore construct the semantics of program Q, i.e.,
$\mathcal{P}[\![Q]\!] = \{(l, [V, \{e_1, e_2\}, \leq, \alpha], l') \mid (l, [V, \{e_1\}, \leq, \alpha], l_1), (l, [V, \{e_2\}, \leq, \alpha], l_2) \in \mathcal{P}[\![\langle P \rangle]\!] \wedge l' \in \{l_1, l_2\}\}^{\ddagger}$.

Obviously, both $\alpha(e_1)$ and $\alpha(e_2)$ would be labeled by $\{(s, s') \mid s' = [s | x = s(x) + 1]\}$. No conflicts occur between events e_1 and e_2. It indicates the events e_1 and e_2 are independent.

5   Laws of Parallel Programs

We can utilize the extended pomset semantics to prove equations and inequations between concurrent programs. All programs about sequential operator constitute a monoid. The commands $Skip$ and $Stop$ are the corresponding *unit* and *zero* respectively. Moreover, All programs form a commutative monoid about concurrency. The *unit* and *zero* is the same as those in the sequential operator.

$$(P_1; P_2); P_3 = P_1; (P_2; P_3) \qquad\qquad (; -associativity)$$

$$Skip; P = P = P; Skip \qquad\qquad (; -unit)$$

$$Stop; P = Stop = P; Stop \qquad\qquad (;-zero)$$

$$P_1 \| P_2 = P_2 \| P_1 \qquad\qquad (\| - community)$$

$$(P_1 \| P_2) \| P_3 = P_1 \| (P_2 \| P_3) \qquad\qquad (\| - associativity)$$

$$Skip \| P = P = P \| Skip \qquad\qquad (\| - unit)$$

$$Stop \| P = Stop = P \| Stop \qquad\qquad (\| - zero)$$

Judging from the refinement relation, the statement $Stop$ would be the greatest element, i.e., $Stop \sqsupseteq P$. Deadlock ($Stop$ or $\langle False \rightarrow SP \rangle$) is regarded the same with divergence ($While\ True\ do\ Skip$) since both of the semantics are an empty set.

Here, We only prove the soundness of $\|$-associativity.

Proof: We define T_1, T_2, T_3 as the semantics for the program P_1, P_2, P_3 respectively. Assume that $(l, [V, V_S, \leq, \alpha], l')$ is an extended trace in $(T_1 \| T_2) \| T_3$.

There exists $(l, [V, V_S^{12}, \leq, \alpha], l_{12}) \in T_1 \| T_2$, $(l, [V, V_S^3, \leq, \alpha], l_3) \in T_3$, $V_S = V_S^{12} \uplus V_S^3$ and $l' \in \{l_{12}, l_3\}$.

As for $(l, [V, V_S^{12}, \leq, \alpha], l_{12})$, there exists $(l, [V, V_S^1, \leq, \alpha], l_1) \in T_1$, $(l, [V, V_S^2, \leq, \alpha], l_1) \in T_2$, $V_S^{12} = V_S^1 \uplus V_S^2$ and $l_{12} \in \{l_1, l_2\}$ based the same reason with above.

Obviously, the extended trace $(l, [V, V_S^{23}, \leq, \alpha], l_{23})$ with $V_S^{23} = V_S^2 \uplus V_S^3$ and $l_{23} \in \{l_2, l_3\}$ would be the element of $T_2 \| T_3$. Moreover, we can conclude that $(l, [V, V_S, \leq, \alpha], l')$ is an extended trace in $T_1 \| (T_2 \| T_3)$ since $V_S = V_S^{12} \uplus V_S^3 = V_S^1 \uplus V_S^2 \uplus V_S^3 = V_S^1 \uplus V_S^{23}$ and $l' \in \{l_1, l_2, l_3\}$. Thus $(T_1 \| T_2) \| T_3$ is the sub set of $T_1 \| (T_2 \| T_3)$. The reverse $T_1 \| (T_2 \| T_3) \subseteq (T_1 \| T_2) \| T_3$ is proved similarly. At last, we finish the proof $(P_1 \| P_2) \| P_3 = P_1 \| (P_2 \| P_3)$.   □

Other laws can also be easily validated. According to the definition of parallel compostition, the law $\| - community$ holds trivially. Taking advantage of the property $S - Stutter\ Addition\ Closure$, all involving $Skip$ could be established naturally. The laws $;-zero$ and $\| - zero$ holds obviously since the semantics of $Stop$ is an empty set of traces.

6 Discussion

Brookes presented the so-called transition trace semantics for a shared-variable parallel language in [6]. The semantic model is adaptive for different levels of granularity or atomicity. The coarse granularity model involving shared variables only assumes that all evaluations of expressions are atomic while the finer granularity model permits the evaluation of the expression step by step in virtue of the implicit thread-local variables and the expression evaluation is no longer atomic. Actually, the finer granularity model also deals with shared variables but the unfinished evaluated result should be stored in thread-local variables since the evaluation strategies are proceeding step by step. Brookes has not mentioned the thread-local variables but here we introduce thread-local variables explicitly to make evaluation atomic again. Accordingly, the expressiveness of our language is at least as powerful as the parallel language in [5]. The assignment command $x := e$ (the expression e involves shared variables) can be expressed in our language. The strategy is that we first read each of the shared variable in expression e and assign it to the thread-local variables respectively, then we compute the value of the expression (utilizing the fresh thread-local variables) and assign it to the shared variable x. For instance, the assignment command $x := x + y$ adopted by Brookes can be reformulated into the form $I := x; J := y; x := I + J$.

In this paper, we do not permit the *action collapsing*, i.e., a set of indivisible actions belonging to the same agent can collapse (or compose) into a big atomic action. It makes our semantic model more concrete than the version with action collapse. The similar concept *mumbling* was investigated by Brookes in [5], where the trace can be mumbling if its environment is interference-free. The conditions of action collapsing are more complicated in non-interleaving setting since our semantics model is based on pomsets. In partial order, a natural lifting of 'contiguity' is not adequate to guarantee the localness of an action collapsing: it is possible that a pair of previously incomparable actions become comparable after the action collapsing. Furthermore, in a sequence an action is enabled only on one state. So a degenerated partial function, a state pair, suffice for action. In a partial order, due to the existence of parallel actions, an action can be enabled on many states and thus requires the full power of partial functions. The action collapsing make the situation more complicated and gaining the semantics of the fresh action is difficult. Thus the version with action collapsing of our pomset model will be investigated in our next work.

7   Conclusion

We have developed Brookes' shared-variables parallel language and presented extended pomset semantics for our language. Not only shared variables but also thread-local variables are allowed in our framework. The introduction of thread-local variables does enhance the expressiveness of our langauge and make it more feasible.

This paper explored the true concurrent model for our shared variable parallel language. The semantics of actions are defined and the condition of independent actions is researched in our framework. The pomsets lift transition traces to the non-interleaving settings and the extended pomset semantics of parallel program is given. Furthermore, the extended pomset fulfill the AT-Refinement closure and S-Stutter Addition closure property. Almost all the classic laws of parallel language suffice but the mumbling property is not included.

In the future, we will allow that some system events collapse into a big action if the environment is interference-free. We also plan to apply this framework to characterize the various memory model [4,7] for multi-core computer. To reason about shared-variable parallel programs, future work includes adjusting separation logic [9,10,11] to our semantics model.

Acknowledgement. This work is supported in part by the Macao Science and Technology Development Fund under the PEARL project(No. 041/2007/A3), National Basic Research Program of China (No. 2005CB321904), National High Technology Research and Development Program of China (No. 2007AA010302) and National Natural Science Foundation of China (No. 90718004).

References

1. Abadi, M., Plotkin, G.: A Logical View of Composition. Theoretical Computer Science 114, 1 (1993)
2. Gischer, J.: Partial Orders and the Axiomatic Theory of shuffle, Ph.D. Thesis, Computer Science Dept., Stanford University (December 1984)
3. Pratt, V.R.: Modeling concurrency with partial orders. Int. J. of Parallel Programming 15(1), 33–71 (1986)
4. Adve, S.V.: Designing Memory Consistency Models for Shared-Memory Multiprocessors. PhD thesis, Computer Sciences Department, University of Wisconsin-Madison (December 1993), Available as Technical Report #1198
5. Brookes, S.: Full abstraction for a shared variable parallel language. In: Proc., 8th Annual IEEE Symposium on Logic in Computer Science. IEEE Comput. Soc. Press, Los Alamitos (1993)
6. Brookes, S.D.: Full Abstraction for a Shared-Variable Parallel Language. Inf. Comput. 127(2), 145–163 (1996)
7. Adve, S.V., Gharachorloo, K.: Shared memory consistency models: A tutorial. IEEE Computer 29(12), 66–76 (1996)
8. Brookes, S.D.: Traces, Pomsets, Fairness and Full Abstraction for Communicating Processes. In: Brim, L., Jančar, P., Křetínský, M., Kucera, A. (eds.) CONCUR 2002. LNCS, vol. 2421, pp. 466–482. Springer, Heidelberg (2002)
9. Reynolds, J.C.: Separation Logic: A Logic for Shared Mutable Data Structures. In: LICS 2002, pp. 55–74 (2002)
10. Brookes, S.D.: A Semantics for Concurrent Separation Logic. In: Gardner, P., Yoshida, N. (eds.) CONCUR 2004. LNCS, vol. 3170, pp. 16–34. Springer, Heidelberg (2004)
11. O'Hearn, P.W.: Resources, concurrency, and local reasoning. Theor. Comput. Sci. 375(1-3), 271–307 (2007)
12. Gastin, P., Teodosiu, D.: Resource traces: a domain for processes sharing exclusive resources. Theor. Comput. Sci. 278(1-2), 195–221 (2002)
13. Mazurkiewicz, A.: Trace theory. In: Brauer, W., Reisig, W., Rozenberg, G. (eds.) APN 1986. LNCS, vol. 255, pp. 279–324. Springer, Heidelberg (1987)
14. Katz, S., Peled, D.: Defining conditional independence using collapses. Theoretical Computer Science 101, 337–359 (1992); a preliminary version appeared in BCS-FACS Workshop on Semantics for Concurrency, Leicester, England, pp. 262–280. Springer, Heidelberg (July 1990)
15. Flanagan, C., Godefroid, P.: Dynamic Partial-Order Reduction for Model Checking Software. In: Proceedings of POPL 2005 (32nd ACM symposium on Principles of Programming Languages), Long beach (January 2005)
16. Yi, X., Wang, J., Yang, X.: Stateful dynamic partial-order reduction. In: Liu, Z., He, J. (eds.) ICFEM 2006. LNCS, vol. 4260, pp. 149–167. Springer, Heidelberg (2006)

Generating Denotational Semantics from Algebraic Semantics for Event-Driven System-Level Language

Huibiao Zhu, Fan Yang, and Jifeng He

Shanghai Key Laboratory of Trustworthy Computing
Software Engineering Institute, East China Normal University
3663 Zhongshan Road (North), Shanghai, China, 200062
{hbzhu,fanyang,jifeng}@sei.ecnu.edu.cn

Abstract. As a system-level modelling language, SystemC possesses several novel features such as delayed notifications, notification cancelling, notification overriding and delta-cycle. We have explored the denotational semantics [15] for SystemC using *Unifying Theories of Programming* (abbreviated as UTP) [6], where algebraic laws can be achieved based on the denotational model.

In this paper, we consider the inverse work; i.e., generating the denotational semantics from algebraic semantics for SystemC. A complete set of algebraic laws is explored. The concept of head normal from is applied in supporting the calculation. We also explore the simulation of algebraic laws and head normal form. Based on this, the mechanical derivation of denotational semantics from algebraic semantics is also studied.

1 Introduction

SystemC is a system-level modelling language, which can be used to model a system at different abstract levels. Modelling and simulation in SystemC gives the designers early insights about the potential design problems that could arise. Compared with traditional hardware description languages, SystemC possesses several new and interesting features, including delayed notifications, notification cancelling, notification overriding and delta-cycle.

In SystemC, processes can trigger events actively while in Verilog [7] events are generated based on the changes of states. In SystemC, events represent some general condition during the execution of the program. An event can be notified on many separate occasions. There are three kinds of event notifications: immediate event notifications, delta-cycle delayed notifications and timed notifications. Delayed notifications can be cancelled via cancel statements before they are triggered. Delayed notifications on the same event override each other and only one delayed notification survives.

Although SystemC comes with a user manual ([9,10]), a formal semantics of SystemC is mandatory for various applications in simulation, synthesis, and formal verification. Müller et al presented an ASM-based SystemC simulation

S. Qin (Ed.): UTP 2010, LNCS 6445, pp. 286–308, 2010.

semantics [13]. That semantics covers method, thread, and clocked thread behaviour as well as their interactions with the simulation kernel process. Gawanmeh et al extended the work in [13] to deal with more complex components of
SystemC [3]. Habibi and Tahar presented a semantics of the main part of SystemC in terms of fixed points [4]. We have also provided an operational semantics
for SystemC [12], where a set of algebraic laws has been explored via the concept
of bisimulation [8]. Meanwhile, we have also studied the denotational semantics
for SystemC using *Unifying Theories of Programming* (abbreviated as UTP) [6].
Algebraic laws [5] can also be achieved based on the denotational model.

This paper considers the inverse work; i.e., generating the denotational semantics from algebraic semantics for SystemC. With the introduction of the concept
of guarded choice, a complete set of parallel expansion laws is studied. In order
to index an instantaneous action to which exact component of a parallel process, the concept of location status (i.e., locality) is introduced. For the aim of
supporting the calculation of denotation semantics, we introduce the concept of
head normal form for each program. The simulation of algebraic laws and head
normal form is studied, which can mechanically support the calculation of head
normal form of programs. We provide the definition for deriving denotational semantics from algebraic semantics. The derived denotational semantics gives us
a way to reason about program properties easily. Based on the derivation strategy and the simulation of head normal form, the simulation of the derivation is
explored, which can mechanically calculate the derived denotation semantics.

The rest of this paper is organized as follows. In section 2 we select a kernel subset of SystemC and present an introduction for the language. We give
the concept of guarded choice with locality in this section. We also investigate
a complete set of parallel expansion laws and its simulation. Section 3 provides
the definition of head normal form for each statement. We also explore the simulation of head normal form. Section 4 focusses on the derivation of denotational
semantics from algebraic semantics. Our approach is based on the concept of
head normal form. We provide the derivation strategy for deriving denotational
semantics. The denotational semantics for programs can be calculated via strict
proof. The simulation of the derivation is explored as well. The simulation ap-
proached are proceeded in logic programming language Prolog [2]. Meanwhile,
we also investigate the derivation of denotational semantics for infinite programs
via approximation approach. Section 5 concludes the paper and presents some
possible future work.

2   Algebraic Laws for SystemC

2.1   The Syntax of SystemC

In this paper we select a kernel subset of SystemC for exploring its semantics. Although it is a subset of SystemC, it still covers the interesting and main features,
such as delay notifications, notification cancelling, notification overriding, channel, concurrent processes and delta-cycle. In this section, we present the syntax
of the selected subset and give a brief introduction of its interesting features.

For simplicity, we omit the syntactic elements for representing the architecture of a SystemC program. The subset language adopts a C-like syntax:

$$PP ::= P \mid PP \parallel PP$$
$$P ::= \textbf{Skip} \mid v := exp \mid chan\_stmt \mid event\_stmt \mid wait\_stmt$$
$$\mid P; P \mid \textbf{if } b \textbf{ then } P \textbf{ else } P \mid \textbf{while } b \textbf{ do } P$$
$$chan\_stmt ::= ch??v \mid ch!!exp$$
$$event\_stmt ::= notify(e_{\Delta 0}) \mid notify(e_{\Delta 1}) \mid notify(e_{\sharp T}) \mid cancel(e)$$
$$wait\_stmt ::= wait(\Delta 1) \mid wait(\sharp T) \mid wait(e\_list)$$
$$e\_list ::= single\_e \mid \textbf{or}_{i \in I}\{single\_e_i\}$$
$$single\_e ::= e \mid pe(ch) \mid ne(ch)$$

For statements such as **Skip**, assignment statement ($v := exp$), sequential composition ($P; Q$), conditional statement (**if** b **then** P **else** Q) and iteration statement (**while** b **do** P), their meanings are similar to the conventional programming language.

Channel output statement $ch!!exp$ is executed in evaluation phase, which generates a request to update the channel. These update requests will be carried out in the following update phase. Channel input statement $ch??v$ assigns the current value of channel ch to variable v.

An event is notified by statement $notify$. An event can be notified immediately (i.e., $notify(e_{\Delta 0})$) or after a period of time (i.e., $notify(e_{\Delta 1})$) or $notify(e_{\sharp T})$). Statement $cancel(e)$ cancels the delayed notifications on event e.

A process may wait for the arriving or firing of an event. These events can be classified into two types; i.e., single events or complex events. Single events can have three forms; i.e., e, $pe(ch)$ and $ne(ch)$, where event e can be generated by event notifications. $wait(pe(ch))$ is fired only when the current value of channel ch is greater than its previous value, whereas $wait(ne(ch))$ stands for the opposite firing case. Complex events can be of the form $\textbf{or}_{i \in I}\{single\_e_i\}$. For the waiting of complex events, if anyone is fired or becomes active, the whole waiting behaviour becomes fired or active.

Different from traditional hardware description language, time delay has two types; i.e., micro time advance and macro time advance. $wait(\Delta 1)$ stands for one unit micro time advancing, whereas $wait(\#T)$ stands for T units macro time advancing.

$P \parallel Q$ means P runs in parallel with Q. Their communication is through channels and variables. Further, their synchronization is based on events.

If there exist branch processes of a parallel process ready to run, one branch will be selected to be executed. The selection is nondeterministic. Channels will be updated when a waiting command is encountered during the current execution. If all branch processes are still waiting, then time will be advanced. Micro time (Delta-cycle) will be advanced first. If that does not activate any processes, then macro time will be advanced. The execution is proceeded by the following steps.

(1) Evaluation Phase. Select a ready process to execute. The order of the selection is nondeterministic. The selected process does its execution until a waiting command is encountered. This sequence of instantaneous commands form an atomic action, which is uninterrupted.

   The execution of a process may cause immediate event notifications to occur. It may also generate pending requests to update channels in the following update phase.

(2) Update Phase. Carry out all pending channel update requests generated in last evaluation phase, which may generate some events $pe(ch)$ or $ne(ch)$. Then go to step (1).

(3) Micro Time (Delta-cycle) Advancing Phase. If there are no processes ready to run and no pending channel update requests, but there exist pending delta-cycle notifications or delta-cycle timeouts, advance the delta-cycle. Then determine which processes are ready to run and go to step (1).

(4) Macro Time Advancing Phase. If there are no processes ready to run, no pending channel update requests, no pending delta-cycle notifications and no delta-cycle timeouts, advance the current macro time by one time unit. And determine which processes become ready to run due to events or timeouts that are triggered at the current time. If there exist processes ready to run, then go to step 1, otherwise advance the current macro time by one time unit again.

2.2   Location Status and Types of Guarded Choice

Example 2.1. Let $\ P = I \parallel J,\ \ I = A_1 \parallel A_2,\ \ J = A_3 \parallel A_4$, where $A_i = notify(e_{i\Delta 0})\ ;\ notify(f_{i\Delta 0})\ ;\ u_i := u_i + 1\ ;\ v_i := v_i + 2\ (i = 1, 2, 3, 4)$. Below is the graph that illustrates the structure of P.

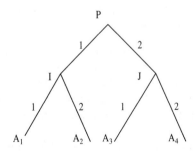

   The behaviour of A_i forms an atomic action. If $notify(e_{i\Delta 0})$ in A_1 is scheduled, A_i $(i = 2, 3, 4)$ cannot be scheduled until the completion of the execution of the statements in A_1. In order to support the parallel expansion laws, we introduce the concept of locality (i.e., location status). For example, if $notify(e_{i\Delta 0})$ is scheduled, we want the expansion laws to correctly indicate the next behaviour should be $notify(f_{1\Delta 0})$, i.e., all $notify(e_{i\Delta 0})$ $(i = 2, 3, 4)$ cannot be scheuled at this moment.

In order to solve this, now we assign a label for each edge. If it is the left edge, the label is 1, otherwise the label is 2. For every point, its thread sequence is the label sequence from the root of the tree to the considered point. This sequence can index the exact component an instantaneous is due to. For example, if the instantaneous action is due to process A_1, the thread sequence is $\langle 1 \rangle^\frown \langle 1 \rangle$. Further, if the instantaneous action is due to process A_2, the thread sequence is $\langle 1 \rangle^\frown \langle 2 \rangle$. □

Now we introduce the concept of location status for a program, which is one of the following two forms:

(1) *index*, which can be $\langle \rangle$ or a non-empty thread sequence.
(2) *null*, which indicates a process is at the state, where the atomic action completes its execution. Further, the environment can get the chance to perform its instantaneous action.

For the aim of linking the various semantics of SystemC, we introduce the concept of guarded choice. A guarded choice is composed of a set of guarded components. The introduction of guarded choice is to support the parallel expansion laws. Guarded choice can be formalized with location status (i.e, *tag*), which is defined as below.

Definition 2.2

(1) h (P, tag) is a guarded component if it can be one of the forms below. Here, b is a Boolean condition and *index* can be $\langle \rangle$ or a non-empty thread sequence.

$$V\ (P, index), \quad wait(e)\ (P, null), \quad \#1\ (P, null), \quad \Delta 1\ (P, null)$$

where, V can be one of the following forms:

$$b\&(x := e), \quad ch!!exp, \quad ch??v,$$

$$notify(e_{\Delta 0}), \quad notify(e_{\Delta 1}), \quad notify(e_{\Delta -1}), \quad notify(e_{\#T})$$

(2) $[\{h_1\ (P_1, tag_1), \ \ldots, \ h_n\ (P_n, tag_n)\}$ is a guarded choice if every element $h_i\ (P_i, tag_i)$ is a guarded component. □

In the above definition, guarded component V $(P, index)$ indicates that the instantaneous action V will be executed. After the execution, the subsequent program P will be at the location status *index*. For event waiting component (i.e., $wait(e)$ $(P, null)$) and delay guarded component ($\#1$ $(P, null)$, $\Delta 1$ $(P, null)$), after the firing of event guard or time elapsing, the subsequent behaviour should be the location status *null*.

Guarded choice can be divided into five types, which can be described as below.

(type-1) $[_{i \in I}\{b_i \& (x_i := e_i)\ (P_i, index_i)\}[_{j \in J}\{ch_j\ !!\ exp_j\ (Q_j, index_j)\}$
            $[_{k \in K}\{ch_k\ ??\ v_k\ (R_k, index_k)\}[_{l \in L}\{notify(e_{l_x})\ (T_l, index_l)\}$

(type-2) $[_{i \in I}\{wait(e_i)\ (P_i, null)\}$

(type-3)   (1) $[\{\Delta 1\ (P, null)\}$

            (2) $[\{\#1\ (P, null)\}$

(type-4) $\|_{i \in I}\{b_i \& (x_i := e_i) \ (P_i, index_i)\} \| \|_{j \in J}\{ch_j \ !! \ exp_j \ (Q_j, index_j)\}$

$\|_{k \in K}\{ch_k \ ?? \ v_k \ (R_k, index_k)\} \| \|_{l \in L}\{notify(e_{l_x}) \ (T_l, index_l)\}$

$\|_{m \in M}\{wait(e_m)(S_m, null)\}$

(type-5)   (1) $\|_{i \in I}\{wait(e_i) \ (P_i, null)\} \| \|\{\Delta 1 \ (Q, null)\}$

(2) $\|_{i \in I}\{wait(e_i) \ (P_i, null)\} \| \|\{\#1 \ (Q, null)\}$

The first type of guarded choice is composed of some instantaneous actions including assignment, channel output, channel input, and event notifications. The selection between them is nondeterministic. The second type is only composed of a set of event guard components. Assume that all the guard events are different from each other. It can be fired when the corresponding event happens. The third type has one delta-cycle time delay or one macro time delay component. The fourth type is composed of a set of instantaneous action components and a set of event guard components. The whole process waits for any of the event guards to be triggered and any of the instantaneous actions can also have chances to be scheduled. The fifth type of guarded choice is composed of a set of event guard components and a time delay component. The process waits for any of the event guards to be fired at the current time point. Time will elapse one delta-cycle time delay or one macro time delay when there are no more event guards to be triggered.

2.3   Algebraic Semantics

In this section we explore the algebraic laws for SystemC. We mainly focus on the parallel expansion laws. Our algebraic laws below are expressed in the form $(P, tag) = (Q, tag)$, indicating that program P and Q behave the same at the location status tag. For simplicity, $(P, tag) = (Q, tag)$ is also written $P =_{tag} Q$.

Firstly we define two functions $\mathbf{par}(P, Q)$ and $\mathbf{par1}(P, Q, i, index)$, which can reduce the number of parallel expansion laws by covering several cases at the same time.

$$\mathbf{par}(P, Q) =_{df} \begin{cases} (\varepsilon, \ null) & \text{if } P = \varepsilon \text{ and } Q = \varepsilon \\ (P \parallel Q, \ null) & \text{otherwise} \end{cases}$$

$$\mathbf{par1}(P, Q, i, index) =_{df} \begin{cases} (\varepsilon, \ null) & \text{if } P = \varepsilon \text{ and } Q = \varepsilon \\ (\varepsilon \parallel Q, \ null) & \text{if } P = \varepsilon \text{ and } Q \neq \varepsilon \text{ and } i = 1 \\ (P \parallel \varepsilon, \ null) & \text{if } P \neq \varepsilon \text{ and } Q = \varepsilon \text{ and } i = 2 \\ (P \parallel Q, \langle 1 \rangle ^\frown index) & \text{if } P \neq \varepsilon \text{ and } i = 1 \\ (P \parallel Q, \langle 2 \rangle ^\frown index) & \text{if } Q \neq \varepsilon \text{ and } i = 2 \end{cases}$$

In the following algebraic laws, U_i and V_j stand for the instantaneous actions. The notation (par-i-j) stands for the parallel expansion laws whose two parallel components are of type i and type j. The first five laws stand for the case that the first component of a parallel process is of type one.

(par-1-1)   Let $P =_{null} \|_{i \in I}\{U_i \ (P_i, index_i)\}$ and $Q =_{null} \|_{j \in J}\{V_j \ (Q_i, index_j)\}$

Then $P \parallel Q$

$=_{null} \|_{i \in I}\{U_i \ \mathbf{par1}(P_i, Q, 1, index_i)\} \| \|_{j \in J}\{V_j \ \mathbf{par1}(P, Q_j, 2, index_j)\}$

(par-1-2) Let $P =_{null} \|_{i \in I}\{U_i\ (P_i, index_i)\}$ and $Q =_{null} \|_{j \in J}\{wait(e_j)\ (Q_j, null)\}$

       Then $P \parallel Q$

       $=_{null} \|_{i \in I}\{U_i\ \mathbf{par1}(P_i, Q, 1, index_i)\}\|\|_{j \in J}\{wait(e_j)\ \mathbf{par}(P, Q_j)\}$

(par-1-3) Let $P =_{null} \|_{i \in I}\{U_i\ (P_i, index_i)\}$ and $Q =_{null} \|\{t\ (R, null)\}$

       Then $P \parallel Q =_{null} \|_{i \in I}\{U_i\ \mathbf{par1}(P_i, Q, 1, index_i)\}$

(par-1-4) Let $P =_{null} \|_{i \in I}\{U_i\ (P_i, index_i)\}$ and

         $Q =_{null} \|_{j \in J}\{V_j\ (Q_j, index_j)\}\|\|_{k \in K}\{wait(e_k)\ (R_k, null)\}$

       Then $P \parallel Q$

       $=_{null} \|_{i \in I}\{U_i\ \mathbf{par1}(P_i, Q, 1, index_i)\}\|\|_{j \in J}\{V_j\ \mathbf{par1}(P, Q_j, 2, index_j)\}$

         $\|\|_{k \in K}\{wait(e_k)\ \mathbf{par}(P, R_k)\}$

(par-1-5) Let $P =_{null} \|_{i \in I}\{U_i\ (P_i, index_i)\}$ and

         $Q =_{null} \|_{j \in J}\{wait(e_j)\ (Q_j, null)\}\|\|\{t\ (R, null)\}$

       Then $P \parallel Q$

       $=_{null} \|_{i \in I}\{U_i\ \mathbf{par1}(P_i, Q, 1, index_i)\}\|\|_{j \in J}\{wait(e_j)\ \mathbf{par}(P, Q_j)\}$

The next four laws stand for the case that the first component of a parallel process is of type two.

(par-2-2) Let $P =_{null} \|_{i \in I}\{wait(e_i)\ (P_i, null)\}$ and $Q =_{null} \|_{j \in J}\{wait(f_j)\ (Q_j, null)\}$

Let $E = \{e_i | i \in I\}$, $F = \{f_j | j \in J\}$, $I' = \{i \mid e_i \in E \wedge e_i \notin F\}$,

   $J' = \{j \mid f_j \in F \wedge f_j \notin E\}$, $IJ = \{(i,j) \mid i \in I \wedge j \in J \wedge e_i \in E \wedge f_j \in F \wedge e_i = f_j\}$

   Then $P \parallel Q$

 $=_{null} \|_{i \in I'}\{wait(e_i)\ \mathbf{par}(P_i, Q)\}\|\|_{j \in J'}\{wait(f_j)\ \mathbf{par}(P, Q_j)\}$

     $\|\|_{(i,j) \in IJ}\{wait(e_i)\ \mathbf{par}(P_i, Q_j)\}$

(par-2-3) Let $P =_{null} \|_{i \in I}\{wait(e_i)\ (P_i, null)\}$ and $Q =_{null} \|\{t\ (R, null)\}$

       Then $P \parallel Q =_{null} \|_{i \in I}\{wait(e_i)\ \mathbf{par}(P_i, Q)\}\|\|\{t\ \mathbf{par}(P, R)\}$

(par-2-4) Let $P =_{null} \|_{i \in I}\{wait(e_i)\ (P_i, null)\}$ and

         $Q =_{null} \|_{j \in J}\{V_j\ (Q_j, index_j)\}\|\|_{k \in K}\{wait(f_k)\ (R_k, null)\}$

       Then $P \parallel Q$

       $=_{null} \|_{j \in J}\{V_j\ \mathbf{par1}(P, Q_j, 2, index_j)\}\|\|_{i \in I'}\{wait(e_i)\ \mathbf{par}(P_i, Q)\}$

         $\|\|_{k \in K'}\{wait(f_k)\ \mathbf{par}(P, R_k)\}\|\|_{(i,k) \in IK}\{wait(e_i)\ \mathbf{par}(P_i, R_k)\}$

(par-2-5) Let $P =_{null} \|_{i \in I}\{wait(e_i)\ (P_i, null)\}$ and

         $Q =_{null} \|_{j \in J}\{wait(f_j)\ (Q_j, null)\}\|\|\{t\ (R, null)\}$

       Then $P \parallel Q$

       $=_{null} \|_{i \in I'}\{wait(e_i)\ \mathbf{par}(P_i, Q)\}\|\|_{j \in J'}\{wait(f_j)\ \mathbf{par}(P, Q_j)\}$

         $\|\|_{(i,j) \in IJ}\{wait(e_i)\ \mathbf{par}(P_i, Q_j)\}\|\|\{t\ \mathbf{par}(P, R)\}$

The next five laws stands for the case that one component of a parallel process is time delay. The first three laws represents the parallel composition of various time forms.

(par-3-3-1) Let $P =_{null}$ $[\{\Delta 1\ (R, null)\}$ and $Q =_{null}$ $[\{\Delta 1\ (S, null)\}$

Then $P \parallel Q =_{null}$ $[\{\Delta 1\ \mathbf{par}(R, S)\}$

(par-3-3-2) Let $P =_{null}$ $[\{\Delta 1\ (R, null)\}$ and $Q =_{null}$ $[\{\#1\ (S, null)\}$

Then $P \parallel Q =_{null}$ $[\{\Delta 1\ \mathbf{par}(R, Q)\}$

(par-3-3-3) Let $P =_{null}$ $[\{\#1\ (R, null)\}$ and $Q =_{null}$ $[\{\#1\ (S, null)\}$

Then $P \parallel Q =_{null}$ $[\{\#1\ \mathbf{par}(R, S)\}$

(par-3-4) Let $P =_{null}$ $[\{t\ (R, null)\}$ and

$Q =_{null}$ $[_{i \in I}\{V_i\ (Q_i, index_i)\}[\!\![_{j \in J}\{wait(e_j)\ (R_j, null)\}$

Then $P \parallel Q$

$=_{null}$ $[_{i \in I}\{V_i\ \mathbf{par1}\ (P, Q_i, 2, index_i)\}[\{[_{j \in J}\{wait(e_j)\ \mathbf{par}\ (P, R_j)\}$

(par-3-5) Let $P =_{null}$ $[\{t\ (R, null)\}$ and

$Q =_{null}$ $[_{j \in J}\{wait(e_j)\ (Q_j, null)\}[\!\![\{t_S\ (S, null)\}$

Then $P \parallel Q =_{null}$ $[_{j \in J}\{wait(e_j)\ \mathbf{par}\ (P, Q_j)\}[\mathbf{par2}(P, Q2)$

In the above laws, $P2$ and $Q2$ stand for the second guarded choice of P and Q respectively. Function $\mathbf{par2}(P2, Q2)$ can be defined as below.

Let $P2 =_{null}$ $[\{t_1\ (P', null)\}$ and $Q2 =_{null}$ $[\{t_2\ (Q', null)\}$

Then

$$\mathbf{par2}(P2, Q2) =_{df} \begin{cases} [\{t_1\ \mathbf{par}(P', Q')\} & \text{if } t_1 = t_2 = \Delta 1 \ \vee\ t_1 = t_2 = \#1 \\ [\{t_1\ \mathbf{par}(P', Q)\} & \text{if } t_1 = \Delta 1 \ \wedge\ t_2 = \#1 \\ [\{t_2\ \mathbf{par}(P, Q')\} & \text{if } t_1 = \#1 \ \wedge\ t_2 = \Delta 1 \end{cases}$$

The next two laws stand for the case that one component of a parallel process belongs to the form of type four.

(par-4-4) Let $P =_{null}$ $[_{i \in I}\{U_i\ (P_i, index_i)\}[\!\![_{j \in J}\{wait(e_j)\ (R_j, null)\}$

$Q =_{null}$ $[_{k \in K}\{V_k\ (Q_k, index_k)\}[\!\![_{l \in L}\{wait(f_l)\ (R_l, null)\}$

Then $P \parallel Q$

$=_{null}$ $[_{i \in I}\{U_i\ \mathbf{par1}\ (P_i, Q, 1, index_i)\}[\!\![_{j \in J'}\{wait(e_j)\ \mathbf{par}\ (R_j, Q)\}$

$[\!\![_{k \in K}\{V_j\ \mathbf{par1}\ (R, Q_k, 2, index_k)\}[\!\![_{l \in L'}\{wait(e_l)\ \mathbf{par}\ (P, R_l)\}$

$[\!\![_{(j,l) \in JL}\{wait(e_j)\ \mathbf{par}\ (P_j, R_l)\}$

(par-4-5) Let $P =_{null}$ $[_{i \in I}\{U_i\ (P_i, index_i)\}[\!\![_{j \in J}\{wait(e_j)\ (R_j, null)\}$

$Q =_{null}$ $[_{k \in K}\{wait(f_k)\ (Q_k, null)\}[\!\![\{t\ (S, null)\}$

Then $P \parallel Q$

$=_{null}$ $\|_{i \in I}\{U_i \text{ } \textbf{par1} \text{ } (P_i, Q, 1, index_i)\}\|\|_{k \in K'}\{wait(f_k) \text{ } \textbf{par} \text{ } (P, Q_k)\}$

$\|_{j \in J'}\{wait(e_j) \text{ } \textbf{par} \text{ } (R_j, Q)\}\|\|_{(j,k) \in JK}\{wait(e_j) \text{ } \textbf{par} \text{ } (R_j, Q_k)\}$

The law below stands for the case that both of the two components of a parallel process belong to the form of type five.

(par-5-5) Let P $=_{null}$ $\|_{i \in I}\{wait(e_i) \text{ } (P_i, null)\}\|\|\{t_R \text{ } (R, null)\}$

Q $=_{null}$ $\|_{j \in J}\{wait(f_j) \text{ } (Q_j, null)\}\|\|\{t_S \text{ } (S, null)\}$

Then $P \parallel Q$

$=_{null}$ $\|_{i \in I}\{wait(e_i) \text{ } \textbf{par} \text{ } (P_i, Q)\}\|\|_{j \in J}\{wait(e_j) \text{ } \textbf{par} \text{ } (P, Q_j)\}$

$\|_{(i,j) \in IJ}\{wait(e_i) \text{ } \textbf{par} \text{ } (P_i, Q_j)\}\|\textbf{par2}(P2, Q2)$

Further, if one parallel part is at the state of the execution of an instantaneous action and another parallel part is of any form. Then the whole process continues the execute of the instantaneous action. The case is expressed in law (par-*II*).

(par-*II*)   Let P $=_{index}$ $\|\{U \text{ } (P', index)\}$

Then $P \parallel Q =_{(1)^\wedge index}$ $\|\{U \text{ } \textbf{par1}(P', Q, 1, index)\}$

$Q \parallel P =_{(2)^\wedge index}$ $\|\{U \text{ } \textbf{par1}(Q, P', 2, index)\}$

The following five laws stand for the case that one component of a process is empty. Another component can be of any forms.

(par-*III*-1)   Let P $=_{null}$ $\|_{i \in I}\{U_i \text{ } (P_i, \text{ } index_i)\}$

Then $P \parallel \varepsilon$ $=_{null}$ $\|_{i \in I}\{U_i \text{ } \textbf{par1}(P_i, \varepsilon, 1, \text{ } index_i)\}$

$\varepsilon \parallel P$ $=_{null}$ $\|_{i \in I}\{U_i \text{ } \textbf{par1}(\varepsilon, P_i, 2, \text{ } index_i)\}$

(par-*III*-2) Let P $=_{null}$ $\|_{i \in I}\{wait(e_i) \text{ } (P_i, \text{ } null)\}$

Then $P \parallel \varepsilon$ $=_{null}$ $\|_{i \in I}\{wait(e_i) \text{ } \textbf{par}(P_i, \varepsilon)\}$

$\varepsilon \parallel P$ $=_{null}$ $\|_{i \in I}\{wait(e_i) \text{ } \textbf{par}(\varepsilon, P_i)\}$

(par-*III*-3) Let P $=_{null}$ $\|\{t \text{ } (P', \text{ } null)\}$

Then $P \parallel \varepsilon$ $=_{null}$ $\|\{t \text{ } \textbf{par}(P', \varepsilon)\}$

$\varepsilon \parallel P$ $=_{null}$ $\|\{t \text{ } \textbf{par}(\varepsilon, P')\}$

(par-*III*-4) Let P $=_{null}$ $\|_{i \in I}\{U_i \text{ } (P_i, index_i)\}\|\|_{j \in J}\{wait(e_i) \text{ } (Q_j, null)\}$

Then $P \parallel \varepsilon$ $=_{null}$ $\|_{i \in I}\{U_i \text{ } \textbf{par1}(P_i, \varepsilon, 1, \text{ } index_i)\}$

$\|_{j \in J}\{wait(e_j) \text{ } \textbf{par}(Q_j, \varepsilon)\}$

$\varepsilon \parallel P$ $=_{null}$ $\|_{i \in I}\{U_i \text{ } \textbf{par1}(\varepsilon, P_i, 2, \text{ } index_i)\}$

$\|_{j \in J}\{wait(e_j) \text{ } \textbf{par}(\varepsilon, Q_j)\}$

(par-*III*-5) Let P $=_{null}$ $\|_{i \in I}\{wait(e_i) \text{ } (P_i, null)\} \| \{t \text{ } (Q, null)\}$

Then $P \parallel \varepsilon$ $=_{null}$ $\|_{i \in I}\{wait(e_i) \text{ } \textbf{par}(P_i, \varepsilon)\} \| \{t \text{ } \textbf{par}(Q, \varepsilon)\}$

$\varepsilon \parallel P$ $=_{null}$ $\|_{i \in I}\{wait(e_i) \text{ } \textbf{par}(\varepsilon, P_i)\} \| \{t \text{ } \textbf{par}(\varepsilon, Q)\}$

2.4   Animation of Algebraic Laws

As mentioned before, the two functions **par**(P, Q) and **par1**$(P, Q, i, index)$ are used to reduce the number of parallel expansion laws. In the animation program these two functions are defined as $par(P, Q, R)$ and $par1(P, Q, i, Index, R)$, where P and Q denote the two parallel programs while R denotes the result of the function. All the programs P, Q and R are represented as a list in Prolog. The ε program is represented as [ ]. *Index* is defined as a list composed by 1 and 2, or it is just *null*. Our animation is proceeded using Prolog.

$par([\,],[\,],[[\,], null]).$

$par(P, Q, [P \parallel Q, null]).$

$par1([\,],[\,], I, Index, [[\,], null]) :- idItem[I], indexs(Index).$

$par1([\,], Q, 1, Index, [[\,] \parallel Q, null]) :- Q\sim=[\,], hn(Q), indexs(Index).$

$par1(P, [\,], 2, Index, [P \parallel [\,], null]) :- P\sim=[\,], hn(P), indexs(Index).$

$par1(P, Q, 1, Index, [P \parallel Q, [1|Index]]) :- P\sim=[\,], hn(Q), indexs(Index).$

$par1(P, Q, 2, Index, [P \parallel Q, [2|Index]]) :- Q\sim=[\,], hn(P), indexs(Index).$

Here, hn defines the form of guarded choice. $hn1$ denotes the first type of guarded choice we defined in section 2. Similarly, $hn2$ and $hn3$ represents the second and third type of guarded choice respectively. The fourth and fifth type is composed by the first three forms, so we use the operator *or* to denote the composition relationship.

$hn1([[V \ \$ \ [P, Index]|Q], Tag]) :- inst(V), prog(P), hn1(Q),$
$\qquad\qquad\qquad\qquad\qquad\quad indexs(Index), tag(Tag).$

$hn2([[wait \ E \ \$ \ [P, null]|Q], Tag]) :- singleE(E), prog(P), hn2(Q), tag(Tag).$

$hn3([[delta \ 1 \ \$ \ [P, null]], Tag]) :- prog(P), tag(Tag).$

$hn3([[\#1 \ \$ \ [P, null]], Tag]) :- prog(P), tag(Tag).$

$hn(P) :- hn1(P).$

$hn(P) :- hn2(P).$

$hn(P) :- hn3(P).$

$hn(P \ or \ Q) :- hn1(P), hn2(Q).$

$hn(P \ or \ Q) :- hn2(P), hn3(Q).$

$hn(P \ or \ Q) :- hn2(P), hn1(Q).$

$hn(P \ or \ Q) :- hn3(P), hn2(Q).$

inst defines five forms of the instantaneous actions.

$inst(B \ \& \ (V = E)) :- bool(B), variable(V), expr(E).$

$inst(Ch \ !! \ V) :- variable(Ch), expr(V).$

$inst(Ch \ ?? \ V) :- variable(Ch), variable(V).$

$inst(notify \ Event \ \$ \ [delta \ T]) :- variable(Event), deltaT(T).$

$inst(notify \ Event \ \$ \ [\# \ T]) :- variable(Event), integer(T), T > 0.$

Now we are ready to consider the animation of parallel expansion laws. We will introduce the animation of par-1-1, par-2-2, par-3-3-2 and par-4-5. First, we consider the case that both of the two components of a parallel process are of type one (i.e., par1-1). Its animation can be described as below:

$parallel(P, Q, R) :- hn1(P),\ hn1(Q),\ par1\_L(P, Q, 1, R1),$
$$par1\_R(P, Q, 2, R2),\ append(R1, R2, R).$$

$par1\_L$ denotes the performance of the program when P (i.e., the parallel component on the left side) is performed. Similarly, $par1\_R$ denotes the case when the right one is performed.

$par1\_L([V\ \$\ [P1, Index1]|P], Q, I, R) :- par1(P1, Q, I, Index1, X),$
$$par1\_L(P, Q, I, R1),\ append([V\ \$\ X], R1, R).$$

Here, the parallel law $par1$ is applied recursively. $append(P, Q, R)$ concatenates list P and Q into list R.

Next we consider the animation of the case that both of the two components of a parallel process are in the form of type two, then its animation can be described as below:

$parallel(P,\ Q,\ R) :- hn2(P),\ hn2(Q),\ par2\_R(P,\ Q,\ R1),\ par2\_L(P,\ Q,\ R2),$
$$par2\_2(P,\ Q,\ R3),\ append(R1,\ R2,\ R3,\ R).$$

$par2\_2(P,\ Q,\ R)$ is used to generate the program components when the events belonging to the intersection of both of the two parallel components are fired. $par2\_R(P,\ Q,\ R)$ generates the program components when the events only in the right branch are fired. The analysis of $par2\_L(P,\ Q,\ R)$ is similar.

For the case that one of the parallel components is $\varDelta 1$ and the other is $\#1$, its animation is as below.

$parallel([delta\ 1\ \$\ [P,\ null]],\ [\#1\ \$\ [Q,\ null]],\ [delta\ 1\ \$\ R]) :- par(P,\ Q,\ R).$

If one of the parallel component is of type four which is the compound of type one and type two and the other is of type five which is the compound of type two and type three, its animation can be described as follows.

$parallel(P1\ or\ P2,\ Q1\ or\ Q2,\ R)$
$\quad :- hn1(P1),\ hn2(P2),\ hn2(Q1),\ hn3(Q2),\ par1\_L(P1,\ Q1\ or\ Q2,\ 1,\ R1),$
$$par2\_2(P1\ or\ P2,\ Q1\ or\ Q2,\ R2),\ append(R1,\ R2,\ R).$$

If one of the parallel component is the empty process ε, which is represented by [ ], and the other is in the form of type two, then the parallel rule is as follows:
$parallel([wait\ E\ \$\ [P,\ null]|Q],\ [\ ],\ R)$
$\quad :- hn2([wait\ E\ \$\ [P,\ null]|Q]),\ par(P,\ [\ ],\ R1),$
$$parallel(Q,\ [\ ],\ R2),\ append([wait\ E\ \$\ R1],\ R2, R).$$
$parallel([\ ], [wait\ E\ \$\ [P,\ null]|Q], R)$
$\quad :- hn2([wait\ E\ \$\ [P,\ null]|Q]),\ par([\ ],\ P,\ R1),$
$$parallel([\ ],\ Q,\ R2),\ append([wait\ E\ \$\ R1],\ R2,\ R).$$
For the animation of other parallel expansion laws, their explorations are similar.

3   Head Normal Form and Its Animation

3.1   Head Normal Form

Now we assign every program P a head normal form at location status tag, expressed in the form $HF((P, tag))$. Our consideration for deriving denotational semantics from algebraic semantics is based on the concept of head normal form.

(1) $HF((v := e, tag)) =_{df} (\, |\!|\{true\&(v := e) \, (\varepsilon, \langle\rangle)\}, tag \,)$

   $HF((\mathbf{Skip}, tag)) =_{df} (\, |\!|\{true\&(x := x) \, (\varepsilon, \langle\rangle)\} \, , tag \,)$

   where, $tag = null$ or $\langle\rangle$.

(2) $HF((X, tag)) =_{df} (\, |\!|\{X \, (\varepsilon, \langle\rangle)\} \, , tag \,)$

   where, $tag = null$ or $\langle\rangle$.

   X can be $ch??v$, $ch!!exp$, $notify(e_{\Delta 0})$, $notify(e_{\Delta 1}$, $notify(e_{\# T})$.

   $HF((cancel(e), tag)) =_{df} (\, |\!|\{notify(e_{\Delta -1}) \, (\varepsilon, \langle\rangle)\}, tag \,)$

(3) $HF((P \triangleleft b \triangleright Q, tag)) =_{df} (\, |\!|\{b\&x := x \, (P, \langle\rangle), \neg b\&x := x \, (Q, \langle\rangle)\}, tag \,)$

   $HF((b * P, tag)) =_{df} (\, |\!|\{b\&x := x \, (P \, ; \, b * P, \langle\rangle)\}, \neg b\&x := x \, (\varepsilon, \langle\rangle)\}, tag \,)$

(4) Assume $HF((P, tag)) = (\, |\!|_{i \in I}\{X_i \, (P_i, tag_i)\}, tag \,)$

   Then $HF((P; Q, tag)) =_{df} (\, |\!|_{i \in I}\{X_i \, (\mathbf{seq}(P_i, Q), tag_i)\}, tag \,)$

   where, $\mathbf{seq}(X, Y) =_{df} \begin{cases} Y & \text{if } X = \varepsilon \\ X; Y & \text{otherwise} \end{cases}$

(5) $HF((\Delta 1, tag)) =_{df} (\, |\!|\{\Delta 1 \, (\varepsilon, null)\}, tag \,)$

   $HF((\#1, tag)) =_{df} (\, |\!|\{\#1 \, (\varepsilon, null)\}, tag \,)$

   $HF((\#T, tag)) =_{df} (\, |\!|\{\#1 \, (\#(T - 1), null)\}, tag \,)$, where $T > 1$.

   $HF((wait(e), tag)) =_{df} (\, |\!|\{wait(e) \, (\varepsilon, null)\}, tag \,)$

(6) $HF((P \parallel Q, null)) =_{df} (T, null)$

   where, T is the result by applying the above parallel expansion laws of $HF((P, null))$ and $HF((Q, null))$ at the location status $null$.

   $HF((P \parallel Q, index)) =_{df} (T, index)$

   where, T is the result by applying the above parallel expansion laws at the location status $index$.

   Further, for some cases, $HF((P \parallel Q, index))$ cannot be calculated by using the above laws, we say it is undefined; i.e., $HF((P \parallel Q, index)) =_{df} undefined$.

The above head normal forms can be used in deriving the operational semantics from algebraic semantics for SystemC.

Example 3.1. Let $P_1 = v_1 := 1 \, ; \, ; notify(e_{2\Delta 1}); notify(e_{3\# 3})$,

$\qquad\qquad P_2 = v_2 := 2 \, ; \, notify(f_{2\Delta 1}); notify(f_{3\# 3})$,

$\qquad\qquad Q_1 = wait(e_2); wait(e_3), \quad Q_2 = wait(f_2); wait(f_3)$

Consider the head normal form for program P, where $(P_1 \parallel P_2) \parallel (Q_1 \parallel Q_2)$.

For program P, its head normal form can be described as:

$$HF((P, null))$$
$$= ([\![\{ v_1 := 1 \ ((P_{11} \parallel P_2) \parallel (Q_1 \parallel Q_2), \langle 1 \rangle \hat{} \langle 1 \rangle),$$
$$v_2 := 2 \ ((P_1 \parallel P_{21}) \parallel (Q_1 \parallel Q_2), \langle 1 \rangle \hat{} \langle 2 \rangle),$$
$$wait(e_2) \ ((P_1 \parallel P_2) \parallel (wait(e_3) \parallel Q_2), null),$$
$$wait(f_2) \ ((P_1 \parallel P_2) \parallel (Q_1 \parallel wait(f_3)), null) \}$$
$$, null)$$

where, $P_{11} = notify(e_{2\Delta 1}); notify(e_{3\#3})$, $P_{21} = notify(f_{2\Delta 1}); notify(f_{3\#3})$
Further,

$$HF(((P_{11} \parallel P_2) \parallel (Q_1 \parallel Q_2), \langle 1 \rangle \hat{} \langle 1 \rangle))$$
$$= ([\![\{ notify(e_{2\Delta 1}) \ ((notify(e_{3\#3}) \parallel P_2) \parallel (Q_1 \parallel Q_2), \langle 1 \rangle \hat{} \langle 1 \rangle)) \}, \quad \langle 1 \rangle \hat{} \langle 1 \rangle)$$
$$HF(((notify(e_{3\#3}) \parallel P_2) \parallel (Q_1 \parallel Q_2), \langle 1 \rangle \hat{} \langle 1 \rangle))$$
$$= ([\![\{ notify(e_{3\#3}), ((\varepsilon \parallel P_2) \parallel (Q_1 \parallel Q_2), \langle 1 \rangle \hat{} \langle 1 \rangle)) \}, \quad \langle 1 \rangle \hat{} \langle 1 \rangle)$$

The analysis of the head normal forms for other programs above are similar. □

3.2 Animation of Head Normal Form

Now we start to explore how to generate the head normal form for programs; i.e., the mechanical consideration of head normal form in Prolog. For program P, we use the rule below to generate its head normal form.

$$hf((P, Tag), \quad (T, Tag))$$

where, (T, Tag) stands for the head normal form of program P at the location status Tag.

For assignment $x := e$ at location status Tag, the generation of its head normal form can be described as below:

$$hf([V = E, Tag], [[true \ \& \ V = E \ \$ \ [[\ ], \ [\ ]]], \ Tag])$$
$$:- hn1([[[true \ \& \ V = E \ \$ \ [[\ ], \ [\ ]]], \ Tag]).$$

The whole clause means that the head normal form of $(v := e, Tag)$ is $[[true \ \& \ V = E \ \$ \ [[\ ], \ [\ ]]], \ Tag]$, which is a list containing two elements, (i.e., the program and its location status Tag). Also, we make sure that its head normal form is in the form of type one.

Conditional can also be expressed as the first type guarded choice composed of two assignment-guarded subcomponents. Iteration has similar structure.

$$hf([if \ EB \ \& \ P \ else \ Q, Tag], [[EB \ \& \ V = V \ \$ \ [P, [\ ]], \ EB \ \& \ V = V \ \$ \ [Q, \ [\ ]]], \ Tag])$$
$$:- hn1([[EB \ \& \ V = V \ \$ \ [P, \ [\ ]], [\ EB \ \& \ V = V \ \$ \ [Q, \ [\ ]]], \ Tag]).$$
$$hf([while \ \ EB \ \& \ P, \ Tag], [[EB \ \& \ V = V \ \$ \ [P; while EB \ \& \ P, [\ ]],$$
$$[\ EB \ \& \ V = V \ \$ \ [[\ ], [\ ]]]], \ Tag])$$
$$:- hn1([[EB \ \& \ V = V \ \$ \ [P; while \ \ EB \ \& \ P, [\ ]],$$
$$[\ EB \ \& \ V = V \ \$ \ [[\ ], [\ ]]]], \ Tag]).$$

Now we start to consider the calculation of the head normal form for sequential composition. For $P; Q$, we first translate program P to its head normal form and then distribute ; to each component of it. The distribution behaviour can be done by a function *seqs*.

$$hf([P; Q, \ Tag], \ R) :- hf(P, [[X \ \$ \ [P1, \ Index]|L], \ Tag]),$$
$$seqs([[X \ \$ \ [P1, \ Index]|L], \ Tag], \ Q, \ R).$$

For the parallel program, we first calculate the head normal form of each parallel component and then the parallel expansion laws we defined before are used to generate the head normal form of the whole parallel process $P \parallel Q$.

$$hf([P \parallel Q, \ null], \ [R, \ null]) :- hf([P, \ null], \ R1), \ hf([Q, \ null], \ R2),$$
$$parallel(R1, \ R2, \ R).$$

$$hf([P \parallel Q, \ Index], \ [R, \ Index]) :- hf([P, \ Index], \ R1), \ hf([Q, \ Index], \ R2),$$
$$parallel(R1, \ R2, \ R).$$

4 Deriving Denotational Semantics from Algebraic Semantics

4.1 Denotational Model for SystemC

For dealing with the feature of shared-variable concurrency, we introduce a sequence type variable $tr1$ for recording the behaviour of state change of a program. Moreover, SystemC has two types of time delay; i.e., micro time delay and macro time delay. Therefore, the structure of $tr1$ can be depicted as Figure 1.

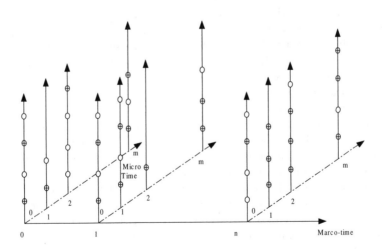

Fig. 1.

At the relative macro time "i" point, time may also advance in Δ time step, standing for the micro-time advancing. Therefore, a sequence of behaviours may be recorded at each Δ time point. These behaviours can be classified into two types; i.e., contributed by the process itself or its environment. In Figure 1, the symbol "$\oplus$" and "$\circ$" stand for the contribution by the process itself and its environment respectively.

In order to record these behaviours, the concept of snapshot is introduced, expressed as $(t1, t2, \sigma, f)$, where σ stands for the contribution of the behaviour and f stands for the flag. "$f = 1$" indicates that the behaviour is contributed by the process itself and "$f = 0$" indicates that the behaviour is contributed by its environment. Here, $t1$ stands for the macro time and $t2$ stands for the micro time. This indicates that the contribution σ is taken at the point with macro time $t1$ and micro time $t2$. Below is the formal structure of trace $tr1$.

$$Element1 = \{(t1, t2, \sigma, f)|t1, t2 \in N \wedge \sigma \in State \wedge f \in \{0, 1\}\},$$
$$tr1 \in \mathbf{seq}(Element1)$$

Here, $\mathbf{seq}(T)$ stands for a sequence type, where each sequence is composed of elements from type T. We select the components of a snapshot using projections; i.e., $\pi_i(sn)$ stands for the i-th element of snapshot sn.

In SystemC, waiting guards can be triggered by events, which can be generated by the process itself or its environment. We use the trace variable $tr2$ to record all the events generated by the process or its environment. $tr2$ has the same time structure, as shown in the above Figure 1. It can be defined as below.

$$Element2 = \{(t1, t2, e, f)|t1, t2 \in N \wedge e \in Event \wedge f \in \{0, 1\}\}$$
$$tr2 \in \mathbf{seq}(Element2)$$

In our semantic model, we introduce two variables $Time1$ and $Time2$ to represent the macro time and micro time respectively. More specifically, $Time1$ and $Time1'$ stand for the start point and the end point of a macro time interval. Further, $(Time1, Time2)$ stands for the starting two dimensional time point and $(Time1', Time2')$ stands for the ending two dimensional time point. We define $\delta1 =_{df} Time1' - Time1$. If $Time1' = Time1$, we define $\delta2 =_{df} Time2' - Time2$.

The execution of an atomic action is represented by a single snapshot. In order to describe the behaviour of individual shared variable assignment, we introduce a variable ttr to model the accumulated change made by the statements of the atomic action. An assignment is simply formulated as storing the result in variable ttr. Meanwhile, the current value of channel ch is also stored in variable ttr. On the completion of an atomic action, the corresponding snapshot is attached to the end of the trace to record its behaviour.

The event generated by channel receiving will not be immediately attached to the end of the trace variable $tr2$. After all the behaviours in an atomic action complete, the process enters into the update phase. Hence we use a trace variable RQ to record new channel states due to the channel receiving.

Three kinds of event notifications are introduced in SystemC for generating events. $notify(e_{\Delta0})$ is used to generate event e, which will be active immediately. For $notify(e_{\Delta1})$, it can generate event e that will be active in one micro time unit. Moreover, $notify(e_{\#T})$ also generates event e. However, it can only be active in T macro time units. For recording the events contributed by the above last two notification commands, we introduce two set type variables, $EN2$ and $EN3$. Here, $EN2$ records the generated events, which will be active in one micro time unit. $EN3$ contains the pairs (e, T), which indicates that event e will be active in T macro time units.

Definition 4.1. Formula P is healthy iff there exists a design $D = (Q \vdash (W \lhd wait' \rhd T))$ such that $P = \mathbf{H}(D)$,

where:

(1) $\mathbf{H}(Y) =_{df} (II \lhd wait \rhd (Y \wedge Inv(tr1, tr2))$

(2) $Q \vdash R =_{df} \neg ok \wedge Inv(tr1, tr2) \vee \neg Q \vee (ok \wedge R)$

(3) $Q \lhd b \rhd R =_{df} b \wedge Q \vee \neg b \wedge R$

(4) $Inv(tr1, tr2) =_{df} tr1 \preceq tr1' \wedge tr2 \preceq tr2'$ □

In the subsequent sections we will use healthy formula

$$\mathbf{H}(\neg Q \vdash W \lhd wait' \rhd T)$$

to explore the semantics of programs. Here, Q, W and T stand for the divergent behaviour, waiting behaviour and termination behaviour respectively.

4.2   Semantic Analysis for Fundamental Components

Firstly we consider the behaviour of program variable assignment. Variable assignment can be classified into two cases; i.e., shared-variable assignment and local variable assignment.

Shared-variable assignment under a Boolean condition can be expressed as:

$$D(b\&(v := e)) =_{df} b \wedge \big(InstEnv \lhd ttr = null \rhd II \; ; \; sassign(v, e) \big)$$

Similarly, local variable assignment can be expressed as:

$$D(b\&(x := f)) =_{df} b \wedge \big(InstEnv \lhd ttr = null \rhd II \; ; \; lassign(x, f) \big)$$

where:

$$InstEnv =_{df} \mathbf{H} \left(\mathbf{true} \vdash \left(\begin{array}{c} \delta 1 = 0 \wedge \delta 2 = 0 \wedge \neg wait' \wedge \\ \bigwedge_{t \in \{tr1, tr2\}} \pi_4(t' - t) \in 0^* \\ \wedge ttr' = \pi_1(last(last(last(tr1')))) \\ same(\{X, RQ, EN2, EN3\}) \end{array} \right) \right)$$

$$sassign(v, e) =_{df} \mathbf{H} \left(\mathbf{true} \vdash \left(\begin{array}{c} \neg wait' \wedge ttr' = ttr[e/v] \wedge \delta 1 = 0 \wedge \delta 2 = 0 \\ same(\{tr1, tr2, X, RQ, EN2, EN3\}) \end{array} \right) \right)$$

$$lassign(x, f) =_{df} \mathbf{H} \left(\mathbf{true} \vdash \left(\begin{array}{c} \neg wait' \wedge x' = f \wedge \delta 1 = 0 \wedge \delta 2 = 0 \\ same(\{tr1, tr2, ttr, X \backslash \{x\}, \\ RQ, EN2, EN3\}) \end{array} \right) \right)$$

Now we consider the semantics for the triggering for $wait(et)$. There are two event triggering cases. The first case is the self-triggering case; i.e., the event is triggered by the process itself, which indicates that the event is generated by the most recent completed atomic actions.

$selftrig(et)$

$=_{df} InstEnv2 \lhd ttr = null \rhd II$;

$update(RQ)$; $(ttr \neq null) \wedge attach$; $selfjudge(et)$

where:

$InstEnv2$

$$=_{df} \mathbf{H} \left(\mathbf{true} \vdash \left(\begin{array}{l} \neg wait' \wedge \delta1 = 0 \wedge \delta2 = 0 \\ \wedge ttr' = \pi_1(last(tr1)) \\ \wedge same(tr1, tr2, X, RQ, EN2, EN3) \end{array} \right) \right)$$

and

$selfjudge(et)$

$$=_{df} \mathbf{H} \left(\mathbf{true} \vdash \left(\begin{array}{l} \neg wait' \wedge \delta1 = 0 \wedge \delta2 = 0 \\ \wedge last(tr2) = (Time1, Time2, et, 1) \\ \wedge same(tr1, ttr, X, RQ, EN2, EN3) \end{array} \right) \right)$$

Here $update(RQ)$ and $attach$ are similar to those in [15] except the introduction of two time variables $Time1$ and $Time2$.

The second case is the environment triggering case; i.e., an event is generated by the environment and this event triggers the waiting behaviour.

$await(et)$

$=_{df} InstEnv2 \lhd ttr = null \rhd II$; $update(RQ)$;

$(ttr = null \vee last(tr2) \neq (Time1, Time2, et, 1)) \wedge attach$; $aawait(et)$

and

$$aawait(et) =_{df} \mathbf{H} \left(\mathbf{true} \vdash \left(\begin{array}{c} et \notin \pi_3(tr2' - tr2) \wedge \delta1 = 0 \wedge \delta2 = 0 \wedge \\ \bigwedge_{x \in \{tr1, tr2\}} Env(x' - x) \wedge \\ same(RQ, X, ttr, EN2, EN3) \end{array} \right) \right)$$

$$trig(et) =_{df} \mathbf{H} \left(\mathbf{true} \vdash \left(\begin{array}{c} \delta1 = 0 \wedge \delta2 = 0 \wedge \\ last(tr2' - tr2) = \langle (Time1, Time2, et, 0) \rangle \wedge \\ same(tr1, ttr, RQ, EN2, EN3) \end{array} \right) \right)$$

Therefore, we can have:

$D(wait(et)) =_{df} selftrig(et) \vee (await(et)$; $trig(et))$

We can also consider the semantics for other fundamental components.

4.3   Deriving Denotational Semantics from Algebraic Semantics

In this section we explore the derivation of denotational semantics from algebraic semantics for SystemC. The derivation strategy is explored. Our approach is based on the head normal form of each process, i.e., we have five types of guarded choices.

Let

$$C(tag) =_{df} \begin{cases} ttr = null & \text{if } tag = null \\ ttr \neq null & \text{if } tag = index \end{cases}$$

If the head normal form of a process belongs to the first type, its denotational semantics can be described as the semantics of the instantaneous action followed by the denotational semantics of the corresponding subsequent process at the new location state. This construction is proceeded by going through all the above instantaneous action.

(1) If $HF((P, tag)) = ($ $\|_{i \in I} \{b_i \& (x_i := e_i)\ (P_i, index_i)\}$
$\|_{j \in J} \{ch_j \ !!\ exp_j\ (Q_j, index_j)\}$
$\|_{k \in K} \{ch_k \ ??\ v_k\ (R_k, index_k)\}$
$\|_{l \in L} \{notify(e_{l_x})\ (T_l, index_l)\},$
$tag\ )$

then

$A((P, tag))$

$=_{df} C(tag) \wedge \begin{pmatrix} \bigvee_{i \in I} (\ D(b_i \& x_i := e_i)\ ;\ A((P_i, index_i))\ ) \\ \vee \bigvee_{j \in J} (\ D(ch_j !! exp_j)\ ;\ A((Q_j, index_j))\ ) \\ \vee \bigvee_{k \in K} (\ D(ch_k ?? v_k)\ ;\ A((R_k, index_k))\ ) \\ \vee \bigvee_{l \in L} (\ D(notify(e_{l_x}))\ ;\ A((T_l, index_l))\ ) \end{pmatrix}$

If the head normal form of a process belongs to the second type, its behaviour can be divided into two cases. The first case indicates that one of the events can be self-fired. The second case indicates that none of the events can be self-fired. Then the process will wait for any of the events to be fired. During the waiting periods, all the events cannot be fired. After that, one of the events will get fired. For the above two cases, if one event gets fired, the subsequent behaviour will be the corresponding process at the location status $null$.

(2) If $HF((P, tag)) = (\ \|_{i \in I} \{wait(e_i)\ (P_i, null)\},\ tag\ )$

then

$$A((P, tag)) =_{df} C(tag) \wedge \begin{pmatrix} \bigvee_{i \in I} (selftrig(e_i)\ ;\ A((P, null))) \\ \vee \\ (await(e)\ ;\ \bigvee_{i \in I} (trig(e_i)\ ;\ A((P_i, null))\ )\ ) \end{pmatrix}$$

where, $e =_{df} \mathbf{or}_{i \in I} \{e_i\}$

Now we consider the case that the head normal form of a process belongs to the third type. The time delay can be divided into two cases; i.e., micro-time and macro-time. The process first behaves the same as the corresponding one unit time delay. After that, the behaviour can be expressed as the subsequent behaviour of the process at the location status $null$.

(3) If $HF((P, tag)) = \|\{\Delta 1\ (P, null)\}$,

then $A((P, tag)) =_{df} C(tag) \wedge (D(\Delta 1)\ ;\ A((P, null)))$

If $HF((P, tag)) =_{df} \|\{\#1\ (P, null)\}$

then $HF((P, tag)) =_{df} C(tag) \wedge (D(\#1)\ ;\ A((P, null)))$

If the head normal form of a process belongs to the fourth type. The analysis can be divided into two cases. The first case indicates that one of the events can be fired. The second case indicates that none of the elements can be self-fired. The process waits for any events to be fired and all the events will not be fired during the waiting period. The waiting period will not let macro and micro time advance. Finally, either any instantaneous action will be scheduled or one events will get fired.

(4) If $HF((P, tag)) = (\quad \|_{i \in I}\{U_i\ (P_i, index_i)\}$
$$\|_{j \in J}\{wait(e_j)(Q_j, null)\},$$
$$tag\ )$$

then

$$A((P, tag))$$

$$=_{df} C(tag) \wedge \left(\begin{array}{c} \bigvee_{j \in J}(selftrig(e_j)\ ;\ A((Q_j, null))) \\ \vee \\ await(e) \wedge hold\Delta(0)\ ;\ \left(\begin{array}{c} \bigvee_{i \in I}(D(U_i)\ ;\ A((P_i, index_i)))\ \vee \\ \bigvee_{j \in J}(trig(e_i)\ ;\ A((Q_j, null))) \end{array} \right) \end{array} \right)$$

where,

$$e =_{df} \mathbf{or}_{j \in J}\{e_j\}$$

$$hold\Delta(0) =_{df} \mathbf{H} \left(\mathbf{true} \vdash \left(\begin{array}{c} \bigwedge_{x \in \{tr1, tr2\}} Instenv(x' - x) \wedge \\ \delta 1 = 0 \wedge \delta 2 = 0 \wedge \\ same(ttr, X, RQ, EN2, EN3) \end{array} \right) \right)$$

If the head normal form of a process belongs to the fifth type. The analysis can be proceeded according to the time delay type. If the time delay is micro time, the analysis can be divided into three cases. The first case indicates that one of the events gets self-fired. The second and third case indicate that none of the events are self-fired. The process will wait for any events to be fired. During the waiting period all these events will not get fired and the waiting period is one micro time unit long. The second case indicates that one event will get fired without micro time advancing. For the third case, one micro time will advance.

(5) If $HF((P, tag)) = (\quad \|_{i \in I}\{wait(e_i)\ (P_i, null)\} \| \|\{\Delta 1\ (Q, null)\},$
$$tag\ )$$

then

$$A((P, tag))$$

$$=_{df} C(tag) \wedge \begin{pmatrix} \bigvee_{i \in I}(selftrig(e_i) \; ; \; A((P, null))) \\ \vee \\ (await(e) \wedge hold\Delta(0) \; ; \; \bigvee_{i \in I}(trig(e_i) \; ; \; A((P_i, null)))) \\ \vee \\ (await(e) \wedge hold\Delta(0) \; ; \; \textbf{phase}\Delta \; ; \; A((Q, null))) \end{pmatrix}$$

where,

$$e =_{df} \textbf{or}_{i \in I}\{e_i\}$$

$$\textbf{phase}\Delta =_{df} \textbf{H} \left(\textbf{true} \vdash \begin{pmatrix} same(tr1, tr2, ttr, X, RQ, EN2, EN3) \wedge \\ \delta 1 = 0 \wedge (\delta 2 = 0 \lhd wait' \rhd \delta 2 = 1) \end{pmatrix} \right)$$

Further, we explore the type that the time delay is macro. The analysis can also be divided into three cases, which are similar to micro time. For the second and third case, the holding behaviour will change from $hold\Delta(0)$ into $hold\#(0)$. For the third type, time advancing will change from micro time into macro time.

$$\text{If} \quad HF((P, tag)) = (\; \|_{i \in I}\{wait(e_i) \; (P_i, null)\}\|\{\#1 \; (Q, null)\},$$
$$tag \;)$$

then

$$A((P, tag))$$

$$=_{df} C(tag) \wedge \begin{pmatrix} \bigvee_{i \in I}(selftrig(e_i) \; ; \; A((P_i, null))) \\ \vee \\ (await(e)hold\#(0) \; ; \; \bigvee_{i \in I}(trig(e_i) \; ; \; A((P_i, null)))) \\ \vee \\ (await(e) \wedge hold\#(0) \; ; \; \textbf{phase}\# \; ; \; A((Q, null))) \end{pmatrix}$$

where,

$$e =_{df} \textbf{or}_{i \in I}\{e_i\}$$

$$\textbf{phase}\# =_{df} \textbf{H} \left(\textbf{true} \vdash \begin{pmatrix} same(tr1, tr2, ttr, X, RQ, EN2, EN3) \wedge \\ (\delta 1 = 0 \wedge \delta 2 = 0) \lhd wait' \rhd (\delta 1 = 1 \wedge Time2' = 0) \end{pmatrix} \right)$$

Remark: If $HF((P, index)) = undefined$,
        then $A((P, index)) =_{df} attach; A((P, null))$

Based on the above definitions, we can have a way to calculate the denotational semantics from algebraic semantics for SystemC.

Definition 4.2. (Calculating Denotational Semantics from Algebraic Semantics)

$$A(P) =_{df} A((P, null)) \ \vee \ A((P, \langle \ \rangle)) \qquad \square$$

The calculation can be divided into two categories according to the location status of a program. The detailed calculation is based on the denotational semantics for each type of guarded choice.

4.4 Animation of Deriving Denotational Semantics

Now we consider the mechanical derivation strategy for deriving denotational semantics from algebraic semantics. For program P, we use the function below to generate the denotational semantics of P.

$$a((P, tag), D)$$

where, D stands for denotaional semantics of program P at location status tag.

If the head normal form of P is of type one which is denoted as $[[V\$[P, Index]|Q], Tag]$, then the denotational semantics is generated as follows

$$a([P, Tag], \ R) :- hf([P, Tag], \ [[V\$[P, Index]|Q], Tag]), \ c(Tag, \ R1),$$

$$denotation([V \ \$ \ [P, Index]|Q], \ R2), \ conjunct(R1, \ R2, \ R).$$

Here, function $denotation(P, \ Q)$ is used to generate the semantics of fundamental components P and is stored in Q. $conjunct(P, Q, R)$ is defined to gengerate the conjuctioin of component P and Q, the result is then stored in R.

Now we consider the case when the head normal form of a program is of type two.

$$a([P, \ Tag], \ R) :- hf([P, Tag], \ [[wait \ E \ \$ \ [P, null]|Q], Tag]),$$

$$selftrigs([wait \ E \ \$ \ [P, null]|Q], R1),$$

$$trigs([wait \ E \ \$ \ [P, \ null]|Q], \ R2),$$

$$conjunct(R1, \ await([wait \ E \ \$ \ [P, \ null]|Q]); R2, \ R).$$

We first calculate the head normal form of program P. Then function $selftrigs$ is used to record the behaviour of the program when one of the events can be self-fired. The analysis of function $trig$ is similar.

If the head normal form of a process belongs to the third type, its behaviour is denoted as follows.

$$a([P, \ Tag], \ R1; R2) :- hf([P, \ Tag], \ [[\#1 \ \$ \ [Q, \ null]], Tag]),$$

$$denotation([\# \ 1], R1), \ a([Q, \ Tag], R2).$$

$$a([P, \ Tag], \ R1; R2) :- hf([P, \ Tag], \ [[delta \ 1 \ \$ \ [Q, \ null]], Tag]),$$

$$denotation([delta \ 1], R1), \ a([Q, \ Tag], R2).$$

Similar consideration can be applied to a program when its head normal form is of type four or five.

4.5 Exploration of Deriving Denotational Semantics for Iteration

In the previous subsections, we have explored the derivation of denotational semantics for finite programs. Now we start to investigate the derivation of denotational semantics for iteration, i.e., including infinite programs.

Let

$$F^0(b, P) =_{df} Chaos$$
$$F^{n+1}(b, P) =_{df} \textbf{if } b \textbf{ then } (P; F^n(b, P)) \textbf{ else Skip}$$

Now we consider the derivation strategy for iteration.

$$A(\textbf{while } b \textbf{ do } P) =_{df} \sqcup_i A(F^i(b, P)).$$

where:

(1) $A(Q)$ stands for the derived denotational semantics from algebraic semantics for program Q. This implies that $A(F^i(b, P))$ stands for the derived denotational semantics for finite program $F^i(b, P)$

(2) The denotational semantics for $Chaos$ can be described as follows.

$$A((Chaos, tag)) =_{df} C(tag) \wedge \textbf{H}(true), \quad A(Chaos) =_{df} \textbf{H}(true)$$

(3) We need to add additional algebraic laws for $Chaos$

$$Chaos \parallel P =_{tag} Chaos, \quad \text{where } tag = null, \langle 1 \rangle, \langle 2 \rangle$$

5 Conclusion

Compared with traditional programming language, SystemC possesses several novel features, including delayed notifications, notification cancelling, notification overriding and delta-cycle. In this paper we studied the calculation (i.e., derivation) of denotational semantics from algebraic semantics for SystemC. We systematically explored the algebraic laws for SystemC and introduced the concept of head normal form. Meanwhile, we also investigated the simulation (i.e., animation) of algebraic laws and head normal form, which aims to support the mechanical derivation of denotational semantics. Based on the concept of head normal form, we provided the strategy for deriving denotational semantics from algebraic semantics. Two pairs of variables (i.e., $Time1$, $Time1'$, $Time2$ and $Time2'$) are introduced to model the timed behaviour. We also studied the mechanical derivation of denotation semantics. The derivation of denotational semantics for infinite programs has also been explored using the approximation approach.

For the future, we are continuing to work on the unifying theories [1,6,14] for SystemC. We plan to embed the achievements in this paper in the framework of PVS [11] to support automatic verification based on the UTP approach.

Acknowledgement. This work was supported by the Open Fund of the State Key Laboratory of Software Development Environment under Grant No. SKLSDE-2009KF-2-05, Beijing University of Aeronautics and Astronautics, and by National Basic Research Program of China (No. 2005CB321904), National High Technology Research and Development Program of China (No. 2007AA0103 02), National Natural Science Foundation of China (No. 90718004), and Shanghai Leading Academic Discipline Project (No. B412).

References

1. Brookes, S.D.: Full abstraction for a shared-variable parallel language. Information and Computation 127(2), 145–163 (1996)
2. Clocksin, W.F., Mellish, C.S.: Programming in Prolog, 5th edn. Springer, Heidelberg (2003)
3. Gawanmeh, A., Habibi, A., Tahar, S.: An executable operational semantics for SystemC using Abstract State Machines. Technical report, Department of Electrical and Computer Engineering, Concordia University, Montreal, Canada (March 2004)
4. Habibi, A., Tahar, S.: SystemC fixpoint semantics. Technical report, Department of Electrical and Computer Engineering, Concordia University, Montreal, Canada (January 2005)
5. Hoare, C.A.R., Hayes, I.J., He, J., Morgan, C., Roscoe, A.W., Sanders, J.W., Sørensen, I.H., Spivey, J.M., Sufrin, B.: Laws of programming. Communications of the ACM 38(8), 672–686 (1987)
6. Hoare, C.A.R., He, J.: Unifying Theories of Programming. Prentice Hall International Series in Computer Science (1998)
7. IEEE: IEEE Standard Hardware Description Language based on the Verilog Hardware Description Language, vol. IEEE Standard 1364-2001. IEEE, Los Alamitos (2001)
8. Milner, R.: Communication and Mobile System: π-calculus. Cambridge University Press, Cambridge (1999)
9. Open SystemC Initiative(OSCI). Functional Specification for SystemC 2.0 (October 2001)
10. Open SystemC Initiative(OSCI). SystemC 2.0.1 Language Reference Manual (2003)
11. Owre, S., Shankar, N., Rushby, J.M., Stringer-Calvert, D.W.J.: PVS Language Reference. In: Computer Science Laboratory, SRI International, Menlo Park, CA (September 1999)
12. Peng, X., Zhu, H., He, J., Jin, N.: An operational semantics of an event-driven system-level simulator. In: Proc. SEW-30: The 30th IEEE/NASA Software Engineering Workshop, Columbia, Maryland, USA, pp. 190–200. IEEE Computer Society Press, Los Alamitos (April 2006)
13. Ruf, J., Hoffmann, D.W., Gerlach, J., Kropf, T., Rosenstiel, W., Müller, W.: The simulation semantics of SystemC. In: DATE 2001: Proceedings of the conference on Design, Automation and Test in Europe, Piscataway, NJ, USA, pp. 64–70. IEEE Press, Los Alamitos (March 2001)
14. Zhu, H.: Linking the Semantics of a Multithreaded Discrete Event Simulation Language. PhD thesis, London South Bank University (February 2005)
15. Zhu, H., He, J., Peng, X., Jin, N.: Denotational approach to event-driven system level language. In: Butterfield, A. (ed.) UTP 2008. LNCS, vol. 5713, pp. 258–278. Springer, Heidelberg (2010)

Author Index

Printing: Mercedes-Druck, Berlin
Binding: Stein+Lehmann, Berlin